Sexuality and
the Body
in Russian
Culture

CONTRIBUTORS

Svetlana Boym
Diana Lewis Burgin
Jane T. Costlow
Helena Goscilo
Barbara Heldt
Catriona Kelly
Eve Levin
Eric Naiman
Cathy Popkin
Stephanie Sandler
Jane A. Sharp
Judith Vowles
Elizabeth A. Wood

EDITED BY
JANE T. COSTLOW
STEPHANIE SANDLER
JUDITH VOWLES

Sexuality and the Body in Russian Culture

Stanford University Press
Stanford, California

Stanford University Press
Stanford, California
© 1993 by the Board of Trustees of the
Leland Stanford Junior University

CIP data are at the end of the book

Printed in the United States of America

Acknowledgments

■ The Amherst College Russian Department, through the Julia A. Whitney Foundation, generously funded the 1989 symposium at which most of the essays collected here were first presented. The Russian Department and the Amherst Center for Russian Culture have continued to support this project, assisting with funds for preparation of the volume for publication. Bates College, through the dean of the faculty, covered additional publication expenses. We are also grateful to Jeanne Stolarski, who coordinated all aspects of the symposium and assisted in the production of this volume with her usual good spirits and flawless efficiency. She and Margaret Ferro typed corrections into final versions of all the essays. The excellent copy editing of Nancy Atkinson made further welcome improvements, and we also thank Peter Kahn for his good work shepherding our manuscript through the production process.

For help with bibliographical information, we thank the reference staff at Frost Library, Amherst College, particularly Michael Kasper.

Many colleagues and friends took time to read and offer comments about the Introduction as it went through several drafts. We particularly thank Diana Burgin, Charles Isenberg, Catriona Kelly, and Eve Levin for their helpful suggestions and criticisms. Helena Goscilo deserves a special acknowledgment, not only for her intelligent and thorough response to the Introduction but also for generously providing some of the more obscure contemporary texts we discuss there and for suggesting several of them in the first place. The responses of Caryl Emerson and Helen Tartar to a much earlier version also encouraged us to attempt the more detailed Introduction that now follows.

J.T.C.
S.S.
J.V.

Contents

Contributors ix

A Note on Translation and Transliteration xi

Introduction
    *Jane T. Costlow, Stephanie Sandler, and
    Judith Vowles* 1

PART I. THE CULTURAL HISTORY OF SEXUAL REPRESENTATION

Sexual Vocabulary in Medieval Russia
    Eve Levin 41

Marriage à la russe
    Judith Vowles 53

A Stick with Two Ends, or, Misogyny in Popular Culture:
A Case Study of the Puppet Text 'Petrushka'
    Catriona Kelly 73

Redrawing the Margins of Russian Vanguard Art:
Natalia Goncharova's Trial for Pornography in 1910
    Jane A. Sharp 97

Prostitution Unbound:
Representations of Sexual and Political Anxieties in
Postrevolutionary Russia
    Elizabeth A. Wood 124

PART II. LITERARY VERSIONS OF SEX AND BODY

Kiss and Tell:
Narrative Desire and Discretion
    Cathy Popkin 139

Loving in Bad Taste:
  Eroticism and Literary Excess in Marina Tsvetaeva's 'The Tale of Sonechka'
    Svetlana Boym   156

Laid Out in Lavender:
  Perceptions of Lesbian Love in Russian Literature and Criticism of the Silver Age, 1893–1917
    Diana Lewis Burgin   177

Monsters Monomaniacal, Marital, and Medical:
  Tatiana Tolstaya's Regenerative Use of Gender Stereotypes
    Helena Goscilo   204

PART III. THE MATERNAL BODY

The Pastoral Source:
  Representations of the Maternal Breast in Nineteenth-Century Russia
    Jane T. Costlow   223

Motherhood in a Cold Climate:
  The Poetry and Career of Maria Shkapskaya
    Barbara Heldt   237

Historectomies:
  On the Metaphysics of Reproduction in a Utopian Age
    Eric Naiman   255

Notes   277
Index   347

Contributors

SVETLANA BOYM is Assistant Professor of Comparative Literature at Harvard University and the author of *Death in Quotation Marks: Cultural Myths of the Modern Poet*, as well as articles on Mandelstam, Mayakovsky, Barthes, Benjamin, and Soviet cinema. She is the author of a play, *The Woman Who Shot Lenin*, and a short film, *Flirting with Liberty*. Her current scholarly project is *Common Places: Mythologies of Everyday Life in Russia*.

DIANA LEWIS BURGIN, Professor of Russian at the University of Massachusetts in Boston, is the author of *Richard Burgin, a Life in Verse*, a biographical narrative poem written in the Onegin stanza about her relationship with her father and how she came to be a Slavist. In a purely scholarly vein, she has written articles on Pushkin, Tolstoy, Dostoevsky, Bulgakov, Solzhenitsyn, and Parnok. Her most recent research has been on the life and creative evolution of Sophia Parnok, whose lyrics she has translated into English verse.

JANE T. COSTLOW is Associate Professor of Russian at Bates College. She is the author of *Worlds Within Worlds: The Novels of Ivan Turgenev* and of several essays on nineteenth-century Russian women's writing.

HELENA GOSCILO, Associate Professor of Slavic Languages and Literatures at the University of Pittsburgh, has written articles on Pushkin, Lermontov, Tolstoy, Bulgakov, and contemporary Russian women's fiction. Her translations include Lermontov's *Vadim*, Nagibin's *The Peak of Success and Other Stories*, *Russian and Polish Women's Fiction*, *Balancing Acts*, and *Glasnost: An Anthology of Russian Literature Under Gorbachev*. Her current projects include book-length studies of Tatyana Tolstaya, current Russian women's fiction, and a volume of interviews with current Russian female authors.

BARBARA HELDT, Professor of Russian at the University of British Columbia, is the author of *Terrible Perfection: Women and Russian Literature*.

CATRIONA KELLY, Research Fellow in Russian at Christ Church, Oxford University, is the author of *Petrushka, the Russian Carnival Puppet Theatre* and of articles on Symbolist poetry and Russian popular culture. She is the co-editor of *Discontinuous Discourses in Modern Russian Literature;* in addition she has translated Leonid Borodin's *The Third Truth* and the prose of Sergei Kaledin.

EVE LEVIN, Associate Professor of History at Ohio State University, is the author of *Sex and Society in the World of the Orthodox Slavs, 900–1700*. She is also Associate Editor of *Russian Review*.

ERIC NAIMAN, Assistant Professor of Comparative Literature and Slavic Languages and Literatures at the University of California, Berkeley, is completing a book on sexuality in early Soviet culture.

CATHY POPKIN, Associate Professor of Russian at Columbia University, is the author of *The Pragmatics of Insignificance: Chekhov, Zoshchenko, Gogol*.

STEPHANIE SANDLER, Associate Professor of Russian and of Women's and Gender Studies at Amherst College, is the author of *Distant Pleasures: Alexander Pushkin and the Writing of Exile*. She is completing a book on myths of Pushkin in Russian culture.

JANE A. SHARP is a former Project Assistant Curator at the Solomon R. Guggenheim Museum, New York City. She recently completed her Ph.D. in art history at Yale University, and she teaches at Vassar College.

JUDITH VOWLES works on eighteenth-century Russian literature. She collaborated with Beth Goldring on a translation of Maria Ioffe's *One Night,* and has translated Sophie Dubnov-Erlich's *The Life and Work of S. M. Dubnov*.

ELIZABETH A. WOOD is Assistant Professor of History at Massachusetts Institute of Technology. She recently completed her dissertation, "NEP and Its Discontents: Gender and Politics in Soviet Russia, 1918–1928."

A NOTE ON TRANSLITERATION AND TRANSLATION

We intend this volume for specialists and nonspecialists alike, and thus the essays transliterate Russian names in their most familiar English spellings, for example, "Solovyov" and "Tolstoy." Russian quotations in the text, as well as all bibliographical information, use the modified Library of Congress system of transliteration except when they are given in Cyrillic. All material quoted from Russian sources is also given in English translation; unless otherwise noted, the translations are by the authors.

Sexuality and
the Body
in Russian
Culture

JANE T. COSTLOW
STEPHANIE SANDLER
JUDITH VOWLES

Introduction

■ "Russians have their own, particular erotic culture; it's just that we don't know much about it."[1] With these words, the contemporary Russian sexologist and psychologist Igor Kon sums up both the premise and purpose of this volume: to demonstrate that there is a distinct and complex subject matter to be found under the heading *Sexuality and the Body in Russian Culture*, to explore why comparatively little is felt to be known about it, and to begin to explore what in fact we do know with some confidence. While sexuality, its practices and discourses, are now more commonly studied by Western scholars, we know far less about sexual life and sexual representations in Russia's past and present, as Kon suggests. The papers collected here make a valuable contribution to a subject that has received little scholarly attention inside or outside Russia, though media attention to the profusion of sexual discourses in contemporary Russia is notable.

We take the terms "sexuality" and "the body" principally to mean not biologically precise events or objects in the physical world, but (following Foucault) rather discursively constituted and changing entities that people have imagined and lived with in various ways throughout Russian history. Sexuality thus includes "the array of acts, expectations, narratives, pleasures, identity formations, and knowledges in both men and women, that tends to cluster most densely around certain genital sensations but is not adequately defined by them."[2] Foucault's work has stimulated the thinking of many of the contributors as well as our own, and it was Foucault's implicit principle—that sexuality would be both symptomatic of and constructed by a culture—that motivated us to organize the Amherst conference and to publish this book. We felt that there were aspects of Russian culture that have been invisible to us because we know little about the culture's ideas of sex. As we explore below, there has also been considerable denial of sex as a valid subject of research until very recently. We take the scantiness of that research itself to be a feature of sexuality in Russian culture and of Slavic studies in the U.S.; following Foucault's "repressive hypothesis," we conclude that the existence in Russia of "an injunction to silence, an affirmation of nonexistence, and by implication, an admission that there was nothing to say about such things, nothing to see, and nothing to know" means that for Russian culture sex and the body are phenomena that can tell us a great deal rather than phenomena that can tell us "nothing."[3] The essays in this volume demonstrate that the repressions and expressions of "bodies and pleasures" (in Foucault's terms) have motivated writers as different as the Church fathers, foreign visitors to Russia, Leo Tolstoy, Lidia Avilova, Anna Barykova, Anton Chekhov, Marina Tsvetaeva, Maria Shkapskaya, and Tatiana Tolstaya; the reception of the *Petrushka* puppet plays and the plays as popular spectacle; criticism of Sophia Parnok's poems and Natalia Goncharova's paintings; a rhetoric of purity to justify control of prostitutes after the revolution; and the metaphysics of some of Russia's most distinguished philosophers.

Why sex *and the body*? In part, we suspected that whatever was specific to Russian ideas about sex might have to do with how Russian bodies are imagined. The images that come to Western (but not just Western) minds are telling: they might include bulky and enduring peasant bodies, a mother's fertile body, and, as a grotesque result of the famines, the labor camps, the wars, and the purges of this century, probably also dead bodies.[4] Participants at the Amherst symposium discussed several instances of pictorial or narrative representation of a body quite apart from its eroticism.[5] But the most intense discussion came when we talked about myths of the mother's body in Russian culture. We asked how particular historical bodies live out and resist the mythification of the maternal, and how this mythification has shaped the problematic imagination of the erotic body for Russia.

Introduction

Crucial to the discussion of sex and the body is the question *whose body*. The papers amply show that there is a volatile and inevitable relationship between sexual experience and gender difference. As others have noted, it is a weakness of Foucault's arguments that he rarely considers gender difference, and his idea of "the body" is in fact a man's body. In writing this introduction, we found the work of Eve Kosofsky Sedgwick, particularly her recent study *The Epistemology of the Closet,* a useful and provocative corrective, for she is able to work with Foucault's insights in order to untangle the relationship between sex and gender with compelling clarity, and to study the power relations between women and men and the injunctions to secrecy that especially coalesce around gay men and lesbians.[6] Sedgwick's lucid analysis of willed ignorances that create complex systems of knowledge and power has reinforced our own commitment to understanding some of the silences that seem to substitute for well-formed questions of sex and the body in Russian culture.

The essays in this volume vastly expand our knowledge of sexuality in Russian culture, while they also suggest areas of ignorance that remain. For this reason we felt that any attempt to place these essays in a comprehensive and connecting narrative or to sketch a history of sexual discourse in Russia would be premature. The essays display a variety of approaches and make differing theoretical assumptions, divergences that produced much lively discussion at the symposium. Rather than risk distorting the particular insights of each essay in an attempt to reconcile these differences, we have tried to provide a framework in this introduction within which to read the essays in all their variety. That framework draws on recurrent themes from the essays, and adds historical background for the eighteenth and nineteenth centuries.

We begin with a brief discussion of Russia's relation to the West. When it comes to ideas about sex and the body, assumptions about what is foreign and what is native are charged with a host of expectations about morality, privacy, and pleasure. We follow with a reading of several attempts at an overview of sexuality in Russia as a way of drawing out and testing the common underlying assumptions about sexuality and the body. These assumptions are not always explicit, and they include the processes by which sex has been coded as transgressive or liberatory, the establishment of heterosexual sex as a norm, and a frequently expressed desire to transcend the body, a desire connected in important ways with the image of the maternal body. We subject the images of the maternal identified by the philosophical and literary traditions to detailed analysis, asking how the discourse of motherhood is consolidated at given historical moments, and how various expectations and taboos make themselves felt in daily life. We discuss a short narrative about a sexual encounter between a man and a pregnant woman to clarify the conflicting but also mutually constitutive patterns of thought about the maternal body and the erotic body. We then consider the interactions between gender and sexuality, specifying how they are fundamentally different but importantly connected categories. We take our examples of cross-gender masquerade from the memoir and popular cartoon traditions.

We conclude the introduction with something that might well have been our starting point—the explosion of curiosity and discourses about sex in the contemporary period. Our survey of the contemporary period is somewhat more detailed than other parts of the introduction, since there is only one essay on the period in this volume (Helena Goscilo's reading of Tatiana Tolstaya), and since a great deal of this new material is little known. We do more, though, than survey this material: to understand how *glasnost* was made to seem "sexy," we ask whether the bodies represented in recent fiction are only or even principally erotic. We also describe how a rhetoric of sexual liberation, particularly movement toward gay and lesbian liberation, has met with resistance. These topics, then, will organize our introduction, and within this structure we refer to the essays in this volume as they create and debate the contexts we are elucidating.

How Does "Russian" Sexuality Differ
from that of the "West"?

In 1767 the great libertine adventurer and authority on matters erotic Count Giacoma Girolama Casanova de Seingalt paid a brief visit to Russia in hopes of repairing his fortunes at Catherine II's court. Casanova enjoyed his customary pleasures and adventures in Russia, in these respects finding the country little different from the many others he visited (with the exception of openly displayed

Introduction

male homosexuality in Russia). His descriptions of public balls, masquerades, dinners, and other social gatherings remind us of Peter I's success in Westernizing Russia, and more particularly in transforming the relations between the sexes.[7] The eighteenth century saw a decisive shift in sexual manners, a shift away from the mores of the pre-Petrine period described by Eve Levin. Peter brought noble women out of the seclusion of the *terem* and obliged men and women to associate with one another in ways long established in Western countries.[8] This policy reflected social and economic theories widely accepted in the West. Broadly speaking, these theories averred that the progress and development of civilizations could be gauged by relations between men and women: primitive societies were characterized by violent, rapacious, and promiscuous male tyranny over women, while in more civilized societies women were treated respectfully, and ideals of mutual love and pleasure were cultivated.[9]

Alongside these Western manners, Casanova found very un-Western customs. Nowhere was this more noticeable than at the baths, that peculiarly Russian institution.[10] Casanova took his beautiful serf mistress Zaira to the baths, "where thirty or forty naked men and women were bathing together without the slightest constraint. This absence of shame must arise, I should imagine, from native innocence; but I wondered that none looked at Zaira, who seemed to me the original of the statue of Psyche I had seen at the Villa Borghese at Rome."[11]

In the face of Russian indifference, Casanova himself documents Zaira's beauty, displaying not only her body but his Western standards of erotic pleasure. His comparison to the famed statue of Psyche in the Villa Borghese suggests the extent to which his views are embedded in a long history of Western culture, one that established standards for the erotic and the beautiful, replete with notions of innocence and corruption, exposure and concealment of the body. Judith Vowles's paper has an extended account of how foreigners saw eighteenth-century Russian society through the prisms of their own cultures.

Casanova's account suggests the tensions and contradictions of Russia's relation to the West. At the Amherst symposium, participants repeatedly returned to this subject, trying to specify what was different about the history of sexuality and the body in Russia. We hardly solved the problem of Russia and the West, but we agreed that this very issue has been central to Russian images of sexual and bodily presence in the world since at least the eighteenth century. The eighteenth century is similarly a crucial period for Western culture: many modern institutions and ways of thinking about sexuality and the body were founded at this time. While Michel Foucault's *History of Sexuality* focuses on the nineteenth century's repressive hypothesis, his writings on the way in which the body became the object of attention in numerous disciplines, including the medical and legal professions, push back into the eighteenth century.[12] Thomas Laqueur summarizes the importance of eighteenth-century changes when he notes, "human sexual nature changed"; his claim is supported by historians and scholars in other disciplines.[13]

Many eighteenth-century Russian writers of love and sex also anticipated and framed the ways in which later writers would treat the subject. The poet Vasily Trediakovsky introduced Western literary erotic texts and genres (the novel and the love song) as a civilizing influence; however his critics perceived his work as corrupting and profane.[14] These dual attitudes persisted throughout the eighteenth century; Western literary models of love and romance were imitated approvingly, but also attacked and satirized for being Western, the male and female dandy (*shchegol'* and *shchegolikha*) being especially vilified as the bearers of new sexual manners.[15] Some writers, like Alexander Sumarokov, advanced both positions, producing numerous charming love songs and successful satires. One of the most severe critiques of how the West had brought sexual corruption and decay to Russian society was Prince M. M. Shcherbatov's *On the Corruption of Morals in Russia* (*O povrezhdenii nravov v Rossii*, 1786–89).[16] His harsh view of Russia's relation to the West finds many echoes in later writers; perhaps one of the best known among contemporary figures is Valentin Rasputin, whose attitudes we explicate at the end of this essay. These two writers from very different times share the assumptions that Russia is pure, unlike the West, which is preoccupied with sex, and thus a source of corruption.[17]

Such assumptions have often taken the form of a claim that the Russian language lacks a vocabulary of the erotic because it lacks the thing itself.[18] Trediakovsky, for example, said that he was obliged to invent a vocabulary that included Western forms for his *Journey to the Island of Love* (*Ezda v ostrov Liubvi*, 2nd ed. 1778).[19] More recently the Russian philosopher Georgy Gachev noted that until the word *seks* ("sex") appeared in common Russian usage, the language was limited to terms that strictly connoted only biological phenomena, only emotional intensity, or only obscene and forbidden acts.[20] The contemporary explosion of published material about sexuality has taken account of a perceived paucity of Russian terms and Russian unfamiliarity with Western vocabularies by including lists of new terms at the conclusion of various books.[21]

We ignore the complaint of language's inadequacy at our peril, since it bespeaks a "nonexistence," in Foucault's terms, beneath which an extensive fund of material about the culture is hiding. But we also should resist taking the claims at equal or face value. Some are dubious: Eve Levin's paper in this volume gives an extensive sampling of the words and locutions used in Church writings during the Middle Ages, and there are many texts attesting to the existence of a rich vocabulary in the eighteenth century.[22] There is a long history of anxiety about importing foreign words, something Russian has long done and intellectuals have long debated. Words like *seks, erotika, gomoseksualist, lesbianka* are becoming more rooted in Russian daily use, and one wonders if, in time, they will grow to seem no more apparently foreign than *teatr* or *akter*.[23]

Any discussion of sexuality and the body in Russian culture must therefore take account of how distinctions between Russia and the West are used to structure arguments and shape narratives on the subject. Mikhail Bakhtin's colleague V. Voloshinov declared in his account of Freudianism that interest in sexuality is a Western phenomenon, characteristic of the development of individualism in Western societies, a decadent sign of a corrupt society. "All periods of social decline and disintegration," he writes, "are characterized by overestimation of the sexual in life and in ideology."[24] Viewed in this light, the essays collected here become a peculiarly Western phenomenon, and a decadent one at that (given the controversial nature of the subject, a point of view with which some Western critics might sympathize).[25]

Against the insistence that sexuality is a Western, not a Russian, phenomenon, one might set Western accounts that claim the opposite. Eighteenth-century foreign travelers, for example, frequently voiced shock at Russian depravity, as Judith Vowles's paper documents. Catherine II's court and her lovers were often cited by foreigners to exemplify Russian decadence; even Casanova called her the most dissolute woman he had ever met.[26] Throughout the nineteenth century Western writers saw Russia as a locus of exotic sexuality, as numerous examples from Mario Praz's *The Romantic Agony* attest.[27] Such attitudes turn up in Russian literature, for example in Leo Tolstoy's *Anna Karenina*, where Vronsky obliges a foreign prince by entertaining him with the expected round of Russian orgies. Similar views persist into the twentieth century; an American sexologist of the 1930s who considered Russia a hotbed of vice, a "country of sexual vices and excesses," was not atypical.[28] In many ways the accusations flung by Russians and Westerners at each other are similar in form and moralistic outrage; the American sexologist's diatribes are little different from, say, Rasputin's attacks on the West. The same distrust and horror of sexuality and the body are shared by American and Russian alike, although each projects the source of corruption and decadence onto the other country (and both reserve particular vilification for homosexuality).

Voloshinov can also be said to represent a strand of Russian thought that seeks to evade the problem of sexuality by defining it as Western. The supposition that sex is *not* a central theme in Russian literature is not self-evident, but rather a key argument in Russian discussions about sexuality. It owes a great deal to attempts to define the nature of Russian culture by defining the difference between Russia and the West, that is, by defining (and rejecting) the nature of the Other, just as definitions of Man have been made in contrast to the Other, Woman.[29]

Versions of Russian Sexuality

Having called into question the Russian idea that sexuality per se is a Western preoccupation, we now offer several accounts of sexuality in Russian culture. We begin with two narratives, one by Nikolai Berdyaev, one by Simon Karlinsky. We will consider a third perspective, that of Georgy Gachev, in a moment, and others will be used as counterpoints to these three, including Vasili Rozanov, Alexandra Kollontai, and a growing group of contemporary Russian feminists who critically engage traditions of writing about sex in Russian culture. Berdyaev and Karlinsky recommend themselves initially, however, because they attempt comprehensive views of their subject, because they embody important oppositions in Russian culture, and because the objects of their discourse (sublimation and heterosexuality for Berdyaev, homosexuality and liberation for Karlinsky) enable interrogation of fundamental categories of Russian thought.[30] Both men address Russia but write out of specifically Western traditions (Parisian emigration of the 1920s and 1930s, contemporary American academic life); both speak from political contexts that, while sometimes submerged in their work, nonetheless inform it (the anti-Sovietism of Russian intellectuals in emigration, the struggles for gay rights in the U.S.); each represents an intellectual tradition that has roots in modern Russian history (Berdyaev, the appeal to Russian spirituality also found in the Slavophiles' hostility toward Westernization; Karlinsky, the commitment to secular, pluralist values associated with figures like Alexander Herzen, and in our century, Andrei Sakharov and Andrei Sinyavsky). Finally, the two writers stand out for their quite different fates among readers, a difference that again enacts the paradoxical status of sexuality as a legitimate question for Russian culture: while Karlinsky appears to have affected a limited audience even among American Slavists, Berdyaev has emerged as a frequently reprinted and powerfully influential thinker in Russia's contemporary cultural revival. In terms of influence, Berdyaev is comparable to Rozanov (in fact, the recent spate of republications from Rozanov's vast legacy has edited out his endorsements of male homosexuality and made him seem even more like Berdyaev).[31]

Nikolai Berdyaev, widely known as a religious philosopher, spoke of himself in a late, semiautobiographical essay as belonging "in all probability, to the *genus* of philosophers of the erotic" (Berdyaev, *Self Knowledge*, p. 449); but in the same pages, he also insisted that sex should not be spoken about. Eric Naiman's paper in this volume explicates well the consequences of this paradoxical attitude. Writing in emigration in Paris, Berdyaev is one of several philosopher-theologians responsible for a twentieth-century renaissance of interest in Russian Orthodoxy; he is self-consciously indebted in his thinking on eros to Jacob Boehme, and propelled more negatively by opposition to Freud. Berdyaev's narrative plots a history of heroic spiritual denial, finding in Russian culture an eschatological essence that grants no legitimacy to the pleasures of world and body. Berdyaev urges us to keep sex private, to cover it up. His is a story that depicts and celebrates the triumph of morality and sublimation over the temptations of the flesh. Ironically, Berdyaev comes to a position not unlike the late Freud's, in his insistence on the values of personality and culture constructed through sublimation of bodily drives.

Simon Karlinsky, on the other hand, is an American scholar who has virtually inaugurated academic discourse on sexuality in Russia.[32] In "Russia's Gay Literature and Culture," he foregrounds a history of homosexuality in Russia, militating against any assumptions that the history of sexuality is linked only (or primarily) to relations *between* genders. Karlinsky could not be further from the quasi-religious urgings toward repression and sublimation found in Berdyaev; he sees nothing to be gained by hiding sexual pleasure or preference. Indeed, in his earlier landmark study of Nikolai Gogol's homosexuality, he charts the tragic path of one who starved himself to death rather than acknowledge his body and its desires. In *The Sexual Labyrinth of Nikolai Gogol*, Karlinsky reads the entire oeuvre of a major Russian writer on the basis of an extended and rich understanding of what kinds of sexual expressions were possible at a particular historical moment (Russia in approximately the first half of the nineteenth century) and what kinds of emotional and physical connections to others a particular person, Gogol, sought, valued, and feared.[33]

Karlinsky's keen sense of historical change, particularly in his essays about Russia's gay literary tradition, provides a view of sexuality quite different from Berdyaev's. Rather than Berdyaev's transcendent and essentializing categories of body and spirit, Karlinsky sees distinct periods in Russian history, and observes the nearly cyclical changes in attitudes brought by time's passage. Periods of relative tolerance for homosexuality include the pre-Petrine era and the nearly 60 years starting just after 1861 (the emancipation of the serfs), the greatest tolerance occurring in the *fin de siècle* period known as Russia's Silver Age. Karlinsky's his-

Introduction

tory moves between prohibition (in the eighteenth century and under Nicholas I) and celebration. His is a plot not of denial and sublimation, then, as in Berdyaev, but of liberation, brought to a tragic dénouement with the October Revolution and the "return of the repressors"—Lenin and his cohort, who inherited a "Victorian, puritanical ethic devised in the 1860's by the utilitarian positivists of that period" ("Russia's Gay Literature," p. 352). One might quarrel with this scheme, particularly if one tried to use the repression or acceptance of male homosexuality as a basis for conclusions about sexual repression and liberation more generally. The Silver Age, as we discuss below, is particularly resistant to categorization: the essays by Diana Lewis Burgin and Jane A. Sharp in this volume suggest that, as far as both lesbian and heterosexual women were concerned, the period was not so liberatory.

The accounts of Karlinsky and Berdyaev shape familiar oppositions (familiar, one notes, not only in Russia): of body versus spirit, of celebration versus repression, of homosexual versus heterosexual love. To some extent these are the oppositions that shape traditional histories of Russian culture, particularly as it moves from the culture of the mid-nineteenth century (characterized by prose, satire, politics, materialism, the *literal* in all its forms and tyrannies) to the 1890s (marked by poetry, metaphor, decadence, play, elusive identity, and flirtation with other worlds). Silver Age culture, for most students of Russia, is marked by the *repudiation* of the materialist ethos of the 1860s, and by the advent of unprecedented freedoms.[34] Partly for this reason, the Silver Age has become a period to which a great number of contemporary Russian thinkers and artists look for inspiration and models—hence a period that may prove pivotal in the renovation of various forms of discourse and creativity. Five essays in this volume (by Svetlana Boym, Diana Lewis Burgin, Barbara Heldt, Eric Naiman, and Jane A. Sharp) attest its importance and document the complexity of the position of women during the Silver Age. A sixth essay, by Cathy Popkin, treats a writer who stood in unusually complex relation to the age (Anton Chekhov). Its more liberal atmosphere facilitated the work of Natalia Goncharova and Sophia Parnok, for example, but Jane A. Sharp's and Diana Lewis Burgin's essays also show that opposition to, or incomprehension of, their achievements was significant. And Cathy Popkin, by reading the narrative strategies in a single Chekhov story, calls into question the separateness of prohibitions on sexuality from celebrations of sexual pleasure; indeed she finds the two to be mutually constitutive and finally inseparable. These essays, among others, remind us how the intricacies of gender and sexuality might temper apparently stark opposition between repression and liberation.

A similar convergence of patterns of repression and liberation characterizes the period of reform after 1861. A description of those years suggests almost immediately why they, too, are important to any study of sexuality in Russian culture. The reform inaugurated in 1861 marks a fundamental redrawing of the class configuration and economic structure of Russia, one that hastened the decay of an agrarian society and the institution of a more urbanized, industrialized country. These changes directly affected the history of sexuality. One paper in this volume, as well as much work elsewhere, focuses specifically on this period: Jane T. Costlow, in her essay on nineteenth-century representations of the maternal breast, suggests connections among anxiety over maternal roles, women's growing place in the workforce, the growth of prostitution, and literary/sexual appropriations of women's bodies.[35] Elizabeth A. Wood's essay in this volume contributes to a growing body of work on prostitution in nineteenth- and early-twentieth-century Russian culture. Catriona Kelly's paper, which discusses developments before and after the period of reform, observes that the misogyny of the *Petrushka* puppet plays intensified during and perhaps because of this period's urbanization. Eric Naiman and Jane A. Sharp both note that the "woman question" motivated subsequent protest against women's involvement in culture.

Most of the work on sexual representations during the 1860s has been anchored by the "woman question"—that is, the question of women's proper role in society, which arose during this time as women's concerns emerged in public discussions. Topics like women in the family, women's physiological role and/or limitations, women's desire for love, and women's rights to education made issues of sexuality part of a broad range of discourses (legal, medical, moral, publicistic, literary).[36] Nikolai Chernyshevsky both condensed many of these troubling issues and expressed the anxiety they produced in his exclamation "Away with these erotic questions!"[37]

Among the most provocative readings of this period, particularly of Chernyshevsky, is Nikolai Berdyaev's *Russian Idea* (*Russkaia ideia*, 1946). Berdyaev's focus on the legacy of Russian Orthodoxy and its impact on the "justification of culture" shapes his surprisingly positive response to Chernyshevsky.[38] Berdyaev reads Russia's nineteenth-century political radicals as faithful sons of Russian Orthodoxy; the nihilists were the monk-ascetics of a new order, governed by the law of castration, as Rozanov put it.[39] For Berdyaev, the great radical movements of the nineteenth century were infused with the same essence of transcendence, or what we might now call repression and sublimation, directed by men for whom the eschatological ends of social transformation negated all justifications of this-worldly pleasure. Berdyaev's narrative produces a picture of Russia in which male brotherhood plays a central role.

Chernyshevsky's portrait of the ideal revolutionary, in his novel *What Is to Be Done?* (*Chto delat'?*, 1863), provides a telling instance of both the sublimations Berdyaev describes and the bonds of love that were sublimated.[40] In chapter 29 ("An Extraordinary Man"), Chernyshevsky recounts a narrative of sanctity that focuses on the denial of bodily pleasures ("I shall not drink one drop of wine. I shall not touch any women," p. 280) and their sublimation in forms of manual labor.[41] Rakhmetov, Chernyshevsky's extraordinary man, becomes a kind of folk hero of labor, endowed with herculean strength and endurance and legitimated by his ability to share the work and material existence of the people, despite his own noble birth. In his sole concession to bodily desire, Rakhmetov smokes expensive cigars. Even without stressing the striking substitution of one form of oral pleasure (cigars) for those Rakhmetov has denied (wine and women), one recognizes in this figure of radical asceticism and power a virulently masculine image. In a novel that seems more centrally about *women's* work (the plot turns on Vera Pavlovna's founding of a sewing collective to help women of all classes gain economic and emotional autonomy), this chapter glorifies masculinity and male labor. The physical bond of men at work displaces the emasculating and decadent association with women. It seems hardly surprising that Rakhmetov's first interaction with Vera Pavlovna involves a refusal: Vera does not ask Rakhmetov to perform the labor with which she needs help (sorting women's garments), an omission that underscores the revolutionary's distance from the tactile, bodily, feminine realm still faintly represented in Vera. It is in fact Vera who succumbs to the oral, gustatory pleasure Rakhmetov denies himself: she's a sucker for clotted cream. The possibility of political radicalism coupled with bodily delight fades, however: it is the radical ascetic Rakhmetov who served as model for future revolutionaries.[42] What Chernyshevsky adumbrates in this portrait of a revolutionary is a rhetoric of revolutionary labor and discipline that will control and discipline (in Foucault's terms) the impetuous, apolitical body.

It is more than a little ironic, then, to find a rhetoric of sublimation and work that uncannily resembles that of the radicals of the 1860s in a contemporary commentator on "Russian Eros," one who owes much of his philosophical allegiance to the "antimaterialist" Russian Silver Age.[43] Georgy Gachev, like Berdyaev, insists on a distinction between sex (narrowly physical) and eros (a broader and more spiritual category).[44] Work, writes Gachev, can be seen as a "form of eros."[45] Gachev might find an association of his essay with Chernyshevsky's views rather unlikely: his elaboration of work and love envisions a deeply idyllic (rather than revolutionary) connection between tiller and soil. Yet he shares both Chernyshevsky's turn from the sexual body to the body at work and his insistent masculinity. Both men inscribe visionary teleologies that erase sexual pleasure as illegitimate; Gachev dissolves the woman's body in a mythology of feminine earth. Chernyshevsky moves toward an ideology of virility and class solidarity in labor; Gachev envisions the maternal as the site of redeemed work. Both men refuse what Berdyaev has called the "justification of the flesh"—something Berdyaev associated with the more decadent aspects of Silver Age culture, but which we might take more broadly to signify an attitude of joy and justice associated with the body and its pleasures.[46]

Gachev's reading of Russian culture stresses the spirit of renunciation that Berdyaev finds essentially Russian and claims as a common thread linking the nineteenth-century materialists with

both the medieval religious period and figures as disparate as
Tolstoy and Berdyaev himself. But this reading of Russian culture,
both of the nineteenth century and more broadly, excises those
historical phenomena that Karlinsky draws to our attention: phenomena in which the bodily and the sexual are both individually
affirmed and tolerated by society at large. We might return to the
lessons of Foucault's study of the institutions and discourses of
sexuality for a moment. It becomes clear how risky it would be
for us to agree too quickly that one historical period was a time of
liberation, another a time of sexual repression, or to see the two
as mutually exclusive; Foucault persuades us that liberation and
repression often go paradoxically and inextricably hand in hand.

This is in fact what a more diverse reading of the nineteenth
century might suggest. Chernyshevsky's portrait of Rakhmetov is
only one aspect of the ethos of this era. Legislative mandates notwithstanding, Karlinsky notes, the latter half of the nineteenth
century was marked by a tolerance of homosexual practice ("Russia's Gay Literature," pp. 350–53). Chernyshevsky insisted on
granting his wife the freedom of sexuality and emotion that had
traditionally been men's prerogative.[47] Chernyshevsky also participated in one of the numerous triangular relationships among radicals and nihilists in the period, relationships that are strikingly
similar to those studied by Eve Sedgwick in the English literary
tradition (the similarity includes the way that a deep but dangerous bond between two men is strengthened, indeed facilitated, by
the presence of a mediating woman).[48] *What Is to Be Done?* became a powerful force in initiating and legitimating companionate
marriage, as well as strong relationships of affection and economic
support among women. Such practices raise important questions
about the nature and languages of friendship and sexuality for
radicals in this era. Companionate marriage, recognition of sexual
desire, tolerance for maternity outside marriage, openly homosexual relationships between men and between women—these all
existed alongside Chernyshevsky's intensely masculine ideal of
sublimating physical labor. The quasi-official rhetoric of Russian
radicalism that increasingly disdained attention to matters of intimate life and personal relations existed in paradoxical tension
with these other practices.[49]

Chernyshevsky's novel might stand, then, as containing all the complicated and occasionally contradictory strands of thought of a period that aspired to fundamental liberation in matters personal, even as it held more repressive potential. The precise configuration of the interactions among these practices, and their relationships to official religious and legal discourse, remains to be mapped. What seems unquestionable is the dangerous linkage of an insistence on Russia as essentially spiritual, hence asexual, that we find in Berdyaev and Gachev, with the privileging of certain moments and phenomena from Russian history as proof of that essence. This is a powerful philosophical and cultural construct that needs to be named as such, and not taken as a "given" or as something natural.

Karlinsky argues against this spiritualization and virtual renunciation of sexuality, and we want to end this part of the introduction with thinkers who share his project of affirming sexual expression and describing the realities of sexual experience. Alexandra Kollontai (1872–1952) was a contemporary of Berdyaev, and a thinker who is also drawing new attention from Russians in the 1990s (in her case, from contemporary feminists). She became a figure of some infamy for the last three decades of her life, in large part because she sought the political and social liberation of women, which could not have been more at odds with the repressions urged by Stalin.[50] Kollontai devoted much of her energy to trying to improve the lives of Russian women; she wrote, "women and their fate have been the preoccupation of my entire life, and it is women's lot that drew me to Socialism."[51] Within her larger agenda of social programs for women and children, Kollontai also offered an analysis of women's second-class status that went beyond the Marxist theory of class oppression: she saw the oppression of women as complexly buttressed by women's sexual vulnerability.[52] She assumed the importance of individuality and self-expression in ways that resemble Berdyaev's and Rozanov's arguments for a spiritual value in sexual experience. But she did not lose sight of the material base of sexual experience, principally because of her strong intellectual debts to the Marxist tradition.[53] Kollontai is most insightful, in fact, when she writes of the complex interworkings of cultural paradigms with an individual's experience of intimate relationship. It is no surprise that she wrote fiction and autobiography in addition to her vast output in journalism, political analysis, and public speaking. The fiction has been scorned even by those who take Kollontai's political writing seriously.[54] Tales like *The Love of Worker Bees* (*Liubov' pchel trudovykh*, 1923), *A Great Love* (*Bol'shaia liubov'*, originally titled *Zhenshchina na perelome*, 1923) offer valuable alternative accounts of sexuality and desire in Russian culture. Kollontai's insights and discoveries are mentioned in some of the essays in this volume, in studies as different as Elizabeth A. Wood's essay on prostitution after the revolution (where Kollontai's views of prostitution are criticized) and Jane A. Sharp's account of Natalia Goncharova's trial for pornography.

Kollontai was never fully forgotten in or after her lifetime.[55] But her feminism has been virtually ignored in Russia, at least until very recently.[56] Kollontai and more recent feminists remind us that the sexual adventures of heterosexual men have, in Russia as elsewhere, sometimes involved violent repression of women. Kollontai's keenest insights are on relations between men and women; when she says sex she means heterosexual sex. She never, for example, lets her fictional heroines who are fed up with selfish and dominating men imagine intimacy with other women, which, as Diana Lewis Burgin and others have shown, was in fact a way of life for some women of this age. Kollontai's views of motherhood as women's most fulfilling emotional experience could also use some critical distance;[57] in fact she participates in the mythic elevation of the maternal so typical of Russian culture, to which we will turn in a moment.

Contemporary Russian feminists, who have in a sense picked up where Kollontai left off after an interval of 60 years, also exhibit a complex set of views about motherhood. The first generation of these feminist activists, of whom Tatiana Mamonova is the best known, often glorified the maternal and identified women with an instinctual desire to create and preserve life.[58] But these feminist writers contextualized women's reproductive capacities rather differently from what we shall see in male writers in a moment: their essays attack inadequate medical and child care, they see women's sexual pleasure as not in conflict with the biological reality of women's capacity to bear children, and in their affirmation of lesbian existence they do not limit women's sexual pleasure to heterosexual (or monogamous) settings.[59] Though there are obvious differences among these writers, there is a strong sense of continuity within this alternative feminist tradition: Mamonova as well as Kollontai are cited in a 1988 essay by Olga Lipovskaya, a feminist activist and journalist living in St. Petersburg.[60] As in Kollontai's writing, the strength of this work is its placement of women at the center of analysis, and the insistent awareness of the material realities that underlie sexual experience for women as well as men. This feminist impulse motivates much of the thinking in this volume.

Sexuality and the Myths of Mother Russia

The importance of the myth of the maternal has most recently been documented by Joanna Hubbs in her book *Mother Russia*; she identifies many Russian writers who draw on these myths, as well as those who claim that the myth of the Mother is the key to Russian culture.[61] The philosopher Georgy Fedotov, for example, writes: "in Mother Earth, who remains the core of Russian religion, converge the most secret and deep religious feelings of the folk." He goes on to describe how pagan cults of Mother Earth are retained but spiritualized in Russian Orthodoxy; the erotic element, says Fedotov, was "obliterated."[62] The importance of understanding how ideas about the maternal function in Russian culture was acknowledged at the conference—indeed, this was perhaps the topic most hotly debated.[63] Essays here by Jane T. Costlow, Barbara Heldt, and Eric Naiman consider the intertwinings of the maternal and the sexual. Each views the veneration of the mother and the maternal as problematic, not axiomatic; beneath and intertwined with idolatry of the maternal they uncover considerable anxiety about the body and sexuality.

Alongside the veneration of the mother in Russia exists a feeling of revulsion toward the maternal body. Writers like Berdyaev could speak reverently of motherhood while being repelled by every aspect of reproduction and pregnancy. Berdyaev's idolatry and repugnance are thoroughly documented here by Eric Naiman, and strongly resemble attitudes found in Tolstoy, whose views Jane T. Costlow's paper discusses and contrasts to women writers who were Tolstoy's contemporaries. What is problematic for Tolstoy is the combination of maternity and sexuality, which should not, in his eyes, coexist in the same body.[64] In *What Is Art?* (*Chto takoe iskusstvo?*, 1898), though the context is a discussion of art, Tolstoy's attitudes toward the maternal body are stated vividly: "Strange as the comparison may sound, what has happened to the art of our circle and time is what happens to a woman who sells her womanly attractiveness, intended for maternity, for the pleasure of those who desire such pleasures. The Art of our time and of our circle has become a prostitute."[65] Tolstoy sees this ruinous situation as the "tragedy of the bedroom" (Gachev, "Russkii eros," pp. 226–27),[66] tragic because what should be limited to the domestic safety of bedroom and family is opened out to spaces of the public, specifically the market.

This juxtaposition of approval for women whose sexuality produces children with disgust for those whose orientation is toward pleasure is hardly unique to Tolstoy, or to Berdyaev, or even to Russian culture. Its stark and disputable opposition is familiar from Victorian culture, for example, and has been critiqued well by feminist scholars.[67] Where Russian examples offer new insight is in the effect this idealization of the maternal has on sexual fantasy. Once again, the philosopher Georgy Gachev offers a peculiarly condensed version of this adult male fantasy.[68] Here is his description of early-twentieth-century writers (Gachev mentions two by name—Ivan Bunin and Mikhail Artsybashev) who were exploring more adventurous erotic motivations and sexual plots:[69] "The Eros that began to raise its head and get up on its hind legs in Russian literature at the beginning of the twentieth century was entirely the eros of the sneaking, voyeuristic adolescent, and not the eros of the confidently male" (p. 241). The sex scenes of this branch of literature move Gachev to still more extreme metaphors. He calls them "an impulse to stick out one's tongue" and goes on: "that is exactly how an adolescent stands behind a door and spies through a crack or a keyhole, his tongue hanging out, licking his lips, breathing heavily—drooling now and then, he spies on the woman as temple [*baba-khram*] reclining naked and keeping unto herself in the next room, like something out of Kustodiev.[70] Nowhere is there powerful possession of a woman, only groping her" (p. 241).[71] Is the position of woman in all this only that of a viewed (or "groped") object? We seem to be in the presence of the familiar dichotomy of sainted motherhood versus despised whore, but as we suggested above its effect is unexpected. Evoking the familial bond substitutes pity for love,[72] purging the erotic of sexual desire; indeed one might argue that the function of this evocation is precisely to create and enforce a taboo. Consequently any representation of sexual desire is likely to be surrounded by shame and horror—it is as if all sex were incest. What results are the attempts (catalogued above) to escape the body and desire by redefining sex as transcendence.

If Gachev rejects certain "adolescent" writers, it is perhaps because they do not evade what they see in the Russian tradition, and because they bring together elements that should be kept apart. What Gachev dismisses as peeping through a keyhole might in fact be a refusal to avert the gaze, an insistence on confronting the taboo. This will to confront a taboo emerges vividly in two papers in this volume that seek out previously ignored points of view about maternal representations in their erotic and bodily contexts. Barbara Heldt finds in Maria Shkapskaya "a sexually empowered motherhood centered in the female body," and Jane Costlow concludes her essay on the maternal breast with three lesser-known women writers who uncover "the economic and erotic exploitation of women's bodies" in the practice of wet nursing.

A narrative that addresses these kinds of conflict as inherent in the images associated with the maternal in Russian culture is Ivan Bunin's "Mordvinian Sarafan" ("Mordovskii sarafan," 1925).[73] Bunin's three-page tale of a man's liaison with a pregnant woman has both characters repeat the myths and clichés about motherhood that they have absorbed from their culture. The mainspring of the affair is their sexual desire, and the rather tawdry circumstances might indeed make it a sordid adolescent tale. What transforms this rather commonplace relationship is the fact of her pregnancy, which makes the affair, at least to him, peculiarly horrible. From the beginning, when he asks, "Why do I go to her, this strange and, what's more, pregnant woman? Why have I formed this connection and why do I keep up this unnecessary and even repellant acquaintance?" (p. 379), to the end, when he can think only of flight, the atmosphere of the story is one of shame, disgust, and horror.

Her pregnancy is initially a problem of description. On first looking her over the man observes her hair, her full breasts, and her stockings, but entirely omits to mention her belly, the most telling part of her body and that which obviously both attracts and repels him. His ambivalence is symbolized by the sarafan from which the tale takes its title: she displays "something strange and terrible" (p. 381), a Mordvinian sarafan, which evokes for the narrator the horror of the encounter and perhaps of sexual desire itself. The sarafan is a coarse peasant dress that contrasts oddly with her rich velvet gown; she holds it up to herself, to her breasts and to her belly, drawing attention to the very part of her body that he has tried not to see. He feigns interest and pretends to admire the garment, but thinking all the while, "there was something gloomy, ancient and funereal, as it were, in that shapeless garment; it evoked something terrifying and very unpleasant for me in connection with her pregnancy and her uneasy merriment. Probably she will die in childbirth" (p. 381). These are his fantasies however; when *she* speaks, it is not of fear of dying in childbirth but fear that her child will die.

As their sexual encounter begins, he now fixates on her belly, a change presumably enabled by his pity for her likely death, her talk of children, and thus Bunin's reconceptualization of their relation as that between a parent and child. Compassion has been substituted for desire (in Gachev's terms, *zhalet'* for *zhelat'*). When the moment he has been waiting for comes, a scene of passion is replaced by a scene of comfort, in which he draws her to him with the words "Calm yourself," and she sinks weeping on his breast. The ensuing sexual activity is elided, perhaps because it has come to seem like incest. By the end, the compassion, the tenderness are gone, leaving the image of bodies whose embrace is imbued with shame.

Bunin's story helps us to make concrete Berdyaev's construction of a history of Russian sexuality marked by denial and spirituality, specifically his (and Gachev's) claims for a redemptive ethos in Russia's maternal asexuality.[74] Nothing is redeemed in this story, for the narrator has no access to the transcendence of the body that the idea of the maternal, rather than the physical presence of a pregnant woman, would seem to have promised. Bunin shows us instead how tightly sexual desire has been trapped in the myth of the maternal, and he links both to death with the deeply symbolic and "horrible" peasant dress. The story has the air of death about it because it belongs to the age of Russian decadence; but Bunin also seeks to create a rarified atmosphere of entrapment and decay, as if to say that if this is the conceptual framework within which Russians imagine sexual desire they will always associate it with taboo and death and, as the story's ending suggests with its fantasy of flight, they will inevitably seek escape.

Gender, Masquerade, and Desire

What, though, if the flight were to be fiercely desired by the woman? Would she seek to escape the myth of the maternal that so powerfully imposes on Gachev, Berdyaev, and Bunin? We want to turn here to two quite different scenarios of sexual desire and bodily presence. They involve a foregrounding not of the maternal but of gender difference itself, and allow us to note some of the patterns of enforcement and anxiety that social norms of gender produce about sexuality. But they are perhaps most useful in specifying how gender and sex are not the same thing.[75] They do so by "making strange" the assumptions we might have about femininity and masculinity. Our readings are meant to contextualize the essays in this volume. In her discussion of a Tolstaya story, Helena Goscilo describes a male poet as a "transgendered Clarissa," whom she links to the more general way Tolstaya challenges the limits of gender. Diana Lewis Burgin's analysis of critical writing about Sophia Parnok reveals a rhetorical slippage between the categories of gender and sexuality, as critics who refuse to be forthright about Parnok's lesbianism place her voice in a no-man's-land between the "masculine" and the "feminine." And Svetlana Boym's essay, on Marina Tsvetaeva, identifies the figure of the "poetess" as an impossible combination of feminine excess and feminine lack, both impinging on the kind of love story Tsvetaeva's prose can narrate. As her essay shows, one solution to the resulting narrative problem is the adoption of an exaggerated femininity as masquerade.

We turn, then, to two examples of "women" dressed as "men."[76] The first of these masquerades comes from the memoirs of Nadezhda Durova, *The Cavalry Maiden* (*Kavalerist-devitsa*, 1836), initially published by Alexander Pushkin when he was editor of

Introduction

The Contemporary (Sovremennik). In 1807, Nadezhda Durova sets off to become a cavalry soldier in the Russian army. She leaves behind a mother whose cruelty she emblematized in the tale of how her mother threw her out the door of a moving carriage when she was an infant. Her horrible memories of how she was coaxed and forced toward feminine stillness, meekness, and submissiveness create fully adequate motivation for Durova's decision to emulate instead the adventurous life of her father. When Durova departs, she is dressed in a Cossack uniform and accompanied only by her beloved horse, Alcides.[77] Thanks to wit, some luck, and the help of strangers (including the Emperor Alexander), Durova leaves behind the world of boredom and enclosure that would have been hers as a woman. She marches off to Poland and battle, accepted as a male soldier and only occasionally shadowed by stories of a mysterious woman granted the right to serve as an officer. She is anxious in the company of women, who are more shrewd in suspecting her sex. One pleasure of Durova's text derives from our possession of a knowledge her fellow soldiers do not have. Durova's rejection of gender brings with it liberation, the liberation of movement and adventure. Her freedom depends, though, on the capacities of dress to cloak the body; on her skill at the soldierly gestures that confirm "identity"; on others' persistent reading of her *surface*, rather than her "depth."

Durova inhabits a world in which bodily appearances create a kind of opacity; she provokes little anxiety (that we can read). If anything, there is slimly veiled attraction, an eroticism between women that Durova's male dress both initiates and makes safe. Women pursue Durova; at least one woman is eager to marry her, and Durova's own intense feelings for some of these women emerge fleetingly in the memoir. A mixture of opacity and recognition thus enables the acting out of what may be Durova's longing to be desired by members of her own sex. We suggest, then, that rather than just reading Durova's memoirs as an exciting tale of a woman who gets to experience the adventures of a man during the Napoleonic wars, we might focus on the way that masquerade facilitated a military man's life in public and a woman's encounters with other women in private. If we recall Karlinsky's contrast of sexual liberation versus sexual repression, Durova's memoirs offer a case study in which the reaction against the repressive norms of gender lead to a life experience of at least partial liberation (Durova did not enter into an enduring relationship with any of the women whom she attracted, as was the case for some other women who fought in European or American wars disguised as men).[78] There is indeed some irony in the fact that it is the army that provides Durova with an institutional framework for her liberation, and not just because of the regimentation we associate with the military: Karlinsky notes that laws penalizing consensual male homosexuality were instituted in 1706 and 1716, which means that the very army that facilitated Durova's own closeness to women would have been a site of greater impediments to men's seeking intimacy with other men. Her memoirs thus point to an asymmetry between the ways that men might have lived homosexual lives and the ways that women might have done so, an asymmetry that the Russian legal system has long codified by prohibiting male homosexuality but passing over lesbianism in silence. Durova's memoirs also provide another case where repression and liberation exist side by side.

In our second example of masquerade, the situation is more political. The time is 30 years later, with the advent of the "woman question" and the growing articulation of women's desire to break with traditional categories of existence. The ambiguity of gender and sexuality now seems to worry Russians more; it first surfaces around the figure of George Sand. Elena Shtakenshneider writes in her diary that George Sand is neither man nor woman, a refusal echoed by the editor of a liberal journal, who wrote, "[the new woman] is not a woman, no, and it is not a man either—it is an entirely new sex, a new organism, which we can legally only consider a transition type."[79] The visual representation of such a "new organism" was essayed in 1859 in *The Spark* (*Iskra*), the satirical supplement to the left-wing journal *The Contemporary* (*Sovremennik*). The cartoon (Fig. 1) depicts a figure of apparently feminine form (her hips and bosom both generously shaped), who wears a simple, light-colored dress and a man's dark hat. She lifts a tumbler in one hand and holds a cigar in the other; her facial features seem neither masculine nor feminine, her hair tucked behind her neck is of ambiguous length, while the broad neck and shadow of an adam's apple suggest, perhaps, masculine strength. Her gesture is accompanied by the following text: "Dear Ladies!

Introduction

Fig. 1. A cartoon from the journal *The Spark* (*Iskra*), 1859, depicting an ambiguously gendered "new organism." Courtesy of the Hoover Institution Library.

This toast is for our emancipation! The time for the rule [*vladichestvo*] of women has arrived; the men are under our heels. Hurrah! May men's power [*vlast'*] be destroyed, like this empty tumbler! (She throws the tumbler. An outburst of applause.)"[80]

The Spark and *The Contemporary* both represent that wing of the Russian intelligentsia that most adamantly supported women's emancipation (an issue still tied, we note, to the emancipation of the serfs, and not yet dismissed as irrelevant in the more radicalized world of post-reform Russia). So, for example, Chernyshevsky's *What Is to Be Done?*, perhaps the fullest and most radical articulation of the midcentury feminist program, was published in *The Contemporary* four years after the appearance of this cartoon. What the 1859 image illustrates, however, is a level of anxiety that is only accentuated by the impossibility of dismissing the image as parody. The parodic association of "emancipated women" and "George Sandistes" with masculine attire had become a staple of the conservative (and not only the conservative) press in Russia.[81] But the full weight of the journalist's anxiety is felt less in the woman's attire (both her dress and hat) than in the representation of the body itself. The powerful neck and dark facial features hint at masculinity, while the wine bottle that stands directly in front of the woman casts a phallic shadow along her otherwise curvaceous form. (She seems, in fact, to discard the supposed emptiness of women's genitals in the empty tumbler, in order to take up the more aggressive phallic stance.) All "essence" of gender is lost in this shadow play of sexuality and power. In the disappearance of gender as essence, the cartoon recalls Durova, but the context is insistently political, which means that gender difference is fundamentally a difference in power: the accompanying script alludes to *political* power (*vladichestvo, vlast'*), while the image itself conveys male sexual prowess. The image's unresolvability (is this a woman "masquerading" as a man, or a man dressed up in corset and hoop skirt?) also marks its difference from Durova, as well as its powerful unsettling of categories that were, even for radicals, crucial.[82] Jane A. Sharp's essay in this volume provides important evidence of the various ways that Russians tried to keep in place the categories and prohibitions resisted by masquerades such as Durova's or more organized efforts like the women's movement. Her account of Natalia Goncharova's later trial for obscenity shows how the legal system tried to punish a woman painter's intrusion into the historically male preserve of nude painting. Goncharova's reworking of the conventions of nude painting were profoundly disturbing to her contemporaries.

This volume includes other essays in which the controlling of sexuality and gender norms is studied in specific historic contexts:

Eve Levin documents the Orthodox church's language of sexual prohibition during the medieval period, and Elizabeth Wood's study of the discourse around prostitution during the early Soviet period shows how metaphors of purity and contamination were mobilized to control women's sexuality. These essays contribute to a history of sexual repression in Russian culture, which is one important aspect of a history of sexuality in Russia, as elsewhere.

Sexual Discourse in Contemporary Russia

For all the talk about greater sexual freedom in contemporary Russia, we have found as much impetus to regulate and discipline the body and its desires in the contemporary period. To be sure, one impulse behind our symposium on sexuality and the body in Russian culture was an impression of richer, more varied, and perhaps freer sexual expression in today's Russia. This is certainly the story told by reports here and there on Russian cultural life since the advent of *glasnost,* and it is a further narrative about sexuality and the body in Russian culture that requires examination, one that shows important contrasts and continuities with what we have already noted. As we examine the ideas of sex and the body that have emerged since 1985 or so, we will consider some that seem explicitly erotic, with particular attention to the figure of the prostitute; others that refuse to idealize or even eroticize the body, instead representing it as ill or dead; and still others expressed in a group of texts and artistic events that flee (in some cases, by magic) the norms of gender and the constraints of heterosexuality.

Contemporary Russian culture seems to have found not so much a wholly new concern for sexuality, as more places where references to sex are possible and useful: criticism of culture and politics increasingly includes analysis of sexual behavior and relies on sexual metaphor; sexual behavior itself merits more explicit description and seems to need more regulation. A *New York Times* op-ed piece urged exporting condoms rather than computers to the USSR, a scholar has suggested the prostitute as an appropriate icon for this age of transition to a market economy, an Astrakhan entrepreneur has proposed a hotel with hourly rates for couples seeking privacy, and one Soviet cultural critic has noted the "eroticization of the entire country."[83] The proliferation of ways of thinking and talking about sex has not passed without some consternation, as one could guess from the exaggerated, alarmed claim that an entire country could be "eroticized" (and the Astrakhan businessman met with such resistance that his hotel plans were stalled). Igor Kon vividly describes the paradoxes of permission and reprisal that govern this proliferation of sexual discourses and commercial activities:

Now we have everything. Pornography. Erotic art. You can get an appointment with a sex therapist as simply as with a stomach specialist. You can exchange a book about Russian sexology for French detective fiction or for knitting instructions. We have a league to defend sexual minorities. Attacks on pederasts. Nudist beaches on the Baltic coast. Fines for appearing in public in shorts in the height of the tourist season in a southern town. Exhibits of erotic photography in the best exhibition spaces of one major cultural center. The refusal of permission for a similar exhibit in a different, no less major cultural center. A discussion in the press and in government bodies of opening a brothel.[84]

Kon's examples are chosen to highlight the variety of views about sexuality and the body in Russian culture today. But it has seemed wildly inappropriate to some that public figures would discuss these supposedly private matters at all while the Soviet economy is collapsing. Don't send condoms, these people would urge, send us food and clothing.[85]

Yet the claim that the discourses of sexuality and of daily life are separate makes sense only if one holds a narrow and quite specific notion of what sexuality entails, and only if one believes that sexual activities performed behind closed doors are not influenced by the desires, prohibitions, and fears that have been formed elsewhere. One view of sexuality that emerged in the first years of *glasnost* echoes age-old Russian views of sex as a Western (and decadent) phenomenon, views we discussed above. This was particularly true in the campaign against prostitution (an early Gorbachev effort to get people to take work more seriously, like the trials of bureaucrats for corruption and the anti-alcohol measures). As Elizabeth Waters has argued, this campaign targeted women who had foreign clientele; not only did this strategy create the false impression that it was not Soviet men who were paying for sex, but it also surrounded the prostitute with an aura of costly and of course imported clothing, as if sex could exist only in luxurious and foreign circumstances.⁸⁶ A popular 1988 literary and cinematic treatment of prostitution used the same images, with the added moral twist of the heroine's eventual death in her shiny Volvo.⁸⁷

Other treatments of prostitution have put aside the glamour to show the seamier side of a prostitute's life. Alexander Galin's drama *Stars in the Morning Sky* (*Zvezdy utrennego sveta*) was a hit in Leningrad and Moscow in 1987 that played New York in 1988. Its gritty, frightening quality was expressed in both the superb acting and in the very language of the play—intensely profane, in a way that at the time felt quite shocking.⁸⁸ More recently, the documentary filmmaker Tofik Shakhverdiev has completed *To Die for Love* (*Umeret' ot liubvi*, 1991), which contrasts two Moscow prostitutes, one who works in a hotel for foreigners and earns hard currency, another whose ruble trade provides badly needed income to sustain her husband (a writer) and their three sons. Neither woman is idealized visually; in fact they are contextualized by images of Gypsy women and children begging on the streets and tales of women who have killed their lovers.⁸⁹ This more disturbing view of exploitation, desire, and violence provides an important answer to the glossy visual representations of women's bodies that have also proliferated recently—they appear on items from keychains to postcards, in journals (like *Ogonek*, where what one Amherst conference participant called "tit shots" have become a remarkably regular feature), and in beauty contests.⁹⁰

The less idealized image of women's bodies has also begun to emerge in literature, for example in the plays and stories of Lyudmila Petrushevskaya.⁹¹ Here one finds references to any and every bodily function and blithe evocations of body parts.⁹² Petrushevskaya's recent story, "Down the Road of the God Eros" ("Po doroge Boga Erosa," 1991), features two aging women and contrasts the cosmetic surgery of one to the sagging skin of the other—yet this is a love story, where the two women compete for the same man.⁹³ But it is less her representation of the body than what seems to some her loveless world that has drawn so much attention to Petrushevskaya: her distanced descriptions of horrifying actions or feelings still seem to unnerve Russian readers, who are not yet estranged from the didacticism of socialist realism (shouldn't the prostitute be killed in the end?). Some of this same anger at apparent indifference to violence has been directed at other contemporary cultural figures, notably women (the filmmaker Kira Muratova, for example, and to a lesser extent Tatiana Tolstaya). They have seemed "cruel," an epithet that echoes A. N. Mikhailovsky's famous description of Dostoevsky as a "cruel talent," and with good reason: Dostoevsky foreshadowed much of the "dark literature" (*chernukha*) in recent Soviet writing, and his novels explored the psychological complexities of sexual desire and sexual dread a generation before the advent of Freudian psychoanalysis.

What is remarkable about the conception of sex in Petrushevskaya's writing is its lack of difference from the other numbly performed acts of desperation in her stories: a woman comes home and throws herself out a window; a woman meets a man and sleeps with him; a woman tells the woman whom her son has left pregnant that she'll have to move out, knowing that the woman has nowhere to live; still another pregnant woman routinely feigns illness to get herself into a hospital because she, too, has nowhere to live. One critic has aptly defined Petrushevskaya's great theme as "the fate of woman in a cruel world"; he suggests that it is something about the world these characters inhabit that makes horrifying forms of behavior seem inevitable and routine.[94] Indeed, Petrushevskaya seems to have her finger on the pulse of the times: the literary critic Natalia Ivanova has written that unmasking the violence in everyday life is contemporary culture's primary task.[95]

A writer who would seem a likely confederate here for Petrushevskaya is Viktor Erofeev; Ivanova concludes another, similarly pointed essay with a discussion of his fiction.[96] Erofeev would have a place in this introduction even without his fiction since he is also an important literary critic who, among other things, has written an impressive essay on the place of the Marquis de Sade in twentieth-century European culture. His stories include explicit descriptions of sexual activities that are not all that far from Sade, and his grounding of some forms of sexual pleasure in the destruction of the human body will certainly discomfit readers in ways that Sade's writings do.[97] Erofeev is not unique in his sexual explicitness nor in the objections raised to his work: among others,

Introduction

Eduard Limonov, writing in the West, has long elicited condemnation from intelligentsia reviewers, and one could guess that in Limonov's case the exploration of gay male and bisexual sensibilities has increased the provocation.[98] Yet to place Petrushevskaya in this context, where attention has been paid principally to sexual explicitness, is to risk quick devolution into a discussion of pornography, especially since the writing of Limonov, Erofeev, and others often depicts the violent sexual abuse of women.[99] As Catriona Kelly suggests in the conclusion of her essay, the sexually explicit pictures marketed in Russia today appeal to a very broad male audience; they ought to be viewed on a continuum with the "high culture" productions endorsed by a writer like Erofeev.

Instead, we suggest juxtaposing Petrushevskaya to Elena Makarova, a prose writer who has drawn far less critical attention, although she has published five volumes of stories. Like Petrushevskaya, and unlike Limonov or Erofeev, Makarova centers narrative attention on women. Compared to the extreme actions of Petrushevskaya's heroines, human conduct seems harmless or mild in her work, but only at a first glance; Makarova's narratives are typically told by a sympathetic, believable woman, as opposed to Petrushevskaya's more suspect women narrators, like the blind, dying woman who abuses her child in "Our Crowd" ("Svoi krug," 1988), to cite a famous example. Makarova frequently shows us the body during illness, the handicapped or malformed body, the body at moments of vulnerability and exposure. She is unflinching in her chronicling of illness and deformity (a striking example is her tale of a sanatorium for adolescent girls with orthopedic problems, "After Six Days Comes Sunday" ["Cherez kazhdye shest' dnei—voskresen'e," 1968]).[100] In this she resembles Petrushevskaya, from whose plays one literary critic cited seventeen illnesses—and the list seemed rather off the top of his head.[101]

One of Makarova's darkest stories is "Preserving Life" ("Na sokhranenii," written in 1974, published in 1989). It takes place in a maternity ward (and cannot help but remind one of Julia Voznesenskaya's *Women's Decameron* [*Zhenskii dekameron*, 1985]).[102] The pregnant heroine has come here because she is hemorrhaging. But the story is less about her experiences, fearful and estranged though they are, than about the appalling indifference to life that reigns in this hospital. The lack of medical treatment and even cleanliness is not shocking (these are all too well known realities of ordinary Soviet medical care). What is stunning is how much the scene reminds one of prison memoirs: the women have as little privacy and control over their fates as those in Evgenia Ginzburg's *Journey into the Whirlwind* (*Krutoi marshrut*, 1967), and the hospital staff are certainly as abusive as prison guards.[103] Here, where the society has supposedly built an institution to preserve and protect life (note the story's title), one finds instead an atmosphere of punishment and denunciation. This is Foucault's nightmare of surveillance come true, prison and hospital in one.

It is also something more, a nightmare of near death. Next to the maternity hospital is a morgue, and when the women go to the window to shout down to visitors (no one is allowed into the hospital), they also glimpse bodies being carried into the morgue. That juxtaposition might be taken as nothing more than a paradox in Makarova's story, like the paradox of women waiting in line for their abortions while one woman has come to the hospital for fertility treatment. But dead bodies appear in too many recent Soviet fictions, particularly those that have something important to say about sexuality and the body, for Makarova's morgue to be taken as a trivial detail. In "The Meaning of Life" ("Smysl zhizni," 1990), Petrushevskaya writes of a doctor kept alive by machines, a condition she ironically labels "complete immortality."[104] In *Polina*, a novella by Nina Katerli that shocked its first audience by telling of a sexually adventurous woman who avoided both marriage and motherhood, readers might now be struck by Polina's recurring memory of dragging her former lover, Boria, from a forest. She gets him to a doctor only to be told that Boria is dead, that he died back there in the forest.[105] This image, of a woman dragging a dead man on her back, is barely visualized in the story, but it is haunting in a more than figurative sense: Polina is also called on to identify the body of her dead father (whom she had never seen previously), as if the story will not let her avoid this physical encounter with the tangibly dead body.

One way to read the recurrence of corpses is as a sign of something in a culture's memories that cannot be repressed; one would not have to look far to conjecture the historical and political reasons why the body that emerges in many Russian texts might be damaged, wounded, aching, dead, decayed.[106] Referring to death became a way to talk about the deadness of various forms of public life in the former Soviet Union; thus Viktor Erofeev wrote a wake for Soviet literature two years before the Soviet government collapsed.[107] A recent essay partly about Stalin's terror (which is also the historical ground for the 1984–86 Georgian film *Repentance*, where a woman insistently digs up a corpse), Mikhail Rykhlin's "Bodies of Terror," is another example of a powerful judgment about Soviet culture's disdain for the body.[108]

Given the complexities of Russia's myth of the maternal discussed above, we might ask whether there are not examples from the *glasnost* period that try to reanimate the dead body without resorting to the mystifying rhetoric of reproduction. A story that does precisely this is Valeria Narbikova's "Around Environ . . ." ("Okolo ekolo . . . ," 1990), in which two men go through elaborate magical preparations to hatch a baby, an android, tenderly named in Russian an "andriusha."[109] In another of her stories there is birth by telephone conversation.[110] Narbikova has commented negatively on the omnipresence of the maternal figure ("such a robust country . . . so many forests, fields, meadows, and everywhere there is mama, you can't go anywhere that there is no mama").[111] We have seen writers who reject any glorification of the mother, like Durova or, among contemporary writers, Tolstaya, as Helena Goscilo's paper demonstrates, but Narbikova sidesteps the maternal trap entirely by reimagining enchanted ways of reproducing. This theme of magic is felt as well in Narbikova's energetic linguistic world, where words spring up out of other words, and the Russian language, which seemed so dead in daily Soviet life, is exuberantly at play (the titles of her stories are all fine examples).

Folk magic plays a surprising and creative role in other recent narratives about erotic desire. Elena Makarova, for example, brings both whimsy and fear to many of her stories when she resorts to folk magic. A splendid example of a story that builds this contrast (and it is a contrast, since the story includes a dying man, a mentally ill woman, and interpolated images of frighteningly red women's bodies in the public baths) is "Herbs from Odessa" ("Travy iz Odessy," 1982), where a young woman seeks a magic potion to cure her grandfather's cancer.[112] And in Makarova's "Preserving Life," the women patients advise each other about folk cures that promise better results than the doctors' medicine (in view of the quality of medical care they receive, one begins to share their optimism about wonder-working concoctions purchased from wise old women). A more sinister example would be Tolstaya's story "Date with a Bird" ("Svidanie s ptitsei," 1983), wherein exotic Tamila lures the young hero with enchanted trinkets, but the experience proves a harsh introduction to the adult world of sex and death. Magic also moves the plots of the extraordinarily creepy tales recently published by Nina Sadur. Sadur brilliantly draws together the workings of folk magic and sexual desire when she writes of the quest for love potions, or of the urge to avenge rejection.[113]

Sadur, Makarova, Tolstaya, and Narbikova are showing us something overlooked by the more sensational accounts of "the eroticization of an entire country"—and their resort to age-old Russian forms of folk magic keeps these writers very far from an anxiety about the West. They tell of a desire to be able to cure the body's ills with which institutionalized medicine certainly has not come to terms; they tell (in Narbikova's android story and in other writers' frequent recourse to images of androgyny) of a wish to have babies outside the norms of childbirth, to have sex outside the norms of gender; they imagine a world of sexual pleasure where black magic makes possible things that grim, daily reality withholds.[114]

Recent writing offers hope, then, in ways that can counter even the most overwhelming fantasies of death. Another encouraging sign has been the flourishing of both feminist and specifically lesbian and gay journalistic and artistic work. These are new and important, if still marginalized, possibilities that challenge the norms of gender and sexuality still dominating in Russian culture. Olga Lipovskaya has produced six issues of *Women's Reader* (*Zhenskoe chtenie*), one devoted entirely to lesbian writing, all including translated and original writings that promote sexual awareness, curiosity, and liberation.[115] A first issue of *Sappho's Lyre* (*Lira Safo*), edited by Anna Vetrova, was circulated in Moscow in 1990. A gay and lesbian newspaper, *The Theme* (*Tema*), has appeared in Moscow, and the summer of 1991 saw not only an international conference but also a gay and lesbian film festival, to which 20,000 tickets were sold and during which a Moscow gay rights demonstration was held (its motto: Turn Red Squares into Pink Triangles).[116] Gay activists distributed condoms to those emerging from the 1990 Communist party conference—and probably not simply, as they claimed, to discourage party members from reproducing.[117] *Ogonek* gave a brief account of the warm reception San Francisco mayor Art Agnos accorded to Roman Kalinin, editor of *The Theme*: a rare example—rare even for such a "liberal" periodical as *Ogonek*—of a mainstream Soviet journal's reporting without condemnation on gay activism.[118]

Has this political activity tangibly affected the production of writers, directors, filmmakers, and artists? It is hard to generalize so soon (and in the face of such intense and volatile change in Russia, perhaps unwise), but individual breakthroughs, especially in the visual arts, should be noted.[119] One exhibit (installed in the Marble Palace, then still a museum of Lenin's life) celebrated "the classical ideal of the male physique—for fun": "All the pieces by the five young artists dealt with male physicality and sexuality. Some were frankly homoerotic. A male performance artist, video crew in tow, swirled through the rooms gleefully impersonating Marilyn Monroe and ridiculing Soviet television clichés. No less campy, the last page of the photocopied catalogue showed a ballerina in a tutu perched atop Lenin's armored car."[120] At least one Petersburg gallery (named after Salvador Dali) that plans to focus on gay and lesbian art has opened as well. Among literary innovations, one could cite the increased publication of poetry by people who identify themselves as feminist activists (for example, the Moscow collection *Seventeenth Echo* [*Semnadtsatoe ekho*, 1990], collected by Olga Tatarinova and showcasing the results of poetry-writing workshops sponsored by the Transfiguration club). Lipovskaya's *Women's Reader* is also notable for its prominent inclusion of poetry and fiction by contributors.

There has been a backlash, of course, which has been reported well by Masha Gessen in *Out/Look*. When homosexuality was thought not to exist, when it was invisible, she argues, it was also safer, and the dawning awareness of AIDS in Soviet society has had homophobic effects similar to what we have witnessed in the last few years in the U.S. (although, as Gessen correctly points out, AIDS is spreading in the former Soviet Union principally in hospitals, where disposable syringes are unavailable and sterilization procedures are inadequate).[121] Conservative Russian writers like Valentin Rasputin continue to legitimate a widely held view that homosexual sex is sick: Rasputin is said to have told a British television reporter: "If you legalize homosexuality the necrophiliacs will clamor for their rights—after all they're a sexual minority too. When it comes to homosexuals let's keep Russia clean. We have our own traditions."[122]

Rasputin's reference to necrophiliacs instantiates once again the recurring corpse of contemporary culture, but his words also return us full circle to the question with which we began our Introduction—just how different is sexuality in Russia from sexuality in the West? Rasputin makes the dangers of this comparison all too painfully felt: the desire to keep Russia "clean" because it has its "own traditions" suggests that "Russian tradition" is itself "clean." This rhetoric can become a slogan on which to build a campaign of persecution and injustice—the Third Reich's desire to purify the Aryan race may be the most famous example and the most murderous, but it is hardly the only one in a history linking national purity and sexuality.[123] The easy alliance between Rasputin (and other conservative writers) and the Russian nationalist, virulently anti-Semitic group Pamyat ought to be kept well in mind here. This is not to single him out, for Rasputin's views unfortunately have a substantial following. But it is the case that Rasputin's writings offer brutally clear statements against sexual liberation and against the more general, political liberation of women as well.[124]

Conclusion

Similar demands for moral reform and a national purity campaign were heard during the Emergency Committee's speech during the attempted coup to overthrow Gorbachev's government in August 1991. To justify their coup, the committee drew a grim picture of the deterioration of society. The violence that some writers have identified as characteristic of Soviet society for 70 years was reconceived as a product of *perestroika*. Among a long list of ills, the committee cited the decline of law and order: "The country is sinking into a quagmire of violence and lawlessness. Never before in national history has the propaganda of sex and violence assumed such a scale, threatening the health and lives of future generations. Millions of people are demanding measures against the octopus of crime and glaring immorality."[125] Among the coup's promises, then, was the eradication of "shameful phenomena discrediting our society and degrading Soviet citizens."[126] Their words augured the "return of the repressors," to use Karlinsky's description of the effects of the October Revolution, and it is not difficult to imagine who the targets of repression and eradication would have been and what kind of social reconstruction would have taken place. The Emergency Committee's representation of themselves as guardians of public morality, their criminalization of "shameful phenomena," their defense of national purity in the name of preserving future generations, and their repeated evocations of the Motherland all reflect a hardy tradition of thinking about sexuality and the body deeply embedded in Russian culture long before 1917.

Yet many representations of the body, especially the female body, since the advent of *glasnost* reflect similar ways of thinking about sexuality and share the same traditions, demonstrating once again that the distinction between liberation and repression is far more problematic than it might first appear. Writers and thinkers trying to create a present and imagine a future look to the past. They turn to writers like Berdyaev, Tolstoy, and Dostoevsky for inspiration and guidance, but, as so many of the papers in this volume demonstrate, there was never a clear break between Soviet and prerevolutionary (or émigré) attitudes toward sexuality and the body.

One such continuity can be found in the claim that Russia, as compared to the West, is "sexless" or uninterested in the erotic. Chernyshevsky's exclamation "Away with these erotic questions!" and his relegation of all sexual activity to the plushly discreet rooms of the Crystal Palace in *What Is to Be Done?* is not unlike the Soviet critic's recent comment that the entire Soviet Union has been "eroticized": both reflect the view that sexuality can be compartmentalized and discrete, that it is something that can be neatly tucked away, or something that has its particular, appropriate place but is now on the loose, flooding the entire country. The papers in this volume demonstrate that the "erotic questions" have always been present in the history of Russian culture, even when they have been most vehemently denied.

The range of subjects covered by the papers in this volume points to some of the many areas one might investigate to document the history of sexuality and the body in Russian culture. Let us turn, then, to the papers for their analyses of particular moments in a history we have only begun to write, that of sexuality and the body in Russian culture.

PART I

The Cultural History of Sexual Representation

EVE LEVIN

Sexual Vocabulary in Medieval Russia

■ As always in summer, it took us two days to reach Kholmogory. There I visited Katya. In the hay loft, while the wood pigeons crooned outside, she softly echoed their sound, murmuring, "Lyooblyoo tibya. Lyooblyoo. . . ." Thinking only how beautiful the word was, I repeated, "Lyooblyoo." Afterwards I felt sorry; what we had both said, she meant. Or so it seemed by her tears, when I told her I was going to Moscow. She sobbed out, "My husband will kill me!"
"What! Does he know?"
"My mother-in-law told him. She knew because I was looking well and happy."[1]

That this passage is from a modern novel, rather than a medieval tale, is readily apparent upon even a superficial reading. And, although the author never uses the word, she leaves no doubt that she is describing a sexual encounter. The author paints a verbal picture of "nature," with birds if not bees. Words of love followed by the significant phrases "Afterwards . . ." and "Does he know?" tell the reader that the two protagonists have engaged in sexual intercourse. The euphemisms convey not only the information about the act itself, but also serve as a vehicle for expressing the attitudes toward sex that the author attributes to her characters. We see readily that sexual intercourse is supposed to be an expression of romantic affection, that attraction outweighs the obligation of a loveless marriage, that sex leads to health and happiness. It is these anachronistic terms for sexual activity and the anachronistic attitudes they express, even more than the modern novel genre, that defy the sixteenth-century Muscovite setting.

Medieval Russian authors could and did write about sex, but in rather different terms. They drew upon a set of sexual values based in Slavic Orthodox Christianity, which shaped both verbal and visual signs. Nearly all literature that survives from pre-Petrine Russia emanated from the Church and shares the ecclesiastical image of sexuality.

In the official view of the medieval Russian Orthodox Church, sex was always suspect, even in marriage for procreation. The ideal life was marked by total abstinence. The desire for sex originated with the Devil, who used this greatest of all temptations to lead humankind astray, beginning in Eden. Childbearing resulted from God's blessing, not from sexual intercourse. Any form of sexual expression was essentially unnatural, unhealthy, and indecent. Sex was also, as Russian churchmen granted, inevitable. Human weakness and propensity to sin led men and women into sexual desire and sexual activity. Thus God, in His infinite mercy, had granted dispensation to human beings to marry, in order to channel the sexual impulses to which they were all too susceptible. Because churchmen could find no logical explanation for God's toleration of sex, they resorted to the authority of Scripture, citing Jesus' miracle at the marriage at Cana.[2]

In its condemnation of sexuality, Eastern Orthodoxy took a much more extreme stand than the Roman Catholic Church in the West.[3] Catholicism also voiced its suspicions of sensual pleasure and its preference for virginal purity over temptations of the flesh. However, St. Augustine, unlike his Eastern counterparts, such as St. John Chrysostom, argued that sexuality was an innate part of God's creation, no matter how corrupt it had become after the Fall. Augustine also coined the doctrine of the "conjugal debt," which became the cornerstone of Western Christian teachings on marriage, granting legitimacy to marital sexual relations. The secular traditions of courtly love that developed in the twelfth century reinforced yet another approach to sexuality in the Western Christian tradition: sexual intercourse could express commitment and bonding, and thus be viewed as a positive good. Thus while the West evolved a more accepting sexual ethic, the Slavic Orthodox world remained isolated from these developments until Peter the Great's introduction of Western norms of social interaction in the early eighteenth century.

Although the Russian Orthodox view of sexuality might strike the modern reader as harsh in the extreme, it was in fact more moderate than many of its heretical alternatives. The Bogomils of medieval Bulgaria, for example, disallowed marriage and procreation altogether. Insofar as the teachings of Russian heretics concerning sexuality are known, they similarly adopted more stringent views than the Orthodox. Avvakum vituperatively condemned what he saw as a new laxity in sexual standards in his time.[4] Upholding traditional sexual morality became part of Old Believer traditionalism.[5] While neither of these heresies formulated its opposition to Orthodoxy around sexual issues, both took stands on proper sexual behavior.

An elaborate system of rules arose to regulate sexual behavior, to forestall the spiritual perils and societal dangers of unrestricted sexual expression. Through penitential materials and didactic tales and saints' lives, medieval Russian clerics instructed the laity about improper sexual conduct. To be sure, a sizable portion of this literature was based on Byzantine Greek originals, but Slavic churchmen thoroughly reworked the texts to reflect native mores and vocabulary. (Law codes are an exception to this rule; in Russia as elsewhere, they tended to use arcane and archaic linguistic forms.) Because ecclesiastical literature was intended to edify more than entertain, it could not appeal to prurient interests. Phrases that had obscene connotations to the medieval mind would not be in keeping with the pious tone of the work, and so were not included. It is not accidental that the retired merchant Afanasii Nikitin put all his most explicit advice concerning the availability of sexual favors abroad into Turkic.[6] This didactic goal necessitated the use of language that was at once unambiguous and decorous, colloquial and literary.

The portrait of sexual imagery derived from ecclesiastical literature is necessarily one-sided, comprising only "proper," high culture.[7] It cannot be doubted that "profane" expressions of sexual ideas also existed in the medieval period. The Russian equivalents of what we call "Anglo-Saxon four-letter words" are equally archaic, as linguistic analysis attests, and clerics warned their parishioners against use of "shameful" (*sramno*) language.[8] However, medieval written sources for low culture are exceedingly few, so it is not possible to reconstruct actual usage of its sexual vocabulary.

Even folklore and ethnography, which can otherwise be valuable in reconstructing traditional society, fail us when it comes to sexual innuendo: in the post-Petrine period, sexual attitudes changed as Western ideals filtered into popular culture, making nineteenth-century peasant culture unreliable as a model for the reconstruction of medieval life.

The literary language of medieval Russia was rich in euphemisms for sexual activity. The most specific references to sexual intercourse use words from the root *blud*. The noun *blud* could mean either the act itself ("fornication," ignoring its antiquated sound) or the desire for it ("lust").[9] In the latter meaning, *blud* was synonymous with *pokhot'*, "desire," as in the penitential question "Did you step on someone's foot in lust?" (*s pokhotiiu* and *blouda radi*).[10] *Blud* was not value-neutral. It connoted sinfulness, as demonstrated by the related word *zabluditisia*, "to stray, get lost"; this word preserves the older, nonsexual meaning of the root, which survives also in the English cognate "blunder."[11] *Blud* described illicit sexual activity. This could be sexual relations outside of marriage, as in the tale of the moral slave who saw his master's wife *tvoriashchu blud*, "doing fornication," with her servant.[12] It could also be used to refer to intercourse between husband and wife at a forbidden time, for instance on Saturday or during menstruation, or in a forbidden manner, *bloudit' sozadi a ne litsem k litsiu*, "fornicate from behind and not face to face."[13] In a reflexive form, it could even refer to masturbation, as in the phrase *kto sam" v sia blud stvorit*, "whoever commits fornication by himself in himself," or to unintentional nocturnal emissions (*s"tvorit" bloud vo sne*, "do fornication in sleep").[14] The etymologically related word *bliad'* meant "prostitute" in both ecclesiastical and secular society, as evidenced by its use as a slander against a female creditor in a twelfth-century birchbark document.[15]

The word *blud* did not distinguish between lesser sexual violations and more serious ones. The latter, such as incest, rape, adulterous sex with a married woman, or sex with a monk or nun, could be labeled *preliubodeistvo*, which corresponds to the English "adultery." The *pre-* prefix denotes intensification. A word meaning "fornication," *liubodeistvo*, did exist, but it was found almost exclusively in biblical texts and their paraphrases.[16] When medieval authors wished to make clear that they were talking about marital infidelity rather than some other sort of sexual sin, they resorted to a native euphemism, *muzh' ot zheny* or *zhena ot muzha* ("husband from wife" or "wife from husband"), followed by some verb implying sexual intercourse.[17] The word *sodomskoe* ("sodomy") and its variants similarly carried a general pejorative meaning rather than a definition of specific non-procreative sexual acts as in the Western tradition. "Sodomy" and "unnatural" intercourse (*neestestvenno*) involved some sort of inversion of "proper" relationships, such as putting the woman in the dominant "male" position, or placing another man in the passive "female" position. Although most sexual acts described as "sodomy" were considered to be serious violations of behavioral canons, this was not always the case.[18]

There were milder, although still negative, descriptions of illicit sex as well. The phrase *laziti na*, literally "enter upon," was used primarily to refer to masturbation and forbidden coital positions.[19] *Paditisia* (from the root meaning "fall"), *bezakonniia* ("lawlessness"), and *priditi v grekh* or *sogreshiti* ("come to sin") will sound familiar to modern ears; they connote wrongdoing, but not utter abasement.[20] The identification of sin as primarily sexual, especially when women were involved, was a standard feature of mainstream Christianity.

Because clerical authors wished to promote sexual abstinence, even in marriage, they regularly portrayed saints, both men and women, as refusing marital intercourse if not marriage altogether. The terms used to describe sexual abstinence all carried positive connotations. *Devstvo* ("virginity") would recall to a medieval listener the frequent epithet of praise for Mary, *devo*. Even couples who had consummated their marriage could decide to forego sexual relations temporarily or permanently, *sokhranitisia*, *v"zderzhatisia*, or *ouderzhatisia* (to "preserve themselves"), or again, they could decide to live *chisto* ("chastely") or *v tselomudrii* ("in full wisdom").[21] These terms were also applied to Mary, as well as other esteemed saints.[22] In a different context, where marriage was not involved, these terms refer to spiritual purity and knowledge. The opposite of purity, in both the sexual and the nonsexual sense, was *skvernost'* ("defilement").[23] Loss of virginity even in the context of a lawful marriage was frequently described as "defilement" or *rastliti devstvo*, "corrupting virginity"—a term akin to that used in reference to the raping of maidens.[24] Overindulgence in sexual activity, whether in marriage or outside it, was denigrated by means of animal similes: "wallowing in fornication [*blud*] in a sty like swine and . . . like cattle."[25]

Medieval Russian authors, unlike their modern counterparts, generally did not use the word *liubov'* ("love") in connection with sex. Love, an elevated emotion associated with God, could not have any connection with the Devil or devilish things such as sex. The reluctance to associate love with sex may explain why the words concerning sex using the *liub-* root, *preliubodeistvo* and *liubodeistvo*, are found primarily in scriptural and juridical contexts. The phrase *stvoriti liubov'*, literally "make love," did not have any sort of sexual connotation; it meant instead "be kind (generous) to" and was usually found in requests for large favors. For example, in the tale of how the pious monk Serapion rescued a prostitute, the newly converted harlot implored him, "Stvori liubov', oche, poimi mia," literally "Make love and take me, father," but meaning here "Be merciful and receive me," as the next phrase expressing hope of salvation makes clear.[26] Words with the root *liub-* remained atypical as descriptors of sexual activity through the end of the seventeenth century, although they could be found occasionally.[27] "Falling in love" (*v"zliubiti*) was portrayed as a bad thing—concentrating on the object of one's affections to the detriment of more important spiritual matters. In the pious tale of Princess Olga's conversion to Christianity, the Byzantine emperor *vozliubi iu zelo* ("fell deeply in love with her") and proposed marriage. Although there would seem (to a modern reader) to be nothing inappropriate in this proposal—both were free to marry, and both were Christian—the narrator characterized it as nothing less than "the slander of the lying Devil."[28]

Instead of talking about love in the context of sexual attraction, Russians could conceive of "wanting" (*khocheti*) a particular person. Forms of the verb *khocheti* in this meaning can be found both in ecclesiastical literature and in everyday speech. The case of Princess Rogneda in the Primary Chronicle account represents an early use of that verb in a sexual sense. In response to Vladimir's marriage proposal, Rogneda replied, "ne khochiu rosuti robichicha, no Iaropolka khochiu" ("I do not want to remove the shoes of a slave's son; I want Iaropolk").[29] Similarly, Mikita wrote on birchbark to Ulianitsa in thirteenth-century Novgorod: "Poidi za m'ne. Iaz" t'be khotsiu, a ty mene" ("Marry me. I want you and you want me").[30] Personal desire was only grudgingly accepted as a justification for marriage in medieval Russia. The chronicler applauded Vladimir's revenge on Rogneda for her rejection. In Iaroslav's Church Statute of the twelfth century, what a maiden or a youth wished (v"skhoshchet') in choice of spouse was upheld only obliquely: if the thwarted child chose suicide, the parents were held responsible.[31] In this way, the language of medieval Russian literature reinforced the view that marriage and sex were not matters for personal preference.

While clerical authors found it difficult to express any sort of approval for sex even in marriage, they needed to have terms for it that did not imply that it was sinful. The sinfulness of marital sex was one of the primary tenets of the Bogomil heresy; the reaction to it shaped Slavic Orthodoxy in the formative period of the tenth century. The monk Iakov, after railing against lust, sin, and sex at length, finally admitted to Prince Dmitri Borisovich that marital intercourse "po apostolu, ne tokmo ne skverno lozhe, ino chestno" ("according to the Apostle, is not only not a defiled state [literally 'bed'], but honorable").[32] The philosophical problem of the legitimacy of marital sex was clearly reflected in the language of a sixteenth-century guide for arranging weddings. Every aspect of the celebration is described in great detail, including preparing the nuptial bed. However, the author cannot bring himself to say what is supposed to happen there. He instructs participants to wish the couple "May the Lord grant you healthful rest," and "then it is done" (da potom prom'shliaet).[33]

Churchmen sometimes fell back on biblical euphemisms for marital sex, such as "lie with" (lezhati s") and "know" (vedati).[34] They doubtlessly sounded as odd to medieval Russians as they do to us. Verbs with the sense of "joining" or "uniting" could take on a sexual implication without an obvious pejorative meaning. For example, sovokupitisia, taking the preposition s" and an instrumental complement, did not have the coarse connotation of the modern Russian reflex, meaning "copulate."[35] The verbs smeshiti ("to mix with"), priblizhitisia ("to come close"), or s"chtatisia ("to join") could be used to imply either the married state or sexual relations, depending upon the context.[36] See, for example, this sentence from the *vita* of St. Konon: "S"chtav" zhe sia s" zhenoiu abiie ne priblizhisia n" ouveshcha dvstvovati" ("He joined himself with his wife, although they did not come close, but instead agreed to remain virgin").[37] These terms could also be used in reference to illicit sex, but then accompanying modifiers indicate disapproval. The verbs *spati* ("to sleep"), *sediti* ("to sit"), and "to be" in the forms of *byti* or *pribyti*, usually with the preposition *s"* and an instrumental complement, could also be used to indicate sexual intercourse in either acceptable or unacceptable circumstances.[38] For example, in the apocryphal "Confession of Eve," the principal says, "our eyes were opened, and I saw my nakedness, and my heart wanted in desire [*voskhote na pokhote*] and it was so [*byst tako*]."[39] As with other usage of the verb "to be" in Russian, the present tense form might be omitted.

When the authors needed to describe the specifics of sexual intercourse—usually in penitential questions—they did so in a laconic, straightforward manner. For example, to describe the forbidden coital position with the woman on top, penitential materials described it thus: "a woman sitting on the man."[40] The dominant "missionary" position was described with the metaphor *na kone* ("on a horse"), whether in approval in the case of marital, male-on-top intercourse or disapproval in the case of lesbian relations.[41] The words for orgasm were *istechenie* (literally "flowing out") and *ispoushchenie* ("pushing out") and their verbal forms; the same terms were used for male ejaculation and female climax.[42] Terms of foreign origin, such as *malakia*, the Greek word for masturbation or intercrural homosexual intercourse, or *afedron* ("anus"), frequently had to be defined for the sake of the parish clergy and the laity.[43] The popular words for the genital organs carried an obscene connotation and so could not be used. Instead, the authors substituted *estestvo* (literally "nature"), *sram* ("shame"), or *ud"* ("organ" or "vessel"), often in the plural. *Udy* was sometimes modified with the words *sramnye* ("shameful"), *tainye* ("secret"), or *detorodnye* ("reproductive") to distinguish usage in the genital sense from other common meanings, for example, church vessels such as the chalice.[44] These euphemisms could be put to good purpose in narrative literature, to imply both specifics and generalities simultaneously. For example, the young bride of an old man warned him, "your organs will weaken and you will not satisfy my fleshly nature" (*udy tvoi oslabeiut, i plotskomu moemu estestvu ne utekha budeshi*).[45] Similarly, in the tale of Peter and Fevronia, Fevronia thwarts the lustful intent of her husband's *boyar* by pointing out, "there is only one nature of women" (*edino estestvo zhen'skoe est'*)—that is, all women are alike genitally.[46]

While deliberate exposure of the genitals drew clerical criticism, nudity might or might not be considered sensual, depending upon the circumstances. "Stealing a look at another's shame" (*ukradom videl chiuzhi sram*), for example, was sinful.[47] Discarded clothing had the same connotation to a medieval Russian audience as it would to a modern American one. The trail of female garb in the cell of Archbishop Ioann of Novgorod sufficed to earn him condemnation for unchastity. The archbishop was innocent, of course; the clothes were left by a demon who was trying to discredit him.[48] Forcibly unclothing a woman was part of dishonoring her. Thus the narrator in the Russian version of the "Tale of Dracula" remarked approvingly that women guilty of premarital or extramarital sex were stripped naked before being impaled.[49] However, nudity in other circumstances bore no sexual connotation at all. *Iurodivye*—men and women "fools in Christ" who wandered from place to place speaking God's truth—went unclothed without arousing any condemnation. Perhaps the most telling example of this phenomenon is the sixteenth-century Muscovite saint Vasilii "the Naked."[50] Nudity during mixed-sex bathing had no sexual implications in Russia, the suspicions of Westerners and Greek Orthodox clerics notwithstanding.[51] Ecclesiastical artists followed the same norms in their icons. When they needed to convey sexuality, they drew a demonic face in the groin, or painted the figure—either male or female—with large, pendulous breasts.[52] Nudity itself was depicted frequently, to illustrate a bathhouse, baptism, or the sufferings of the martyrs, but in those cases the figures exhibit no sexual features.[53]

Just as specific visual signs indicated the presence or absence of a message about sexuality in iconography, certain literary motifs alerted the audience that the issue of sex would arise in a story. The most obvious omen was the appearance of a demon, preceded by a phrase such as *nenavidia zhe dobra rodu chelovecheskago supostat Diavol* ("the Devil, hating what is good for the human race").⁵⁴ This image carried over into iconography, where demons or serpents, adorned with large breasts or faces in the groin, tempted humans into sexual sin.⁵⁵ Demons could cause a variety of mischiefs, not only sexual misconduct. However, when the demon appeared in the form of a young and licentious woman, the demonic temptation to sin could be only sexual. More rarely, the demon took the form of a youth, to tempt a man into homosexual sex, or a man, to tempt a pious woman.⁵⁶ Another possibility was that a demon could incite a weak but not evil man to desire a proper, even saintly, woman, as in the case of Fevronia discussed above. By this literary device, churchmen promoted the view that sexual desire was a malevolent force that originated outside the individual, waiting to pounce at any hint of weakness. This conception is perhaps best illustrated by the most common term for nocturnal emission, *vo sne iskushenie besovskoe* ("a demonic temptation during sleep").⁵⁷ Through use of this demonic image, the authors reinforced the conception of sex as sinful and dangerous, a bar to salvation.

Another omen of future sexual temptation was beauty in a woman. Didactic texts warned that female beauty was the source of (male) fall into sin: "Avert your eyes from a beautiful [*krasna*] woman; do not look upon another's fairness; in female fairness many have been lost [*zabludisha*]."⁵⁸ Prostitutes were frequently described as having a "beautiful face" (*krasotoiu licha*).⁵⁹ Physical descriptions rarely exceeded generalities in strictly ecclesiastical literature, although they became more common in historical writings of the seventeenth century.⁶⁰ This omission reinforced the ecclesiastical opinion that external, bodily matters were at best unimportant and at worst a source of temptation.

In most instances when a positive female character was described as "beautiful" (*krasna*), she later encountered a man who was tempted, because of her beauty, to have sex with her. Typically, the heroine was as wise as she was beautiful, and consequently was able to avert "defilement." For example, in the *vita* of St. Ripsimia, because she was *ouna i blgorodna i krasna* ("young and noble and beautiful"), a man had *pokhot'* ("desire") for her and tried to rape her. The saint was saved from this fate through timely martyrdom.⁶¹ The *vita* of St. Barbara similarly suggests that her beauty caused men to lust after her, despite her spiritual calling.⁶² Tatiana, the virtuous wife of Karp Sutulov, thwarted the amorous advances of her husband's colleague, her confessor, and the archbishop when they lusted after her beauty.⁶³ In one tale from the Paterikon, a beautiful, but wise and loyal, wife not only diverted her would-be seducer from his intention, but inspired him to pay her husband's debts.⁶⁴ The clerical authors did not intend to suggest that beauty was somehow evil. Indeed, despite the misogynistic tendencies of medieval Christianity, they did not want to suggest that women were evil, either. But they did want to warn their audience that both beauty and women, especially when combined, could lead to sexual sin.

In addition to beautiful women and demons in disguise, churchmen identified two other circumstances associated with sexuality: paganism and drunkenness. In this context churchmen particularly decried dancing. Dances were connected with festivals of pagan origin, and involved physical contact between the sexes. Because paganism was regarded as the worship of demons, it seemed logical to the medieval Russian mind that the demons would lead their followers into sexual activity. For example, in one didactic tale, a monk whom a demon led to fall in love (v"zliubi) with a pagan priest's daughter renounced his clerical vows, his baptism, and his faith for her sake.⁶⁵ In this way, sex was associated with alien, non-Christian (pagan or heretical) beliefs. Churchmen labeled drinking the source of all sorts of trouble, including paganism and sex. While modern Western society tends to excuse misconduct—particularly in sexual matters—which occurs while "under the influence," the medieval Russians considered alcohol use to be an intensifying factor in any offense. Furthermore, drinking would often take place in a "party" atmosphere, where overindulgence in drink, food, merriment, singing, dancing, and other "demonic" behavior abounded.⁶⁶ It is not accidental that the author of *Domostroi*, a sixteenth-century guide to family and household management, condemned in order "fornication, impurity, obscene speech, shameful speech, devilish songs, dancing," and a host of games and amusements, from horse racing to horoscopes.⁶⁷

In sum, churchmen's disapproval of indulgence in physical sensation found clear expression in the choice of words and motifs used to discuss sexuality. The vocabulary is predominantly negative, but the fact remains that the cultural spokesmen of medieval

Russia did discuss sexual behavior at great length and in great detail. This willingness to talk about sex, even while condemning it, stands in contrast to the dominant tradition of later Russia and the West as well, where disapproval of sexuality was expressed mostly through silence.

Through a study of the words and contexts used by medieval Russian authors to convey messages about sex to their audiences, the differences between modern and medieval Russian approaches to sexuality become readily apparent. As scholars of the Victorian era have noted, the language used to talk about sexuality embodies attitudes about sex and about women, the "other" in the perspective of male-centered culture. These scholars have also demonstrated that language not only reflects attitudes but also shapes, defines, and ultimately dictates them.[68]

While much of the content of post-Petrine attitudes toward sexuality derives from Western European and popular "low" culture rather than medieval ecclesiastical sources, many nineteenth- and twentieth-century authors drew inspiration from the literary traditions of the medieval period. Perhaps the most telling example is Leo Tolstoy's tale of sexual temptation and morality, *The Kreutzer Sonata* (*Kreitserova sonata*, 1889). In this novella, Tolstoy reiterates the medieval position that sexual desire was a dangerous emotion antithetical to spiritual love. It is not accidental that the first character to voice this opinion is described as "Domostroi zhivoi," "a living Domostroi."[69] Thus an understanding of how medieval Russian high culture viewed sexuality becomes a necessary first step for the analysis of sexuality in modern Russia.[70]

JUDITH VOWLES

Marriage à la russe

■ At the beginning of the eighteenth century Peter the Great wrought a transformation in Russian society by bringing women of the upper classes from the seclusion of the *terem* and encouraging men and women to associate with one another in ways based on the "new notion of women as partners in love relationships that extended beyond the physiological bond between the sexes."[1] A century later, however, foreign observers still found Russian manners and morals wanting. Charles-François-Philibert Masson (1762–1807) spent ten years in Russia and lamented:

A Russian youth will never feel his blood boil, and his heart palpitate, at the idea of a rising bosom. He never sighs after secret charms, at which he scarcely dares to guess; for from his infancy he has seen and examined everything. The Russian maiden will never have her cheek overspread with an involuntary blush at an indiscreet idea or curiosity, and her husband will have nothing new to shew or to teach her, nor will marriage have any novelty for her. Love is here a stranger to those delicate and exquisite approaches which constitute its true charms, and to those preludes to pleasure more delightful than pleasure itself. Where poignant sentiments do not ennoble the happiest of human passions, it becomes mere momentary impulse, too easily gratified to be highly prized.[2]

Masson's opinion was echoed, from a different perspective, by Catherine Wilmot (1773–1824), a young Anglo-Irish woman who, with her sister Martha (1775–1873), spent several years in Russia, where they were the guests of Princess Ekaterina Dashkova (Martha Wilmot, 1803–8; Catherine Wilmot, 1805–7).

Catherine Wilmot wrote of the "Russian maiden" to her sister Alicia on February 18, 1806:

> As to such innocent, virtuous, humble, rational, rosy, white robed Nymphs as you, the Lanthams, Penroses, & Glanmirites, there is no such rank in society here and consequently no such beings. The more I know of these matters the less I am surprised at Englishmen being in such a hurry to marry the moment they return from their travels. There is that gentlemanlike fine young man S——n who stared poverty in the face to marry my favorite Sarah C——n and he has gone the round of Nations; there is Lord King, & 40 others I could name.[3]

The Wilmots' diaries and letters and Masson's *Mémoires secrets sur la Russie* contain a wealth of information about Russian women and the relations between the sexes at the turn of the nineteenth century. At the same time their moralizing observations of Russian society lay bare their own manners and morals, assumptions and prejudices, values and discretions.

All three were well acquainted with Russian society. Masson made a successful career in Russia, first as a private tutor attached to the court and then in military service. In 1796 he incurred Paul I's wrath and was arrested and deported. He spent the last years of his life in France, where he wrote his sensational and scurrilous *Mémoires secrets sur la Russie*. His book was translated into several European languages and achieved an immediate *succès de scandale*.[4] Masson's publicly displayed rancor, his slanderous and unreliable anecdotes, his extravagant statements and sweeping condemnations present a sharp contrast to the private correspondence and personal journals of Martha and Catherine Wilmot. The sisters wrote only for their own eyes and the amusement and edification of their friends and family in Ireland. Their minutely recorded accounts of Russian daily life display their good nature and wit, their powers of observation and intelligence, and, too, the good breeding and good manners of eighteenth-century ladies.

The rakish and gallant Frenchman's observations complement the more modest writings of these two respectable young women. By the end of the eighteenth century a feminine ideal founded on modesty and virtue had largely displaced an earlier recognition and acceptance of female sexuality and female authority.[5] On encountering a general's mistress in respectable society, Martha

Wilmot is shocked into silence. "We have been inundated lately with subjects of this nature," she declares. "Such a mingle of pride & meanness as is the Russian Character! Well I will not write what I think & what I know of it" (*Russian Journals*, p. 289). Presenting her refusal to write as an act of disdain of such manners and thus making a virtue of her silence, she reveals the extent to which sexual matters had by the end of the century become a forbidden realm for women. Like the Wilmots, Masson comes "from a country where the manners and morals exact the strictest decency," but where the two sisters avert their eyes and purse their lips he does not scruple to speak of the libertinism he sees in Russia.[6] Nevertheless all three share the same assumptions about the proper relations between the sexes. They embody the manners and morals of a culture increasingly organized around sexual differences that dictated and justified the division of the world into separate spheres of activity and codes of conduct for men and women. Russian society provoked shock and alarm by throwing into question differences that took their legitimacy and authority from being perceived as natural and universal. The uneasy attempts of Masson and the Wilmot sisters to describe what they see bring to the surface hidden aspects and underlying tensions in the sexual arrangements of their own countries. When they speak of Russian women, they advert to those subjects that most determine their own situations as speakers: female sexuality and female power and authority. Together Masson's chapter "Female Government" and the more scattered remarks on women and marriage in the Wilmots' letters and journals provide a critical context for interpreting their views on the deplorable state of Russian matrimony. Masson's account of the "masculineness of the women" and the Wilmots' views of female conduct and the peculiarities of Russian marriage reveal a society with sexual manners very different from their own. While modesty obliges the sisters to fall silent, Masson focuses on the influence of those peculiarly Russian institutions the baths and slavery (as both he and the Wilmots term serfdom) to explain Russian "libertinism."

Masson asserts that a complete reversal of the proper and natural relations of the sexes has taken place; Russian women have usurped male prerogatives and assumed a superiority over the men. So alien are such women to his conception of the feminine that he evokes legend to explain the "masculineness of the women":

> The existence of the Amazons appeared to me no longer a fable, after I had seen the Russian women. Had the succession of empresses continued, we might perhaps have seen that nation of female warriors locally produced, and in the same clime where they formerly flourished. Great energy is still observable in the women of the Sclavonian nations, [of] which their history furnishes many proofs. That feminine activity, which love, tenderness, and domestic cares absorb in other countries, the women of the north, who are born with more cold and robust constitutions, employ in search of sway and in political intrigue. They frequently experience a physical necessity of inspiring love, but their hearts seldom feel a want of returning it. (*Secret Memoirs*, pp. 254–55)

The robust and cold natures that Masson attributes to Russian women fall outside the parameters of woman's nature as defined by eighteenth-century science. By the end of the century medical science had described/prescribed Woman as universally and naturally softer and weaker than Man, and, on this basis, elaborated theories about the natural social roles and functions of men and women.[7] Masson's contemporary, the distinguished French physician Pierre-Jean-Georges Cabanis, gave an influential and typical account of the connection between female physiology, woman's place in society, and love. Women are physically weak, Cabanis declares:

> This muscular feebleness inspires in women an instinctive disgust of strenuous exercise; it draws them towards amusements and sedentary occupations. One could add that the separation of their hips makes walking more painful for women. . . . This habitual feeling of weakness inspires less confidence . . . and as a woman finds herself less able to exist on her own, the more she needs to attract the attention of others, to strengthen herself using those around her whom she judges most capable of protecting her.[8]

Physiological differences and characteristics dictate the natural role and function of women as wives and mothers within a separate sphere removed from the rougher and harsher world in which men, stronger and hardier, thrive. The Russian women plainly contradict nature and science in body and deed, challenging the very basis for the social arrangements of his own country, especially masculine authority. Later Masson will declare in one of his many contradictions: "The girls appear as reserved and modest as the women do impudent. They are born susceptible of the most profound and gentle sentiments: it is with difficulty, that examples and the general corruption render them depraved" (p. 267). He discards his earlier physiological arguments and insists that the feminine ideal is natural to Russia also, as though unable to endure the implications of the scenes he himself documents in "Female Government," and unable to acknowledge that the behavior of Russian women might be as "natural" as the feminine activities of "love, tenderness, and domestic cares." Masson's revulsion for Dashkova, who was "masculine in her tastes, her gait, and her exploits, [and] was still more so in her titles and functions of *director* of the academy of sciences, and *president* of the Russian academy" (original emphasis, p. 255), is characteristic of his attitude toward Russian women who run their estates, command troops in their husbands' absence, and in general engage "in business by no means suitable to their sex" (p. 257). He emphasizes that women's influence over their husbands was not the result of women's attracting others to "strengthen" themselves as Cabanis describes. "The reader," Masson insists, "must not suppose that this submission [of husbands to wives], which became almost general, was that gallant and chivalrous deference which has sometimes been paid to ladies: those whom I have cited as examples were old, ugly and ill-tempered" (p. 256).

The Wilmots, as women, stand in a very different relation to women and to society, and this is reflected in their account of female activities. To find Russian women running their own estates and managing their own affairs does not disturb them. They are astonished only by the extent of Dashkova's industry, "for she helps the masons to build walls, she assists with her own hands in making the roads, she feeds the cows, . . . she is a Doctor, an Apothecary, a Surgeon, a Farrier, a Carpenter, a Magistrate, a Lawyer . . ." (*Russian Journals*, p. 201). But they do not interpret her behavior, nor that of other women landowners they meet, as unnatural or masculine.[9] Cabanis's confident pronouncements about female physiology might be compared with the prescriptions for female decorum to be found in the abundant conduct literature of the time.[10] These prescriptions for women's conduct hint that female weakness and dependency were dictated as much by social and economic arrangements as by nature. The Scottish physician Dr. John Gregory, author of one of the most widely read English conduct manuals for women, *A Father's Legacy to His Daughters*, cautions his daughters to enjoy good health in "grateful silence," for "we [men] so naturally associate the idea of female softness and delicacy with a correspondent delicacy of constitution, that when a woman speaks of her great strength, her extraordinary appetite, her ability to bear excessive fatigue, we recoil at the description in a way she is little aware of."[11] It is a short step from "grateful silence" to a more active dissemblance of physical weakness and delicacy designed to please, an important consideration, Gregory declares, given women's economic dependency on men. Although he considers women "not as domestic drudges, or the slaves of our pleasures, but as our companions and equals" (p. 7), nevertheless "your sex" are dependent on men, and must conduct themselves accordingly. Thus, while he describes "that system of conduct which I think will tend most to your honour and happiness," he also "endeavour[s] to point out those virtues and accomplishments which render you most respectable and most amiable in the eyes of my own sex" (p. 8).

In Masson's eyes Russian women are neither respectable nor amiable; the Wilmots are inclined to agree. But where Masson sees Russian women assuming a superiority over men, the Wilmots see women merely gaining a measure of independence from men. Catherine Wilmot writes to her sister Harriet on October 21, 1806:

You must know that every Woman has the right over her own Fortune totally independent of her Husband & he is as independent of his Wife. Marriage therefore is no union of interests whatsoever, & the Wife if she has a large Estate and happens to marry a poor Man is still consider'd rich while the Husband may go to Jail without one farthing of her possessions being responsible for him! This gives a curious sort of hue to the Conversations of the Russian Matrons which to a meek English Woman appears prodigious independence in the midst of a Despotic Government! (*Russian Journals*, p. 234)

The difference she and her sister observe between the situation and demeanor of Russian and English women brings out the connection between comportment and dependency in their society. Throughout their letters the Wilmots must repeatedly remind their readers that Russian women, at least of the upper classes, can possess property and money in their own right, otherwise the conduct of Russian women appears incomprehensible. Under the English common-law principle of coverture a woman's property and person were merged with her husband's on their marriage. This "union of interests" meant that in effect married Englishwomen had neither recourse to the law nor economic powers; they could neither possess property in their own right nor engage in economic activity, such as signing contracts or engaging in business for themselves.[12] Russian women present a striking contrast; they can and do possess property and individual legal standing. "This is the reason," Martha Wilmot writes,

that one so often hears two Ladies perhaps young pretty & coquettish talking to each other about the sale of Lands, purchase of *Souls* (slaves), "My husband's Estate, after which we shall go to my Estate where I intend to make improvements" &c. &c, then talking of Mme Such a one's affaires at the Senate being in good or bad train, of her oats, her wheat, her barley &c. being sold to advantage this year & very frequently of her *Whisky distillery* being insufficient to deffray the expences of her Toilet. (Pp. 271–72)

Catherine Wilmot reports, "When a party of Ladies talk together in a group one is sure of affairs, affairs, affairs, being the subject" (p. 235).

Such independence permits a married Russian woman, having her own means, Martha Wilmot writes, to live "Separated from her Husband *in the Russian way*, that is keeping different establishments but on very good terms & writing Letters to each other by every Post" (original emphasis, pp. 286–87). This arrangement, so different from the "union of interests" of English society, leads her to ponder the connection between domestic happiness and female independence in a journal entry dated Sunday, August 17, 1806:

The full & entire dominion which Russian Women have over their own fortunes gives them a very remarkable degree of liberty & a degree of independence of their Husbands unknown in England. Is this the reason that *Domestic* happiness is much more frequent there than here? I do not think it is. Morals are purer, and that's the real cause. Here a Woman's powers to dispose of her own wealth is a great check on her husband's inclination to forsake her or to Tyrannize. (Original emphasis, p. 271)

Her reluctance to regard female independence as undesirable and destructive of domestic happiness puts her at odds with the more common claims of her contemporaries, who, as Masson does, tie female dependency to love and tenderness. Samuel Richardson, the English novelist, could argue against women's possessing even an allowance because "it makes a wife independent, and destroys love, by putting it out of a man's power to lay any obligation upon her that might engage gratitude, and kindle affection."[13] Martha Wilmot refuses the argument that demands female dependency as a prerequisite for domestic felicity, but her assertion that morals are purer in England accepts the argument in a different form. As Mary Poovey has shown, "the ideology of separate spheres both generated and depended on an arrangement of social and property relations that positioned women as moral superiors *and* economic dependents."[14] Women possessed and preserved their moral superiority by being restricted to the domestic sphere, where they "raise the virtues, animate the bliss, and sweeten all the toils of human life," protected from the harsh masculine world of business and material endeavor.[15] This noble and virtuous calling was fulfilled only by exchanging active power in the public world for a more spiritual superiority and influence in the private realm. Such moral superiority could be lost, as indeed Masson believed the Russian women had lost it, their virtue as tainted by their business activities as by any libertine act.

Martha Wilmot speaks generally of morals being purer, but the demand for moral purity fell most heavily on women—hence the preoccupation with regulating female conduct to be found in such books as Gregory's and in the Wilmots' observations. The moral standards reflected in Catherine Wilmot's assertion "As to such innocent, virtuous, humble, rational, rosy, white robed Nymphs as you, the Lanthams, Penroses, & Glanmirites, there is no such rank in society here and consequently no such beings" (p. 217), and in such praise as her sister bestows on the young Countess Orloff for "the modesty & dignity of her Conduct & the sweetness of her disposition in the interior of her family" (p. 344) are upheld throughout their letters and journals. "As to Manners (& now I speak of the young Women particularly)," Catherine Wilmot writes to her friend Anna Chetwood on March 23, 1806, "they are the most abrupt, superficial & ignorant I ever happen'd

Marriage à la russe

to meet with in my Life" (p. 224). To their readers the sisters' descriptions of female manners speak eloquently, however indirectly, of female virtue. Martha Wilmot's journal entry of September 26, 1804, compares the young women of Moscow unfavorably to those of Smolensk:

> I find there is less of the *fire and fume* of a good education amongst the damsels of Smolensky than amongst the Muscovites who bewilder you to *shew off* their 4 or 5 languages, their musical ability & their profound knowledge of the great science of dancing. The Smolenskovites are consequently less affected & I am tempted to add *better bred*, as a tincture of diffidence is at least mingled with the *fearless inquisitive* fatiguing manner of half the fair damsels of my acquaintance at Moscow. (Original emphasis, p. 130)

Gregory's admonitions provide a gloss on the behavior of the Muscovite girls. "One of the chief beauties in a female character," he writes, "is that modest reserve, that retiring delicacy, which avoids the public eye, and is disconcerted even at the gaze of admiration" (*Father's Legacy*, pp. 26–27). In everything they do the Muscovites lack the modesty and reserve necessary to virtuous women. On the love of dancing Gregory warns, "I would have you to dance with spirit; but never allow yourselves to be so far transported with mirth, as to forget the delicacy of your sex.—Many a girl dancing in the gaiety and innocence of her heart, is thought to discover a spirit she little dreamed of" (pp. 57–58). He is equally prudent on the dangers of lively conversation, insisting, "this modesty, which I think is essential in your sex will naturally dispose you to be rather silent in company. . . . One may take a share in conversation without uttering a syllable. The expression in the countenance shews it, and this never escapes an observing eye" (p. 28). He adds that while women are "our companions and equals," nevertheless they should guard against excessive liveliness, for while "on some occasions it might render you more agreeable as companions, . . . it would make you less amiable as women: an important distinction, which many of your sex are not aware of" (pp. 36–37). Paradoxically the very modesty thought so natural to and so deeply rooted in women is also imagined as so fragile and so easily corrupted that elaborate distinctions and codes of conduct are required to guard it from destruction. Women are to be carefully scrutinized for any expression or intimation or even bare appearance of sexuality, which can be detected in the most innocent behavior. The Wilmots report that the young Englishmen of their acquaintance agree with their opinion of the women; nothing escapes their eye, and they will seek wives among the innocent, white-robed nymphs of England. They prefer the diffidence of the Smolensk women to the liveliness of the Muscovites; in their own country women who behave with such little reserve violate the demands of decorum and modesty. Within the Wilmots' and Gregory's code of manners love of self-display, pleasure and enjoyment, vivacity and loudness indicate a lack of modesty and virtue.[16] Yet although they place a sexual construction, however indirectly stated, on such behavior, the conduct of the Muscovites need not be read as a mark of immodesty and ignorance of "good" manners. As Catherine Wilmot suggests, describing the "curious sort of hue" of "the Conversations of the Russian Matrons," in a society where women are not schooled to marriage and dependency, and do not have to live by an elaborate code of behavior regulating female conduct and female virtue, manners may be very different.

Where a woman can "exist on her own" she need no longer "attract the attention of others" to strengthen herself as Cabanis claims she must, nor need she learn to follow Gregory's advice on how to appear "most respectable and amiable in the eyes of my own sex."[17] In such circumstances the insistence on preserving modesty and virtue and protecting purity from outside corruption is also lessened. The Wilmots find society as wanting as female conduct. Catherine Wilmot describes the general corruption:

Accomplishments are taught the Girls more than ever was known before, & that one can perceive the advance of by the Stile of their Mothers. The latter are to a Woman Gamesters but cannot always explain themselves in french. However the trophies of their Celebrity are generally recorded with Credit in the annals of Galantry, & this is no sort of impediment to their Consideration in the beau monde. (P. 217)

The general libertinism she and her sister find in Russian society places them in the delicate and difficult situation of seeing too much, and they generally confine their remarks on what they witness to the privacy of their journals.[18] Since she cannot directly speak of such matters without affronting her own modesty and running the risk of tainting her own virtue, she employs highly stylized language to describe "the annals of gallantry" and distance herself from her subject. But the two sisters cannot dismiss Russian society as merely libertine, as that "slight specimen of Russian manners" that compelled Martha Wilmot to silence demonstrates. A respectable gathering at General Kissiloff's house included

Genl Kissiloff's Mistress, a french Woman who was in the room all the time & with whom the young & pretty little Mlle Bavanoff, who is really well manner'd & highly accomplish'd appear'd to be in habits of intimacy in the presence of Mme Bavanoff who convers'd with her a great deal herself. Mlle Kissiloff with whom we were conversed with her likewise. In short she appear'd very nearly as Mistress of the House, & very nearly did the honours as such!!! We have been inundated lately with subjects of this nature. Such a mingle of pride & meanness as is the Russian Character! Well I will not write what I think & what I know of it. (P. 289)

The presence of the general's mistress in the company of respectable and cultivated women confounds her. The Bavanoffs, mother and daughter, as well as the general's own daughter, whose manners and education lead Martha Wilmot to expect good morals and the enforcement of the moral code, treat the general's mistress not only politely but with friendship. These women fail to uphold crucial distinctions separating the innocent from the fallen, the virtuous from the corrupt. Their modesty is not affronted, nor their virtue sullied. They do not shun in deed what Martha Wilmot shuns even in words. They should, in her view, have enforced the proper distinctions, as does happen in another story she relates, of the Orloff family and Count Alexis Orloff's mistress, Marie Bakmeteff:

She married young, & in a very high rank of life. She quitted her husband (a woman's fortune in Russia is always at her disposal) & attach'd herself to Count Alexis O[rloff] who she accompanied into Germany. . . . There was no colouring cast on this act, but on her return with him & his daughter she took her former place in society, liv'd in a small house close by his, & frequently accompany'd his family in her excursions to the Country &c. &c. &c. (P. 345)

As in the Kissiloff household, the collapse or absence of social boundaries between family and mistress erases distinctions crucial to the Wilmots' society. The daughter finds herself in the company of her father's mistress, a situation described as placing her "amidst scenes which would have corrupted a common mind"

(p. 315). On her father's death the young princess shows that her mind "has preserv'd all its purity & risen superiour to every seduction" (p. 315) by changing her relation to Mme. Bakmeteff; the young princess "treated her politely but banish'd familiarity with her" (p. 345). Having established the necessary moral distinctions between herself and Mme. Bakmeteff, the princess then creates a world more appropriate for a young woman: "Her prudence of conduct and sweetness of disposition keep her surrounded by respectable old relations & young girls who have been educated with her. Her bonne (a child's maid & nothing more) accompanys her almost everywhere, & the good old woman who has lived with her from the day of her birth exists but in her adoration of her" (p. 344). The rigid and punitive code of sexual morals behind this charming picture of feminine society fell most heavily on women. Reflecting the double standard characteristic of her code, Martha Wilmot does not propose that General Kissiloff or Count Orloff should be excluded from society. But such women as the young princess are rare, and from the Wilmots' accounts it appears that Russian women did not generally maintain the elaborate codes of behavior and social distinctions designed to preserve and protect female virtue. Just as they need not enforce differences between the sexes by shaping their activities and behavior to an ideal based on weakness and dependency, so they need not enforce moral and social distinctions between virtuous and fallen women.

Russian society repeatedly presents the sisters with such violations of their sexual code. Boundaries and distinctions between the sexes, between women, between worlds are repeatedly blurred or overthrown. In a rare moment of directness Martha Wilmot writes in the privacy of her Moscow journal, Monday, May 10, 1807, "Respecting Morals there is a good Specimen in the next Street to us. A Prince Zenovia, into whose yard we look from our Windows, has Let a wing of his House as a Brothel & lives *with his family* in the remainder of his Palace!!!" (original emphasis, p. 294). Her shock and outrage are directed less at the existence of brothels than at the casual juxtaposition of worlds that should be kept strictly separate. The view from her window forces her to see too much, offends her modesty, and threatens her own innocence and virtue. To preserve her own character and her own

Marriage à la russe

modesty she must avert her gaze; a closer view of such scenes and a more detailed account of Russian sexual manners can be seen only through Masson's eyes.

Masson agrees that modest, innocent young women are rare, "flowers thinly sown and blooming in secret" (*Secret Memoirs*, p. 269). Like the Wilmots, he admires those "who have had a good education, whom the manners of their families, and the care of a prudent governess, or respectable mother, have formed to the graces without moulding to vice" (p. 269). But where Martha and Catherine Wilmot speak as women who aspire to such an ideal and whose criticisms of the conduct of Russian women are a defense of their own virtue and moral superiority, Masson speaks as a man alarmed by the loss of feminine solicitude and by female encroachments on his masculine world and privilege. His description of the Russian women who run estates, command armies, and direct academies without appealing to male protection or assistance as "old, ugly and ill-tempered" sets the tone for his remarks on sexual manners. Female independence not only makes women unlovable, it also gives them "bold and masculine tastes and manners" (p. 263). "It was not at the court and in domestic affairs only, that the women assumed a superiority over the men," he writes. "Nowhere did so many women arrogate to themselves the right of making the first advances, and being the active party, in affairs of love" (p. 263). Imagining the relations between the sexes to be reversed, Masson in his description of Russian women simply inverts the characteristics and manners he considers proper and natural to each sex. He describes the women behaving not as women living in a society with very different social and economic structures and, consequently, with very different manners, but as men would behave in his own society. The perspective of a man who once enjoyed "superiority" and is now unwillingly subject to it reveals the bleaker side of male gallantry and the more violent aspect of a society that idealizes the feminine.

The same set of manners and morals that positioned women as weak, dependent, and in need of protection also asserted that the source of that protection, the stronger man, was also the source of danger. Martha Wilmot's defense of female independence raised the shadow of male tyranny, infidelity, and abandonment as a danger to dependent women. Gregory warns his daughters that they live in a "wolfish" age and must beware of men, whom he portrays as vicious and predatory creatures.[19] His assertion that women are "designed to soften our [men's] hearts and polish our manners" (*Father's Legacy*, p. 6) alludes to explicit and widely accepted theories that the history of civilization was also the history of rape and seduction. Whatever corruption the refinements of civilization might bring, women can only benefit; through the arts of love they can exert influence over men, from whom in a state of nature they are, as weaker creatures, in constant danger of violence, rape, and enslavement.[20] In Masson's view the sheer physical strength and abilities of Russian women abrogate their need to be amiable and cultivate the arts of love in order to gain protection. Moreover, Masson asserts, Russian women are not merely unamiable but act as men; they have become the "active party" in matters of love and men the passive, feminine object of their attentions. Masson adduces two examples of the "masculineness of the women" to demonstrate the dangers of female sexuality to men. Describing the women who accompanied the Russian army, Masson claims: "Potemkin's seraglio was always composed of handsome Amazons, who delighted in visiting the fields of battle, and admiring the handsome corpses of the Turks, as they lay stretched on their backs, their scymetars in their hands, and with an air of defiance still in their countenances" (*Secret Memoirs*, p. 257). This grim pleasure was repeated after the battle of Ochakov, when the bodies of the dead soldiers were piled up and frozen over until the thaw. Throughout the winter, Masson writes, "round these pyramids the Russian ladies used to take the air in their sledges, to make their observations" (p. 257).

In these alarming stories Masson emphasizes that women have become the observers. Unlike the Wilmots, who avert their gaze from fallen women, brothels, and other such disgraceful scenes, these women boldly stare. Inverting the roles of a society in which women, being dependent, must always be conscious of being observed by men, Masson imagines that Russian women become the observers of men, that they see and know too much. He blames the Russian baths and slavery (serfdom) for depraving society and corrupting the women: "The habit of treating men thus [as slaves] and that which both sexes have in mixing together in the public baths, deaden, at a very early age, that modesty which is natural

Marriage à la russe 67

to women, and I have seen some as bold as the most impudent men" (p. 258). His account of these institutions reveals the fear that female knowledge undermines the significance of sexual difference, the very foundation of his society, and the basis for "natural" male superiority.

Immediately upon his arrival in Russia Masson sets out to see the famous baths. "Young, and coming from a country where the manners and morals exact the strictest decency," Masson writes, "I had promised myself that I would contemplate at my ease the treasures of which my eye had never yet caught more than a furtive glimpse."[21] Unlike the Wilmots, also young and strictly brought up, he, being a man, can set out to make his observations without risk to modesty or reputation:

> I figured in my mind the voluptuous baths of Diana and thought of nothing less than surprising the nymphs like another Acteon. Accordingly one day I descended the banks of the Neva with a friend, toward a public bath; but I had not occasion to go far, before I was convinced that the Russian belles were accustomed to expose their charms to the eye of the passenger. A party of women of all ages, tempted by the heat of the month of June, had not thought it necessary to go so far as the precincts of the baths. They had stripped themselves, and were swimming and sporting near the banks of the river. This spectacle, to which I was not accustomed, made the most lively impression on me; and I stopped, and leaned over the quay, without my presence proving any interruption to the sports of the bathers. (Pp. 265–66)

He gains his object and does view the "treasures" that would be carefully concealed in his own country, but he is perplexed at how to account for the scene. He comes to his adventure in the spirit of Acteon surprising Diana and her nymphs bathing, a myth told by Ovid that was used in the seventeenth and eighteenth centuries to motivate the painting of the female nude. Where Ovid emphasizes that Acteon comes on Diana unawares and devotes the greater part of the myth to Acteon's punishment, the pictorial treatment of the myth more commonly offered an occasion for the display of the female body viewed unawares.[22] Taken aback by the bathers' indifference to his stares, Masson changes his interpretation of the scene. Since his own society places such significance on the display or concealment of the body, he places a sexual construction on a scene that obviously has no such a meaning for the bathers. When his original framework fails and he cannot imagine himself Acteon because the nymphs are in no way disconcerted by his gaze, he claims, "the Russian belles were accustomed to exposing their charms to the eye of the passenger." Interpreting their behavior sexually, he can now represent their actions as immodest display. However, a lengthy footnote with further details of the women's appearance and an account of an alarming incident suggests that his explanation of their behavior is not as satisfactory as he might wish. Having committed himself to reading the scene as one of sexual display and activity, he cannot escape the unpleasant consequences of his interpretation:

> The sight of the budding breasts that some of the youngest artlessly exposed was almost paid for by having to see the disgusting spreading objects shamelessly displayed by the old women, whose wrinkled skin formed a thousand folds which were least of all love's hiding place. One of these old women, seeing some men of her acquaintance bathing a little way off, swam over to them, and began a fight with one of the young lads comparable to the fight between Salmacis and Hermaphroditus. The young man not knowing how to swim, the old woman had the advantage of him, and seizing him by the beard with one hand, and by the ... with the other, she ducked him repeatedly, to loud laughter from both groups, as well as the spectators. This scene took place near a part of the shore, where persons of all ages and sexes were walking, and the young ladies in the neighbouring houses might enjoy it from their windows.[23]

The English translator surpasses Masson's delicacy and omits the description of the young and old breasts, the classical allusion, and the discreet elision. Yet these provide the key to Masson's alarm. In the main text he was able to put a pleasurable construction on the scene before him, and to transform disappointed expectations of taking female modesty unawares into moralistic enjoyment of immodesty. He cannot, however, imagine the old women as objects of desire; not only can he not impose a pleasurable sexual construction on these old bodies, they spoil his pleasure in the young girls. Moreover the sexual interpretation he persists in placing on their behavior, whether considered artless or shameless, becomes terrifying when one of the old women approaches a young man.

To account for the scene Masson turns to Ovid once again. In interpreting what is no more than a wrestling match, he uses the myth of Salmacis and Hermaphroditus, a story of female desire for the modest and innocent male body that has given the fountain of Salmacis its evil reputation of making "men weak and feeble."[24] The beautiful youth Hermaphroditus is seen and desired by the nymph Salmacis when he comes to her pool to bathe. When the youth repulses her advances, the nymph pretends to abandon the pursuit and retreats to the bushes to watch as he, "as if no one were looking at him," undresses and enters the water. Salmacis immediately grasps him to her, but "he refused her the joy she wanted most." They struggle in vain until she finally beseeches the gods, "May no day ever come to separate us!" Her prayer is answered and their bodies become as one, "no longer two beings, and no longer man and woman, but neither, and yet both." Hermaphroditus curses the fountain so that "every one hereafter, who comes diving into this pool, emerge half man, made weaker by the touch of this evil water." The myth expresses Masson's fear that sexual differences and distinctions may be lost, and with it male superiority and power. The young man's humiliation and defeat when the old woman seizes him by the beard and genitals, the two symbols of his manhood, show the youth to be as weak and feeble as Hermaphroditus. Masson is especially concerned that this overthrow of sexual difference, and the defeat of male superiority, has been observed. Although he himself happily set out to make his observations at the baths and leans over the quay to enjoy the naked bathers, he is nevertheless outraged that the tussle between the old woman and the youth is visible to all, regardless of age or sex. He is particularly perturbed at the thought of young ladies at their windows observing the scene as Acteon secretly observed Diana and her nymphs. Masson feels, as Martha Wilmot did on encountering the general's mistress, and as Catherine Wilmot did on seeing a brothel from her window, that important and necessary distinctions have not been maintained. But what the Wilmots feel as an affront to their own modesty, Masson experiences as a loss of masculine power.

Although Masson insists on placing a sexual construction on the whole scene, he is perhaps as fearful that it has no such meaning. Thus, observing that even when a man wishes to bathe separately, a woman often washes and soaps him and applies the birch twigs, he adds, "she acquits herself of all these matters down to the last detail and with all the indifference possible."[25] The woman's indifference to difference can only alarm a man whose position, power, and privilege in his society are rooted in the definition, elaboration, and enforcement of sexual difference. Ostensible concern with female modesty, whether that of young ladies at their windows or of women of the lower classes bathing in the river, conceals fears that women's indifference to male observation and women's knowledge of the male body lead to the loss of male superiority.

Masson's fears become even more acute when he writes of slavery, that other corrupting institution. The widespread institutionalization of women's possessing real power over male slaves is even more disturbing than a moment of horseplay among the lower ranks of society. To a general repugnance for slavery Masson brings particular fears about women as slave owners. He inverts contemporary political arguments that compared women's dependency on men and their legal and economic situation to that of slaves.[26] In a country built on slavery Masson declares that women are inevitably "engaged in business by no means suitable to their sex. To buy, sell, and exchange slaves, assign them their tasks, and order them to be stripped and flogged in their presence, would be as repugnant to the feelings as to the modesty of a woman in a country where men are not degraded to the level of domestic animals, and treated with the same indifference" (pp. 257–58). The indifference that most concerns him, however, is not for the difference that sets men and animals apart, but for the difference that sets men and women apart. His example of women's treating men as domestic animals is of a woman landowner intent on fishing who orders her male slaves to strip and go into the water. When they do so, Masson relates, "she gave them their orders, directed the fishing, and with a truly comic air of scorn watched their members shrivel from the cold and the water."[27] The English translator renders this last line "and she gave them direction in their fishing with all the unconcern imaginable" (p. 258) and obscures Masson's fear that the weakness natural to women is also natural to men. The passive indifference of the women scrubbing men's bodies here becomes a more active attitude of contempt and ridicule.

Masson's depictions of men as slaves and how they cease to be considered as men by women slave owners show how much the definition of their humanity is tied to the respectful acknowledgment of their sex. He writes, women "live from their childhood in the greatest familiarity with a herd of their slaves: a thousand private and even secret services are performed for them by male slaves, whom they scarcely consider as men" (p. 258). As proof he offers an anecdote of a Russian lady out walking who orders her two strong manservants to take her arms and hold her up while she relieves herself behind a bush. This parody of male protection and support of the weaker sex provokes her French female companion to remonstrate with her for performing such an act before two men. To which the Russian lady replies, "These are my slaves; they were brought up with me: I'd like to know it if they have the audacity to think I have anything but a petticoat under my skirts, or think that I am a woman to them, or they are men to me."[28] She denies them knowledge of the body and sexuality, just as these were conventionally denied to women. By denying them knowledge of her as a woman, and by not thinking of them as men herself, she takes their manhood from them, strong as they are.

Having blamed slavery and the baths in extravagant detail for corrupting women, Masson is still able to write that the Russian bathing customs, which are "shocking, and which are so to all people who wear clothes and are no longer savage, are yet by no means the effect of corrupt hearts, and do not indicate libertinism" (p. 266). And he insists that women's treatment of their slaves "must not be ascribed to libertinism, or gross licentiousness" but to living in circumstances that "afford them daily opportunities of satisfying, and even anticipating, their curiosity respecting all the mysteries of nature" (p. 258). Like his contradictory assertions about the cold, robust constitutions of Russian women and the modest reserve and gentleness of the girls, his conflicting views indicate the difficulty of contemplating the possibility that sexual differences may not be as important or as powerful as he believes. Ironically such statements suggest that he, rather than the Russian women, is concerned with sexuality and pleasure. His belated denial of libertinism and licentiousness is based on the belief that "the habit of seeing every thing unveiled continually . . . from an early age deadens the senses, and cools the imagination" (p. 266). It is the veil of modesty that would allow the Russian youth to experience pleasure, to "feel his blood boil, and his heart palpitate, at the idea of a rising bosom" and allow the Russian maiden to "have her cheek overspread with an involuntary blush at an indiscreet idea or curiosity." Ironically the pleasures that Russian men and women do not know, the "delicate and exquisite approaches which constitute [love's] true charms" and "those preludes to pleasure more delightful than pleasure itself," are denied them because they know too much (pp. 266–67). Cast over the body, the veil of modesty inflames the imagination and in the very act of concealing becomes the veil of erotic pleasure.[29] Sexual purity leads the Wilmots to reproof, silence, and averted eyes, but it also leads Masson, coming from "a country where the manners and morals exact the strictest decency," to the Russian baths. Both he and the Wilmots are led to see depravity and immorality everywhere, placing sexual constructions on scenes and conduct innocent of such meaning.

Masson's lyrical portrait of the mysteries of love and marriage and the Wilmots' charming picture of "innocent, virtuous, humble, rational, rosy, white robed Nymphs" are founded on the strict application and enforcement of sexual differences in every area of life. The veil of modesty and of pleasure tends to conceal (and is perhaps used to conceal) the social and economic realities of marriage. Observing Russia through the veil of their own manners and morals, Masson and the Wilmots find themselves unable to see clearly or completely. The silent blushes of the Wilmots, Masson's inflamed imagination, and the moral indignation of all three shape their accounts of Russian mores as much as the realities of Russian life.

CATRIONA KELLY

A Stick with Two Ends, or, Misogyny in Popular Culture

A Case Study of the Puppet Text 'Petrushka'

■ This essay is a preliminary study of some theoretical and practical problems raised by the analysis of misogynistic elements in Russian late nineteenth- and early twentieth-century popular culture. I am specifically concerned with the representation of women and women's sexuality in *Petrushka*, an orally transmitted dramatic tradition. It would be as well to stress at this early stage that I am not discussing the subject in a way that could be glossed as "The Image of Women in the Puppet Theater." The isolation and cataloguing of misogynist elements in popular culture would not only, I feel, be a crude exercise; it would also appear to distance the material from the educated observer's experience. Instead, I have used examples and quotations from popular texts in order to contextualize the two issues that do concern me. The first of these is the question of women's involvement in popular culture. How did the women who watched the puppet plays react to them? This is by far the more problematic section of the article. It is, of course, impossible to canvass the text's original audiences on their views; details of performance history and reception are scanty. But I hope at least to raise some points of meditation or contention, if not to give any definite answers.

My second concern is the relation between popular culture and high culture, one aspect of what has been termed "the circulation of social energy."[1] I am not going to adopt a comparative method, analyzing the "(in)authenticity" of high literary texts based on the popular tradition. Study of incidental formal or conceptual differences between literate and orally transmitted texts would mask the fact that there is often a startling similarity between these two seemingly separate traditions. Popular culture often directly and overtly articulates assumptions that lie behind the apparently respectable and sophisticated façade of high culture. Moreover, popular culture tends to be used by educated observers, whose demeanor often resembles that of some traveler or anthropologist studying an exotic tribe, as a "pathetic imaginative space," a means of escape from their own intellectual predicament.[2] The paucity of evidence has of course done nothing to hinder this process. Sentiment and nostalgia have dogged many studies of popular culture or "folklore"; there has been emphasis on the "natural," the "traditional," the "uncorrupted"; or there has been quietistic, pseudo-objective, and relativistic acceptance of cultural patterns that, by implication, are justified by their ancientness. As we shall see, the presentation of women in the *Petrushka* texts as passive objects of male desire has been regarded by many commentators as just such a time-honored and inevitable phenomenon.

My analysis of direct reactions on the street and indirect reactions in the study will be explicitly feminist. Feminism is well qualified to lay bare the (often reactionary) assumptions that lie behind folkloristic orientations, since it is essentially a critical discourse. Sentimental affection for pure, uncorrupted, and venerable practice, the "wisdom of ages," is vulnerable to attack by feminism's critical gaze, for, as Rosalind Coward says, "it is rare, not to say impossible, to find a feminism which attributes women's subordinate position to some natural, god-given and therefore unchangeable sexual role."[3] In its attack on this concept of "naturalness," which lurks beneath the writings of many observers of the popular tradition, the type of feminism that I shall practice shares the standpoint of James Clifford's "ethnographic surrealism" and other recent orientations in cultural criticism, but is more politically explicit in its ambitions. "Self-reflexivity," or self-consciousness, is understood as a necessary part of historical analysis, but as something subordinate to the task of understanding beliefs about gender, rather than important in itself. I make no attempt to imitate the post-Romantic tradition in which a myth of the multifaceted self is used to parade diffidence and reinforce writerly authority.

To conclude this introductory section I should briefly indicate two areas of difficulty that rapidly made themselves obvious. The first is the sheer size of the subject. Even denominating it by geography and language on the one hand and by epoch on the other leaves one with an enormous amount of material, ranging from the most improvised and widespread forms, such as jokes, to highly organized types of dramatic spectacle and ritual. This explains my decision to concentrate on drama and confine my attention to what was performed in towns. My choice may seem artificial given that misogyny is not exclusively an urban phenomenon, but it is justified, I believe, by the differences between the urban and rural manifestations of misogyny. One of the most important consequences of urbanization was the disappearance of traditional public rituals and their replacement by new forms of social encounter whose purpose was entertainment rather than celebration. In rural theater and theatricalized ritual the genders had been separated; the Christmas plays and mumming shows included female characters, but these were always played by men in drag; the women for their part had their own rituals, such as the procession with a straw doll, known as *Kostroma*, and the preparation of brides for marriage, from which men were excluded. (One important exception was the marriage ritual in which the bride made a dumb show of her reluctance to be taken from her family.)[4] In the popular dramas of the town fairgrounds, such as harlequinades, pantomimes, and puppet shows, men shared the performance space with women, who were included not only among the fictional characters but among performers, operators, and entrepreneurs. And in contrast to the village plays, where sexual politics were an issue of secondary importance, the popular dramas of the city often focused on marital and extramarital conflicts, which were indeed among the most favored subjects.[5] On the other hand, despite the participation, both active and passive, of large numbers of women in the urban spectacles, the way in which women were represented was often hostile, sometimes more so than in the village spectacles in which men alone acted. Moreover, though the urban entertainments tended to be, in a broad political sense, antiauthoritarian and socially subversive, in the sense of sexual politics they were, literally, violently conservative; the authority of man over woman was asserted. The center of my analysis, the puppet play *Petrushka*, is, like its English counterpart *Punch and Judy*, a vivid illustration of the problematic character of popular culture. It combines verbal and physical abuse directed at establishment figures, such as policemen, priests, and army officers, with verbal and physical abuse of a racist and sexist nature. The club (*dubinka*) used by Petrushka was indiscriminate in its choice of targets, a synecdoche of the popular culture's conflicting values; hence my choice of the proverbial Russian formula of ambivalence, "A Stick with Two Ends," as the title of this essay.[6]

The second difficulty, besides the tendency of the material to escape in all directions, is that of methodology. Russian urban popular culture is in general a neglected area; some outstanding work was done by Soviet scholars in the 1920s, but under Stalin the whole area became an ideological minefield, and only recently has study of the subject begun again in Russia. Even now attitudes are uneasy; published studies often take the form of art-historical catalogs, and analysis of the material is generally avoided or takes place according to the stereotypical principles discussed below. Problems stem not only from political but also from aesthetic considerations; the word *kul'tura* still imparts a value judgment that the English word *culture* has lost.[7] Lest I be suspected of bilious anti-Soviet prejudice, let me add that in the West the situation is no better; here scholarly documentation is virtually nonexistent and it has become customary simply to state that the material is not available.[8] In the circumstances it is not surprising that the subject of women and popular culture has scarcely been aired. For example, Jeffrey Brooks's recent exhaustive study of popular and mass literature, while mentioning the existence of a women's readership, does not give detailed information on its composition and tastes.[9] Specifically feminist studies are also thin on the ground, and most of those that have come to my attention have dealt with material of rural origin.[10] I am able, therefore, to point to few specific positive theoretical influences, and have mostly had to confine myself to indicating where I feel that existing approaches have been unhelpful or misleading. The partisan character of fair-

A Stick with Two Ends

ground entertainments and the important questions of representation and of reception that it raises have made many intellectual critics uneasy to the point of incoherence; often they have preferred not to deal with these questions at all. An analogous problem is that of worker violence, which provoked acrimonious debate among historians a few years ago.[11] I have no illusions of being able to give a definitive answer to these thorny questions; I hope simply to outline them as they arise in *Petrushka*, and to show how various critical interpretations of the text have ignored or whitewashed them. At times this approach may seem unduly apophatic or scholastic, for which I ask advance indulgence.

Since it is by no means certain that *Petrushka* is familiar to everyone, I had better begin by a brief description of it.[12] Like *Punch and Judy*, *Petrushka* is or rather was an orally transmitted dramatic text of episodic structure performed by a single operator inside a cloth booth, working with one or two glove puppets per scene. It concerned the adventures of a grotesque and immoral puppet hero bearing that name. His distorted body, with a large nose and chin and beady eyes, symbolized his aggression, which became woefully clear when, after a boastful introduction to the public, he made use of the club with which he was armed in order to beat viciously or even to kill a series of other puppet characters upon little or no provocation. While resting between exertions Petrushka would insult his victims and the public.

The diapason of Petrushka's violence was wide, and his victims included male figures (a policeman, a soldier, a German, a Gypsy, a Jew) as well as women; as with any orally transmitted text, there was no canonical version, and the choice of secondary characters varied from show to show. However, among the characters most popular with puppeteers was a female puppet, Petrushka's Wife or Bride, whose conventional names (if she had a name at all) were Parashka, Malanya, and Akulina (for these almost any other name of obviously plebeian origin might be substituted).

As the uncertainty over her name suggests, Petrushka's female companion generally played a much less significant role than her English counterpart Judy or than Guignol's wife, Madelon, in the French tradition.[13] Though nineteenth-century observers recorded that *Petrushka* usually included a fight between the hero and his bride, no transcriptions of such a scene have been published in variants of the text recorded in Moscow or Petersburg. Possibly such scenes do survive in archival variants as yet unpublished; possibly the scene, like the stick-fight between two Arabs to which Benois refers, was a wordless pantomime that some observers did not bother to record when they took the text down.[14] But if no fight scene survives in recordings made in and around the capitals, there is a version recorded in Chernigov that includes a screaming row between Petrushka's Ukrainian and Southern Russian counterpart, Vanka, and his wife. The two trade insults about each other's drinking; finally, the husband lays into his wife, who calls for help:

WIFE: Och, you drunkard, you drunkard: you've drunk all my cattle away.
VANKA: Just like ye drank my mittens away, you and your gossip Regodulia.
WIFE: Let's go home.
VANKA: I'm not going there.
WIFE: Have ye forgotten who I am?
VANKA: Well, who are ye then?
WIFE: I'm a pope's daughter.
VANKA: Eh, there's posh. And I'm the coachman on the corner's chicken's confidant.
WIFE: Let's go home, 'fore I scratch yer eyes out.
[*Vanka grabs the bottle and starts to beat his wife.*]
VANKA: Take that, and that!
WIFE: Help, good people! My husband's killing me![15]

More commonly the Bride's role was to be the butt of crude personal remarks and jokes made by Petrushka and by the "Musician" (the puppeteer's partner, who stood outside the booth playing a hurdy-gurdy). After his opening monologue, Petrushka would usually begin the action by boasting to the Musician and the public that he was about to be married. He would drag his Bride on by the arm and present her, and her looks were then the subject of discussion between him and the Musician; the following extract comes from a show recorded in the early 1900s:

MUSICIAN: Well, she's pretty enough . . . but snub-nosed.
PETRUSHKA: Musician, you're lying! Just look at her button eyes! Her rosebud mouth! What hands!! What lips!! What a neck!![16]

The joke at the expense of Petrushka's Wife or Bride was shared by the puppeteers, who used to manufacture puppets of particularly vile appearance for this role. This description comes from an inventory of the puppets used in a version recorded in the 1920s: "*Vanka's Bride* (no name). Round-faced, berouged, full-figured. Dressed in pink blouse and green skirt, red headscarf and scrap of muslin. . . . Speaks in high little voice (no swazzle [squeaker] used: [male] performer speaks for her in a high voice."[17] The puppeteers would also jokingly refer to her as "the beauty" (*krasotka*). (Petrushka's strikingly ugly appearance, on the other hand, was not the subject of such teasing.) Her clothes also attracted mockery; she is normally represented as what has come to be known as a "fashion victim"; as one commentator put it, "all the Bride's modish fripperies were grossly exaggerated, it stands to reason."[18]

Sometimes the jokes at the expense of Petrushka's Bride were more explicit than those quoted above. There is a standard scene in which Petrushka boasts of his dowry; in a version held in a Russian archive, though unfortunately not published in full to date, many of the items are what one scholar coyly calls "unprintable."[19] D. A. Rovinsky records that there was a popular scene or series of scenes (which do not seem ever to have been transcribed) going under the title of *Petrushka's Marriage*, played as a coda to the main drama if the public paid extra. In this Petrushka, too impatient to wait for his wedding night, persuades his Bride to sate his lust in advance.[20] In another scene, from the same 1920s version as the description of the Bride-puppet, Vanka-Petrushka slobbers horribly on his consort, and the references to "dancing" are obvious double entendres:

FEED [*doffs hat and bows to Vanka and his Bride*]: My respects to you both. And is she any good, Vanya?
VANKA: You bet she is, and comely too!
FEED: Show us how much you love her, Vanyusha!
VANKA [*cuddling and kissing his Bride*]: O my pretty lass, my comely lass! Sweetie-pie!
FEED: Duckiekins.
VANKA: Duckieuckiekins! [*embraces her tightly and kisses her*]
FEED: Vanichka [*sic*], can you dance though? If a man gets married, he's got to know how to do all kinds of dances.
VANKA: I can dance all right. . . . [*tenderly to his bride*] Take my arm, duckiekins. . . . [*The dancers cuddle and kiss and eventually vanish inside the booth.*][21]

In short, then, standard scenes of the *Petrushka* show represented violence and violent licentiousness that were directed against a woman. As I have indicated elsewhere, linguistic factors might emphasize the Bride's subordination.[22] In most versions she does not speak at all; where she does (as in the Ukrainian version) this may provoke terrible retribution. Equally, the antagonism between man and woman might be underlined by emphasis on her alien social origins: she might be a priest's daughter or a merchant's daughter, rather than sharing Petrushka's working-class status. Both these aspects of *difference*—linguistic and social— are paralleled in the characters from ethnic minorities, many of whom are incompetent in the Russian language as well as being drawn from the petty trading, rather than the laboring, classes. Armenians and Jews, for example, are always street traders or shopkeepers who speak with thick accents.

However, the most important feature by which women were characterized was their sexuality. In the scene cited below (found in two extant versions recorded in the vicinity of Petersburg around the turn of the century), the Bride is a working-class girl who expresses her disapproval of Petrushka's treatment of her directly—though with none of the verbal wit that marks the hero's speeches. She complains that he has not written to her and then spits on him. When promised a gift of clothing, however, she becomes malleable and surrenders to the hero's sexual advances:

MATRYONA: I forgive you. So will you promise to buy me something, then?
PETRUSHKA: I will, I will, I will buy you something, anything. I'll go to the market on Nevsky and buy you a bonnet and some bootees.
MATRYONA: Oooh, I do love you for that.
PETRUSHKA: And I love you too. Give us an Easter kiss, then. [*They kiss three times, and Petrushka mutters*] What sugary lips! ... Mmm![23]

In both of these versions a second female character, Katerina, "milady," appears. First she dances with the Barin ("Toff"), and then Petrushka takes her back home, saying "Hush, hush, hush, the staircase is steep, the passages are narrow, my chickabiddy, my bangabangbang [*trambambulechka*], my little bellybutton."[24]

Contemporary observers record that *Petrushka* was as popular with women as with men. D. V. Grigorovich, for example, who gives a very early account of a performance (1842), describes the composition of the audience as "apprentices, wet nurses, and children."[25] Petrushka's opening monologue, too, addressed itself to a mixed audience: "Good day to you boys, babies, hold your noise! Bonjour, shake your tresses, you sharp-eyed young misses! Bonjour, bonjour, flap your ears, you painted old dears!"[26] There is no reason to suppose that specially "soft" versions of the text were played to female audiences; the only scene from which women are said to have been excluded was "Petrushka's Wedding."[27] As contemporary illustrations reveal, the social class of women spectators was no different from that of the men.[28] Females seem to have enjoyed the show as much as the males, though their role was more passive; there are no records that they took part in the banter between hero and audience that invariably succeeded Petrushka's appearance in the booth.

Yet if women were on more or less equal terms with men as far as their representation in the audience went, they most certainly were not in terms of the representation on stage. The working-class men in the audience could see a spectacle whose hero represented them. Though Petrushka often had no specific occupation, and where he did he was represented as a cook or a waiter rather than a factory worker, many of his experiences were familiar to his public. Some scenes, such as that in which Petrushka was called to order by a policeman and that in which he was forcibly conscripted, represented incidents possible or even likely on the Russian streets. Others dealt with the problems of male popular life in the abstract: for instance a scene in which the hero negotiated terms with his stupid employer the Barin handled the problems of employment in general. Puppeteers were capable, too, of adapting the text to immediate circumstances; so the journalist V. Doroshevich records a version played on the island of Sakhalin in which Petrushka was represented as a callous parricide eventually incarcerated for his crime.[29] Many accounts confirm the direct identification of men with Petrushka: there were cases even after the revolution when performances of the show were used as political surgeries, at which members of the audience would complain to Petrushka of their dissatisfaction with the authorities.[30]

What the men watching *Petrushka* saw was not only a reflection of their own lives; it was also a dream of impossible power. The hero exploited other members of the subordinate classes without their having the chance to retaliate. He attacked figures of authority without the severe consequences that would certainly have ensued in life. The Policeman and the Soldier would be murdered, to the delight of the crowd, and the hero would get away with it. Sometimes the show ended with the hero's death at the hands of the Devil or in the jaws of a hairy dog, but as he immediately popped up again in the next show the punishment was not severe. Never worsted in a physical sense, the hero came off best with all his antagonists in a verbal sense, too: he alone had the right to make jokes. As in Freud's model of joking in the popular tradition, the laughter of men watching Petrushka was aggressive and active.[31]

For women spectators the situation was more complicated. They saw a spectacle that can hardly have been wish fulfilling: it credited women neither with extraordinary power nor with wit. Why, then, did they laugh?

The question might at first seem simple, even naive (that term conventional academic discourse finds so convenient as it rejects, without examining them, unexpected assaults on accepted orthodoxies). But simple questions can sometimes be remarkably useful in the pursuit of women's history, which is generally better served by counterintuitive strategies than by acceptance of what seems immediately obvious.[32] The question "Why did women laugh?" can be countered with answers such as "Well, everyone laughs at jokes against themselves, don't they?" But such answers are by no means self-evident: they are underpinned by a belief in overall social consensus. They reflect no sense of the volatility of street interchanges, the mechanism by which a humorous insult can become a dangerous piece of provocation.[33] The use of "everyone" also denies the possibility that women might be, in any circumstances, a socially marginal group; it fails to recognize that socially marginal groups, and socially dominant groups, might have different reactions to social interactions, such as laughter.

In fact, this apparently straightforward question is central to current feminist debate on historical analysis and cultural criticism.[34] At the core of the debate is the issue of how much weight should be given to the asymmetrical power relations between men and women. According to some readings, the women watching a spectacle such as *Petrushka* would have laughed because it would never have occurred to them to do anything else. The assumptions of female inferiority inculcated by upbringing would have been insuperable, and the figure of the Bride would have simultaneously reproduced, and constructed, general assumptions, common to both sexes, about female behavior.

Such explications have a long and honorable history, stretching at least from Madame de Staël's "Les femmes qui cultivent les lettres" (1800) to such neo-Freudian analyses of relations in culture as E. Ann Kaplan's "Is the Gaze Male?" (1983).[35] They have enjoyed particular popularity among observers of Russian culture, who have argued not only that beating and sexual exploitation were current in nineteenth-century working-class life but also that this situation was accepted by victims.[36]

Arguments of this kind carry a great deal of weight. The problem for a historian, indeed, is that they carry too much weight, allowing little room for the possibilities of variation. First, synchronic variability seems little accounted for. How, using such paradigms, may we distinguish the power structures expressed in a melodrama, say, from those expressed in a comedy, and account for the fact that comedy can see the assertion of male power as transgressive? In a version of Petrushka recorded in the 1920s, for example, the Musician rebukes the hero for his rude treatment of the Bride:

PETRUSHKA: That's enough, off you go, put the samovar on, I'll come and have some tea later. Get out. [*He chases her off.*]
MUSICIAN: What d'you think you're doing?
PETRUSHKA: Didn't do it on purpose.[37]

By referring to male dominance as an overall social phenomenon, we can understand why women did not throw bricks or kick over the booth, but not why they laughed, as opposed to watching with rapt and earnest attention.

The other problem with such feminist approaches to reception is that they also make it rather hard to account for diachronic alterations in conditioning. Kaplan herself states, "many of the mechanisms we have found in Hollywood films which echo deeply embedded myths in Western culture are thus not inviolable, eternal, unchanging, or inherently necessary." But she concludes the same paragraph with a sentence that seems, on the contrary, to preclude any possibility of change and variation: "We have participated in and perpetuated our domination by following the pleasure principle, which leaves us *no options* [my emphasis], given our positioning."[38]

To advocate that some account of historical change should be given does not mean reverting to nineteenth-century notions of progress. In women's history, the idea of progression seems to be more useful. Should one, then, lay out a Foucaultian map of protean shifts in repressive structures?[39] This would risk another kind of oversimplification: the image of one prohibitive nexus of discourses succeeding another as smoothly and inevitably as beads on a necklace.[40] It would be more productive to search for places where the inevitability of patriarchally determined reactions might be pulled apart. As a recent programmatic statement by French historians has put it, the task is to explore "ruptures," sites of change and conflict, rather than to construct narratives of unalterable power relations, whether these are seen in terms of dominance by one gender or of equilibrium between the two.[41]

It is easy enough to accept such suggestions in the abstract; a more complex question is that of where, in the field of popular representations of the female body and of sexuality, we might begin to search for such "ruptures." One possible point of attack might be this. *Petrushka* assumes that women are different, physically and sexually, from men. But no separate viewpoint is offered to women spectators: they, while being "different," as women, from men, must at the same time accept, as spectators, an evaluation of this "difference" identical to the evaluation made by men in the audience.

Having accepted this place of entry into the contradictions and discrepancies in the nineteenth-century patriarchal system, we might then proceed in two ways. On the one hand, we might accept that women spectators of *Petrushka* could only watch the text in the same way as men. They might look for dislocations and contradictions between this context, with women as "male spectators," and other contexts in which they were supposed to act as "women." On the other hand, we might argue that women spectators of *Petrushka* were so conscious of their difference as "women" that they were unlikely to have accepted the text's invitation to watch as "men"; then we might investigate the contradictions that arise between the text and its interpretation. We might expect some conflict and uncertainty on this occasion, one where women's feelings of difference were not accommodated.

I am going to follow the latter course here, positing that some or all of the women spectators of *Petrushka* may have reacted differently from the men, and trying to speculate on the ways in which this different reaction may have been manifested. The reason for this decision does not lie in any reification of "the female mentality" in an absolute sense, but in an apprehension of the immediate circumstances in which Russian working-class women were likely to construct their views of themselves. The adoption of a "male position" as a spectator or reader is not an act that is dependent solely on the expectations in a given text: it is also linked with a broader social context. Many educated women readers of the nineteenth and twentieth centuries have been the products of post-Enlightenment educational systems. They have been exposed to teaching that has assumed the "neutrality" (in fact often the maleness) of intellectual activities such as reading.[42] Recognition of a perspective specific to women in the act of reading is likely to require a conscious effort of detachment from the processes current in education and upbringing. By contrast, the female working-class public in nineteenth-century Russian towns had been little exposed to formal education. It was dressed in ways that differentiated it rigidly from the male public; it did jobs of work also differentiated by gender; and its domestic routine was differently organized. As Roger Chartier has put it, this was "a public for whom complementary tasks within the home were the very condition of survival for the family group."[43] To argue that such women read *Petrushka* in a "male" manner would be to place this set of textual relations outside any other relations in which working-class women would have been involved.

We are to see the performances of *Petrushka* before women spectators, then, as a clash of expectations: women who have a definite sense of their difference from men are confronted with men's view of women. The dynamics of reaction can be posited in different ways: two of them might be labeled "compensatory" and "subversive."[44] (This is not to suggest that there are only two possible strategies, representing symmetrically opposed or mutually exclusive solutions.) "Compensatory" is my term for a process by which women might feel their status to be enhanced by adopting a position that an external observer would regard as degrading. An example from outside Russian culture has been given by the anthropologist Victoria Goddard, who has traced Neapolitan women's acceptance of apparently inferior employment to a complex of attitudes about status in the family.[45] It might well be productive to ask whether Russian women's acceptance of their sexual effacement in public had status-enhancing possibilities of this kind. Are we perhaps seeing a process whereby the popular oral tradition adopts the Western notions of female gentility that had been current in Russian printed texts for more than a century? Or is Russian Orthodoxy's stress on the spiritual value of resignation (*smirenie*) the key factor here?[46]

What about "subversive" strategies? An enticing example of this type of differential interpretation is given by an anecdote cited by the British anthropologist Nigel Barley. Barley relates how a woman in an Indonesian village left her husband after his adultery, but was then sent back to him by her own family. Despite the closing of social ranks on all sides, she found a method of exacting revenge. When doing his washing, the task of a good wife, she "seized a large rock and humming to herself . . . began pounding the crotches of his underpants one by one. . . . She had returned to wifely duty but still managed to have the last word."[47]

There is no available evidence, in the case of the Russian street theater, for a similarly overt process of subversion. That is not to say that Russian working-class women were incapable, in other contexts, of protests about oppression.[48] Nor is it to say that the traditions of Russian popular theater have *invariably* conformed to the Freudian view of popular humor, according to which women can only be the passive object of male sexual jokes. Eighteenth-century comic interludes, with their female trickster figures, and nineteenth-century obscene proverbs in the female voice are two instances of popular texts in which women adopt actively humorous roles.[49] But there are no records that such protests took place at fairgrounds—though they could have, since the circumstances of production and reception (unlike those surrounding a film or a book) involved direct participation.

It would be tempting to attribute the absence of records to bias in the recorders. Most of the lorists and travelers who have left us reports of *Petrushka* were men; besides, as the second part of this paper will demonstrate, the Russian and Soviet traditions of folklore study have been gender-blind to a significant degree. But there is cause to suspect that the problem of women's involvement in the fairground puppet shows goes beyond bias in recording. As mentioned previously, the fairground entrepreneurs included women; there may also have been some women players of *Petrushka*. The puppeteer Zaitsev, for example, lived with a woman who was herself a puppeteer.[50] No version by a woman puppeteer survives (or, at any rate, has been published), so it is impossible to establish whether women's shows differed from those of their male colleagues. But evidence does exist regarding a parallel group, ethnic minorities. The Soviet scholar T. Bulak has revealed that Jewish *Petrushka* showmen played comic scenes poking fun at Jews, just as their Russian and Ukrainian counterparts did; they had, indeed, a larger repertoire of comic Jewish characters than their counterparts had.[51]

We cannot easily posit a separate public tradition of interpretation of fairground spectacles by women. The only room to speculate is on the question of women's *private* interpretation of a male-centered text. Compensation or subversion may have worked as strategies by which women spectators distanced or mocked the material that they watched. It is possible that a show of submission was Russian women's most productive strategy for manipulating their male partners, as it sometimes was for manipulating their male employers. Alternatively, being presented as a compliant sex object may have been an ironic and refreshing contrast to the burdens of dealing with financially incompetent and physically incapable males, which must have been many women's actual lot in life.[52] Or perhaps Russian women laughed because they found men's representations of women ludicrously unlikely and inappropriate. Whichever way, I think it is worth considering the *possibility* that the adjustments and accommodations made by female spectators were not precisely those made by male spectators.

Recognition that the reactions of urban working-class women to cultural phenomena may have been dynamic, rather than static, is important because their condition, like that of "Oriental" women, has often been used as a negative counterimage to the condition of "enlightened," elite women. They have been seen as the objects of crusades, or else as a comforting reminder of the successes notched up by liberation movements in their campaigns to better women's lot.[53] But one cannot, of course, take the arguments for historical and gender variability too far. Popular culture does not offer a means of escape to a more harmonious and palatable reality: the pressures on women in oral tradition resemble those on women in literate culture. The woman spectator was no better off in the oral theater than in the written theater. There is a tendency, even in certain quarters of feminism, to polarize a "good" (that is, pro-female) oral tradition and a "bad" (male-dominated) written tradition. Lissa Paul, for example, writes: "Historically, the warm, mimetic culture of pre-Socratic Greece (presided over by Mnemosyne and the muses) was suppressed by Plato and his old boys' network in favour of his new rational mode of thinking and the recently invented phonetic alphabet."[54] I am less interested here in criticizing the rather dramatic telescoping of four centuries of Greek history than in the polarization of "warm mimetic culture" and (by implication cold) "old boys' network." To my mind this polarization can only exist in comfortable ignorance of the tradition that is eulogized. The tension and ambivalence within the popular-cultural tradition must be recognized.

There is also a second, and possibly more important, type of tension that historical readings should recognize: that between the world of the text and the "ethnographic present" of the observer. It is not enough to catalogue the facts of an alien tradition, however distant it may seem in historical or geographical terms, without some sense of the purpose of the catalogue: every critical act wrenches the text out of one context and into another. The critic is forced to make judgments about historical topics—here the *Petrushka* show—in accordance with a whole range of different, nonauthentic, considerations. In his book *The Great Cat Massacre* Robert Darnton has recently asserted, "by picking at the document where it is most opaque, we may be able to unravel an alien system of meaning."[55] Though in general agreement with the procedure suggested, I am eager that the sense of "unraveling the alien" should not leave us simply with a collection of colorful historical anecdotes and an admiration for the skill of the unraveler.

It may be important to know about how the worldview of Paris printworkers caused them to slaughter dozens of cats in the late eighteenth century, but it is just as important to meditate on why we like reading about such things (delight in the forbidden?).

A historical reading that would take proper account of gender issues in cultural texts of the past would, then, neither assume that men and women have always behaved in the same way nor take refuge in a celebration of the past for its own sake. It is here that my critique of earlier interpretations of *Petrushka* begins. Though outwardly there is no standardization of approach among different commentators on or users of *Petrushka*, all (women as well as men) in fact adopt either a reductive or a relativist approach, either ignoring the representation of sexual politics or justifying it because it is "traditional."[56]

Leaving aside those studies that deal simply with the genesis and origins of the text and those that confine themselves to cataloguing the different characters and scenes that appeared in the text, the analyses to date have conformed to three main patterns, the first two of which ignore the issue of misogyny and the last of which sees it as inevitable.

The first pattern characterizes A. Lunacharsky's observations on the popular theater, dating from the 1920s, and M. Gorky's comments on it at a slightly later date.[57] Petrushka's victims are seen here as class enemies; his subversion is therefore laudable. There is no attempt to explain the presence of women and foreigners among the victims; by implication, they are class enemies like the rest, and misogyny passes without comment. As has emerged from my analysis, class antagonism between Petrushka and his Bride is certainly evident (as it is also between him and his victims belonging to different races). But the "class war" reading cannot explain the linguistic distortions that characterize the speech of ethnic minorities and women in the puppet texts, or indeed other manifestations, such as costume or manners, that also indicate gender and race difference. Nor does it explain why women should be presented above all as sexual beings. Rather than arguing that the racist and sexist elements in the puppet theater are products of class antagonism, I would see the emphasis on class difference as simply a rationalization of prejudice or an articulation of self-interest; analogous were the taunts of "class traitors" thrown by Russian male workers at their female coworkers when the latter argued that shorter hours were more valuable than higher pay, and the views held by male workers that their female colleagues were retrograde, "creatures of a lower order," "backward and uncultured."[58]

Many of Lunacharsky's contemporaries adopted a different approach, which was to catalogue the formal features of the text, such as "oxymoron," or absurd contrast. This formalist reading, of which P. G. Bogatyrev was the most distinguished proponent, avoids the political and moral problems presented by popular culture altogether. Leaving aside the obvious fact that this approach's apparent neutrality was to become essential for folklorists who wanted to continue serious work in the Stalinist era, the avoidance of value judgments inherent in it was extremely useful in that it provided a way of recognizing and enumerating popular-cultural phenomena; the well-bred disgust inspired by, for example, obscenity was irrelevant to it. But while the study of folklore is impossible without some knowledge of its structural patterning, to confine oneself exclusively to this reduces it to a limbo of clinical acceptability. The problems with which I am concerned do not exist for such readings, for in terms of their structural function, all Petrushka's enemies are the same; they punctuate the scenes by their entrances and exits. The facts that they may be offensive caricatures and that they may exit when brutally murdered are irrelevant.[59]

The third critical orientation, inspired by Mikhail Bakhtin's book *François Rabelais and His World*, is more subtle and more wide-ranging than the first two, more conscious of a social and historical dynamic, and rightly enjoys most popularity at the moment.[60] It affords a more adequate explanation of the politics of *Petrushka*, stressing that its subversion of normality is temporary; it also illuminates the construction of the text, since it is clear that the contrasts and associations on which it depends are of characteristically carnival type: death and resurrection, eating and sex, eating and death.

Satisfactory as this approach is in most ways, however, it fails to address the problem of misogyny in a sufficiently critical manner. It does not *avoid* the problem; it explains it inadequately. Bakhtin is, for example, surely wrong when he argues, "in the world of the carnival all hierarchies are canceled," since we are dealing rather with a *substitution* of one hierarchy for another than with a cancellation of all.⁶¹ Equally questionable is his argument that the violence and abuse of the text are justified as manifestations of fertility cult. The beatings are "merry," and the distortions of the woman's body suggest capacity for breeding:

> The popular tradition is in no way hostile to woman and does not approach her negatively. In this tradition woman is essentially related to the material bodily lower stratum; she is the incarnation of this stratum that degrades and regenerates simultaneously. She is ambivalent. She debases, brings down to earth, lends a bodily substance to things, and destroys; but, first of all, she is the principle that gives birth. She is the womb. Such is woman's image in the popular comic tradition.⁶²

The problem with this approach is that there is in fact little evidence that women were primarily associated with fertility in the urban popular comic tradition of the nineteenth century.⁶³ If there *is* a link between women and fertility in the nineteenth-century popular tradition, this link is negative (in *Petrushka* they are seen as *in*fertile, childless, and sexually attractive only in a hedonistic sense). It is, besides, important that the text classes Petrushka's female victims among a whole series of antagonists, victims of his violence, who cannot be accommodated in a fertility-cult model: the German, the Jew, the Gypsy. Like the seventeenth-century Roman spectacle in which Jews were rolled in barrels through the streets, the violence in *Petrushka* appears to reflect a broader context of institutionalized violence and oppression pretty accurately.⁶⁴

The lack of evidence that puppet shows had any connection with fertility rites in the minds of those who watched and played them has not deterred other commentators, for whom the religious function of the texts transcends time and context. Olga Freidenberg, for example, traced the street shows of her own time to the cults of the archaic world: "Every cart and every portable temple is essentially a wagon of Thespis, 'the divine'; and the fusion between its character as temple and as theater is especially obvious when it is transporting the puppet theater or the vertep, the temple-box where the puppet-gods live."⁶⁵ Another commentator, Anna Nekrylova, has argued that Petrushka himself is not a real-life figure but a modern incarnation of the Sun God of primitive ritual; his red hair and red shirt indicate this symbolically.⁶⁶

The violence and abuse of women can be accommodated quite neatly by this argument; it, too, is seen as ancillary to the enactment of fertility ritual, an association that goes back to Frazer, Cornford, and Viacheslav Ivanov, from the last of whom I now quote: "In [Dionysiac religion] is developed the rich symbolism of the sacrifice, which goes back entirely to the sole principle of substitution, the presentation of an animal sacrifice instead of a human sacrifice. Thus in Arcadia the sacrifice of girls is replaced by beating them before an idol of Dionysus."[67] I find this reading of urban popular cultural forms as survivors of the "primitive" disturbing. It may be productive or amusing (though fast becoming a banality) to analyze the survival of archaic ritual beliefs in high culture, to assert, as Stephen Greenblatt does, that "literary professors are salaried, middle-class shamans," or for that matter to dwell, as others have done, on the occultic powers of doctors or ballet critics.[68] But to continually emphasize such elements in the urban popular culture of the nineteenth century is to risk confirming prejudices about it, rather than working toward an understanding of it.[69] A further and perhaps more serious objection is that the search for ultimate origins indicates a fatalistic acceptance of misogyny and of gender roles, which makes this seem inevitable or even laudable, enshrined by tradition and custom. Moreover, as Olga Freidenberg's obsessive use of the word "paleological" suggests, such theories are often constructed using a frame of reference taken from theories of evolutionary biology, specifically from a tradition in which Haeckel's theory of recapitulation is misused to determinist ends.[70] Discrimination according to gender is, therefore, seen as not only culturally but *biologically* inevitable; in a manner, in fact, that is quite inimical to the radical, critical model of feminism with which we began.

In summary: critical work on *Petrushka* has either ignored the abuse, verbal and physical, that is endured by the female character, or has explained that it is insignificant, whether because sanctioned by tradition or because the woman deserves it, being a class enemy. Both critical orientations have parallels or reverberations in literary appropriations of *Petrushka*. The first, in which misogyny was seen to be sanctioned by cult and tradition, characterized the symbolists' reworkings of the fairground genre, such as the Stravinsky-Benois *Petrouchka*; the second, in which women are seen as guilty by their association with reactionary political ideas, was central to the literary adaptations of the fairground theater in the 1920s.[71]

Here I shall briefly discuss one of these traditions, that of the 1920s. The agitprop puppet plays of the period took over Petrushka as a hero, but altered him almost out of all recognition; in some plays he was represented as the scourge of ideas unacceptable to the new Soviet regime, in others, yet more improbably, as a verbose and boring *raisonneur*. Carnival elements in the plays were also filtered out almost completely: Petrushka lost his long nose and his gross appetites, his crude jokes and insults were censored, and the antiauthoritarian scenes were excised. Significantly, almost the only element in which the new plays resemble their predecessors is in the representation of women, who are almost invariably identified with political reaction and unseemly longing for petit bourgeois delights. In one play, Volpin's *An Amateur Performance*, for example, the existence of a village cooperative is seriously threatened when a local *kulak* sends along his daughter to distract the assistant so that he can get on with polluting the cooperative goods. Like Petrushka's Bride, the daughter is from a disparate class background; like her, she is obsessed with fashionable fripperies. As with Malanya, her seduction is achieved by means of a gift: cosmetics.

STOREKEEPER: You're—you're a goddess.
NYURKA: Oooh, enough of your compliments.
STOREKEEPER: Nyurochka, what are you saying. It ain't . . . Oooh whoops scuse me, mean to say isn't, a coompliment, it's plain to see.
NYURKA: No need to be so formal with me.
STOREKEEPER [*embracing her*]: My lovey, my little orange, my goldilocks, my eau-de-cologne, my lapdog, my lemon . . . [*Kissing her with every word*] Actions speak louder than words, I'm told [*goes into the co-op and comes out with a jar of "Metamorphosis" skincream, which he gives Nyurka*]. So I've got you a pressie, if I may be so bold.
[*Nyurka looks at the jar*]
NYURKA [*screams with delight*]: Lord love a duck, some men are a dream, "Metamorphosis"! It's vanishing cream![72]

In another play, *Whack on the Nut*, by Lev Mirianin, Petrushka is momentarily taken with a French Mamzelle, but when she (understandably) expresses her reluctance to submit to his advances, he subjects her to a torrent of abuse. Here the fact that Mamzelle is a hanger-on of the White generals Denikin and Wrangel, who appear in immediately preceding scenes, is sufficient to brand her as a class enemy. But the writer has also taken on board the linguistic distortions associated with women and underdogs in the street tradition; the Mamzelle speaks with a comic French accent.[73]

In general the authors and theorists behind the agitprop theater movement adopted a radical or even hostile attitude toward the popular traditions of the fairground: "We do not need the old *Petrushka*. It is pointless and senseless," G. Tarasov wrote.[74] Yet they took over the fairground's hostile stereotypes of women without any adaptation, merely adding to them more stereotypes in the same mold. The purpose of reforming Soviet society is seen as being the work of clear-sighted men, fighting heroically to overcome the false consciousness of their womenfolk, who cling like mad to their despicable three Cs: comfort, clothes, the Church.

The prevalence of misogyny after the revolution had support on both paternalist and populist grounds. Official Bolshevik cultural policy, paternalist in its insistence on knowing better than the masses what was good for them, fostered a paternalist attitude to women. Besides, a feeling that a good bit of solid misogyny would give literature by intellectuals popular appeal among the working-class or peasant lads was widespread in the 1920s. A recent article by Alexander Zholkovsky has cited many examples of misogyny in Mayakovsky's poetry; it is interesting how many of these can be traced to popular speech and street comedy.[75] Since then, the tradition of exploiting a perceived popular attitude to women as "creatures of a lower order" has continued, breaking down the distinction between "official" and "unofficial" Soviet literature: the benighted and oversexed peasant women "she-animals" represented by such 1920s realists as Lydia Seifullina come from the same stable (I choose my words) as the range of vapid women castigated in countercultural street abuse by such authors as Dmitri Savitski and Eduard Limonov.[76]

In a poem of Ivan Elagin's, the figure of Petrushka is used as a protagonist in a critical examination of Soviet society—he appears in the role of mindless Soviet yob.[77] I know however of only one reexamination of *Petrushka* whose point was to throw light on sexual politics. In a song by the young guitar poet Veronika Dolina, the puppet wife's position is seen to be one that can be endured only by "shutting her eyes":

> Puppeteer, puppeteer, grey-eyed puppeteer,
> The way you're looking makes my head spin round.
> And she keeps staring, but she mustn't stare,
> She must come to terms with her puppet husband.[78]

This rather timid questioning of tradition stands alone so far. There is no straight reversal of inherited plots, where Petrushka's victims get a chance for revenge in the manner of Percy Press's *The Boot on the Other Foot*, or *Judy Femme Fatale*, and nothing resembling Lorca's reworking of Petrushka's Spanish counterpart Don Cristóbal, who is killed by an explosive fit of rage when his wife bears five children by five different lovers.[79] Nor, casting one's net wider, is there any text resembling Blake Morrison's *The Ballad of the Yorkshire Ripper*, which uses an assemblage of dialect terms of abuse for women in order to question male hostility, rather than to reinforce it.[80]

Is this situation likely to develop, given the fluidity of cultural affairs in the former Soviet Union? The suspension of censorship and administrative regulations has certainly given a new freedom to cultural debate; there are signs that a movement for women's rights may be gaining ground. Younger Soviet women are increasingly concerned to explore the history of women under Soviet rule. True, the new revisionist histories of women to date tend to be as crude and reductive in their explanations of discrimination as were the official Soviet histories that preceded them. Setbacks are often simply attributed to "socialism," an explanation that is as absurd as the traditional Marxist-Leninist view that women's ills were to be attributed to "capitalism."[81]

The oversimplification of history is particularly evident in contemporary arguments about popular tradition. One current unhelpful received opinion in the former USSR is that a return to traditional popular values will benefit women. Right-wing practitioners of "village prose," such as Vasily Belov and Valentin Rasputin, advocate a return to "peasant family life," by which is meant a kind of idealized nuclear family that never actually existed in the villages of the past. Another unhelpful current idea is that, conversely, many negative phenomena, such as the explosion of sexually explicit photographic material, have come about as a consequence of pressure from the urban working classes.[82]

The development of a sophisticated understanding of popular culture must be a central part in the creation of any new version of women's history. At present there are few signs that such an understanding is likely in the immediate future: there still seems a long way to go before popular culture, especially in the hands of intellectuals, stops being a most dubious weapon: a stick with two ends indeed, both of which can be used with equal efficacy in the subjugation of women.

JANE A. SHARP

Redrawing the Margins of Russian Vanguard Art

Natalia Goncharova's Trial for Pornography in 1910

As long as a woman refrains from unsexing herself let her dabble in anything. The woman of genius does not exist; when she does she is a man.[1]

■ This paper presents an account of censorship in Russian art that has no parallel in the modernist era, even if it sounds hauntingly familiar to readers in America today. Yet the events that are described here have been relegated to the marginalia of Russian art history; it could go without saying that they do not figure at all in general studies of modern art. Histories of radicalism in the visual arts draw upon the careers of David, Courbet, Pissarro, and others whose reputations were based as much on their political activities as on their innovations in the visual arts, while studies of vanguard art in Russia now focus more exclusively on formal innovation and the origins of abstraction. Recent efforts to secure a stylistic canon for Russian modernist art are based understandably on the perception that Russian art history is underdeveloped, inadequate, and in need of serious correction in order to counterbalance the long history of Soviet repression and control over access to paintings and documentary material. Ironically, formalist methodologies that have measured both the inimitable originality of individual masters and, concomitantly, the extent to which they continue a tradition of innovation—difference and similarity simultaneously—have a last stronghold in the history of the Russian avant-garde. This paper argues for a shift in critical perspective. It is hoped that by reexamining the public reception of Natalia Goncharova's nude life-studies, an event that has been marginalized by exclusionist discourses in the West and in the former Soviet Union, greater insight will be gained into the differences (other than stylistic) that distinguish artists within the generation termed the "avant-garde."

Goncharova's trial identified her as a radical artist in two senses. Within the broader context of vanguard assaults on the high-art establishment, her trial identified her as part of a collective exhibition group united in opposition to the academy (more specifically to the standards of judgment applied to student work in the Moscow School of Painting, Sculpture, and Architecture). In December 1910 she exhibited paintings in the first exhibition of the Jack of Diamonds group while other members of this group appeared as witnesses at her trial. But despite her prominent participation in and identification with this vanguard group, *the fact of her trial* singles her out from her colleagues. The nude was favored by many vanguard artists; yet Goncharova has the distinction of being the only Russian artist ever tried before for pornography in the "high" genre of the nude life-study. Her trial therefore also diagrams her difference in the context of critical reviews of similar work by vanguard artists. Here, social assumptions regarding feminine practice in the visual arts doubly marginalized her, making Goncharova's difference in gender function simultaneously as a sign of radical difference in vanguard art. In the limited critical response to Goncharova's one-day exhibition, Goncharova's identity as a woman and as a producer of images of female nudity was seen as contradictory, and her behavior therefore as criminally "sexed."

In view of the marginality of this issue in modernist discourse (it is entirely absent in histories of Russian art), it is not surprising that this "incident" has gone unnoticed. Yet her trial proclaimed with unsurpassed clarity a fact of life in prerevolutionary Russia—that in acquiring reputations as social radicals, artists experienced very real consequences for their actions, whatever their intentions. It is likely that a few of the consequences (notably, denunciations in the press, which preceded legal action in Goncharova's case) were anticipated by artists. Therefore their actions, including their decisions to exhibit specific works, need to be understood as part of their reciprocal dialogue with a public, which involved provocation and punishment. Goncharova's trial represents a critical moment in this dialogue: her work in the genre of the nude defined a boundary for the censorship prerogatives of the police and courts.

The record of events leading up to the trial is somewhat ambiguous, and is based on limited documentation. According to two of the several accounts in the press,[2] Goncharova exhibited 20 to 22 paintings on the evening of March 24, 1910, in a closed session for members of the Society of Free Aesthetics (Obshchestvo Svobodnoi Estetiki) in Moscow, which she and Mikhail Larionov attended. Larionov's account of the incident implied that a member of the press managed to infiltrate the meeting by dressing as a lackey. At any rate, an inflammatory article denouncing Goncharova's work appeared the next day in *Voice of Moscow* (*Golos Moskvy*), a daily newspaper.[3] The article declared Goncharova's "nudes" "so completely decadent in their manner of depiction [*sploshnoi dekadentskii poshib*] that the secret anatomical divisions of the Gesner Museum would pass up these images of disturbing perversity." Among the pictures named, *God* (no. 6) and *Same* (no. 13) were reported to have "surpassed the pornography of secret postcards." The reviewer immediately underscored the relevance of Goncharova's gender to his judgment by ominously warning: "It is most disturbing that the painter is a woman under the influence of a perverse form of vulgar decadence that has caused her to exceed all boundaries of morally correct behavior."[4] This notice was followed the next day by a poetic caricature of the meeting, entitled "Our Aesthetes" (*Nashi estety*), which likewise connected the membership of the society (the poet Valery Briusov was then its chairman) with Goncharova's pictorial style:

Literary blabbermouths
Half-witted poetics,
Uncensored and impetuous
Prophets of aesthetics,
Symbolist-declaimers,
Decadent artists,

Though in art—reformers,
Bootmakers in creativity . . .
They wail as if through brass trumpets,
And at their uncensored ravings
Only the poor walls blush
In the literary circle, etc.[5]

As a result of these statements, the police immediately confiscated Goncharova's nudes and began an investigation into the activities of the society.

Despite the foul play that led to the "arrest" of her pictures, Goncharova and members of the society's committee that organized Goncharova's March exhibit (V. Ia. Briusov; Dr. I. I. Troianovsky; V. O. Girshman; a professor of the Moscow Conservatory of Music, K. I. Igumenov; the artist V. A. Serov; and the writer whose work had been discussed at the meeting, B. N. Bugaev [Andrei Belyi]) were charged under article 45 "for the public display of blatantly corrupting pictures" ("iavno soblaznitel'nye kartiny"). Accounts of the trial, which took place in Moscow on December 22, 1910,[6] indicate that the case was based on the connection made by the reviewer and the court between the society's reputation for "decadent behavior" and Goncharova's depictions of the nude figure. Goncharova was defended by the sculptor K. F. Krakht, with members of Jack of Diamonds called as witnesses. Owing in part to the liberal views of the judge, and principally to the fact that the meeting had been closed to the public, Goncharova and those who stood trial with her were acquitted.[7]

It is Larionov's defense of Goncharova, published in Nikolai Riabushinsky's art journal *The Golden Fleece* (*Zolotoe runo*), that explains the rationale for official seizure of the pictures.[8] His statement reveals that Goncharova had been accused of "subverting young people in the audience." Since this was obviously a fabrication (as members of the society, the audience were drawn mainly from Moscow's artistic elite and were probably already sympathetic to Goncharova's work), Larionov argued that the principal issue at stake in Goncharova's trial was freedom of expression in the arts.[9]

The incident occurred during a period when censorship policies were being revised, and this no doubt prompted Larionov and others to ascribe great importance to the outcome of the trial.

Censorship laws had been relaxed by decree on November 24, 1905; however, temporary rulings issued as soon as March 18 and April 26, 1906, reversed the November decree as it applied to drawings and prints. By the end of 1913 it was widely feared that the enactment of new censorship laws would return literature and the arts to practices of the prerevolutionary period.[10] The large number of articles in newspapers describing trials, executions, and confiscation of printing materials and publications, subsumed under a generic category called "repressions" (*Repressii*), gave this aspect of public life particular prominence during the prewar years.[11]

Although a few (male) artists had been tried and imprisoned for publishing politically subversive material, Goncharova's trial was unique for an artist (whether male or female) during the interrevolutionary period.[12] The responses it elicited suggested that it would redefine state censorship policies for "high" art. Because the trial was called to justify the seizure of specific works of art, it would set a precedent recognizing the local police and courts as the *de facto* censors of independent exhibitions. This situation appears to have arisen as a consequence of the decentralization and expansion of the art market in the capital cities. The rapid proliferation of artistic groupings during the prewar years (1907–14) had moved artistic production and consumption successfully beyond the control of the Academy (and its appointed officials) and involved a wider public. At the same time, local government and police authorities began to intervene by confiscating works with increasing frequency. These activities, in effect, replaced the Academy's prerogative to regulate the art market through its policies of exclusion and expulsion with the local police and court system. This shift was in process in 1910, and it raised the stakes for those defending the "autonomy" of artistic expression since the confiscation of a painting might well be followed by trial, fines and/or imprisonment (as was always the case for literature).

The ideological power exercised by the police and courts was as much the issue debated in Goncharova's trial as was the question of pornography in her art. This is underscored by Krakht's and Larionov's defense of Goncharova insofar as both countered the accusations made against her by developing a strategy that would evacuate radical meaning from her work. Both represented Goncharova's art as "free" or nonideological in order to defend her against the prior view advanced by the prosecution, which linked politics with morality. Like Larionov, Krakht argued that the charge of pornography had falsely politicized and misrepresented the content and purpose of Goncharova's art. But his statement, in contrast, emphasized the significance of her gender in the attempt to censor her nudes: "Krakht views this affair as an insult to a woman-artist [zhenshchina-khudozhnitsa] whose whole life has been dedicated to the pursuit of pure art and who never has directed her art to pornographic ends. Moreover, this affair is crucial for artists generally, since it reflects an attempt to impose a process of censorship on free art."[13]

Krakht's redundant reference to Goncharova as a "woman-artist" (in khudozhnitsa, the grammaticial suffix alone indicates feminine gender) emphatically connects Goncharova's gender with the moral issue of pornographic representation in her art and engages the wider debate over women's social roles. Goncharova's imputed transgression is informed by issues relating to women's rights and debate over the regulation of pornography, prostitution, and sexual freedom during the period in question. Paradoxically, although feminists were among the most active advocates of outlawing prostitution and pornography (both were legal and regulated by government institutions in Russia as in other European countries),[14] there were other bases in Russia's recent historical past for the conservative perception that feminism condoned "immoral" sexual behavior. The long historical association of politically radical women with "immoral" sexual conduct probably informed the reactionary viewer's response to Goncharova's representations of the nude figure. Studies of one of the major feminist causes during the prerevolutionary period, the legalization of higher education for women in Russia, indicate that the government sought to legitimize its discriminatory policies by exposing a linkage between the "radical" life-styles and political beliefs of a generation of women who either sought or received higher education abroad (at periods when the Russian government prohibited them from attending institutions in Russia). Many of the government decrees made a specific point of denouncing the practice of "free love" among the highly educated women who were targeted as political radicals.[15] These decrees were designed, in fact, to dissolve the political alliances many of the 1860s and 1870s generation of women had with various anarchist and communist groups but often focused on their sexual politics for moral and legal justification.[16] Further prominence was given to the sexual dimension of "the woman question" by the radical political activity and well-publicized sexual views of Alexandra Kollontai (and others) during these years. In that Kollontai's most important work, *Social Bases of the Woman Question*, was published in St. Petersburg in the year preceding Goncharova's trial,[17] it is likely, if not inevitable, that conservative critics would have ascribed the views of prominent advocates of sexual freedom and socialist politics to any woman transgressing contemporary norms of feminine social behavior. Moreover, Goncharova did not conceal her close relationship with Larionov, and this may have affected the reviewer's response to her as a radical on the sexual front at least.

Although no sources have surfaced to suggest that Goncharova was involved in any of the factions within the feminist movement in Russia and we have no indication of her political views then, feminist activism intensified during this period. In December 1908, the First All-Russian Women's Congress took place, the result of an effort to create a unified women's movement in the Russian empire, and thus threatened the class-sanctioned and exclusive rights men had to higher education, suffrage, and so on.[18] In this context, it is important to underscore that Goncharova's only recorded reaction to the incident does not reveal any self-consciousness at all regarding the relevance of her gender (or life-style) for critical perceptions of her work. On the contrary, she identified her work in the genre of the nude very much as part of a mainstream vanguard assault on the academy.

Goncharova's response to the accusations launched against her was published as part of a sympathetic press interview within a week of the confiscation of her paintings.[19] The article suggests that Goncharova did not consider her nudes provocative; it states that she was "stunned by the unexpected reactions to her work." The article then transcribes Goncharova's statement of her aesthetic concerns. She claims here for the first time an alliance with Cézanne and Picasso and rejects the "impressionist" tendencies with which she had been identified in the press up to this point, thus transposing the moral and political issues at stake into a debate over style. As a distinct and separate issue, she denies that her motivations for exhibiting work under the auspices of the society were in any way subversive: "And as for the Society of Free Aesthetics, their meetings are in no way secretive. They are simply intimate gatherings of people who are interested in new forms of art. Occasionally guests participate by reading new verse, lectures, and so forth."[20] This text, Goncharova's first public statement as a "radical" or "vanguard" artist in the press, is remarkable, yet ambiguous in light of the charges made against her. It reads as a defense of her own artistic integrity and as a disavowal of any specific political agenda. One can only infer that as a central figure in vanguard circles, she managed to avoid the issue of gender difference, or that it did not problematize relations with her peers. Her defense assumes that she occupies a prominent position among artists of her generation, just as her decision to exhibit the nudes manifests her confidence that such work was acceptable to the society's membership. Goncharova's statement places her in the vanguard mainstream, particularly in its implication of the separateness of life experience from practice in the visual arts. But it is also possible to see in Goncharova's response a tactic—a plea of innocence informed by the possible consequences of her challenge.

The reporter's account of the controversy also evades the issue of the artist's gender in the accusation of pornography by recreating the context for Goncharova's work in the genre of the nude:

The first two pictures [two female nudes] are studies from live models painted during a class in the school of Goncharova, Larionov, Mashkov, and Mikhailovsky, where Goncharova was teaching. The model in the first study was standing with one foot on a chair, her arms thrown back behind her head, and in the second pose, with her arms folded across her waist. This same model was painted by the whole class at the same time, consisting of about 25 people of both sexes. As for the third picture, it represents a stone idol; the picture is inspired by archaic art: Hindu, New Zealand, finally, and more closely, by Russian so-called *Kamennye Baby* [literally "Stone Women"] that have been found in our southern steppes. The Stone God is depicted with those attributes with which he is always depicted, and these naturalistic details are, of course, not the main focus of attention for the ordinary uncorrupted viewer, as they were not in ancient Greek and Roman sculpture, which were covered with fig leaves only later when they entered papal collections.

The specific context for Goncharova's work in the genre of the life study has been explored further by Gleb Pospelov in his writings on the Jack of Diamonds. Pospelov identifies the "school" mentioned in the review as Ilya Mashkov's and A. N. Mikhailovsky's studio, which they founded in 1902 (on Malyi Kharitonevsky pereulok in Moscow). He indicates that Goncharova and Larionov must have been invited by Mashkov to share in the teaching sometime between 1908 and the spring of 1910.[21] These classes provided a unique opportunity for Goncharova and Mashkov to experiment with the genre of the nude based on life study, since neither had finished their coursework at the Moscow School of Painting, Sculpture, and Architecture. Pospelov's history is the first to place Goncharova effectively within the modernist mainstream, locating her work of the period 1908–10 in a specific Moscow vanguard environment. He also notes that Goncharova's paintings of the nude figure were censored, yet neither he nor any scholar has questioned the issue of her difference, particularly in relation to the response elicited by Mashkov's work in the genre. Critiques of Mashkov's nudes also appeared in the press, but even these are overwhelmed by the implications of Goncharova's actual trial.[22]

Unlike other reviews of "provocative" nudes, the critique of Goncharova's nudes is centered on the fact of her gender. Even the sympathetic account cited above describes a scenario that was so unusual for its inclusion of a woman—not as model or even as student, but as instructor—that it defies comparison. Goncharova's practice in the genre of the nude challenged the very basis on which the social construction of femininity obtained its authority at the turn of the century. It has been established that the nude was, until relatively recently in the history of modern painting, forbidden territory for the woman artist. Studies of the careers of women artists during the nineteenth and early twentieth centuries document the difficulties they faced in obtaining the privilege reserved for their male colleagues in the Academy: painting from the live model—male and female.[23] In Russia, as in England and France at the turn of the century, women artists' access to the genre was limited to the private studio. Indeed, because women figured so marginally in the Imperial Academy, it is practically impossible to trace a history of women's representation of the nude figure before Goncharova's trial.[24] Male models were used exclusively in Academy studios, which suggests that women were not admitted to life-study classes until after Serov introduced the use of the female model into his classes at the Moscow School of Painting, Sculpture, and Architecture at some point between 1897 and 1909. In view of the inadequate "history" of feminine practice in the genre, Goncharova's limited, one-evening exhibition is a critical marker; her nudes were the first by a vanguard woman artist to reach a public, and the first by any modern Russian artist to cause a public scandal resulting in a trial.

In part, the controversy can be explained by the scenario of Goncharova's evening exhibition. As a result of the virtual exclusion of women from practice in the genre of the nude life-study, Goncharova's paintings engaged the issue of contexts for their public display. Specifically, her exhibition challenged the engendering of spaces designated for viewing work in the genre. In Russia, of the contexts regarded as suitable for viewing representations of the nude figure, the one deemed most appropriate for viewing by the female spectator involved a wide public and was an urban event—the salon. The other spaces frequented by mixed audiences by 1910 were commercial galleries and, of course, the private office or home. Goncharova's semiprivate showing, in the context of an elite (if still marginal) literary gathering of mixed gender and social class, fell outside the boundaries of both, and foregrounded the exclusionary character of the genre. That much of the actual trial was concerned with defining the nature of public viewing, the political orientation of the meeting, and the moral bearing of the (woman) artist betrays the extent to which the three issues were connected. This conjunction of interests can be explained in part by the shifting nature of the nonacademic art world and the increasing visibility of women, both as producers and as spectators. The first two major dealers in St. Petersburg and Moscow were women: Nadezhda Dobychina and Klavdia Mikhailova respectively. Moreover, reports in the press and a few rare summaries of the constituency of audiences at public debates and exhibitions emphasize the presence of women.[25]

But as a few recent revisionist histories have demonstrated, there is a more profound sense in which practice in the genre of the nude was regulated to exclude the female artist. Of the spaces that have been mythologized in the painting of modernity, the artist's studio is particularly prominent. Its representations, from Courbet to Picasso, map out a territory of mastery associated primarily with the male artist and most frequently allegorized in the form of the female studio nude. Griselda Pollock has observed that particularly as regards the tradition and history of the studio nude, or life study, woman figures "as object for art rather than a producer of it."[26]

Feminist approaches to modernist art history, such as Linda Nochlin's and more recently Griselda Pollock's, explain the absence of documentation of work by Russian women artists in the genre of the nude. Goncharova was perhaps the first woman modernist to turn to the life study as a vehicle for experimentation, but even so, it is clear that she did not particularly favor it. This distinguishes her from somewhat younger women artists like Lyubov Popova and Zinaida Serebriakova, who a few years later would work extensively in the genre, and who perhaps enjoyed greater freedom to do so. Ilya Zdanevich's catalogue of 1913 documents Goncharova's lack of interest in and/or lack of professional access to the nude. Only five paintings from the period 1905 through 1910 are listed as "nudes" or "live models": *Study (Nude Girl)* (*Etiud [golaia devushka]*), 1906; *Female Life-Study* (*Naturshchitsa*), 1908; *Pink Female Life-Study* (*Rozovaia naturshchitsa*); *Female Life-Study*, 1909; and *Female Life-Study*, 1910. Even taking into account the possibility that works such as *Red-Haired Woman* (*Ryzhaia zhenshchina*) or untitled "Studies" may have included a few life-studies, they constitute a small fraction of her entire oeuvre. The fact that no nudes created after 1910 appear in the catalogue suggests that the process of the trial may have discouraged her from painting in the genre, although she did continue to exhibit her earlier life-studies.

I have been able to identify only two of Goncharova's female nude life-studies (Figs. 1 and 2) at the present time. These images seem to correspond with the paintings described in the passage quoted above. A comparison of the facture (*faktura*) of these works with that of *Water Nymph* (*Rusalka*) (Fig. 3), also a nude (though probably not drawn from life), suggests that they were painted about the same time (late 1908 to 1909). The identity of *God* (*Bog*), one of the confiscated paintings, is more difficult to

Fig. 1. Natalia Goncharova, *Female Nude (Life Study) (Naturshchitsa)*, 1908–9, oil on canvas, Tomilina-Larionova Bequest, State Tretyakov Gallery, Moscow.

Fig. 2. Natalia Goncharova, *Female Nude (Life Study) (Naturshchitsa)*, 1908–9, oil on canvas, Tomilina-Larionova Bequest, State Tretyakov Gallery, Moscow.

Fig. 3. Natalia Goncharova, *Water Nymph (Rusalka)*, 1908, oil on canvas, Museum Ludwig, Collection Ludwig, Cologne. Courtesy of Museum Ludwig.

establish. Whereas written accounts refer to it as a male figure,[27] the only known paintings by Goncharova of pre-Christian divinities appear to have female attributes (breasts). These paintings include the image that both Ilya Zdanevich and Mary Chamot identified as the confiscated picture in question, *God of Fertility (Cubist Treatment) (Bog plodorodiia [kubisticheskii priem])*, of 1909 (Fig. 4).[28] It is possible that Zdanevich and Chamot confused

Fig. 4. Natalia Goncharova, *God of Fertility (Cubist Treatment) (Bog plodorodiia [kubisticheskii priem])*, 1909, oil on canvas, Tomilina-Larionova Bequest, State Tretyakov Gallery, Moscow.

this painting with another painting, a depiction of a masculine divinity, not identified by Zdanevich and presumably now lost. Otherwise we have to assume that Goncharova repainted *God of Fertility*, since no representation of the genitalia (male or female) can be discerned at the present time.[29]

Fig. 5. Alexei Venetsianov, *Toilet of Diana (Tualet Diany)*, 1847, oil on canvas, State Tretyakov Gallery, Moscow. Courtesy of the State Tretyakov Gallery.

Fig. 6. Ilya Mashkov, *Studio Nude* (*Obnazhennaia v masterskoi*), 1908–10, oil on canvas, State Russian Museum, St. Petersburg. Courtesy of the State Russian Museum.

Goncharova's treatment of the female nude figure in the first two images (Figs. 1 and 2) is without question unconventional in terms of most standards for the nude, from the early-nineteenth-century paintings by Alexei Venetsianov (Fig. 5) to those of her contemporaries, including Ilya Mashkov (Fig. 6). Though Goncharova depicts typical academic studio poses, her handling of each pose, particularly the compositional relation of the figure to the frame, challenges both academic and vanguard representations of the female nude. These pictures are fairly large, though not unusually so for Goncharova. The first measures 111 by 83 centimeters and the second 118 by 96 centimeters; the torso of the first nude is larger than life size. Of the two paintings, the first pose is more confrontational than the second. Here, the viewer is deprived of all narrative structure in the image, including the studio context for the act of painting. The model's body, depicted frontally, completely fills the canvas. Her unforeshortened knee is delimited by the lower right corner of the frame in such a way that no sign of the chair or stool on which her foot "rests" appears within the composition. The posture of the second figure is more relaxed, but again the whole length of the body is compressed into the vertical axis of the canvas.

Equally striking, however, are the discrepancies that arise from a study of Figure 1 in light of the first critic's description of the two figures. This critic, by referring to the Gesner Museum, suggested that Goncharova's rendering of the female anatomy was too clinical or literal. Yet in fact the pubes in both works is depicted only as a shadowed plane, the genitalia represented schematically as a line. This seeming discrepancy suggests that these works exhibited profoundly disturbing tensions through their formal structure, and the activation of the gaze. Indeed, in the first canvas, the alignment of the genital area with the lower border of the frame gives such prominence to this part of the figure that it would make the question of realism of detail irrelevant. While the model's head forms the physical boundary at the top of the canvas, the sign of her sexuality is framed by the lower boundary; hence the viewer's gaze is directed along the vertical axis of the picture plane between the upward lifting of the head and arms at the top and the shadowed wedge of the genital area at the bottom. The angle of the knee that projects forward into the lower right-hand corner directs the viewer's gaze both out of the picture plane and back to the central axis of the canvas and the figure, forcing the viewer to complete the image's compositional dynamic. In the second image, although pubic hair is visible the model's body is depicted at a 90-degree angle, facing away from the viewer; only her torso turns toward the frontal picture plane. Overall, Goncharova's emphasis here is on the lower extremity of the body.

Redrawing the Margins of Russian Vanguard Art   115

By enlarging the scale of the legs and feet in proportion to the torso, and exaggerating chiaroscuro contrasts through planar modeling in tones of black and grey, she creates the illusion of tangible weight and mass. Regarding Goncharova's choice of scale and suggestion of mass in the lower half of the body (which makes this model resemble Goncharova's peasant women) one could speculate that she seemed all too real to her conservative viewers—like Manet's *Olympia*, a successful subversion of the classical tradition, but painted by a woman.

The way in which Goncharova has manipulated the viewer's gaze within these images, and her nearly complete exclusion of narrative or contextual detail from them, undermines the assumptions of masculine empowerment and control that define the genre of the academic nude. Konstantin Semiradsky's extremely popular voyeuristic and monumental compositions, such as *Choosing Between the Slave Girl and the Precious Vase* (Fig. 7), epitomize the

Fig. 7. Konstantin Semiradsky, *Choosing Between the Slave Girl and the Precious Vase*, late 1880s, oil on canvas (location unknown). Reprinted, by permission of Flegon Press, from Alexander Flegon, *Eroticism in Russian Art* (London, 1976).

academic genre at the end of the nineteenth century. These large-scale compositions are characterized by effusive brushwork and transparently titillating themes, in Semiradsky's case, often connected with the orgy or harem. In part, because they are so explicitly concerned with the re-creation of atmospheric illusion and sensory experience, Semiradsky's paintings explicitly illustrate the transferal of erotic and economic power to the male subject.

In *Choosing Between the Slave Girl and the Precious Vase*, the gaze of the viewer is identified with the narrative appropriation of the female form through the conventions of the one-point perspectival system. This system posits a viewer located at a specific point outside of the work whose gaze is materialized in the painted surface of the canvas and, in this case, in theme. The explicit nature of Semiradsky's work requires that the (masculine) viewer's gaze replicate the relation between subject and object set forth in the painting's iconography. Though the painting's didactic narrative transforms the female nude into a commodity and an object of erotic desire, she is clearly not represented as a desiring subject. The exchange of woman for vase diagrams, and eroticizes, possession of the woman/vase—and her "lack" as a sexual subject. Indeed, the gaze turned toward this model, as activated by the conventions of perspective and this particular narrative iconography, renders the dispossession of female sexuality far more explicitly than most images by the same painter. But it therefore clearly reveals why the high genre of the academic nude became so acceptable in Russian bourgeois society; it reinforced or prescribed real relations of dominance and subordination among members of the class for whom such work was produced.

The appropriative action of the gaze as demonstrated in Semiradsky's work is practically continuous in academic and vanguard nude compositions, notably in those painted by Goncharova's contemporary Ilya Mashkov. In his *Studio Nude* (Fig. 6), dating from about the same period as Goncharova's two female life-studies (1908–10), the viewer's gaze directed toward the female figure is acted out in the composition through the presence of a (male) studio bystander to whom the nude presents herself in a posture resembling that of Goncharova's torso figure (Fig. 1). But Goncharova's torso and the standing nude (Fig. 2) as well are remarkably different in that they skew this viewer-object, or active-passive, dynamic. Here the fact of the artist's own gender intervenes, presenting the male viewer with the paradox of a female subject as producer of unconventional images of female nudity. Not only do Goncharova's female nudes (particularly the torso figure) thwart the thematic contextualization of the studio nude in terms of composition, but further, the woman's gaze in the torso figure (Fig. 1) is assertively directed away from the viewer, deflecting the viewer's appropriative gaze. In this work the woman does not appear objectified—created "to be looked at"—rather, she is depicted as a subject with a gaze, mirroring that of the female artist-producer.[30]

Although this disruption of the gaze may have been enough to cast Goncharova's two life-studies as subversive, her transgression in the genre was even more complex. Goncharova's nudes were perceived as most marginal, in view of her gender, insofar as they appeared to double as the mass-produced pornographic or erotic "postcard." The viewer managed to ascribe features and functions that characterize the *carte* to her nudes. Yet it is not difficult to demonstrate that both in intent and in formal aspect, the resemblances between Goncharova's paintings and the *sekretnaia kartochka* are contrived. While her torso figure might share the frontal pose in common with a few explicit images (Figs. 8, 9), such superficial similarities are challenged by the absence in Goncharova's work of any of the paraphernalia one comes to expect from the pornographic—and academic—nude (Fig. 10).[31] Rather, the critical differences apparent in Goncharova's nudes, in the operation of the gaze and in the iconography, questioned the scopophilic objectives that justified the production of both categories of images. What was perhaps most shocking about Goncharova's paintings was that they pointed up censorable similarities between the high art of the academic nude and "boulevard" pornography. Her nudes revealed the hypocrisy of a culture that enfranchised both categories of nude images, academic and pornographic, but could not tolerate the feminine engendering of the gaze on the nude.

Goncharova's nudes, then, represented a marginal challenge to the Tretyakov Gallery nude that exceeded their possible re-

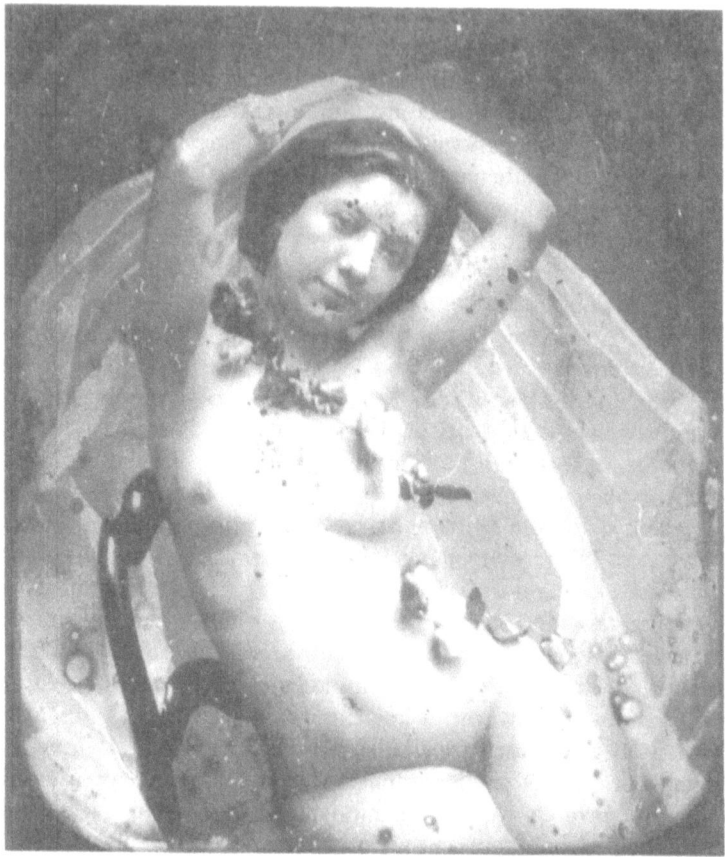

Fig. 8. Daguerreotype, late nineteenth century. Reprinted, by permission of Kunstverlag Weingarten, Germany, from *Die erotische Daguerreotypie, Sammlung Uwe Scheide* (Weingarten, 1989).

semblance to the mass-produced pornographic cards. The compositional and iconographical differences that characterize Goncharova's images as "unconventional" were deemed subversive because they contradicted essentialist views regarding "feminine difference." Predictably, these "differences" were not debated at the time of Goncharova's trial. Indeed, it is the absence of this discourse that works to represent the nude as if it were naturally

Redrawing the Margins of Russian Vanguard Art

Fig. 9. Daguerreotype, late nineteenth century. Reprinted, by permission of Kunstverlag Weingarten, Germany, from *Die erotische Daguerreotypie, Sammlung Uwe Scheide* (Weingarten, 1989).

and inevitably the domain of the male artist. Essentialist views of feminine practice in the visual arts were so entrenched at the time of Goncharova's exhibition that even her most subtle critics preferred to ascribe masculine traits to work that did not conform to their expectations for a woman artist. Yakov Tugendkhold, for example, discussed the singular power of Goncharova's peasant images in terms of gender distinctions, opposing her synthetic

Fig. 10. Daguerreotype, late nineteenth century. Reprinted, by permission of Kunstverlag Weingarten, Germany, from *Die erotische Daguerreotypie, Sammlung Uwe Scheide* (Weingarten, 1989).

"feminine" intuition about form to her "masculine" analytical expressivity:

Her personality, as strange as it seems, is more masculine than feminine. . . . The basic characteristic of Goncharova's talent is her masculine, sharp, energetic expressivity. . . . In essence, her analytic abilities dominate her gift for synthesis, her masculine eye dominates over her feminine lyricism. It's not by accident that in her catalogue she affirms her "deep interest in the petty bourgeois banalities [*meshchanskie poshlosti*] that reign in our era," which only confirms my earlier observation that the vulgar wench "Al'donsa" appeals to her more than the poetic "Dulcinea."[32]

Following Tugendkhold's argument of masculine versus feminine, dominance versus subordination, one is led to conclude that Goncharova has subverted the "proper" expression of her own gender by adopting a "masculine" method or approach to painting.

Tugendkhold's critique is based on the assumption that creativity and the production of a strongly expressive style is incompatible with being female. His dilemma (he feels that Goncharova is nevertheless a singularly great artist) can be understood by engaging recent feminist criticism that seeks to explain how the social construction of femininity has affected concepts of "women's art." Clearly the term *khudozhnitsa* never signified simply the practice or profession of being an "artist." As a number of writers have demonstrated, key art-historical terms assume a masculine subject: the term "male artist" sounds as absurd as does the term "mistress" used for a woman artist of stature.[33] Like the term *poetessa* (see Boym's essay in this volume), the term *khudozhnitsa* (and doubly so *zhenshchina-khudozhnitsa*) signifies both surplus and lack. The "woman artist" is an artist with a suffix and a sex. Goncharova's nudes were censored because they visibly manifested the artist's sexual identity—in effect, disrupting the ideological sublimation of sexual difference within the visual arts. Since it was assumed that a woman artist could not manifest her own individual identity (and sexuality)—indeed such images do not appear to have existed before Goncharova's nudes—critics such as Tugendkhold transferred the gender-specific discourse of originality and "master style" to Goncharova, casting her as a "nominal transvestite."[34]

Tugendkhold's analysis demonstrates the degree to which Goncharova's particular *handling* of her subject raised the issue of the sexual identity of the producer. Recent studies show how male modernists have obsessively worked and reworked the genre of the nude, staking their claim as vanguard innovators on the representation of the female body. Carol Armstrong has argued that what is at issue in the formal treatment of the nude is "the elision between the erotic and the representational appropriation of the female body."[35] Goncharova's paintings and the fact of her trial reveal how difficult it was during the early part of the twentieth century to conceive of a female subject active in the visual arts. An appreciation of this context is critical to understanding modernist innovation in the genre, since it makes the formal appropriation of the nude (and eroticization of form) appear as the natural and, indeed, inevitable consequence of masculine "mastery." Goncharova's paintings challenged the context for producing images in the genre of the nude at the vanguard margins of the masculine tradition by claiming it for her own development specifically as a woman artist. Her nudes presented the contemporary viewer with images that, by virtue of their source (and ambiguity of address), required the active interpretation of a female subject's gaze, and challenged the engendering of concepts of originality. This interpretive position was untenable in Russia in 1910; it demanded that viewers reconsider their assumptions regarding "woman's art" and, more seriously, women's subordinate roles in Russian society.

Three years later, in March 1914, Goncharova's paintings were again the subject of public scrutiny. On this occasion, the artist was accused of blasphemy in her depiction of Christian iconography. A single review in a newspaper, linking the artist's status as a member of the vanguard with the fact of her gender, was sufficient to cause the censoring of her large, public one-person exhibition, the first ever mounted for an artist of her generation. Like the text cited at the beginning of this essay, this review maps out the territory within which gender distinctions obtained radical value in vanguard art. In particular, Goncharova's critic reveals the extent to which a woman's gaze (positing an active subject and producer of images) interfered with and threatened the tradition of patriarchal authority defined by specific categories of images. The anonymous author of "Futurism and Blasphemy" ("Futurizm i koshchunstvo") makes the connection clear: a woman has no place in the restoration of religious art as a monumental genre of painting in Russia. Goncharova's difference in gender heightened his concern that avant-garde (here, futurist) artists, both male and female, were engaged successfully in the process of introducing noncanonical forms of representation into canonical Christian iconography. Thus, again, Goncharova's gender could serve as the pretext for a criminal action, as is implied in the veiled threat concluding the review: "Let the futurist [*futuristka*] exhibit as many women's portraits, cats and other things resembling cabinets and rubbish as she likes; but let her not touch with her dirty hands the subjects of religious devotion belonging to the whole Russian people."[36] In contrast to the charges of 1910, all charges against the artist in this instance were dropped as a result of the mobilization of the artistic community on her behalf. Yet both incidents occurred because Goncharova's "mastery of gaze" and handling of specific subject matter was viewed as criminal—a consequence of her "unsexing." In both cases, Goncharova was charged with presenting for public consumption the spectacle of a female subject transfigured, posturing as masculine.

In 1910, Goncharova's work in the genre of the nude life-study, and in 1914, her religious iconography, attained "radical" value by exposing the prejudices of conservative members of her audience regarding gender and its significance in establishing the (il)legitimacy of vanguard art. Because it is impossible to gauge Goncharova's specific intentions in painting the nude figure, the fact of her trial must be understood as a critical measure of her "radicalism." However, her trial also reaffirms an issue that should be a part of any study of the avant-garde: various sections of her audience enjoyed the power to authorize and legitimize their interpretations through the press and the legal system. The possibility of censorship, a condition of activity in the arts in prerevolutionary Russia, set Goncharova's work as "free" or "autonomous" against the political and moral agenda of the state. This situation intensified the artist's need to affirm the autonomy of form and questions of aesthetic taste. By contrast, the fact of censorship and legal prosecution gave the social and political context for the artist's activities a new measure of importance. In the event of Goncharova's exhibitions (1910 and 1914) and trial (1910) the artist's sexual identity and moral character were placed within an explicitly ideological field of interpretation.

ELIZABETH A. WOOD

Prostitution Unbound

Representations of Sexual and Political Anxieties in Postrevolutionary Russia

> *To redo everything. To construct in such a way that everything becomes new, that our false, dirty, boring, and disgusting life should become a fair, clean, cheerful, and beautiful life.*
> —Alexander Blok, "Intelligentsia and Revolution"

■ In the black evening and white snowstorm of Alexander Blok's poem "The Twelve" (*Dvenadtsat'*, 1918), even the prostitutes meet in the streets to set their prices:

> ... And we had a meeting ...
> ... In this building here ...
> ... Discussed—
> Resolved:
> For a time—ten, for a night—twenty-five ...
> ... Not to take less from nobody ...
> ... To bed! ...

The snowstorm turns the old world upside down, mowing down pedestrians, driving out the old order. In the upheaval Petrukha, one of the Twelve, kills his former girlfriend Katka in a fit of jealousy at her apparent profligacy. She bears the attributes of a prostitute (stockings, new money, French chocolates). At the same time she symbolizes Russia, the mother country. An end to religion means the soldiers of the new order do not fear to put a bullet through "fat old Russia" itself. Yet even as they liberate themselves from crosses and the old religion, they remain vulnerable to the larger forces of the snowstorm with all its hidden gusts of chaos and, I will argue, uncontrolled sexuality.

The twilight of the Old Regime in Russia and the Bolsheviks' assumption of power in October 1917 came at a time of significant upheaval and challenge to fundamental social and political identities. As historian Leo Haimson has noted, Russia at the time of the revolution was "a society out of joint," one that faced "steadily growing contradictions" in the relations of various social groupings to each other and to the state.[1] Sheila Fitzpatrick has also discovered identity confusions that resulted as different groups in society assumed new roles and positions after the revolution.[2] Anxiety within the Communist Party manifested itself in the pervasiveness of rhetoric concerning the bourgeois threat and fears of a resurgence of the old order.

These anxieties, I argue, came to be presented in sexual terms, with particular emphasis on the prostitute as a danger to the new order. Like their counterparts in Western Europe in the late nineteenth and early twentieth centuries, revolutionary and reformist leaders in Russia invoked the prostitute as a leading symbol of decadence, social decay, urbanization, and the exploitation inherent in capitalist social relations.[3] The prostitute's victimization came to dramatize the plight of the nation itself.[4]

In the discussion that follows I explore some of the deep-seated anxieties concerning prostitution and sexuality that appear in Bolshevik publicistic writings. I argue that the sexual nature of this social phenomenon could be emphasized or de-emphasized depending on the circumstances. Prior to the revolution of 1917, for example, Bolshevik theorists dismissed prostitution as merely a symptom of the greater evils of capitalism and bourgeois exploitation; they rejected the melodramatic stories of bourgeois reformers. After 1917, however, writers in the popular press rehabilitated that very melodrama by telling stories of the redemptive powers of the revolution, its powers to save fallen women.

In 1921 the introduction of the New Economic Policy evoked significant new anxieties among the Bolshevik leadership and the rank and file that it would lead to the resurgence of capitalism and the rise of a new bourgeoisie.[5] In the face of these anxieties party leaders, especially those in the women's section of the Communist

Party, wrote insistently about the sexual dangers of the prostitute and the vulnerability to NEP of both society in general and working women in particular. In this context the uncontrolled sexuality of the prostitute served to dramatize the anarchy and danger of market relations.

Yet as the regime stabilized its leading position in the new nation, Bolshevik administrators denied the sexual threat of the prostitute and moved to prescribe rational, administrative approaches to this phenomenon. New campaigns were initiated not to fight prostitution so much as to combat venereal disease, truancy from the main labor force, and income generated outside the state sector of the economy.

In each of these different contexts the invocation of the prostitute served to heighten the tension inherent in the given situation. She was never simply a sex worker, but always a symbol, a metaphor. The issue of prostitution thus had multiple meanings, meanings that could be sexualized or desexualized depending on the context.

Apocalypse and Danger

Prerevolutionary liberal reformers in Russia used a variety of synonyms for the terms "prostitute" and "prostitution" borrowed from Western Europe: "fallen women," "white slavery," women who have "perished," the "traffic in women." The terms of the debate centered on regulation (*reglamentatsiia*) versus abolition (*abolitsionizm*), issues borrowed directly from the West, specifically from Victorian discourse.[6]

In contrast to the reformers, Russian Marxists took great pains to claim that prostitution was not the issue at all. Rather, they argued, prostitution had to be viewed as a *consequence* of capitalism, a dependent variable that arose from poverty and exploitation. If the causes of prostitution—wage labor, private property, marriages of convenience—could be eliminated, then so too would the need for certain women to prostitute themselves in exchange for money.[7]

V. I. Lenin, who otherwise wrote little on the issue of sexuality, invoked the prostitute as *double victim*: she was a victim both of the bourgeois property system and of its moral hypocrisy. As long as wage slavery existed, he was convinced, prostitution would invariably continue: "No 'moral indignation' (hypocritical in ninety-nine cases out of a hundred) about prostitution can do anything to prevent this commerce in women's bodies."[8] In the first issue of a new newspaper for workers (*Rabochaia pravda*, July 13, 1913), he singled out for criticism those Western leaders who met in 1913 for the Fifth International Congress Against Prostitution: "We may judge . . . the disgusting bourgeois hypocrisy that reigns at these aristocratic-bourgeois congresses. Acrobats in the field of philanthropy and police defenders of this mockery of poverty and need gather 'to struggle against prostitution,' which is supported precisely by the aristocracy and the bourgeoisie."[9] Lenin rejected here (and elsewhere) the notion of an abstract morality, one that would operate on a supraclass level. All morality, he argued, is class-based. The only acceptable morality is that which strengthens the hegemony of the working class.[10]

The new Bolshevik order claimed its legitimacy in large measure on the basis of its commitment to building a new social order and to uprooting bourgeois perversions.[11] Bolshevik revolutionaries assumed that the introduction of rational, scientific, and above all work-oriented values in society would drive away their opposites, the dark scourges of prostitution and depravity. The Commissariat of Enlightenment would lead the "dark" (i.e., ignorant) masses into the light of scientific socialism. Abject forms of prostitution would naturally disappear. In 1918 Alexandra Kollontai, the leading Bolshevik feminist, explained: "With changing conditions of work, with the growth of material security of women workers, and with the changing of the earlier, indissoluble, hypocritical church marriage . . . into a free, comradely union, that other disgusting, dark, debasing human evil and scourge of hungry working women—prostitution—will also disappear."[12] Vadim Bystriansky, an editor of *Pravda* and *Leningrad Pravda*, addressed the same issue in his *Communism, Marriage, and the Family*: "Communism will not know prostitution, that open wound of the class structure, which under capitalism has taken on the dimensions of a massive tragedy, just as the original kinship system did not know prostitution."[13]

In contrast to the Marxist logic of these social-democratic theorists, texts written for popular consumption after 1917 often portrayed the revolution as a storm cleansing and purifying society. "The cleansing wave of revolution is pronounced over her head," a women's section organizer wrote of a prostitute brought to court in a mock trial written for agitation purposes.[14] In another story written for a popular audience entitled "From the Darkness to the Light," an illiterate working woman who had worked as a prostitute prior to the revolution is saved by the Bolshevik party, whose organizers teach her to read, cure her of syphilis, and train her to become a factory organizer. In this story the revolution of 1917 is portrayed as the Last Judgment itself: "To some it brought a death sentence, others it returned to life."[15] The revolution could thus "save" the fallen woman, bringing her back to life.

This great national event of the revolution brought not only cleansing but also danger. If negative forces were unleashed by the destruction of the old, what forms might they take, what havoc might they wreak on Russian society? In 1923 after a conference of party propagandists Trotsky explained: "It was, anyhow, clear to all that some great process was going on, very chaotically assuming alternatively morbid or revolting, ridiculous or tragic forms, and which had not yet had time to disclose its hidden possibilities of inaugurating a new and higher order of family life."[16]

The period of transition (between the revolution and the attainment of communism) carried particular dangers in the sexual realm because of the destruction of the old without a corresponding substitution of new forms. The old Bolshevik Lepeshinsky lamented: "What can be put up against this theory [of free love]? Parental authority? There is none. The authority of religion? There is none. Traditions? There are none. Moral feeling? But the old morality has died and the new has not yet come into being. The old form of the family has by and large been thoroughly destroyed, while the new does not yet exist."[17] The commissar of internal affairs in the Northern Region during the civil war found the current time to be one of "inexpressible bacchanalia":

> The old rotten structures of the family and marriage have caved in and are moving toward complete destruction with every day. Yet there are no guiding principles for creating new, beautiful, healthy relations. . . . Free love is understood by the best people as free debauchery. The most responsible, political people, leaders of the revolution, themselves appear

Prostitution Unbound

to be helpless in this area and clearly cannot make ends meet. . . . There are many grounds for deformed relations. We must sound the alarm.[18]

The Introduction of NEP and Renewed Anxieties

Fears that the prostitute would undermine the new society emerged not only in 1917 in the aftermath of the October Revolution itself but also in 1921 in the context of the transition to the New Economic Policy. Even with great effort to create a new society the boundaries of the new republic were not invulnerable. One commentator noted: "In the transition period, according to the French proverb, the dead still try to grab onto the living; the miasma of rotting capitalism still continues to contaminate the public atmosphere. Among the products of that decay of the old society we find as well prostitution, alas as yet unextirpated in Soviet Russia."[19] The open wounds of capitalism, the miasma contaminating revolutionary society—these images depict prostitution as ulcerating, polluting, breaking through the new body politic with contaminations from the old, even after the revolution.

The introduction of NEP in 1921 gave rise to an outburst of renewed anxieties linking capitalism and prostitution because of the acknowledged defeat of the preceding "war communism" (1918–20) in solving contemporary economic problems. Lenin and his advisers explicitly referred to NEP as a "retreat" and a return to "state capitalism." One immediate effect of the new policy was massive unemployment, which affected women workers disproportionately. It also provided some individuals (especially the so-called "NEPmen") with new opportunities to get rich. To many this represented a new danger: needy women would be forced to sell their bodies, and rich men would buy them.

Vera Golubeva, deputy director of the women's section of the party, commented on the difficulties this situation entailed for the whole endeavor of organizing women: "With the transition onto the rails of the New Economic Policy the question of women's emancipation has become enormously more complicated. . . . The cutbacks in production and the growing dissolution of family bonds have engendered massive unemployment and poverty among women, prostitution, and children's homelessness."[20] Activists in the women's section were often at a loss how to continue organizing women workers under such circumstances, as we see in the following letter to the editor of the women's party journal *Kommunistka* from the head of the Belorussian women's section:

> We stand before the fact that the great majority of women workers are being thrown onto the streets, women who will be forced to turn to prostitution as one means of income. . . . A wave of prostitution is flooding all social organizations. The women's section of the party, whose immediate task is supposed to be the fight against this phenomenon, finds itself helpless. The propaganda of new morality without concurrent practical activity—this is a laughable and pitiable measure, powerless to obtain real results.[21]

For activists such as these, calling attention to prostitution strengthened their argument that NEP itself threatened women's economic and social position in the new society.

In the summer of 1922 Kollontai wrote a long article for *Kommunistka* explicitly attacking the New Economic Policy as "the new threat."[22] In her analysis, NEP-based unemployment was once again making women dependent economically and socially on men. They were being forced to choose between prostitution and marriage, a return to "that domestic bondage from which the revolution was supposed to have freed [them]." The revolution had supposedly swept away "doll parasites" like harmful moths (*babochki vreditel'nitsy*) in a summer storm.[23] Now, however, when women constituted some 70 percent of the unemployed, prostitution and concubinage threatened the whole outcome of the revolution for women: "Once a woman ceases to work in production, once her labor is no longer taken into account by the responsible organs, what kind of a 'comrade' can she be?! And then how can you talk about women's equality in the family and in marriage?"[24]

Kollontai's portrayal itself contains a certain misogyny, an antipathy toward any kind of dependence by women, especially their dependence in the realm of sexual relations.[25] A series of drawings that appeared in the following issue of the journal portrayed the "new threat" as the revival of such doll parasites, women who subverted any kind of work ethic and commitment to the new order: "Motherhood repulses them; housework they leave to the servant. As for participating in public life and in construction they don't want to, don't know how to, and cannot."[26] Associating with doll parasites, moreover, would pull others (presumably males) into the "swamp of philistinism." Only the women's section of the party could return women to socially useful work as an antidote to idleness.

The legalization of free trading constituted an additional source of anxiety in contemporary discussions. If poverty and riches might both be exacerbated by the New Economic Policy, then what was to keep an unemployed woman from trading in the only object that was purely her own "property," her physical body? Bystriansky pointed out: "On the soil of the vitality of the commodity economy, prostitution too continues to drag out its miserable existence; sometimes women's bodies too serve as an object for 'free trade.'"[27]

Public outcry against the NEPman focused on his economic activities, while the "NEPka," his girlfriend or wife, was castigated for her sexual dependence. Economic and sexual anxieties were thus intertwined. Yet they also demonstrated an apparently ingrained gender difference. Men, if left unfettered by strict Communist control, would resort to economic misdemeanors; women, on the other hand, would commit sexual transgressions.

Taming Prostitution Through Medical Discourse

While political and especially economic issues were often portrayed in sexual terms in the early NEP years, official policy statements on prostitution tended to purge it of its sexual content, presenting it as a social rather than a sexual concern. In the intervening years between the revolution and NEP, officials had insisted, for example, that efforts were to be waged only against prostitution as a general social phenomenon, not against the individual prostitute.[28] While in practice individual prostitutes were among the first to be sentenced to the newly created First Camp for Forced Labor established by the Petrograd Soviet in 1919, they were ostensibly imprisoned not for their unbridled sexuality, but rather on grounds of "labor desertion," their failure to hold a job in the state sector of the economy.[29] The introduction of NEP, however, meant that the prostitute could no longer be charged with labor desertion since unemployment was rampant and the state could no longer guarantee jobs as an alternative to prostitution. Administrators were forced to develop a series of new measures to combat prostitution and the spread of venereal disease. In this context the primary transgression came to be categorized along medical and social lines. Prostitution itself was not made illegal. Rather the transmission of venereal disease (whether knowingly or unknowingly) was made a punishable offense, as were pimping, keeping a brothel, recruiting women into prostitution—that is, exploiting their labor for financial gain.

Governmental measures taken against prostitution included the creation of an Interdepartmental Commission for Combatting Prostitution, medical programs for the treatment of prostitutes and others with venereal disease, bans on the employment of women as waitresses in private rooms in drinking establishments, educational programs, and the establishment of new, higher standards for membership in the party.[30]

Particularly under the auspices of the Health Commissariat, vigorous efforts were made to bring the evils of prostitution into the public eye in order to show the masses their ignorance and their need for Bolshevik teachings. This was done through public skits known as "agitation trials," in which scripted scenes were acted out by local amateurs, usually factory workers and doctors. In such trials the ignorance of midwives, backward peasants, and mothers, as well as prostitutes, was demonstrated in order to show the superiority of systems of knowledge and expertise established by the Bolsheviks.[31]

In addition, medical asylums known as *profilaktorii* were established where the prostitute could be housed, treated for her illnesses, and trained in a new trade. Women incarcerated in these institutions could come and go as they pleased except during the hours of 3:00 to 10:00 P.M., when it was feared that they would be drawn back to their old professions. Once they were pronounced cured, they were given new jobs and their employers were told about their past so that they could be carefully supervised. The Bolshevik regime, which had initially rejected medico-police regulation as no more than bourgeois hypocrisy, turned to forms of institutional solutions that in many ways resembled precisely the lock wards and Magdalene Societies of Victorian England. The new medical institutions were designed to redeem the fallen woman and make her a useful and productive member of society.

Prostitution Unbound 133

Conclusions

In a variety of ways, then, prostitution served both to *dramatize political anxieties and concerns* and to *create new areas of expertise*, new reasons to educate the public about correct norms of behavior in the Soviet workers' republic. The legislation of prostitution issues thus came to aid in defining the *boundaries* of the new republic and to indicate who the boundary keepers were to be.

While prior to the revolution Bolshevik leaders had tended to see prostitution primarily in terms of the victimization of certain women, after the revolution they roundly criticized prostitution for its harm to the new body politic and opened up extensive struggles against prostitution, campaigns that rivaled in intensity those carried out by prerevolutionary reformers. Prostitution had to be combated, the new leaders argued, because it interfered with economic production by distracting workers from their tasks. It lowered productivity by infecting workers with disease. And it encouraged individual economic accumulation outside of the state sphere: "The prostitute is a person with her own profession. But in the conditions of Soviet reality that profession is excluded. It should not exist. It is the profession of an alien [social] structure."[32]

At the same time the new government ministries, and the Health Commissariat in particular, clearly sought to prove their domination over this issue and especially over the education efforts surrounding it as a means to establish the extent of their authority within the country as a whole. In a context of scarce resources the commissariats of health, labor, and social welfare engaged in countless propaganda battles to show that their work was vital to the survival of the nation as a whole. Prostitution had particular symbolic value in emphasizing the harms of the New Economic Policy and the benefits to be brought by the individual commissariats.[33]

Why was it that the image of the prostitute proved so useful for mobilization in the context of political anxieties, especially given the revolutionaries' original dismissal of this issue? Two key phenomena need to be considered here: first, the preexisting marginalization of the prostitute, which the Bolsheviks accepted, and second, her sexuality as itself anxiety-producing because of its very marginality.

As Julia Kristeva has argued at length in her study *Powers of Horror*, there are certain "defilements" that the individual or the collective seeks to "ab-ject," to "jettison from the 'symbolic system.'"[34] "It is not lack of cleanliness or health that causes abjection but what disturbs identity, system, order. What does not respect borders, positions, rules. The in-between, the ambiguous, the composite."[35] In this work Kristeva self-consciously adopts Mary Douglas's notions of the body as constitutive of cultural configurations that form crucial boundaries within the social. Kristeva goes one step further, however, to examine "those females who can wreck the infinite."[36] While her focus both here and elsewhere is primarily on the threat/attraction of the maternal body, one can apply a similar analysis to the activity of prostitution, which also becomes manifest as an abjection, something that disturbs identities, systems, and orders. In the Russian context both Bolshevik officials and literary fellow travelers called attention to prostitution, constituting different meanings for this abjection as a means to dramatize identity disturbances and changes (positive as well as negative) arising in the revolution. At the same time the process of legislating prostitution, of developing official policies concerning the prostitute and her client, allowed these same revolutionary leaders to face their own fears and to establish the boundaries of the new body politic in formation. As Kristeva also argues, rites of purification designed to eliminate the threat of defilement serve to elucidate boundary definitions, to provide a "hyphen" between what she calls "the unnamable" (that which is defiled) and "the absolute" (the prohibition or law), thus strengthening the political and cosmic "order" of society.[37]

When the unnamable threatens to overwhelm society, then even nonsexual issues become sexualized (as we have seen in relation to the New Economic Policy especially). When there is a movement toward strengthening the hegemonic social order or toward creating a *new* hegemony (Kristeva's "absolute"), then prohibitions against prostitution take on new strength, and that unnamable sexuality is brought forward, named, discussed, contained; it becomes an issue of regulation and ordering.

The findings in this essay also evoke the work of Michel Foucault, particularly his notion of a "great sexual sermon" that emerged in eighteenth-century Europe through developments in pedagogy, medicine, demography, and psychiatry.[38] The mobilization of the issue of prostitution in this period in late tsarist and early Soviet history suggests a modification of this theory. While there may have been sexual sermons both before and after the revolution, "prostitution" served a particular role as a hyphenated, unstable category that could be sexualized (for dramatic emphasis) or desexualized (to emphasize control), depending on the moment and the context. This "sermon" did not then emerge in a linear fashion but in an irregular rhythm of expansion and contraction, sexualization and desexualization. Ostensibly nonsexual issues such as the collapse of the tsarist order, anxieties concerning the new freedoms, and the introduction of the New Economic Policy could be portrayed in more sexualized terms in order to dramatize their threatening, decaying, or subversive nature. In other contexts the same issues of prostitution and sexual disorder could be tamed through the use of apparently neutral medical and scientific discourses with an emphasis on work, education, and rehabilitation rather than on sexuality per se.

In this way prostitution dramatized and sexualized the threat inherent in the snowstorm and the dark night, in the transition to communism and in the resurgent capitalism of the New Economic Policy. At the same time, however, it was a territory that the Commissariat of Health and other commissariats of the new government hoped to conquer through agitation trials, rehabilitation (both forced and voluntary), and education. A newer, cleaner postrevolutionary Russia would be freed from indeterminate, uncontrolled forces such as prostitution.

PART II

Literary Versions
of Sex and Body

CATHY POPKIN

Kiss and Tell

Narrative Desire and Discretion

■ This paper is a meditation on kissing and telling, both as the sequence that produces Anton Chekhov's story "The Kiss" ("Potselui"), and as a kind of model for storytelling in general.

The expression "kiss and tell" names an indiscretion, the exposure of intimacy to publicity. It also names a desire, an irresistible desire to tell of desire no longer resisted. More precisely, "kiss and tell" links two indiscretions, two irrepressible desires, casting one oral function as the necessary complement of the other—as if without the indiscretion of the kiss there is nothing to tell; and without the indiscretion of the report pleasure is incomplete, desire has not been fully stilled, or rather, if anything, has been freshly aroused by the kiss.

Moreover, the more illicit the kiss and, consequently, the more proscribed the narrative indiscretion, the more urgent the desire to be indiscreet. The sexier the kiss, in other words, and the greater the need to be discreet, the more irrepressible the desire not to be.

Hence the old joke about the orthodox rabbi who indulges a long-cherished desire for blasphemy by going out to play golf on Yom Kippur, the highest of holy days. He tees off: beautiful drive, birdies the hole, and proceeds, delighted, to the next, which he aces, and so on, until he miraculously finishes some seven under par. Meanwhile, on the celestial sidelines, Moses, having observed the errant rabbi birdie and eagle his way through the most extraordinary game of his life, looks uncomprehendingly at God.

"What?" he protests, "You reward him for this insolence?!" God, who has been ignoring the meddlesome Moses for eighteen holes, finally turns to him and, in His infinite wisdom, asks the prophet in turn: "But who can he tell?"

This reflects not just an interesting psychological fact but a significant narrative one as well. Desire, like narrative, is double. One wants first to do the dirty deed and then to tell someone. One longs to produce both the story and the discourse, the content and the expression, the signified and the signifier. Narrative is the product of two violations—the original unspeakable indiscretion (actual or fictional) and the speech that betrays it. Storytelling is born of restraint doubly abandoned; if the secret is not divulged, there is, in effect, no story. Ross Chambers even postulates that, ultimately, there can be no secrets "because a secret exists only as discourse, and the discourse which 'realizes' the secret is that which destroys it as a 'secret' (as something unspoken)."[1] This amounts, essentially, to a restatement of Barbara Herrnstein Smith's rejection of the story/discourse dichotomy on the grounds that pure story independent of any discursive treatment is inconceivable.[2] Whether or not one insists on the logical priority of the secret or kiss, however, Chambers's suggestion of mutual entailment is pertinent. In what follows we will be concerned with the ways in which kissing is fundamental to storytelling and storytelling in turn is an inextricable part of kissing.

Kissing is a good figure for the conception of narrative not only because, like telling, it is consummately oral, but also because, like good story, it creates the desire to go on. Kissing awakens more desire (for unless it is taken synecdochically for sexual activity *in toto*, kissing, like storytelling, *excites* desire), and telling attempts a kind of seduction of its own.

"Narratives portray the motors of desire that drive and consume their plots," submits Peter Brooks, "and they also lay bare the nature of narration as a form of human desire: the need to tell as a primary human drive that seeks to seduce . . . the listener."[3] Narrative, in other words, not only reports the kiss but also operates like one. It expresses desire, indulges it, and ideally stimulates it in the receiver. The kiss, then, is not only narrative content but also a metaphor for both text production and reception. Like the kiss, the narrative transaction involves two parties, and for it to succeed, both must be desirous: the "desire to narrate" seeks "desire for narration."[4]

What this seduction model implies is that the teller must "arouse" the listener in order to awaken and sustain the "desire for narration." And while the desire to tell seems assured, a virtual prerequisite for the existence of narrative, the desire to *get* the story, to hear it out, is contingent on the quality of the tale. What makes something worth listening to? Yuri Lotman, who defines an "event" in narrative as the crossing of an inviolable boundary, suggests that the more unlikely, the more unanticipated that infraction (the more illicit, in other words, the kiss), the more eventful the story and the more worth reading it is likely to seem.[5] The stolen kiss, in short, not only wants to be reported, but that report is just as eagerly awaited. (With such complicity between teller and listener, it is no wonder that scandal and gossip travel with such ease.) Thus it is not perversity alone that prompts the Marquis de Sade to figure narrative interest and effective storytelling as titillation; his storytellers may be prostitutes with lewd experiences to convey (story) and considerable skill in erotic delivery (discourse), but the listeners themselves are the most degenerate libertines of them all.[6]

Not that we need to discuss the narrative transaction in such a way that all interest becomes prurient. But we might provisionally allow that a story must be at least figuratively "sexy" enough to arouse interest. Moreover, as we will see, some of the most decorous writers themselves pose the question of tellability in singularly erotic terms. Ultimately, it seems, what's worth telling (and what's worth reading) is connected with desire, with what's worth getting worked up about. Good narrative creates a state of appetite and arousal; it excites our "passion for meaning," our burning desire to get the story.[7] "We are all like Scheherezade's husband," E. M. Forster concedes. We submit to narrative proliferation primarily because of our feverish and primitive drive to find out "what happens next."[8]

Scheherezade has a particularly strong incentive to keep her audience entertained—as she sustains arousal (in the form of narration), she wards off death. Her prolonged nocturnal performances, in which she tenders stories as an alternative to sleep and a substitute for sex, find their counterpart in the Russian folk tradition in a slightly less momentous transaction than Scheherezade's bid for approval as reprieve, but in the guise of a deal all the same: narrative entertainment in exchange for a night's shelter. Story after story in Alexander Afanasiev's collection of folk tales features a "guest" who will "pay" for lodging by providing ongoing nocturnal narration/stimulation. Of particular interest in this regard is "How the Husband Cured His Wife of Stories" ("Kak muzh otuchil zhenu ot skazok"), in which the wife, who "passionately loved stories," would admit to their home only those who knew how to "tell tales" (*skazyvat'*).[9] These strange gentlemen would essentially go to bed with the couple and while away the night with tales. Since this puts the husband at a certain disadvantage, he comes up with a plan to rid her of this obsession. One evening he introduces a peasant who has promised to *skazyvat'* all night long, and sets the condition that any interruption will terminate the performance altogether. When this peasant fulfills his end of the bargain by repeating the opening line over and over and over—by perpetually starting a story that never progresses—the desirous listener, impatient for her stimulation and eventual satisfaction, and intolerant of boredom, demands more excitement. At this signal, the husband jumps up and beats her senseless for her expression of desire—"He beat her and beat her and beat her and beat her, until she began to hate stories and swore off them for good."[10]

In this sadistic entertainment of his own (apparently no less reiterative than the peasant's cherished first line), the controlling husband has successfully banished his wife's passion for narrative, the nocturnal interloper. One only wonders what will occupy their liberated nights now—kissing, as befits a conjugal pair, or sleep. Like good sex, good stories replace slumber: they keep you awake. Boring stories, conversely, are soporific, and sleep becomes the index of the collapse of desire, narrative and sexual.

Chekhov, who will concern us primarily here, sets up a particular sleep/talk economy to calibrate narrative worthiness. In "Peasant Women" ("Baby"), for instance, the enterprising Dyudya, who maintains a lucrative trade in a wide range of commodities and services, exacts a story each night from his transient boarders, almost as part of his calculation of the payment for their lodging.[11] Delivered nocturnally as they are, the stories must represent adequate reimbursement for the listener's forfeited sleep. Chekhov, who worried that his own peasant subject matter might prove too boring (and who had his own profit motive for publishing this story), makes it clear that good stories recounted by Dyudya's lodgers make for a night well spent.[12] The contribution on this particular night is, not incidentally, a kiss-and-tell story of dramatic proportions. Similarly, in the frame narrative that links "The Man in the Case" ("Chelovek v futliare"), "Gooseberries" ("Kryzhovnik"), and "About Love" ("O liubvi"), nights are eagerly whiled away with edifying tales, and the listeners refrain from turning in for fear that someone will recount something interesting in their absence (vol. 10, pp. 42–76). Stories—by implication the three pieces of Chekhov's that are told in these sessions—are more valuable than sleep and much more exciting.

But only up to a point, after which it is emphatically "bedtime." *Pora spat'*, rules the vigilant Burkin more than once in the "Man in the Case" trilogy (vol. 10, p. 54). *Pora spat'*, decrees the mother in peremptory dismissal of the children's "trivial" tragedy in "The Event" ("Sobytie," vol. 5, p. 428). And we need only recall the agony and exasperation of the beleaguered guest in "Pecheneg" when he is kept awake all night by the narrative exertions of his excruciatingly boring host (vol. 9, pp. 325–34). In Chekhov's world, people have even been known to kill the source of the noise that keeps them awake ("Sleepy" ["Spat' khochetsia," vol. 7, pp. 7–12]).

Alternatives to repose come in two basic kinds—stimulating and irritating. Wakefulness as an index for the reception side of tellability stresses vividly the responsibility of the teller to make the story worth the sacrifice, a delight rather than a nuisance.

"The Kiss," in which a shy officer's imaginative life is transformed by a fleeting kiss bestowed by mistake in a darkened room, poses all the questions that obsess Chekhov as storyteller: has something happened, or not? Was it extraordinary, or not? And is it worth telling, or not? (vol. 6, pp. 406–23). Not known for his erotic subject matter, but deeply concerned with what's interesting enough to tell, Chekhov elaborates a dynamic of eros and discretion to explore the narrative transaction—an exchange that relies on erotic entanglement on several levels—in the context of a culture that privileges discretion.

The story opens with the troops of an artillery unit settling in for a night's encampment. As the men are about to retire to much-needed rest and repose, a messenger on horseback arrives to summon the officers to "tea" at the home of a local landowner-general.

Although this unexpected invitation presents the possibility of event and excitement, something worth telling, the officers are singularly unenthusiastic. They remember all too well that last year another local dignitary had issued a similar invitation and ended up "entertaining" the weary combatants all night long with tiresome tales of his own youthful exploits—stories that, like the eternal drone of the Pecheneg or the repetition of the same line all night long by the folktale peasant, arouse only exasperation rather than interest or desire to hear more. Would this year's "tea" be a reprise of that last one, sleep forfeited for boring tales? Protocol demands their attendance, however, so the officers make their obligatory way to von Rabbek's estate.

But there is an important departure from last year's precedent: women. There are so many lovely women taking up the guest rooms, in fact, that the general and his family are unable to invite the officers to stay the night. (The hosts themselves are, in any case, less than keen on this military "incursion," having issued the invitation solely out of their own sense of social obligation.) Thus, the officers will not be unduly detained or forcibly deprived of sleep by endless boring stories. But in view of the female element, they might well initiate some alternatives to slumber of their own. . . .

The man singled out for the kiss-and-tell adventure, though, is an unlikely hero. Ryabovich is distinguished only by his utter lack of distinctiveness. A man of "indefinite" appearance, he is described in grammatical superlatives as the *most un*superlative character imaginable. And this most modest, most unremarkable, most stoop-shouldered nonentity is further defined in terms of *in*activity. He has never danced, never played billiards, and never even *imagined* embracing a woman.

Thus Ryabovich is positively overwhelmed by the flutter of activity at the general's—the whirling feminine figures, the animated faces around the table, the languorous smells of the May night. Unable to focus on anything, overstimulated into a state Chekhov diagnoses clinically as "psychic blindness," he follows several officers through a great maze of empty rooms and corridors to the billiard room. There he watches their game, ignored (indeed not even noticed, except when bumped unceremoniously with a cue), until he feels his own superfluity so acutely that he decides to return to the main festivities.[13]

But he loses his way in the series of empty rooms and ends up in a completely unfamiliar, pitch dark chamber; he stops in confusion. Suddenly, he hears the sound of feminine footsteps in the dark, the rustling of a lady's finery; a woman whispers breathlessly, "At last!," puts her arms around his neck, and plants a resounding kiss near his lips. Realizing her mistake right away (clearly she has been expecting someone else), she emits a cry and disappears abruptly from the room, but emphatically not from Ryabovich's heart and mind and newly begotten life-story.

Heart pounding, he returns to the party transformed—or at least activated. He had left undistinguished and utterly unnoticeable and has now reemerged, he is certain, with that unmistakable "just kissed" look. He spends the rest of the evening grinning expansively, marveling at this unprecedented event, and wondering which of the fair ladies present has so indiscreetly shared this intimacy with him. His gaze rests first on one, then on another, but each physical attribute that attracts him initially then falls short, and in the end he can only construct some abstract composite of one lady's curls, another's shoulders, and so on, a charming creature to be sure, but, alas, nowhere in evidence.

But he takes home with him a previously unknown joy, a sensation of peppermint coolness near his left moustache, and a light trace of oil on his neck. As he falls asleep he tries again to reconstruct the elusive image, but the successive body parts he calls up in his imagination's memory (twice removed from the real thing) are vagrant images that dissolve with amazing rapidity. There remain only the sounds of the incident (which, unlike the sights, the darkness did not obscure).

He awakens the next morning to the call of duty, the peppermint coolness lost, but the joy intact. As the troops march off to their next venue, passing the von Rabbek estate in the process, he tries to visualize "her" asleep, but, again, in vain. Most of the rest of the text is taken up with the counterpoint of that day's march and Ryabovich's personal absorption in his fantasies about his "unknown lady" (*neznakomka*). Normally bored by the familiar routine (to the point of sleeping in the saddle), today he is ardently staging scenarios with his composite lady (whose features continue to elude him), and he begins to fashion a narrative sequence: war, parting, reunion, first child. . . .

Finally, many pages later, after a full day's march and maneuvers (and an oddly extended digression on Chekhov's part on the structure of an artillery column), Ryabovich finds himself at nightfall, seized with an irrepressible urge to tell his story, which by now consumes him utterly. However, his nocturnal narrative performance (which we will return to in greater detail) is very short, and the splash it makes is very small. His bunkmates evidently regard both indiscretions, the kiss and the tale, as trivial, and an anguished Ryabovich vows never to tell secrets again.

For several pages (covering several months), camp life proceeds apace, and while Ryabovich no longer tells his story, he lives the life of a man in love (the fiction the kiss has engendered), begging "her" pardon when he goes out on the town with the boys, and nodding knowingly when others recount romantic adventures (much as soldiers lean into accounts of battles, the narrator remarks, in which they themselves have participated).[14] Finally, when at summer's end they return to the village, Ryabovich passionately anticipates the reunion he has been staging mentally for months. But there is no immediate sign of the general or his bewitching houseguests, and in the end, Ryabovich realizes with newfound clarity that he will never see her again.

Indeed, he has never really seen her before! Perhaps this is fortunate, since in Chekhov's world, the *sight* of beauty seems to inspire more sadness than desire.[15] Though she appears and reappears in Ryabovich's reveries and in Chekhov's text, this obscure object of desire has no appearance. In fact, though Ryabovich proves himself inordinately adept at inserting her into various narrative roles (adoring wife, devoted mother), he is ever unable to endow his putative partner with a body. He spends the first hours after the encounter imaginatively dismembering the women guests, eliminating most of their physical traits, rearranging the remaining ones, and finally discarding them as well. At one point late in his daydream, it is true, an image of some sort is reported to lodge in his brain, but it is never described. She remains resolutely a function, "the one who kissed him" (*ta, kotoraia tselovala ego*; vol. 6, pp. 418); whatever physical attributes he has conjured up are scrupulously withheld.

The darkness of the room not only motivates the mistaken-identity plot and realizes concretely Ryabovich's "psychic blindness"; it also allows Chekhov to keep the physicality of the incident securely invisible. For him bodies are things that go bump in the night, and if actual physical intimacy, a kiss or something else vaguely sexy, is required to generate a good story, then Chekhov is inclined to keep the body contact more or less remote and give its subsequent narrative treatment top billing. Most of the kisses in Chekhov's stories are reported retrospectively (and more or less discreetly) in character speech.[16] The compelling tale of passion run amok that pays for the night's lodging in "Peasant Women" is, again, sex at one remove: the telling of it is the only thing that takes place in the present, the object of its passion is now dead and buried, and its euphemistic presentation ("Well, to make a long story short . . . from that morning on we began to live as husband and wife"; vol. 7, pp. 343–44) is amply motivated by the raconteur's personality and the mixed company in attendance. The one "current" affair, Varvara's dalliance with the priest's son, takes place offstage, and it too exists in Chekhov's text as tale only, attested to with colloquial delicacy: Varvara alludes to "strolling" or, at worst, "messing" around (*guliala*; vol. 7, p. 350).

Aptly, only those who have kissed (or "sinned," as Sophia puts it; vol. 7, p. 350) have a story to tell (Matvey Savvich, the storytelling traveler, and Varvara, the wandering young wife), and Varvara's sexual transgression even gives her the authority to construct a further plot ("Let's murder Dyudya and Alyosha!"; vol. 7, p. 351). If sexual indiscretion is, as it appears, almost a necessary evil for the birth of narrative, this leaves Chekhov in the distasteful position of having to represent moments of daring intimacy. Hence, in "The Kiss" he resorts to his demure version of Erica Jong's "zipless fuck."[17] Chekhov's obfuscations are employed not, however, to maximize pleasure, but to minimize, even erase the disturbing bodies and images and focus on their traces, their stories.

Interestingly, the only explicitly sexual image or body in this story of rampant desire is the invention of an inveterate liar.

Lobytko, the bunkmate whose response to Ryabovich's story is to invent one of his own, fabricates a pitch dark train compartment complete with a mysterious and fiery woman with red, red lips and enormous breasts. His credibility is promptly shattered by the third bunkmate's skepticism about such vivid color in the dark, and the lips and breasts are erased straightaway. But even Ryabovich's genuine erotic experience—the kiss itself—is oddly lacking in bodily sensation. We get the sounds—of her steps, clothes, voice, and even lips (all we are actually told is that a kiss "resounded"; vol. 6, p. 412)—but no sense of touch. At best there is a hint of an aroma from her skin; the whole atmosphere of the story is in fact evoked by sound and smell rather than excited by sight or touch. The physical sensations that are repeated in concrete descriptive terms—the anointed feeling on Ryabovich's neck and the spot of peppermint coolness near his lip—are only aftereffects, traces perceived in retrospect, in absence, after the stimulus is gone; they are sensation conferred retroactively (*nachträglich*).

The kiss, the moment of ostensible presence and plenitude, is blank and dark. "Her" disappearance, her absence, catalyzes everything, far more than her presence accomplishes. Only after she has withdrawn does Ryabovich cathect—take her as an object of desire. This is only logical: desire implies lack. But Ryabovich had lacked her before the kiss and was nevertheless as desireless as he was featureless. At the beginning of the story he craves sleep, nothing more. Watching the other officers dance, talk, and embrace the ladies, he experiences no sense of deprivation, no envy, no desire, only a vague melancholy (vol. 6, p. 411), formless, objectless, unnarratable. Ryabovich himself has no story and very little in the way of identity. This timeworn scenario of *mistaken* identity begins, finally, to lend him one. He becomes a neophyte romantic hero—a man with a role; a man with desire; a man with an alternative to sleep.

Just as language arises through lack, the signs designating absent objects, so is Ryabovich's story contingent upon the disappearance of its object, and so is Chekhov's model of sex one of withdrawal; hence his characteristically laconic ("lacanic") treatment of "her" presence. In this great *fort-da* game, Ryabovich names, recalls, and imaginatively masters her elusive, bodiless presence.[18] Lacking his object, alternately inventing and effacing her, he constitutes *himself* as a kissing, telling, desiring subject; self-creation is an aspect of the self-aggrandizement central to the kiss-and-tell boast. Ghost-bride that she is, "the one who kissed him" brings a tangible legacy-dowry: she bequeaths him a story to enact and to tell.

But what about his story, the delivery of which is marked by urgency, brevity, and a distinct lack of success? Here is the performance as Chekhov gives it:

"A strange thing happened to me at the von Rabbek place," he began, affecting an indifferent, ironic tone. "I went off to the pool room, see, . . ."
He began to tell the story of the kiss in great detail and within a minute fell silent. . . . In that minute he had told everything, and he was stunned that the whole story took so little time. He had felt that he could go on talking about the kiss until morning.

[The story complete, bunkmate #1 smirks skeptically; bunkmate #2 raises his eyebrows and remarks, without looking up from his *European Herald*, that she must be some kind of psychopath; and #1 tells his tall tale about the "similar" thing that supposedly befell him in a train; and Chekhov continues:]

This offended Ryabovich. He walked away from the trunk, got into bed, and promised himself never to confide in anybody again. (Vol. 6, pp. 420–21)

The story's reception is considerably less enthusiastic than its production. Merzlyakov dismisses it without interrupting his obviously more worthwhile reading, and Lobytko supersedes it with a "similar" but purportedly more worthwhile contribution of his own. Is Lobytko's story any better? As Merzlyakov makes clear, it is a patent lie. But truth is hardly the final guarantor of tellability. Ippolit Ippolitych, Chekhov's teacher of geography and most indefatigable commentator ("The Teacher of Literature" ["Uchitel' slovesnosti"]), contributes much that is true ("In the summer it is hot," "in the winter it is cold," "people sleep in beds"; vol. 8, pp. 318–19), but nothing that is even remotely tellable. Besides, although Ryabovich has truly been kissed, the bulk of his private narrative is composed of an elaborate fantasy. In the economy of the narrative transaction, fictionality is not necessarily a shortcoming, and Lobytko's innovation has certain advantages: it is, we surmise, longer, and it is certainly more "fleshed out"—both in the suspense it builds and the bodies it sketches. Most importantly, though, it is *there*; it is transcribed for us. Ryabovich's account, by contrast, though it should be climactic in this kiss-and-tell sequence, is suppressed. To what do we attribute Chekhov's discretionary ellipsis? Why, having done his best to downplay the immediacy of the kiss, does he omit Ryabovich's narrative version as well, as little space as it would require? What makes it so untellable?

Perhaps the very brevity of the account makes it inadequate; as the narrative equivalent of premature ejaculation, Ryabovich's truncated performance fails to give pleasure or even arouse interest among the textually inscribed listeners (and it certainly can't do much for the reader since it has been excluded altogether). Even Ryabovich is more mortified than satisfied by his brief narrative exertion.

But since excessive brevity was a reproach frequently leveled at Chekhov's own work, its invocation as grounds for so summary a dismissal here is hardly neutral. Not incidentally, Chekhov foregrounds his own idiosyncratic narrative misdemeanor (telling a tale in record time) in the context of a story that was uniquely criticized as unnecessarily long.[19] From the very outset, the reader accustomed to Chekhov's spareness wonders about the markedly un-Chekhovian rash of factual detail that opens the story and that raises immediate questions about the inclusion and exclusion of material in narrative. Especially significant in this regard is the extended treatment of troop movements, which, I think, functions implicitly and explicitly as a disquisition on its own problem, namely, "Is all this really tellable? And if not, then what is?"

This digression opens with an explanation of why the whole scene holds no interest for Ryabovich: whereas to the uninitiated a march such as this is mysterious and intriguing, to the participants it is "utterly familiar and thus utterly uninteresting" (vol. 6, p. 417). There follows a long series of descriptive facts, each prefaced by "Ryabovich knows," indicating that none of this would be tellable to him. To us, presumably, it could be of interest, but since we are burning with desire along with Ryabovich to advance the erotic action, it works more as a test of our patience and an even greater incentive to consider the issue of what's worth telling.

While Ryabovich regards this scene indifferently, his mind races to what really captivates him, the romantic story-line. Posing es-

Kiss and Tell

sentially the same question of tellability about the kiss sequence, Ryabovich considers the extent to which the kiss "adventure" is significant or even interesting and soberly rules negatively on both. "But soon he threw logic out the window and abandoned himself to daydreams" (vol. 6, p. 418). Clearly to him the kiss is extremely compelling as subject matter.

After isolating the two spheres of possible attention and measuring their relative interest, the text proceeds to juxtapose them in alternating paragraphs, confronting reality with daydream, troops with trysts, the boring with the interesting, the ordinary with the extraordinary, punctuating the whole extravaganza with periodic cries of "Put on the brakes!" that may check the progress of the artillery brigade down steep hills but do little to retard Ryabovich's private narrative. That this great love story enjoys only private success, however, undercuts the ready opposition of ordinary/extraordinary, boring/interesting, that the text sets up. For while being kissed by a woman is unquestionably an extraordinary event for Ryabovich, it is, as he himself concludes, the most normal, ordinary, everyday sort of thing; and while to Ryabovich, the eternal outsider, "the thought that he was an ordinary [*obyknovennyi*] person and that his life was ordinary" comes as a great solace (vol. 6, pp. 419–20), it hardly makes for tellable tales. In Lotman's terms, we remember, the more unusual and unexpected, indeed, indiscreet and forbidden the incident, the more eventful and the more interesting the tale. In Chekhov's own terms, which he sets up at the beginning of this digression, what is familiar holds no interest, a point explicitly and repeatedly demonstrated by the digression itself. So what is good news for Ryabovich is simply no news for anyone else. No wonder Chekhov forfends him from telling his story out loud.

To underline the point, Chekhov interposes throughout the account of the march (which we begin to realize is not a gratuitous digression at all) other kissers-and-tellers whose sordid little liaisons and their self-aggrandizing remarks about them—the commander's announcement of his visit to "Alexandra Yegorovna," or the skinny general's inane comments about the stout "Lopukhova"—are utterly conventional and extremely tedious. The men, we are told, make a practice of humoring the general, who thinks he's being inordinately witty on this subject (vol. 6, pp. 416, 419).

But without the privileges of rank, his stories would likely be as rudely spurned as Ryabovich's ill-fated tale.

Even the party scenes are laced with trivial but persistent examples of the same dynamic—"uninteresting," untellable material that can evoke only "insincere" interest (vol. 6, p. 409); Lobytko himself, who is supposed to be such a specialist in seduction, spouts "uninteresting nonsense" and is not perspicacious enough to read the reaction he gets (an indifferent [*besstrastnoe*] "is that so?") as a clue that his narrative advances are leaving his object cold (vol. 6, p. 410). As we already know, the inner compulsion to tell in no way ensures a tale's tellability. Ryabovich's performance has amply demonstrated that the desire a story generates is not necessarily proportional to the desire that generated the story.

But if telling is the necessary complement—the completion—of the kiss, why doesn't Chekhov's story end after Ryabovich has indulged his narrative compulsion, particularly given that it produces no new desire in his listeners? Having lost his narrative virginity but failed to arouse his interlocutors, Ryabovich takes a monastic vow of silence never to engage in this kind of intercourse again. But his autoerotic activity does continue and indeed intensifies in his private narrative in the weeks to come. Desire has not been stilled, and Ryabovich still hopes for some answering passion.

If we retrace the shape of Ryabovich's desire and discretion, we note that between the kiss and its report, Ryabovich's passion is primarily for discursive treatment; after his narrative failure, however, he longs essentially for more story. At first, when his longing is awakened by the great labial mistake, he feels that discretion is of the utmost importance: he hopes no one will notice the event or its peppermint traces. But then the enigma—what had happened? who was it?—gets the better of him, and he engages zealously in the hermeneutic activity of producing a plausible narrative. Aside from a few nocturnal sighs and murmurs, however, he keeps it to himself. Finally, though, quite worked up by the kiss and his mute rehearsals of it, like so many other Chekhovian kissers—like Gurov ("The Lady with the Little Dog"), who is unable (*ne uderzhalsia*) to refrain from voicing his secret ("If only you knew what a charming woman I met in Yalta"; vol. 10, p. 137); or Alekhin ("About Love"), who *must* tell his tragic love story (vol. 10, p. 67); or Zhenya ("The House with the Mansard" ["Dom s mezoninom"]), who extricates herself from Monsieur N.'s open arms to run openmouthed to her family ("we have no secrets from each other—I must now tell mama and Lida everything"; vol. 9, p. 189]); or Nikitin ("The Teacher of Literature"), whose kiss is practically just a formality to motivate "informing papa" (vol. 8, p. 322)—Ryabovich is moved by the "irresistible urge" to tell his companions, despite not having exchanged so much as a word with them until now (vol. 6, p. 420). As Tolstoy's irascible Pozdnyshev explains, "It's keeping quiet about it that's painful."[20] But though Ryabovich tries his best to disguise the excitement in his voice, he is overstimulated and gives a brief, artless performance.

But the story cannot end here because his desire is not satisfied (nor, incidentally, is ours—we have become interested, and our "passion for meaning" stands unrequited). After his dismal failure to engender interest, Ryabovich's sense of discretion is renewed, but his hunger for sequel, for more kissing, is redoubled, especially when the opportunity arises to return to the scene of the original indiscretion. As they arrive in the village, his "heart beat[s] wildly," he gazes "greedily" at the place, "expecting an invitation every second" (vol. 6, p. 422), and cannot understand how his fellow officers can be preparing for sleep. He lies down, stands up again, lies down, jumps up again, and finally, unable to control his impatience, runs off to the general's place.

Here, in this closing sequence, although his desire to see "her" remains unfulfilled, his passion is finally cooled. He returns to the river path near von Rabbek's estate, avidly seeking the sounds and smells we have heard so much about—but they have faded with the season. Noticing that the general's household has hung linens out to dry, and finding himself, in spite of everything, "between the sheets," Ryabovich touches one.[21] It is clammy and cold. Here, in the first truly tactile experience of a whole story ostensibly about kissing, his desire dissolves. Amidst these dank "winding sheets," Ryabovich realizes that the whole kiss episode was just a stupid mistake, his ardor subsides, and, not coincidentally, the story ends. For the death of desire signals the death of narration. Thus, even when the long-awaited invitation from the general comes after all, Ryabovich responds by lying down to close the story resolutely in bed. When both enticements (kissing and telling) collapse, there remains only sleep. And between sleep (all anyone longed for on page one) and sleep (all Ryabovich embraces in the end), desire has been born and extinguished in an Oblomov-like swell of activity. Ryabovich's only mistake, it seems, was to imagine that his desire was anything to lose sleep over, that it was tellable, narrative-worthy. His only real indiscretion was not his being kissed, however passionately, or even his boasting about it, but his formulating a narrative that was just plain not sexy enough.

So if Chekhov is discreet about both his character's physical intimacy and Ryabovich's narrative version of it, if he both obscures the actual kiss as too immediately erotic and withholds the resulting tale as not erotic enough, it is to explore the space of tellability, the distance between the obscene and the boring. Indeed, the space between not sexy enough to tell and *too* sexy to say out loud is not vast, particularly in the decorous Russian tradition, where the boundaries of the obscene are drawn close in, the realm of narrative safe sex lying somewhere in between Pozdnyshev's introductory "I must tell" and his parting "excuse me for doing so."[22] Certainly the constraints of censorship have done much to uphold these discretionary norms, making many Russian writers into masters of euphemism who relate intimacy through intimations and hope that though the text is tactful, the reading will not be.

But Chekhov's reticence about kissing is self-imposed, whether in deference to his compatriots' sensibilities or simply out of his own delicacy. His flirtation with the "unmentionable" does not, in any case, involve the upper limits of the permissible, the more obtrusive indices of exclusion that prohibit anything too provocative (whether sexually explicit or politically inflammatory) from text and from view. Chekhov is more drawn to investigate the other extreme of the forbidden, the less dramatic but nevertheless consistent power of veto over prospective subject matter: the inclination to exclude material that is not provocative *enough*, not "sexy" enough to engage the attention, arouse interest, and stimulate desire for more. No external agency is required to enforce this exclusion; when a story falls below this threshold, the audience disperses quite on its own, as a deflated Ryabovich discovers.

If storytelling is born of discretion doubly abandoned (first indulging in the kiss, then indulging in the report), it is ultimately shaped by discretion doubly imposed: some kisses are too sensational to mention, others too ordinary (and about as sexy as an artillery brigade trudging endlessly along). If Ryabovich nonetheless tells his unremarkable kiss and Chekhov belabors the troops, perhaps it is a meditation on the perils of indiscriminate chatter. For while Ryabovich's experience seems to confirm that without the indiscretion of the kiss there is nothing to tell, and without the indiscretion of the report the original pleasure is incomplete, it also suggests that without the answering arousal of the listener, both of the foregoing pleasures are undone. If the listener responds with William Labov's indifferent "so what?" (or, in Chekhov's own terms, an apathetic "is that so?"), as, in effect, Ryabovich's audience does and Chekhov feared his might, then the seduction has been unsuccessful.[23]

Chekhov, famous for his portrayals of failed communication, exhibits particular concern for the pitfalls of the narrative enterprise. Interestingly, his greatest anxiety about the seduction is not the scandal, but the yawn.

SVETLANA BOYM

Loving in Bad Taste

Eroticism and Literary Excess in Marina
Tsvetaeva's 'The Tale of Sonechka'

■ "Woman ... Love ... Passion ... Woman from the very beginning could only sing about love. Without love woman in poetry is nothing ... Woman ... Love ... Passion ...," proclaims Valery Briusov in his speech during the infamous "evening of poetesses" organized in 1920 and ironically described in Marina Tsvetaeva's essay "The Hero of Labor."[1] "Woman ... Love ... Passion" is a kind of amorous triangle that reduces the whole scope of literature by women to "crimes of the heart" and thus presents female writing as a cultural curiosity and as exoticism. The culture stereotypes of "women's art," with its stigma of aesthetic inferiority, are deeply ingrained and appear to haunt both women writers and women critics. Here an attempt will be made to disrupt Briusov's love triangle by examining cultural constructions of the lover's discourse and the boundaries between love, eroticism, and sexuality in the Russian context from a cross-cultural perspective. Since the relationship between the poet and her lover is always adulterated by language, the issue of how love stories are to be told will be the center of my attention. Why is it that "women in love" produce what has been often conceived as "bad writing," or writing in bad taste? What are the aesthetic preconceptions that turn a female lover's discourse into something akin to kitsch? What is at stake in the couplings of aesthetics and gender, of literary excess and female eroticism?

In her diary notes written in 1919, Tsvetaeva complains about a certain lack of native cultural vocabulary of "love" in Russia: "*Beloved*—sounds too theatrical, *lover* is too frank, *friend* too indefinite. . . . What an unloving country!" ("*Vozliublennyi*--teatral'no, *liubovnik*--otkrovenno, *drug*--neopredelenno . . . Neliubovnaia strana!").² This statement might sound like an international poetic commonplace; after all, Tsvetaeva is always looking for love as an "element" and not as an "affair," an element (*stikhiia*) that in Russian is related to poetry itself (*stikhi*). But the statement also points to important cultural differences in the conceptions of love, passion, and their representation in the Russian context. The term "sexuality" exceeds the cultural paradigm of "love and passion" as proposed by Briusov. In the nineteenth-century literary tradition and in the turn-of-the-century Symbolist creation of the metaphysical "Russian eros," there is a particular reluctance to separate love and sexuality. There is a certain fear—not so much a fear of sex as a practice, but a fear of sexuality as an autonomous sphere, independent from social, religious, or metaphysical preoccupations and connected to the "West." In other words the threat of "sexuality" is not a private matter but a public danger coming from the West.

In this respect, the critique of one of the major theorists of sexuality, Freud, offered by a member of Bakhtin's circle, V. Voloshinov, is culturally revealing. According to Voloshinov, whose work is roughly contemporaneous with Tsvetaeva's writings, Freud overestimates the sexual side of human behavior at the expense of the social side.³ (Voloshinov's account does not do justice to the variety of Freud's work, including his cultural theories as expressed in *Civilization and Its Discontents*.) Furthermore, Voloshinov sees this emphasis on sexuality and privileging sexuality over other spheres of human existence as an expression of *Western* "bourgeois individualism," which predictably leads to absurdity, decadence, and other dead ends. Voloshinov claims that the conflict considered by Freud to be an individual's internal (*dushevnyi*) conflict of consciousness and unconscious is in fact located on the level of "everyday ideology" (*zhiteiskaia ideologiia*) of the particular society, with its contradictions between official and nonofficial discourses. I would suggest reading Voloshinov's critique of Freud not only as a Marxist critique of psychoanalysis but also as a Russian cultural critique of Western individualism, a kind of cross-cultural reading or even misreading that hinges on the notions of "sexuality," "self," and "society." This way one could turn Voloshinov's argument against itself, and read his somewhat obsessive critique of Freud's "sexuality" as a reflection and an enactment of Russian and Soviet "everyday ideology" that consistently de-emphasizes the sexual dimension of the individual. It is not by chance that the Russian concept of *poshlost'*—that which is, according to Vladimir Nabokov, culturally untranslatable— refers to artistic triviality, banality, lack of spirituality, and sexual indecency.[4] Hence representation of sexuality in Russian culture is at a particular risk of being not only immoral but also distasteful, not *comme il faut*, to use a French expression frequently employed by the heroes of Russian novels.

Michel Foucault places the word "sexuality" in quotation marks, stressing that it does not refer merely to natural (or unnatural, for that matter) practices common to all human beings, but also signifies a specific cultural construct that is correlated with "different fields of knowledge, types of normativity and forms of subjectivity in a particular culture."[5] According to Foucault, "sexuality" can be discussed in three contexts: in relation to the discourses, representations, and sciences that refer to it; in relation to the systems of power that regulate its practice; and in relation to the "forms within which individuals are able, are obliged, to recognize themselves as subjects of this sexuality."[6] Moreover, "sexuality" as a presumably autonomous sphere, conceived separately from moral, emotional, cultural, and historical elements, is not a transhistorical constant but a nineteenth-century Western European and American construct. Is it, then, possible to suggest that for a variety of complex reasons, including a different cultural conception of the self and a lack of history and of a plurality of secular lover's discourses, "sexuality" as a nineteenth-century individualist construct developed in Russia somewhat differently from the way it did in Western Europe and the United States? Or do we have to readjust accepted intellectual histories of Russia and rescue some of the untold stories about "sexuality" and its powerful constructions? Would those stories challenge some Western theoretical models? Foucault's history of "sexuality" could be regarded only as a starting point for a study, not its definitive grid; Foucault's works de-emphasize, if they do not silence, the history of female "sexuality" and eroticism, as well as the history of certain "pleasures of the text" associated with it. Both feminine eroticism and literary conventions in describing eroticism and sexuality are left between the lines of Foucault's text.

From the point of view of Foucault's contemporary Roland Barthes, this double omission wouldn't be surprising. Eroticism, in Barthes's view, is connected to literariness and pleasures of the text; moreover it "embarrasses" both the psychoanalytic and sociological discourse on sexuality as well as the linear narrative.[7] "Erotic body" reveals itself in "figuration," not in "representation"; erotic text is neither mimetic nor teleological; it does not describe any consummation but rather enacts effects of desire by suggestion, fragmentation, disguise. Hence Barthes raises a question not only of the relationship between desire and sexuality but also about ways of confronting and representing this desire and its fragmentary literariness. Hélène Cixous, one of the major theorists of literary eroticism, describes the utopian concept of "écriture feminine" as a bodily writing that does not allow one to separate body and writing, desire and aesthetics.[8] Yet this "bodily writing" should not be taken literally as a utopian writing that manages to fulfill the body without estranging it. Rather, the term suggests a nonlinear, metaphorical writing imbued with feminine eroticism that "multiplies the effects of desire" and remains antiauthoritarian, nonfinalizable, antiteleological. This conception of literary eroticism might be seen as yet another French export of the 1970s. However, in an attempt "to invent her literary pedigree"—to borrow Jorge Luis Borges's expression—the French writer rediscovers Marina Tsvetaeva, whom she considers to be one of the earlier practitioners of "écriture feminine." Cixous reads Tsvetaeva poetically and in a foreign language—only in French. Russian eroticism has its own tragic accents, separations, and fragmentations, which are due to historical facts of life and not only to literary facts.

Foucault himself urged us to problematize further the modern term "sexuality," to examine it in a broader context of the "techniques of the self," of the interplay of private and public powers, and we might add, of the conceptions of pleasure, desire, emotion, and passion, as well as their social decorum. After all, the boundaries between "sexuality" and love, eroticism and emotion, body and soul, desire and spiritual need, are volatile and shifting, like the boundaries between countries.

Marina Tsvetaeva's *The Tale of Sonechka* (*Povest' o Sonechke*, 1937), an unconventional love story written in Russian and in French, invites us to rediscover a few pages in the forgotten history of female literary eroticism with all its digressions, silences, fragmentations, paradoxes, double entendres, and poetic excesses. The novella is also a story of exile that crosses the borders of Russia and France through desperate lover's discourse. *The Tale of Sonechka* describes multiple relationships between women: between a woman writer and her stereotypical cultural other, the poetess; a woman poet and her female beloved; a woman playwright and her actress-heroine. It is an attempt to reinvent love and "women in love" from a feminine perspective. Yet it remains to be seen whether any form of love or passion can exceed its cultural inscriptions and whether self-conscious texts of the woman poet can completely estrange the ghostwriting of the grotesque "poetess."

The word "poetess," like the word "sexuality," will be used here in quotation marks. It does not refer to women's nature or to the nature of feminine writing. Rather "poetess" designates a specific cultural mask, or, to use Tynianov's term, a specific "literary personality" whose caricaturesque portrait can be found in many Russian, European, and American texts of the nineteenth and twentieth centuries. The "poetess" is an impure poet; a poet plus an excess; a poet plus a feminine suffix, a mark of cultural inferiority and artistic nonbelonging. She is only an impostor in the world of letters. Obviously, the notion of the "poet" is not at all monolithic, shared as it is by everyone. It is rewritten differently by each major poet of the time and in each artistic manifesto. However, in terms of gender, there seems to be a good deal of agreement: the poet is either virile or asexual (the latter acquired the poetic name of "spiritual androgyny"). We read the texts written by a "poet" differently from those composed by a "poetess." In the mind of the reader, the word "poet"—grammatically masculine in all European languages that preserve grammatical gender—is often perceived as culturally neutral and unmarked, that is, as above and beyond sexual difference. Masculinity, in this case, simply signifies normality, universality, and linguistic convention. On the other hand, the "poetess" is seen as a deviation from the norm, clearly marked and excessive. As we shall see, the root and the suffix of the word "poetess" are perpetually at war.

Marina Tsvetaeva suffered many poetic insults. Anna Akhmatova commented that Tsvetaeva's writings often fall into "tastelessness" (*besvkusitsa*).[9] Osip Mandelstam in his essay "Literary Moscow" used Tsvetaeva as a perfect embodiment of the grotesque figure of the "poetess": "Adalis and Marina Tsvetaeva are prophetesses, and so is Sophia Parnok. Their prophecy is like domestic needlework. . . . The feminine poetry continues to vibrate at the highest pitch, offending the ear, offending the historical, poetical sense [*chut'e*]."[10]

In "Literary Moscow," Mandelstam poetically synthesizes the attributes of the cultural mask of the "poetess." These include excessive lyrical exaltation, perpetual lovesickness, abusive use of metaphor, and lack of a sense of history or historical responsibility. The "poetess" is an exalted weaver who by mistake picked up the wrong medium for domestic knitting—words instead of threads. She is also incapable of stepping out of her little emotional home into the supposedly disinterested objectivity of language. The "poetess" can excel only in textiles, not in texts. Moreover, the love songs of the "poetess" are her expressions not simply of love but also of her lack of historical sensitivity and civic duty.

According to Mandelstam, the "poetess" parodies the very kernel of true poetry, defined as "the ideal of absolute virility" (*sovershennoi muzhestvennosti*), "male force and truth" (*muzhskaia sila i pravda*):

To the lot of women in poetry has fallen a tremendous share of parody, in the most serious and formal sense of the word. Feminine poetry is an unconscious parody of both poetic inventions and poetic remembrances. The majority of Moscow poetesses have been hit by the metaphor. These poor Isises are doomed to an eternal search for a forever-lost second part of the simile, which would return to the poetic image-Osiris its primordial unity. (P. 328)

Thus the "poetess" is an unconscious parody of a poet. The discourse of parody was the center of attention among both Russian formalists and the Bakhtin circle. Tynianov, for instance, saw it as part of the driving force of literary evolution, as a rhetorical device indicating evolutionary shifts in genres and discourses.[11]

Bakhtin regarded parody as a privileged form of double-voiced speech, as a dialogue that helps to estrange authorial pretensions from the parodied discourse.[12] Yet Mandelstam's "poetess" does not call into question the authorial pretensions of "a poet." The word "unconscious" here is very significant; the "poetess" lacks precisely that authentic artistic subjectivity, that genius, that would enable her to turn upon the poetic tradition and critically comment on it. In the European and American traditions, women, by nature, or rather perhaps by culture, play in poetry the role of muses, addressees, or beautiful *love objects*, but almost never the role of *speaking subjects*. To paraphrase Edgar Allan Poe, the most poetic subject in the world is the death of a beautiful woman, and any woman poet is forever haunted by the beautiful corpse of a female heroine, over whom she often has to step in order to write.

Mandelstam's "poetess" presents a grotesque *conglomeration of lack and excess*. The poetess's excessive use of metaphor and propensity for exalted love songs is based on her cultural uprootedness, her radical and irretrievable lack. This is a loss predating possession, a loss of the primordial unity of the masculine image (Osiris), in Mandelstam's poetic rewriting of the myth. We remember that according to the legend, one missing part of Osiris that the goddess never recovered was his phallus. Hence in the "poetess" a sexuality and aesthetics are intertwined. "Poetess" helps us to reconstruct an early-twentieth-century cultural myth of the feminine that can be traced in the works of many Russian, European, and American writers of the time as well as in the writings of psychologists and psychoanalysts, including Freud, who is Mandelstam's and Tsvetaeva's contemporary.

It is curious that Freud's well-known and controversial essay "On Femininity" (1931), which claims to approach its subject not from the literary or stylistic viewpoint but from that of "sexual functions," defines femininity in a structurally similar way, as a combination of lack (lack of penis, and lack of inventiveness, originality, social responsibility) and excess (a propensity for hysteria— from the Greek word for uterus, or womb), with its overwhelming theatrical manifestations, fantasies, and love obsessions.[13] Woman in Freud is an "unconscious parody" of a man, a non-subversive parody which does not question but rather consolidates penile powers. Sexual genius (libido), first defined by Freud as "bisexual," later becomes unequivocably male. At the end of his essay Freud himself confesses his doubts and advises the audience to "turn to poets" and consult them on the subject of femininity before science can give deeper and more coherent information. "Femininity," as Freud once observed, remains a "riddle"; indeed it is a riddle in which sexual functions, cultural preconceptions, scientific observations, and poetic mythifications are intimately interwoven.

Thus the "poetess" is not a uniquely Russian cultural myth but a commonly shared European and American phenomenon with diverse culturally specific manifestations. The "poetess" is not a genius by definition; rather she is seen as a sort of literary *nouveau riche* who lacks the genetic blue blood of the artistic aristocracy. ("Genetic" has the same root as "genre," "gender," "genius," and "genitalia.") If we are to trace the genealogy of the twentieth-century myth of the "poetess" and her inevitable "lack of taste" we will have to reconsider the conception of "good taste" as developed in seventeenth-century France and reexamine Kantian foundations of the aesthetic based on the judgment of taste. In seventeenth- and eighteenth-century Europe the so-called "skepticism of tastes"—best expressed in the famous Roman proverb translated into English as "There's no accounting for tastes"—is gradually superseded by a more defined conception of a "good taste." The imposition of the ideals of good and bad on the plurality of sensual pleasures has connections to moral philosophy. According to Hans Georg Gadamer, there is a classical and classicizing element in the conception of taste that dates back to Greek notions of ethics of measure from Pythagoras to Plato, the ethics of proportion, restraint, balance, which is clearly reflected in the Kantian description of the beautiful.[14] As Mandelstam's poetic rewriting of this paradigm demonstrates, the Greek notion of measure and beauty, which has directly and indirectly shaped Kantian views, is linked to the conception of ideal virility. The Kantian "beautiful" is not to be confused with the agreeable, with its lack of "vigor," its languid appeal to the senses, and its propensity for decoration.[15] Moreover, genius was also conceived as "a virile spirit"; hence the gendered metaphor is at the very core of aesthetics.

Perhaps it is not by chance that the Russian word *poshlost'*, which signifies simultaneously artistic triviality, bad taste, sexual indecency, and lack of spirituality, is feminine in gender. In Sasha Cherny's 1910 poem entitled "Poshlost'," *poshlost'* becomes personified as a tacky salon goddess.[16] She is presented as a middle-aged, sexually loose woman, a pretentious amateur painter of watercolor roses and a *nouveau riche* who is enamored of tacky bric-a-brac and foreign fashions. Sexual indecency, excessive "feminine" propensity for decorativism, "cosmopolitanism," and pretentious artistic practices in bad taste are joined together in this grotesque figure of Madame Poshlost'. Any woman poet, and especially a woman poet in love, both in life and in the text is perpetually haunted by the caricaturesque figure of Madame Poshlost'.

Once we begin to disentangle the cultural preconceptions behind the exotic configuration of "women, love, and passion," we see why the story of feminine love told in the first person the way the story is culturally engendered is doomed to a peculiar "stylistic miscarriage" that is at the same time irreducible to matters of style. "For a woman to be a poet is an absurdity" ("Byt' poetom zhenshchine—nelepost'"), Alexander Blok supposedly said to one of the most distinguished women poets of the time, Anna Akhmatova; and she ironically, yet reverentially, rewrites his lines in one of her famous poems dedicated to Blok.[17]

Tsvetaeva's prose writings arouse much criticism, even from the otherwise favorable Tsvetaeva scholars, like D. S. Mirsky and Simon Karlinsky. Mirsky, for instance, calls her prose "the most pretentious, unkempt, hysterical and altogether the worst prose ever written in Russian."[18] Thus, there is something in the very structure of Tsvetaeva's prose works, especially the *Tale of Sonechka*, that insults the notion of "good taste" and appears shocking to many literary critics. It reveals itself in its excessive "hysteric" lyricism, "the excess in the world of measures," overflowing subjectivism, and the impossibility of distinguishing between writing about the self and writing about others. Tsvetaeva's prose goes beyond many acceptable boundaries of genre and does not allow us to draw comfortable distinctions between criticism and autobiography, prose and poetry, fact and fiction. In these eclectic, intergeneric writings Tsvetaeva does not simply describe but also acts out the roles of lover and analyst, critic and poet, poet and "poetess." First we will observe Tsvetaeva's ambivalent attitude toward the cultural myth of femininity as manifested in her essays:

on the one hand, her attempt to distance herself from the traditional feminine heroines—be it a "beautiful woman or a poetess"—and on the other hand, her infatuation with aesthetically obscene "oversweetening," an overly romantic "feminine" discourse in which she partakes and which she tries to reinvent against all critical taboos. Finally, the *Tale of Sonechka* will enable us to explore the links between literary femininity and aesthetic conventions, as well as the relationship between feminine love story and feminine sexuality in the Russian context.

In her essay "The Hero of Labor," Tsvetaeva mocks the very idea of the "evening of poetesses." She claims she has always been appalled by anything that bears a mark of "female separatism ... and the so-called women's question," except for (she continues unpredictably) "its military resolution" in the legendary kingdom of the Amazons and the no less legendary Petrograd Women's Battalion. As Karlinsky remarks, "Tsvetaeva might have wanted to dissociate herself from any kind of feminism in response to the trend in the Soviet Union towards segregating women poets into a somewhat inferior critical category."[19]

What is particularly interesting in the essay is Tsvetaeva's ambiguous perspective. On the one hand, she sees herself as a member of the universal fraternity of poets, and on the other hand she also belongs to the sorority of tragic female heroines. Her description of the "poetesses" presents a kaleidoscope of visual impressions with occasional brief comment on their poetry. For instance, she says about a "poetess" named Susana that she was such a beauty that she did not seem to write poetry at all. This is an interesting twist: from a subject of discourse, the "poetess" is turned into an object for sight. This objectified feminine beauty is a reduction to absurdity of the poetess's mask, a reduction that reveals all the hypocrisy of Briusov's patronizing enterprise of organizing the "evening of poetesses." Tsvetaeva's description alternates between ridicule and sympathy. Her gaze shifts constantly between distance and involvement, between her estrangement from "poetesses" and her identification with them. Contemporary film critic Laura Mulvey calls the ambiguous viewpoint of a female author that includes the perspectives of a woman director and a woman spectator "a bisexuality of the gaze."[20] Tsvetaeva's prose stages the drama of female authorship and female spectatorship.

In the essay "Natalia Goncharova" (1932), Tsvetaeva addresses again the question of the relationship between art and gender. The focus of the essay is the contrasting juxtaposition of the two Goncharovas.[21] On the one hand, Natalia Goncharova the wife—first of Pushkin and then of Lanskoi—is an exemplary feminine beauty (*krasavitsa*), empty and wordless (*beslovesnaia*), "without a soul, intelligence, or a heart." Her biography is "the everyday [*zhiteiskaia*] biography," that is, a biography consisting entirely in the events of everyday life. On the other hand, Natalia Goncharova the artist does not condescend to beauty, just as Natasha Rostova in *War and Peace* "does not condescend to intelligence." Her biography is "purely masculine," "a biography of the creator through the creation." Tsvetaeva writes that the other side of the beauty is not the beast, the monster, but "the essence, the personality, the mark" ("sushchnost', lichnost', pechat'"). This quote curiously paraphrases some of Flaubert's pronouncements in which he opposes the artist to the woman. Unlike "a woman," who is intuitive, natural, voiceless, and entirely absorbed in everyday life, the artist has to be a monster in everyday life, a sort of "homme-plume" (man-pen), a martyr of writing. Thus, it appears at first glance that Tsvetaeva shares the common cultural metaphors of femininity and masculinity. Yet it is crucial to note that Tsvetaeva's "pure masculinity" is exemplified by female artists and writers (Goncharova, George Sand, and others). Hence, what interests her is not "pure masculinity" per se but rather a "purely masculine side" of the split *female* personality.

In Tsvetaeva's imagination, the image that links her and Goncharova is that of Goncharova's grandmother swinging in Tsvetaeva's yard (they happened to be neighbors in Moscow) because she did not wish to meet her potential fiancés: "The grandmother is swinging on the swing in the garden because she does not want any fiancés! The grandmother who does not want fiancés because she is swinging on the swing in the garden! The grandmother escaping from a wedding into the air. Tossing not the bonnet [*chepets*] but her own self into the air! . . . My verses written at age fifteen, aren't they the swing of Goncharova's grandmother?" (p. 117).

Here of course we recognize the famous literary bonnets of Griboedov's women from *Woe from Wit* (*Gore ot uma*, 1823–27), the pathetic feminine pieces of clothing used to express women's patriotic cheer for heroic men: "The women shouted 'hurrah' and tossed their little bonnets [*chepchiki*] into the air."[22] This can be characterized as a revisionary intertextuality, a polemical rewriting of the images of femininity, which is practiced by many women poets. The flying bonnet turns into a flying feminine self, a feminine self flying away from traditional feminine roles and prescriptive family romances and marriages, or not even necessarily flying *away* from something but simply enjoying flight for its own sake. Tsvetaeva wishes to adopt Goncharova's grandmother and become her granddaughter-in-art (not in-law) and the blood sister of Natalia Goncharova. The Natalia Goncharova of the essay incarnates Tsvetaeva's exemplary artist. The peculiar kind of artistic "bisexuality" Tsvetaeva advocates here is female virility, a flight away from the fragile and beautiful heroine-poetess with her seductive disguises designed by sympathetic male artists.

In the *Tale of Sonechka*, a tale about love, theater, and revolution, Tsvetaeva stages a large repertoire of gender roles, and plays many of them herself.[23] To quote Sonechka's nanny: "It's a revolution now, a great cataclysm [*velikoe sotriasenie*]. . . . One does not distinguish men from women, especially among the deceased" (p. 265). In fact, most of the characters of the novella have ambiguous sexual identities. All the relationships among the characters, who are professional actors, poets, and playwrights, are at least triangularized. Hence, it is possible to talk not only about bisexuality but about a general fluidity of sexual identities.

In the center, however, is Tsvetaeva's ideal tragic couple: a poet and an actress ("a woman, an actress, a flower, a heroine"). (To avoid lengthy discussion of the author and narrator and their conflation and differentiation in the autobiographical fiction, I will call the self-styled autobiographical narrator of the *Tale of Sonechka* Marina, while referring to the author as Tsvetaeva). For Marina, Sonechka exemplifies unliterary femininity: the unidealized, the unstructured, and the excessive.

In Tsvetaeva's novella, Sonechka appears in two feminine roles: she speaks like a "poetess" and functions like a traditional female addressee of the poet. But both of those roles are rewritten by the playwright Marina. Sonechka is unashamed of being aesthetically obscene, and of transgressing the norms of established "good taste." One day she confesses to Marina her love for "bad poetry": melodramatic gypsy romances and popular urban songs, what we might now call "kitsch"—something like "And I sharpened my knife in the dark, for the count was devilishly handsome" ("A ia v pot'makh tochila nozh, a graf byl demonski khorosh"). According to Marina, this is the reason why Sonechka is "unloved by men" and intellectuals: her peculiar, deeply feminine intelligence goes beyond "pseudo-feminine pseudo-Beatrice and pseudo-Carmen." Even her name "Sonechka," a diminutive from Sophia, appears significant, almost symbolic. It is one of those unpremeditated, uncanny coincidences that easily yield to allegorization. According to the philosopher of the Russian Eros, Vladimir Solovyov, Sophia is the name of the Eternal Feminine, Feminine Wisdom, the symbolist muse, which then metamorphosed into Blok's famous Beautiful Lady (*Prekrasnaia Dama*). The name "Sonechka," flaunting its endearing diminutive suffix, belongs to a different discourse. It is a feminine term of endearment, an element of feminine "speak" inappropriate for an incorporeal, ideal Beautiful Lady. It is a part of Sonechka's own discourse, which, as Tsvetaeva writes, was full of diminutive suffixes, imploring and endearing.

Marina recreates by memory the long monologues of her beloved, which form almost one third of the tale. For instance:

And Marina, while loving your poems so much, I madly, hopelessly, disgustingly, shamefully love bad verses—those verses, Marina, which nobody wrote but everyone knows, . . . like "The blue balloon is turning and spinning / blue balloon, stay with me / it is turning and spinning and wishing to fall / a young man wishes to kidnap a girl." No, no, Marina, I can't, I'll sing it to you! (She jumps, tosses her head and sings the same.) . . . And now, tell me, Marina, do you understand it? Can you love me the way I am? Because it's just bliss (she recites as if asleep)—a balloon—in the blue of the sky—is spinning, a fire balloon, in the net of blue silk, and it itself is blue, and the sky is blue, and he looks at it and is scared to death that it might fly away forever! And from his glance the balloon is beginning to spin more and more, and it is about to fall down and all the fire balloons will die. (Pp. 305–8)

Sonechka's speech reveals all the mannerisms of the actress and "poetess": extremely passionate diction, immoderation, excessive use of exclamations, repetitiveness, flights of fancy. It curiously intertwines various clichés from literary and popular culture, even paraphrasing Pushkin's poem "I Loved You" ("Ia vas liubil," 1829) and popular "cruel romances" in one line. Sonechka is a professional actress, and potentially an exemplary "poetess," since the "poetess" is primarily seen as an actress, a heroine of her own masquerade. Sonechka's monologues display genuine poetic insights, emotional generosity, and a passion for cheap melodrama that comes from Dostoevsky's hysterical and sentimental heroines whom she impersonated on stage. As Karlinsky remarks, it is possible that Tsvetaeva never read *Netochka Nezvanova* since she was generally not interested in Dostoevsky, yet the discourse of Dostoevsky's exalted girls in love with each other—one of the first such instances in Russian literature—enters the novella through Sonechka's speeches. For Marina the poet (and not the "poetess," as Sonechka argues), Sonechka becomes a living embodiment of what used to be the empty and idealized female addressee of male lyric, the muses, and the beloved. However, the relationship between Marina and Sonechka goes beyond the traditionally unbalanced relationship between the eloquent poet and his ideally silenced beloved, the female beauty as embodied in Tsvetaeva's mythology in Pushkin's wife, Natalia Goncharova the first. Unlike her brother poets, Tsvetaeva lowers her voice and allows us to hear Sonechka's speech with all its childish cuteness, diminutive suffixes, sighs, and exclamations. Marina starts as a playwright writing parts for Sonechka and ends up speaking in Sonechka's voice. Sonechka often exposes Marina's aesthetic credo rather as Alice B. Toklas exposes Gertrude Stein in Stein's *Autobiography of Alice B. Toklas* (1932). Among other things, Sonechka comments on the impossibility of calling Marina "poetess" or a member of the intelligentsia because her life and writing exceed those notions: "How can one call Marina a member of the intelligentsia? [*intelligentnyi chelovek*] This is almost as stupid as to call her a poetess. What a disgusting thing to say!" (p. 293).

This radically modified relationship between the poet and *her* addressee, and the continual transvestism of all the characters, influences the very structure of the novella. In fact, Tsvetaeva writes: "In my tale there were no characters. There was love. It (she) characterized the action" ("Deistvuiushchikh lits v moei povesti ne bylo. Byla lyubov'. Ona i deistvovala—litsami," p. 354). Thus the novella is not structured like any literary genre; it is structured, or rather obsessively unstructured and destructive, like love itself. Tsvetaeva's prose is full of contradictions: it is both excessively lyrical and novelistically polyphonic, written in Russian and French; it consists of seemingly disjointed fragments from diaries, letters, and postcards, multiple parentheses, and discontinuous recollections; it participates in many genres, such as the epistolary novel, the memoir, the essay, the novella, but does not belong to any of them. In this respect it can be compared to another generic monster—Mandelstam's autobiographical prose, particularly *The Noise of Time* (*Shum vremeni*, 1925), *The Egyptian Stamp* (*Egipetskaia marka*, 1928), and *The Fourth Prose* (*Chetvertaia proza*, 1930–31?).

Tsvetaeva herself is aware that the structure of love goes against the grain of the conventions of literariness: "I know, I know, that with my love I 'diminish' the 'effect' . . . ," she writes in one of the parentheses, using estranging quotation marks around the word "effect" (p. 227). Her writing with the urgency of love seems more like an emotional exorcism, a lament, than a composition of a "work of art." It seems that in our culture the lover's discourse is always aesthetically compromised: it is situated in the rift between the abstractions and poetic generalizations of "high culture" and the sentimental kitsch of "lowbrow culture." It is possible to claim that Tsvetaeva structurally reinvents feminine love in her obsessive intergeneric narrative. The logic of the novella is what in Russian is scornfully called *zhenskaia logika* ("feminine logic"), an expression that is commonly used to characterize something irrational, illogical, anarchic, capricious, inconsistent, paradoxical, and excessively emotional. But in Tsvetaeva's writings this cultural stigma of "female logic" is reevaluated. It does not simply exceed but transgresses gentlemanly literary taste.

However, in terms of Tynianov's concept of literary evolution, defined as a continuous shifting of the boundaries between literature and *byt*, Tsvetaeva's prose appears to be very innovative. It questions the established notion of literariness and mixes high and low genres, including examples of "bad verse," lowbrow urban folklore, and the excessively emotional "feminine" speeches of Sonechka. In this way, she self-consciously (unlike the Mandelstamian "poetess") parodies the traditional literary relationship of genders, which usually consists of a male poet addressing a silent

Loving in Bad Taste 171

or silenced female love object. As if haunted by a ghost of the beloved, the novella becomes aesthetically obscene, or as Tsvetaeva self-consciously remarks, "oversweetened." Sonechka is not only Marina's muse, but also an author and an exemplary "poetess," one of those female literati who are so often ridiculed and insulted by male poets, but one whom Marina nonetheless cherishes in herself and refuses to exorcise. The playwright Marina no longer censors the voice of the "poetess"; instead, she falls in love with it.

But what kind of love relationship is described in this text? Is it a love affair with love, a romance with feminine lover's discourse, or a love affair with Sonechka as a person? Can we really distinguish between them in any of Tsvetaeva's relationships with women or men? Is the relationship between Marina and Sonechka "sexual" or Platonic? How does it participate in Russian cultural myths of love and sexuality?

The novella has inspired a lot of criticism for both aesthetic and ideological reasons—it was aesthetically obscene for some critics and not radical enough sexually for others. On the one hand, it is saturated with feminine eroticism and excessive sentimentality, characteristics that seem to repulse some readers, and on the other hand, its depiction of sexual relationships between women has enraged others. The novella does not present a fully sexual relationship between two women. Furthermore, it declares the impossibility of a happy ending in the relationship between women, claiming that Sonechka was doomed to fullfill her "women's fate . . . to love a man, whoever he may be and him alone" (p. 347). Sophia Poliakova has read the novella as "Tsvetaeva's theater of oneself" and as revenge on Sophia Parnok.[24] In a similar vein, Karlinsky infers from the novella that Tsvetaeva's relationship with Sonechka Holliday took the form of a passionate schoolgirl crush and did not have the "dimension of unbridled sensuality" that characterized her affair with Parnok. Indeed, there is a muted intertext in *Tale of Sonechka*—the poetic cycle "Girlfriend" ("Podruga," 1914–15), dedicated to Sophia Parnok, which Tsvetaeva, as Diana Burgin suggests, never published, as if attempting to erase Sophia Parnok from her artistic corpus and from her personal memory. In my opinion however, the novella, with its complex intergeneric status, both invites and challenges a biographical reading, never allowing clear distinctions between biography and what Boris Tomashevsky calls "biographical legend."[25] The interpretation of the novella as an act of personal revenge does not take into account Tsvetaeva's erotic textuality, the painful pleasure of writing and loving. It is a "theater of oneself" in the sense that it is an act of self-dramatization, one could almost say of self-melodramatization, in which Tsvetaeva's life as a person and her life as a poet are closely intertwined. At the same time, Tsvetaeva's theater is not monologic: it is permeated by the discourse of the other and by the other's erotic presence. Perhaps, rather than focusing on Tsvetaeva's potential homophobia, or what constituted her cultural prejudices, especially concerning the relationships between women, it would be more challenging to discuss what can be called "gynophobia," or aesthetic misogyny, a prejudice against writing in the feminine that structures our whole aesthetic value system and therefore perpetuates a certain understanding of gender and sexuality.

The novella continues to be a perfect site for the contemporary critical debate that reveals the historicity of the conceptions of sexuality and gender as well as the politics of sexual orientation and conventions of literariness. Tsvetaeva's self-mythification, as well as her mythification of feminine sexuality, both gives us some insight into the very process of mythmaking and shows how difficult it is even for the most unconventional woman poet to escape pervasive Russian cultural myths.

From the outset, Marina confesses that describing Sonechka and their relationship presents a linguistic problem. She has to use the vocabulary of three languages because Russian lacks the words to relate her love story. Among other things this suggests the lack of female discourse of love written by women, and not simply translated from French and from the feminine, as is Tatiana Larina's letter in Alexander Pushkin's *Eugene Onegin*. Tsvetaeva frequently uses the French word *amant* ("lover"), which is linked to *amour* ("love") and to *âme* ("soul"). Of course, the "soul" (*dusha*) in Tsvetaeva is never incorporeal but, as she puts it in the *Tale of Sonechka*, "soul with flesh" (*dusha s miasom*). The French vocabulary does not prevent Tsvetaeva from partaking in Russian cultural paradigms and transforming them through her own, Tsvetaeva's, syntax.

Loving in Bad Taste 173

From the first pages of the book Marina both defers and anticipates the description of Sonechka. Characteristically, in their first encounter the two women blush. This hot blush is a blush of passion, of mutual recognition and embarrassment. This embarrassment is a combination of self-consciousness and loss of control, a recognition of one's own physicality and the physical bond with the other. The uncontrollable fire is Marina's key metaphor for Sonechka—from the fire of embarrassment to the fire that burned her to ashes. The other central image is its opposite—the ocean, which has literal and poetic meaning, referring on the one hand to a specific place on the ocean where Marina is writing her memoirs and on the other hand to a poetic image of Sonechka's tears and laughs, which generate the overflow of narrative. The description of Sonechka in itself is a perpetual aesthetic embarrassment; it is at once fragmentary and overflowing, incomplete and excessive. It is not by chance that Tsvetaeva was regarded by Hélène Cixous as a predecessor of what 50 years later was to be called *l'écriture feminine*, not to be confused with the discourse of the "poetess."

The novella constantly circulates around the possibility of the physical relationship between Marina and Sonechka, obsessively trying to justify the lack of it in two languages—Russian and French. In the following passage I translate only the Russian and leave the French:

We never kissed, only when saying hello and goodbye. But I often embraced her with a gesture of protection, seniority . . . in a fraternal embrace. . . . No, this was a dry fire, pure inspiration, without an attempt to discharge, spend, realize. A sorrow with no remedy. . . . Je ne me souviens pas de l'avoir embrassée hors de le baiser usuel, presque machinal du bonjour et de l'adieu. Ce n'était pas de la mauvaise—ou bonne—honte, c'était—mais la même chose que avec le tu: je l'aimait trop, tout était moins. . . . Commençant par baiser une âme, on continue par baiser une bouche et on finit par baiser—le baiser. Anéantissement. Mais je l'embrassais souvent de mes bras, fraternellement, protectionnellement, pour la cacher un peu à la vie, au froid, à la nuit. C'était la Révolution, donc pour la femme: vie, froid, nuit. (Pp. 230–31)

The paragraph reiterates and paraphrases a number of poetic paradoxes—including François Villon's "dying of thirst near the stream"—and the Romantic notion of love as insatiable. Here we observe a familiar constellation of the metaphors of fire and water, a peculiar coupling of two languages, and a curious, untranslatable ambiguity of the French *baiser/embrasser*, where *baiser* means both a kiss and sexual intercourse. Interestingly, the feminine fraternal embrace is a woman's protection of another woman from the Revolution, from that kind of revolutionary brotherhood that for a woman signifies "life, cold, night."

Within the novella the kiss is associated with casual unloving relationships with men, in which an overabundance of kisses covers up a lack of words and a lack of love. Sonechka tells Marina the story of one of her failed theatrical love affairs, this one with her young student admirer, whom she kissed in excess to compensate for the lack of words: "Everything lasted for a very short time. We had nothing to talk about. At first I was talking, talking, and talking, and then I fell silent. Because one can't, I can't stand it when in response to my words there are only eyes, only kisses" (p. 243).

Hence in the novella the substitution of kisses for words and words for kisses is thematized; the first kind of relationship—a casual affair between a man and a woman—is called *poshlost'*, and is opposed to the second kind of relationship, that exemplified by the true love between Marina and Sonechka, with its continuous flow of verbal caresses. The novella itself can be read as an excess of lover's discourse that substitutes for the loss of the heroine and addressee, Sonechka, who first leaves Marina and then dies prematurely. But the overwhelmingly "oversweetened" dialogues between Marina and Sonechka do not simply compensate for their lack of physical contact. Neither do they merely present an ideological statement on the (asexual) nature of relationships between women—this would be a trivialization of the poetic and emotional force of the work. These dialogues recapture and redeem that culturally ostracized feminine erotic discourse that tends to exceed narrative and sexual conventions. To regard that discursive excess as a "sublimation" of a failed sexual relationship would be an oversimplification; indeed the relationship between Marina and Sonechka is not conventionally sexual, it is both more and less than that.

The paradox of possession (*obladanie*) and nonpossession is also exemplified in the numerous acts of gift giving and theft in the novella. Marina and Sonechka give each other material and

Loving in Bad Taste

immaterial things, things to wear and thing to write. Thus Marina mentions several times that she "plagiarizes" Sonechka, steals lines from her, while Sonechka promises to give Marina as a gift her favorite book, *Netochka Nezvanova*, which, symptomatically, someone later steals from her. Marina offers Sonechka a number of symbolic gifts: the dress that supposedly was given to her by Sophia Parnok, and the coral necklace. One of the most erotic moments of the novella occurs when Marina offers Sonechka a dress that belonged to her grandmother. Marina's description of Sonechka's undressing, however, focuses not on the romantic beauty of feminine forms but on the poverty of Sonechka's underwear, which is treated here with almost maternal endearment.

The farewell present that Marina gives Sonechka, a token of their mutual possession and foreboding of their mutual loss, is the coral necklace. The corals turn into a love fetish—both Marina and Sonechka cover it with kisses and tears; it is a kind of materialization of that hot blush with which they greeted each other during their first encounter. Furthermore, the necklace is linked to the story of a mythical Undine, a story of two women—not in love with each other, but in love with the same man—which ends tragically. Apart from the presents, Marina often perceives Sonechka herself as a gift. Thus physical nonpossession is redeemed by Marina's possession of Sonechka through language, and the novella demonstrates that this fragile possession can turn out to be more durable than the physical one.

Hence the relationship between Marina and Sonechka can be read in light of *Lettres à l'Amazone* (1932), where Tsvetaeva argues that after the relationship of maternity, love between women is the "truest" kind of love. The relationship between Marina and Sonechka follows many conventions of a Romantic love affair, and in this respect it shares some features with Tsvetaeva's other romances with men and women. Moreover, Tsvetaeva is quite conscious of this *erotic intertextuality* in the novella, and she reveals her Romantic references as well as her stylization of Sonechka as a heroine of her eighteenth-century plays. In fact, the novella vacillates between stylization of the characters of what she calls "Jacobin Moscow" and quite precise description of postrevolutionary poverty and *byt*. The element of being in love with love, and in love with the words of love, characteristic of all Tsvetaeva's infatuations, is definitely present here. Yet what distinguishes the *Tale of Sonechka* is the fact that Marina's relationship with her female addressee is based on dialogue with the beloved and not on the traditional lyrical appropriation of the beloved by the poet. This dialogue is realized here to a much larger degree than in any other of Tsvetaeva's love stories. Marina allows her lover to speak in her own voice, and she lets that feminine discourse dominate the novella. In the *Tale of Sonechka*, "unbridled sensuality" is displaced into discourse.

Tsvetaeva's narrative is indeed very telling: it both reinforces some cultural stereotypes of women's Romantic love and exceeds them, by attempting to speak feminine eroticism in the feminine, by problematizing the "lover's discourse" in the Russian tradition, and by challenging self-consciously aesthetic and social preconceptions. Ultimately, Tsvetaeva's *Tale of Sonechka* is not a story of "sexuality" in the Foucauldian sense of the word. One wonders in general whether this kind of "sexuality" and literariness are inevitably in conflict. Yet Tsvetaeva's novella remains one of the most unconventional love stories ever written in Russian, the one that combines modern eroticism and "outmoded" Romantic pathos and challenges the aesthetic conventionality of a "poet" with no "ess," a poet lacking the suffix.

Maximilian Voloshin once suggested to Tsvetaeva that she should adopt a male pseudonym, like Petukhov, who would be author of the poems about Russia, or even several pseudonyms: genius twins, brother and sister Kryukovs, the creators of Romantic verses.[26] Unlike many famous women poets of the time, including Gippius and Parnok, who started writing under male pseudonyms, Tsvetaeva refused. She wished to keep her female identity, but to stretch it, to push it to the limit, deviating from the established conventions of literary femininity and literary maleness.[27] Hers was an uncommon one-woman show, a polysexual masquerade that staged a continuous passionate dialogue between poet and poetess.

DIANA LEWIS BURGIN

Laid Out in Lavender

Perceptions of Lesbian Love in Russian Literature
and Criticism of the Silver Age, 1893–1917

■ The entry on "Lesbian love" (*Lesbiiskaia liubov'*) in the 1896 Russian *Encyclopedic Dictionary* reads: "Lesbian love—a form of perversion of sexual feeling, an unnatural attraction of a woman for another woman. Named after the island of Lesbos; generally, rather widespread in ancient Greece. According to legend Sappho suffered from L. love."[1] This short definition contains much culturally marked information and echoes a number of common *fin de siècle* theories and stereotypes about female same-sex love. First, it defines a kind of love in purely sexual terms and reduces an intimate relationship between two women to a sexual practice. Second, it calls that sexual practice perverse and unnatural. Lesbian love becomes a pathological condition, an illness, something a woman "suffers from." This view encapsulates the most current theories on female homosexuality offered by late-nineteenth-century German sexologists, whose main works, we now know, had been translated into Russian starting in the 1880s.[2] Third, the definition suggests that Lesbian love, a "bad" kind of love, is far removed from Russia in time and cultural space. It got its name from a small island off the coast of Asia Minor, an isolated place, cut off, so to speak, from the mainland of human love and sexuality, and it characterized an ancient, pagan, exotic, and un-Orthodox civilization, "not us, but other" (*ne svoi, a chuzhoi*). Furthermore, there is the suggestion that Lesbian love may all be a legend.[3] Finally, and on an entirely different note, the definition associates Lesbian love with literature, specifically with Sappho. This association suggests that Russian writers were familiar with the most recent literary speculation and writing in France, for as Joan DeJean has shown, a homosexual Sappho only emerged in the last third of the nineteenth century in French writers' fictions of her.[4] In Russian literature of the 1890s Sappho was perceived to be either heterosexual or, because of her status as a great poet, immune to such "perversions" as Lesbianism.

The 1896 Russian definition of Lesbian love, then, shows us that its writer's understanding of this term was quite up-to-date, expressive of the most current medical ideas about Lesbianism coming from Germany and suggestive of contemporary literary depictions in France. Yet a Lesbian presence in Russian literature and culture at the time the definition was written cannot be observed. While it has been argued that *fin de siècle* Europe saw "the most open practice of female homosexuality in modern times" (DeJean, *Fictions*, p. 265), Russian Lesbians of the period tended to shy away from the social spotlight. In Western Europe, especially in France, Lesbian writers appeared during the *belle époque* in the wake of an emerging feminist movement.[5] Whatever contributions Lesbians have made to Russian feminism have either not been noted by historians or, more likely, are impossible to determine because Russian cultural norms and community standards strongly discouraged and continue to discourage any politics of the personal. If a Silver Age Russian feminist were also a Lesbian, she would have kept that fact of her biography quiet and would herself have considered it irrelevant to supposedly important political concerns.[6] Simon Karlinsky has noted, moreover, that homosexuality was anathema to all Russian radical and revolutionary movements, women's liberation among them.[7]

Lesbian writers did finally appear on the Russian scene in the period 1905–17. Karlinsky has characterized this time as one of "unprecedented freedom of expression unique in Russian history. It was in this liberalized atmosphere that Russia's gay writers could step out of their closets" ("Literature and History," p. 3). In the case of Lesbian writers, however, the "liberalized atmosphere" of the times was less felt in literature than in literary society, where "all kinds of emotional excesses were . . . the fashion."[8] The only openly Lesbian poet of the Silver Age was Sophia Parnok (1885–

1933), whose first book of poems will be the focus of the last part of this essay.[9]

One of the biggest obstacles confronting the investigator of Russian Lesbian writing, in the sense of writing done by Lesbians, is the hidden nature of this population of writers. This is true even in a period such as the Silver Age, when Lesbian writers can be identified (if in some cases only on the basis of what Marks has called, in the French context, "a network of anecdotes—formalized gossip that gives pleasure"; "Intertextuality," p. 353) and assumed to have had at least a modicum of consciousness of their affectional preference and its relevance to their creativity.[10] It is far easier and less risky to identify and deal with Russian writing that concerns Lesbians and Lesbian love. Here too, however, one has to take into account that *Lesbian* writers of such texts have commonly attempted to disguise their Lesbian subject matter.

Lesbian writers employ camouflage tactics most frequently in personal forms, especially love lyrics. These tactics may include expressing Lesbian relationships in allegorical terms (for example, a love between two personified feminine abstract nouns), and changing the sex of the Lesbian poetic speaker or, less commonly, that of her female addressee, from female to male. The use of the last two devices "heterosexualizes" Lesbian love lyrics and makes them "innocent" (*nevinnye*), as Russians are wont to say, but it also diminishes their sexual and affectional particularity. The latter evolves from the emotional, spiritual, and erotic interaction of *two women* apart from whatever gender roles these women may or may not choose to play in the relationship.[11] In my opinion the Lesbian poet who in her writing disguises her love for another woman as the love of a man for a woman in an effort, however understandable in a homophobic society, to "normalize" that love always risks distancing herself from her specific sexuality and making the lyrical expression of her sexuality in that sense less authentic.[12] She also plays right into the widely held heterosexist stereotype of the "mannish" Lesbian and of Lesbian relationships as perforce pale imitations of heterosexual ones. These stereotypes help to create the very literary and cultural norms that constrain Lesbian creativity and the expression of Lesbian desire in literature.

As DeJean notes in her study of Sapphic fictions, the direct expression of female desire is rare in literature, of desire expressed by one woman for another rarer still. This is one of the reasons why Sappho's remaining fragments, in a few of which Lesbian desire *is* openly expressed, still make the powerful or disturbing impression on many readers that they do. It also explains why all Lesbian poets have been drawn to Sappho as a source of creative empowerment, and why so many male poets have sought either to trivialize Sappho, heterosexualize her, or masculinize her and co-opt her for themselves.

This essay seeks first of all to identify some Russian Lesbian texts of the Silver Age and reveal how Lesbian love is treated in them, that is, how the writers "read" this culturally and literarily marked *fin de siècle* theme. Second, through a close examination and interpretation of Silver Age critical reviews, it will attempt to shed some Lesbian feminist light on how Lesbian writing and writers were perceived by their contemporaries. Finally, since the subject of Lesbian writing has been explored in depth in other national literatures while having been almost ignored by Slavic scholarship, this study is also intended as an attempt to break a scholarly silence.[13]

My essay thus has two interrelated parts. The first focuses on different sorts of Silver Age perceptions of Lesbian love: those of a novelist, a highly respected decadent poet and critic, an equally esteemed symbolist poet and Russian translator of Sappho's complete fragments, and an "eye-witness" who published a recollection of the period's most notorious Lesbian couple (the poets Sophia Parnok and Marina Tsvetaeva) at an evening party in Moscow. The purpose of commenting on such a variety of literary and cultural perceptions is to create as broad a context as possible for examining, in the second part, the reviews of Sophia Parnok's first collection, *Poems* (*Stikhotvoreniia*, published in January 1916).

As an openly Lesbian poet, Parnok was a double anomaly in the eyes of Silver Age critics. Many present-day Russian readers may consider her in the same light. Sophia Poliakova, the editor of and general commentator on Parnok's works, seems to be preparing such readers for the "shock" of an openly Lesbian poet when she calls Parnok a "stranger" (*inostranka*)—again, we note the geographical and cultural distancing of the Lesbian as if she were not native to Russia—"who spoke about things one was supposed to be silent about in order not to risk offense to prevailing artistic practice and moral norms."[14] The Silver Age critical responses to Parnok were written by people who expected adherence to such norms from a Lesbian poet. Prevailing artistic practice demanded from Parnok either concealment of her Lesbian identity and sexuality and/or a conventionalized, decadent treatment of lesbianism. Parnok's Lesbian lyrics met neither of these demands, and in fact challenged *fin de siècle* stereotypes of Lesbians. The critical responses to her work are especially interesting, therefore, for what they reveal about the operation of homophobia and anti-Lesbian stereotyping in Silver Age literary culture.

Silver Age Perceptions of Lesbian Love

L'âpre sterilité de votre jouissance
Altère votre soif et roidit votre peau,
Et le vent furibond de la concupiscence
Fait claquer votre chair ainsi qu'un vieux drapeau.
—Baudelaire, "Les Femmes Damnées"

The dominant literary tendencies of the Russian Silver Age, decadence and symbolism, began to emerge in the 1880s under the influence of the French movements of the same name. Among their other innovations, the French decadent poets Baudelaire, Verlaine, and their *fin de siècle* followers can be credited (or damned) with the invention of literary Lesbianism. In developing Russian images of Lesbians, writers of the Silver Age generally followed the example of these French decadents, who had used sensationalistic portrayals of Lesbian sexuality as one tool for shocking the bourgeoisie.[15]

Like their Victorian fathers, the decadents and symbolists in France and Russia continued to worship purity as the highest manifestation of femininity and demonstrated both a fear of and a morbid fascination with female sexuality running free without male control. The idea of women who expressed themselves sexually without the presence or need of a man evoked apparent horror in them while possessing for them the ghastly allure of the "unnatural." The latter notion lay at the center of decadent aesthetics and contributed to the decadents' obsession with infertility, which was prized as a beauty, albeit a beauty that was evil, negative, and necessarily damned (DeJean, *Fictions*, p. 275). Hence, the decadent myth of the Lesbian as the beautifully infertile, unnatural female, the *femme damnée*. While seeming to elevate Lesbian love to the status of an ideal, however, decadence at heart degraded it because, as Shari Benstock has pointed out, it was "constructed by men whose exploitation of the exotic and erotic elements of this love masked deepseated misogyny."[16] Deeply hostile to any female sexuality that did not conform to its own aesthetic tastes or was not controlled or crafted by men, decadence proved far more limiting than liberalizing for women and Lesbian writers.

The effects of the decadent sensibility on the interpretation of Lesbian love in Russian literature are illustrated in Lidia Zinovieva-Annibal's 1907 novel, *Thirty-Three Monsters* (*Tridtsat' tri uroda*). The book deals as much with aesthetics as with Lesbian love, focusing on the issue of male artists' distorted perceptions of female beauty. The plot dramatizes a Lesbian actress's desire to expose her bisexual beloved (the narrator) to the eyes of thirty-three artists whose portraits of her (the monsters) deform their object. The narrator explains: "Each of these thirty three ... had painted his mistress. Excellent! I grew used to myself being in their presence. Thirty three mistresses! Thirty three mistresses! And I was all of them and yet all were not me."[17] The monstrous portraits take possession of their female object, who only partially submits to their seduction. Yet her infidelity, and the monsters' artistic rape of her beauty, lead to the dissolution of her Lesbian relationship and her lover's suicide. This fateful outcome proves, in the language of decadence, the morbidity and self-destructiveness of Lesbians and the sterility of their love. It was the Lesbian who desired the artists to possess her beloved in the first place and in fact acted the role of a procuress-pimp, condemned to bring about what she believed was the predestined artistic deformation of her female lover.

Zinovieva-Annibal's perception of Lesbian love is ambiguous. On one hand she has moments of psychological and political insight. The narrator, for example, says that she was all of the artists' mistresses "and yet all were not [she]." This acknowledges her basic bisexuality, which in itself could have caused the breach with her Lesbian lover. In recognizing this truth, however, the narrator conveys an implicitly anti-Lesbian message when she remarks: "The thirty-three abominations were truthful. They were the truth. They were life. . . . Such are women. They have lovers" (*Abominations*, p. 113). This implies not only that art is superior to life, but that male art and artists are more desirable and powerful than Lesbian artists (the narrator's lover, we recall, is an actress).

Whatever importance Zinovieva-Annibal gave her novel's artistic theme, *Thirty-Three Monsters* was immediately identified as a "Lesbian novel" and entered Russian literary history as such.[18] It introduced the vocabulary and stereotypes of French literary Lesbianism into Russian literature and culture. The Lesbian lovers depicted in the book bear a grotesque resemblance to the *femmes damnées* of Baudelaire and Verlaine. Their hothouse relationship—as decadent Lesbians, they never go outdoors into nature—is based on a dominant-submissive interaction ("I was weak and subservient. . . . Servility I found pleasant," p. 107) with a sadomasochistic component ("Let her beat me. I don't care. I love her," p. 105), and a morbidity that borders on necrophilia—a favorite decadent "forbidden passion": "I imagine to myself that here is Vera, dead, totally motionless, lying on the table in a coffin . . . and I too, of course, can no longer live. But for some reason this gives me pleasure, a terrible amount of pleasure" (p. 106). The Lesbian actress Vera is described as narcissistic and "strange"; she "detests society and detests men" (p. 95), worships beauty, and has a face "full of suffering and tears and evil passion" (p. 96). The narrator conceives of herself in the relationship as a pubescent hermaphrodite, "half-boy, half-girl," her body just beginning to mature. This suggests that Vera's desire for her emulates ancient Greek pedophilia. Finally, and perhaps most tellingly, the novel portrays Lesbian sex as limited to theatrical, weepy, and frenzied kissing. On one occasion the performance of sex is punctuated by Vera's playing to the rafters: "She kept kissing me, weeping and crying with that voice that so excited the theatre-goers in the boxes. . . . She kept wailing: 'I must surrender you to the people. Magnanimity! Magnanimity! This is what has made man distinct from beasts!'" (p. 98). Vera's compulsion to sacrifice her lover may be inexplicable, but the message it conveys is clear: if the Lesbian does not give up her lover "to the people," she will fail to pass the magnanimity test and risk losing her humanity. After this, one can almost understand why being taken by 33 male artists in their art seems more stimulating to the narrator than Vera's lovemaking. Thus the reader is coaxed into the novel's misogynistic and anti-Lesbian moral: sex is insufficient without the male member, be it a penis or a paintbrush.

Zinovieva-Annibal does seem to understand that Lesbian love is tolerated in the world (the 33 artists) only insofar as it can be exploited to fill male needs. Yet the portrait she draws to reveal this supposed truth is itself smudged, if not at times obscured by the perspective of the decadent male eye from which it is drawn. If Zinovieva-Annibal sensed the deep hostility of decadent aesthetics to women and Lesbian love, she was unable to respond to it critically and to make those aesthetics less deforming to women. The poet Zinaida Gippius, who reviewed the novel, was correct in concluding, "*Monsters* is false to women" (review, p. 61).

Decadence was not the only barrier to self-expression that confronted women and Lesbian poets in the supposedly liberalized atmosphere of the Silver Age. They also encountered, and in too many cases accepted and promulgated, male-defined notions of what "female poetry" was. "The female lyric," wrote the decadent poet, classicist, and critic Innokenti Annensky in his 1909 essay, "Contemporary Lyricism," "is one of the achievements of that cultural labor that modernism shall bequeath to history."[19] Annensky makes a separate-but-equal division of lyricists into the he's (*oni*) and the she's (*one*), which reflects and validates the strict gender apartheid that reigned in Russian culture and literature during the Silver Age. The rigid separation of male and female writing and lyricism both trivialized and obfuscated the interpretation of women writers and distorted perceptions (including self-perceptions) of Lesbian writers. The creation and promulgation of distinct and normative male/female categories in writing, categories that worked by analogy with the intermediate-sex theory of Lesbians popular in medical literature of the period, tended to isolate Lesbians as creative hermaphrodites, or neuters, who fit into neither female nor male lyricism.

Annensky may not have known the affectional preferences of the poets he treats in "Contemporary Lyricism," at least three of whom were, or probably were, Lesbians. He also adheres to cultural standards for critical prose and avoids naming Lesbian love even when it is present in lines of verse he quotes. His treatment is tasteful and discreet, the very opposite of Zinovieva-Annibal's novelistic sensationalism. Annensky's critical approach to Lesbian love, however, reminds one of some of Sappho's commentators, who "find themselves in the delicate position of attempting to disprove Sappho's homosexuality without actually naming that which they claim she was not" (DeJean, *Fictions*, p. 2).

Annensky begins his survey of female poets with Zinaida Gippius (1869–1945) and Poliksena Solovyova (1867–1924). First he separates them and tactfully acknowledges Gippius's superior talent by adding the epithet "poetess of the first rank" after her name. Then he links them on the basis of their common use of an exclusively male persona in their lyrics: "Gippius always writes about herself in the masculine gender," and "Allegro also writes about herself in the masculine gender."[20]

In Gippius's love lyrics the poet's male persona is often used to mask the Lesbian desire of her female self.[21] It has this function in the poem "Ballad" ("Ballada"), a lyric dedicated—sororally, not romantically—to Poliksena Solovyova, which narrates the poetic persona's impossible love for a mermaid. Annensky quotes the following stanza ("Lirizme," p. 12):

Я зверь для русалки, я с тленьем в крови.
И мне она кажется зверем . . .
Тем жгучей влюбленность: мы силу любви
Одной невозможностью мерим.

I'm a beast for the mermaid. I have rot in my blood.
And she seems like a beast to me . . .
The stronger in-love-ness: we measure love's force
By its impossibility.

Annensky appears oblivious to the Lesbian encoding this stanza contains in the idea of an impossible love between two opposites (mortal/immortal, self/other) who nevertheless are generically the same (both are "beasts"). The generic sameness of the lovers belies the heterosexual disguise of the poetic persona. By dedicating this poem to a sister poet, Gippius might be communicating, and at the same time seeking, solidarity with someone who understands the "impossible love" she illustrates.[22] "Ballad" contains to my mind an early encoded treatment of Lesbian love in Russian literature. Annensky seems, very faintly, to allude to this possibility when he argues that the impossible love of the poetic persona for the mermaid exemplifies "love as curiosity" and illustrates Gippius's "avidly curious soul" (p. 12).

While Annensky does not discuss the possible Lesbian implications of Gippius's and Solovyova's male personas, he emphasizes that both poets fail to hide their femaleness behind them: "The masculine mask of [Gippius's] remarkable lyrics could hardly deceive a single attentive reader" (p. 12). Solovyova's lyricism is also "purely feminine, severe, modest, [and] tender" (p. 16). From these remarks the poetic personae of the two Lesbian poets emerge as futile and vaguely hermaphroditic. They later acquire a negative tinge when the critic introduces another poetess, Tatiana Shchepkinaya-Kupernik (1874–1952), by saying, "finally we have found a poetess who is not ashamed to speak of herself in the feminine gender" (p. 17).

From Annensky's essay few readers of the time would have been likely to perceive a Lesbian theme in Gippius's or Solovyova's poetry—a perception that, indeed, neither poet would have wished. Yet Gippius's advocacy "of androgyny and psychological unisex" (Karlinsky, "Literature and History," p. 3) and Solovyova's Lesbian orientation were well known in Silver Age intellectual and artistic circles.[23] Annensky's treatment of these Lesbian poets might have titillated those in the know while maintaining the poets' self-imposed invisibility as Lesbians.[24]

Annensky includes a third Lesbian poet in his survey, Liudmila Vilkina-Minskaya (1873–1920).[25] In her 1906 volume, *My Garden (Moi sad)*, which contains several short stories and 30 sonnets (including a handful of Lesbian ones), Vilkina adopts the culturally approved decadent style for expressing her Lesbian material. Her Lesbian lyrics provided fodder for the Silver Age's two main approaches to female same-sex love: the sensationalistic and the discreet. The cover of *My Garden* signals the suggestive themes in the book. It shows two young women in décolletage embracing on a garden bench (see Fig. 1), and resembles Simeon Solomon's 1864 canvas, *Sappho and Erinna in the Garden of Mytilene*. The Foreword of *My Garden*, written by Vasili Rozanov, a Russian champion of platonic male homosexuality (as "Ideal Love"), makes the suggestiveness of the cover illustration explicit.[26] Rozanov warns Vilkina's readers, "I am surprised that her parents and husband (the only 'lawful' circumstances of her life) have failed to lock this eternal threat to their order . . . in an attic room."[27]

Fig. 1. Illustration on the cover of Liudmila Vilkina-Minskaya's *My Garden*. Reprinted from *Moi sad* (Moscow, 1906).

Annensky views Vilkina's conventionally decadent Lesbian "I" ambiguously. Rising to Rozanov's challenge, he seems bent on reversing Vilkina's other male patron's judgment on the "unlawful" poetess, almost as if he were jousting with Rozanov to protect Vilkina's purity, not from the taint of eroticism, but from that of Lesbian love. On one hand, Annensky draws attention to the *heterosexual* eroticism in Vilkina's lyrics; on the other, he describes the Lesbian encounter depicted in his favorite sonnet ("the sonnet I like best") as "totally unerotic," while granting it his critical imprimatur.

To my mind the eros in Vilkina's poem is not so much absent as abstracted; it is expressed indirectly through a kind of allegory in which two "daydreams" (*mechta*, a personified feminine noun) interact amorously, rather than the two female companions (*podrugi*) whose dreams they are. In the stanza Annensky quotes, the Lesbian poetic persona speaks of her daydream seizing her female companion's more passive, virginal daydream:

> С волнением нежданным пред тобою,
> О, бледная подруга, я стою.
> Как ты чиста! Влюбленною мечтою
> Ловлю мечту прозрачную твою.
>
> In unexpected agitation
> I stand, pale girlfriend, here before you.
> How pure you are! My amorous daydream
> Seizes on your limpid dream.
> (Vilkina, *Moi sad*, p. 29)

The "agitation," "pale girlfriend," and "amorous dream" in this stanza are all commonplaces found in *fin de siècle* elegiac lyrics depicting yearning, but basically innocent, Lesbian interactions.

Such interactions were thought by some influential nineteenth-century German Hellenists to characterize Sappho's love for the girls she mentions in her lyrics. Whether or not Lesbian poets of the *belle époque* agreed with these male defenders of Sappho's purity, they were drawn to Sappho herself in their search for a "native lesbian poetic tradition."[28] According to Benstock, "the discovery of the fragments of Sappho's poetry in the 1890's" enabled some Lesbian writers "to redeem Sappho from male authors" (*Women*, p. 53). Russian literature did not have a tradition of controversial Sappho scholarship and literary speculation such as existed in Germany and France. Nevertheless, 1914 saw the publication of the first Russian translation of Sappho's complete fragments, done by the decadent/symbolist poet Viacheslav Ivanov, husband of Zinovieva-Annibal. Ivanov had studied in Germany and was an admirer of the renowned nineteenth-century German Hellenist Ulrich von Wilamowitz-Moellendorf. A proponent of the theory that Sappho's relations with the girls in her school (and in her poems) were analogous to the "Ideal Love" model preached by Plato, and therefore devoid of sexuality, Wilamowitz staunchly upheld the purity of Sappho against the erotic fictions of the French decadents, notably Pierre Louÿs in his 1895 "Songs of Bilitis."

We do not know where Ivanov stood in the European controversy about Sappho's sexuality. His introduction to his translations of Sappho's poetry, aimed at a general audience, repeats the popular if now widely discredited theory that she headed a school for girls on Lesbos, and he explains Sappho's attitudes "to her young female roommates [*sozhitel'nitsy*]" as an instance of how she "combined in a distinctive way [*svoeobrazno*] the warmth and intimacy of an older female friend with the exactingness and strictness of a lofty female mentor."[29] Ivanov's translations attempt to be faithful to the original and retain the Aeolian poet's meters. In trying to achieve formal authenticity, however, Ivanov added words and lengthened or shortened lines, practices that undercut the accuracy he strove for and sometimes cross the boundary between translation and fiction-making. The resulting transmutations gave Ivanov's Silver Age readers a decadent and sexually ambiguous Sappho who reflected the hallmarks of the translator-poet's own style and is curiously at odds with the asexually pure image of her that he defends in his introduction.

A few examples will suffice to reveal the decadent tenor of Ivanov's Sappho translations. The fragmentary line about Eros's descent, "coming from heaven clad in a purple chlamys" (*elthont' eks orano porfurian perthemenon khlamun*),[30] becomes Ivanov's more gorgeous short poem:

С неба сходит, покрыв
Плеч белизну
Алой хламидой.

He comes from heaven, having clad
the whiteness of his shoulders
in a scarlet mantle.
(*Alkei i Safo*, p. 111)

Ivanov renders the fragment "may you sleep on a tender female companion's breast" (*dauois apalas etaras en stethesin*; Barnstone, *Sappho*, p. 40) as the lushly provocative:

> На персях подруги усни,
> Не персях усни сладострастных.
>
> On the breast of your girlfriend sleep,
> Sleep on her voluptuous breast.
> (*Alkei i Safo*, p. 128)

Ivanov's translation of Sappho's most specifically Lesbian and, therefore, most controversial poem, "Equal to the gods seems to me he whosoever" (*Fainetai moi kenos isos theoisin*; Barnstone, *Sappho*, p. 10), follows the practice of the vast majority of Russian and other translators of the poem, beginning with Catullus, of making the "man" referred to in the second line a specific individual rather than the indefinite "any man whosoever" of the original. As a result, the focus of the poem is displaced from the desiring female "I" to the desiring male "rival."[31] By giving his translation the title "Love," moreover, Ivanov injects considerable ambiguity into the poem: which love is meant, the man's for the young woman? the female poetic speaker's for the man? or her love for the young woman? This ambiguity does not translate faithfully the unambiguous expression of the poetic speaker's desire for the young woman, and it diminishes the power of that expression.

Finally, Ivanov adds two phrases, indicated here in brackets, to the final stanza of the "Hymn to Aphrodite" (Ivanov's title), the only complete poem of Sappho extant:

> О, явись опять—[по молитве тайной]
> Выволить из новой напасти сердце!
> Стань, [вооружась, в ратоборстве нежном]
> Мне на подмогу.
>
> O appear again—[in answer to my secret prayer]
> To help my heart out of a new misfortune!
> Come stand, [arming yourself, in tender battle raiment]
> To my aid.
> (*Alkei i Safo*, p. 84)

The interpolation "arming yourself, in tender battle raiment" turns Sappho's revered Aphrodite into a typically decadent, hermaphroditic Amazon fantasy.

Ivanov's translations of Sappho deserve fuller treatment than I can give them here.[32] Some indication of the way Ivanov perceived

Laid Out in Lavender

Sappho was necessary, however, because his translations were read enthusiastically by Parnok, who did not know classical Greek. The discovery of Sappho, even in a distorted Russian decadent variant, proved creatively important for Parnok. After reading Ivanov's Sappho, she began writing Sapphic stanzas and writing out or completing some of Sappho's fragments, thus creating her own Sapphic fictions.[33] She included three Sappho imitations in her first book. One of these asserts her spiritual and lyrical kinship with her "companions in Sappho's school":

> Не забыла, видно, я в этой жизни
> незабвенных нег незабвенных песен,
> что певали древле мои подруги
> в школе у Сафо.

> In this life I clearly have not forgotten
> unforgettable songs' unforgettable blisses,
> that in olden times my companions would sing
> in Sappho's school.
> (Parnok, no. 38, pp. 131–32)

The Sappho poems in Parnok's first book reveal one strategy the latter poet employed to write her Lesbian existence into art, which strategy had been used by Lesbian poets in France but not, prior to Parnok, in Russia. In the 1915 "Like a small girl you appeared in my presence ungracefully," the most sexually explicit poem in *Poems*, to which all Parnok's critics paid special attention, Parnok writes out the fragment in which Sappho remembers her lover, Atthis: "You appeared to me a graceless little girl" (*smikra moi pais emmen efaineo kakharis*; Barnstone, *Sappho*, p. 24). In doing so she recalls how *her* "graceless little girl" (Marina Tsvetaeva) first entered her house:

> Девочкой маленькой ты мне предстала неловкою.
>   —Сафо

> "Девочкой маленькой ты мне предстала неловкою"—
> ах, одностишья стрелой Сафо пронзила меня!
> Ночью задумалась я над курчавой головкою,
> нежностью матери страсть в бешеном сердце сменя,—
> "Девочкой маленькой ты мне предстала неловкою."

> Вспомнилось, как поцелуй отстранила уловкою,
> вспомнились эти глаза с невероятным зрачком . . .

В дом мой вступила ты, счастлива мной, как обновкою
поясом, пригоршней бус или цветным башмачком,—
"Девочкой маленькой ты мне предстала неловкою."
Но под ударом любви ты—что золото ковкое!
Я наклонилась к лицу, бледному в страстной тени,
где словно смерть провела снеговою пуховкою . . .
Благодарю и за то, сладостная, что в те дни
"Девочкой маленькой ты мне предстала неловкою."

> Like a small girl you appeared in my presence ungracefully.
> —Sappho

"Like a small girl you appeared in my presence ungracefully"—
Ah, Sappho's single-line shaft pierced to my very core!
During the night I leaned over your curly head pensively,
Motherly tenderness stilled passion's mad rush in my heart,—
"Like a small girl you appeared in my presence ungracefully."

I recollected you dodging my kiss with some subterfuge,
I recollected your eyes, pupils incredibly wide . . .
Into my house you came, happy with me as a novelty:
Colorful slippers, a sash, maybe a handful of beads,—
"Like a small girl you appeared in my presence ungracefully."

But 'neath the mallet of love you are gold—and so malleable!
Leaning, I cradled your face, pale in our passion's shade,
Where it appeared death had passed like a snowy-white powder-
puff . . .
I'm also grateful to you, sweetness, because in those days
"Like a small girl you appeared in my presence ungracefully."
(Parnok, no. 59, pp. 141–42)

I shall confine myself to one observation about this poem's metapoetic structure, which demonstrates the empowering presence of Sappho for Parnok, a crucially important element in the poem that none of Parnok's critics noticed. The Sapphic poetic persona in this lyric is spurred on in her love affair by emulation of her externally mediated artistic object of desire, Sappho.[34] DeJean has argued that the French-American Lesbian poets Renée Vivien and Nathalie Clifford Barney, leaders of the Saphô 1900 movement, "established Sappho as the origin of all sapphic desire and redefined female same sex love as 'through the desire' of the other, always an attempted union with the woman who gave it her name"

(*Fictions*, p. 284). Parnok seems to have developed a similar notion of Sappho in Russian literature.

The Parnok-Tsvetaeva love affair, which inspired many of the poems in Parnok's first book and may have galvanized the poet into putting the collection together, was the talk of Moscow artistic circles in 1914–15. The women lived their love openly and even flaunted it. One contemporary recalled them at an evening party in Moscow, and his or her *tableau vivant* of these Lesbian lovers is culturally revealing: "The two of them sat embracing each other and took turns smoking from the same cigarette. For me [Tsvetaeva] was at that time *une lesbienne classique*. Which of them dominated? What had Sophia Parnok written? I don't know."[35] The onlooker's perception is rife with decadent stereotypes. He or she *assumes* that the women's relationship is based on rigidly defined dominant-submissive (male-female) roles, and she or he is curious mainly about who played the more exotic, and unnatural, man's role. At this time in her life, just before the publication of her first book, Parnok was clearly more visible in society as a Sapphist than a Sappho. (Tsvetaeva may even have been initially attracted to Parnok in part because of the latter's reputation.) At any rate the viewer disparages Parnok as a poet and suggests that possibly she had not written anything. He or she perceives Tsvetaeva as a Lesbian in the French literary mold (foreign to Russia, with all the glamorous xenophobia and homophobia that implies), and, remembering this impression from long ago, is careful to limit Tsvetaeva's "classic lesbianism" to a particular period of her life. This gives the impression that Tsvetaeva was not really a Lesbian then, or ever, but merely playing a role, going through a phase, self-consciously and rebelliously cultivating a decadent image.

However free Parnok and Tsvetaeva were to flaunt their affair in Moscow literary society, Tsvetaeva nevertheless felt it impossible to publish her cycle of Lesbian love lyrics to Parnok, "Girlfriend" ("Podruga," written in 1914–15). As a result, this revolutionary work passed into the secret drawer for more than 60 years.[36] As Parnok acknowledged in one of her poems to Tsvetaeva, the 1916 "To blush for verses that you wrote" ("Krasnet' za posviashchennyi stikh"), Tsvetaeva's "seed" did not die in the closet with the manuscript of love lyrics it produced. Parnok had taken into herself irrevocably the "fire and moisture and wind of [Tsvetaeva's] murmurs of love," and the first "ears of corn" shot up in *Poems*, whose publication coincided with the end of the two poets' creatively competitive love affair.[37]

Critical Responses to Parnok's First Book of Verse

Que tu me plais, o timbre étrange!
Son double, homme et femme à la fois,
Contralto, bizarre mélange,
Hermaphrodite de la voix.
—Théophile Gautier

Ten years had passed between Parnok's first published poem (1906) and *Poems*. The reasons for her prolonged wandering without a book to call her own are various, but the fact that she was creating in a poetic culture with only camouflaged or negative examples of Lesbian writing can hardly have encouraged her productivity. As we have seen, despite the Silver Age's liberalized sexual mores, or perhaps because of them, it was still unthinkable for a poet of the period to publish Lesbian love lyrics without some mask for their contents, usually a culturally approved, anti-Lesbian decadent morbidity or a masculine persona for the desire-expressing Lesbian "I."

Parnok does not resort to decadent images or language to express her Lesbian desire. Her love lyrics are rooted in life experience, and they illustrate that "the experience of loving a woman is for the [female] narrative voice, *the* experience of awakening" (Marks, "Intertextuality," p. 361). Although this is most true of her later collections, in *Poems* Parnok began the process of emerging from her long poetic hibernation and stirred to the creative potential of her own Lesbian life. About a third of the poems in the collection are love lyrics. In them the Lesbian poetic persona, like Sappho's, writes as a woman about women who have attracted her, whom she has loved, who have loved her and abandoned her. She writes most passionately about her Marina (Atthis), in whose "desperate name blows the wind of all storm-tossed coasts" (Parnok, no. 9, p. 114).

There are five extant reviews of Parnok's first book, of which I shall examine four in some detail.[38] The first is an unpublished anonymous reader's report from the publishing house Lights (Ogni). The author, whom I shall call Anonymous (his or her sex is unknown), begins by placing Parnok in the sexually marked company of Zinaida Gippius and Mirra Lokhvitskaya. The latter, whose first volume of poems appeared in 1896, had been dubbed by one critic "the Russian Sappho," not because of her Lesbian orientation—Lokhvitskaya's Sappho fictions and imitations are aggressively heterosexual—but because of the unabashed eroticism of her "*sweet songs* of love."[39] Anonymous contrasts Parnok to the other two female lyricists in her group: unlike the world-embracing Lokhvitskaya, she "like Gippius, prefers solitude," but "she does not seek Gippius's kind of solitude," she wants solitude "where God is nearby."[40] The critic ends this part of the review with an oblique reference to Parnok's Lesbianism and connects it with the impression that he or she finds conveyed in her lyrics: "In the world of people" the poet's "soul seems to lose its kinship with the Divine Principle. Earthly, *too earthly* passions possess her and she sings them loudest and most of all" (emphasis in the original). By contrast, Anonymous had noted that Lokhvitskaya "wants to sing loudly the joys of love."

Anonymous exaggerates the presence of "too earthly passions" (i.e., Lesbian sex) in Parnok's book. There are only three or four fairly explicit poems among the 60 in the collection. The majority of the love lyrics express what Russians call "the most various tender feelings" (*vsiakogo roda nezhnye chuvstva*), that is, manifestations of love between women (Lesbian or heterosexual) that the culture does not consider primarily "sexual" and therefore accepts as "normal." Yet the small number of frankly erotic Lesbian poems in the book gives Anonymous the impression that Parnok is obsessed with "too earthly passions." While this extreme sexualization of Lesbian love reflects the decadent and medical stereotypes of the age, it also reveals a classic case of homophobia. For Anonymous, Lesbianism is taboo, and "any mention of [it] is so charged that it expands to fill a much larger space than it actually occupies."[41]

Anonymous's fondness for decadent "lavender" prose reaches a climax in his or her comment on the poem "Like a small girl":

And the aroma of autumnal decay unwholesomely encircles and intoxicates the sinful soul with the languorous charms of sweetly impure excitements. There are many poems in which the tender music of affectionately tremulous words interharmonizes with the mysterious serpentine rustle of barely noticeable depravity. In "Like a small girl you appeared in my presence ungracefully," with its most cunning address to a female lover and most intimate tremors of the bedroom, . . . the same chord of decay sounds, just as the smell of rot . . . distinguishes the color of the woods in fall.

The first published review of *Poems* was written by Adelaida Gertsyk (1874–1925), a poet, translator, memoirist, critic, and close friend of Parnok's. The latter frequented the fashionable Gertsyk-Zhukovsky literary salon in Moscow and was also a member of a small group of poets who gathered around Gertsyk, inspired by her cultlike adoration of Bettina Brentano von Arnim.[42] Although Gertsyk's review is positive, as one might expect given her personal sympathy for Parnok, it misunderstands the Lesbian theme in her lyrics. The misunderstanding arises in part because Gertsyk cannot find a language to deal with Lesbianism straightforwardly. She is forced to fall back on euphemisms, allusions, and the critical clichés of her Silver Age culture. We do not know whether those clichés represented her own point of view.

If Anonymous brought to Parnok's poems an obsession with decay, then Gertsyk attempts to read out of them evidence of prevailing ideas about gender attributes and roles. She hopes to reveal the poet's "profound awareness of the antagonism between the male and female principles," but her notions of masculine and feminine are arbitrary and/or clichéd.[43] She claims, for example, to see a contradiction in Parnok's verse between the poet's "masculine" sound of "bitter irony and impassioned reproach" and her "endlessly tired and utterly feminine soul," which "search[es] for chains and thirst[s] for captivity." The latter notion represents a common enough feminine stereotype, but the idea that irony and reproach are inherently "masculine" seems arbitrary and suggests that Gertsyk is trying to "gender" Parnok's lyrics, as Anonymous sexualized them. She seeks a "masculine" equipoise to the "feminine" qualities that Silver Age thinking allows her to identify in Parnok's verse. Gertsyk's reason for reading Parnok's lyrics as a struggle between male and female principles remains mysterious, however, unless the idea of warring genders, which comes from outside the lyrics, is her way of alluding to the Lesbian nature of some of the poems without naming it.

Gertsyk eventually reaches the conclusion that Parnok's poetic persona is insatiable and alone—also part of the decadent stereotype of Lesbians. She finds illustrations of the poet's insatiability and aloneness in one poem where the poetic speaker is incredulous that a brief intimacy is ending: "Is this the end? My eyes are not yet sated, / My lips are still less sated than my eyes" (*Uzhel' konets? Glaza nenasytimy, / usta moi nenasytimei glaz*; no. 50, p. 137).

Insatiability and aloneness lead Parnok, Gertsyk says, to "the world of woman," which the poet celebrates "in refined Sapphic stanzas, close to their ancient models in form and spirit."[44] Gertsyk passes over the specific Lesbian contents of Parnok's Sapphic stanzas and presents these poems as elegant exercises in form, but her implication that the poet's insatiability, aloneness, and focus on women all suggest she is a Sapphist reflects the homophobia of Gertsyk's age. The Sapphic poems in Parnok's collection speak—with one exception, which has a male addressee—to Lesbian companionship, love, creativity, and satisfied passion.

Gertsyk tries to fit Parnok's poetic persona into Silver Age literary culture's favorite opposition between male and female lyricism. The Lesbian poet emerges from this scheme as a sad hermaphrodite struggling with "herimself" in a world of "half-shades and fading autumnal colors." "Truly this is autumnal poetry," Gertsyk concludes, "with its sad and whimsical flowers, overhanging willows, and subtle, stifling odor of decay."[45]

Parnok's good friend and fellow poet, Vladislav Khodasevich, wrote the second published review of *Poems*.[46] In an attempt to establish a context for assessing the work of a woman poet, he begins by noting the recent phenomenon of "poetry of the female soul," as exemplified for him in the verse of "several gifted poetesses, . . . Anna Akhmatova, A. Gertsyk, Marina Tsvetaeva, the deceased N. G. L'vova, and the semi-mythical Cherubina de Gabriac." Khodasevich says these poetesses created a demand for "feminine-ness" (*zhenskost'*), which encouraged an increased supply "not only of female [*zhenskie*] but also typically ladies' [*damskie*] verse." He characterizes the latter as "a whole rain of mannerisms, fractures, caprices, affectedness," and identifies the writers of "ladies' verse" as "youthful offspring of Sappho." Here Khodasevich expresses a view of Sappho, which has had a long career in Western literature, that trivializes her work. Sappho becomes the poet *not* to emulate if one would be a genuine poet, a viewpoint exactly opposite to that held by turn-of-the-century *Lesbian* poets, including Parnok.

In the second half of his review Khodasevich begins by praising Parnok for being untouched by the prevailing "bad fashion" for "femininity." His view of the poet is precisely the contrary of Gertsyk's. Far from reflecting a soul torn by gender conflicts between the "male and female principles," Khodasevich's Parnok is above gender, or without it; she is "not a man and not a woman, but a human being." Clearly Khodasevich considers this a compliment, and it is, in the subjective context he and other male poets and critics had established where feminine verse represents "bad" verse. Nevertheless, Khodasevich's praise places Parnok in a category that suggests his unawareness of (or wish to ignore) the poet's clear and realized desire to inscribe her gender and her sexuality in her poems. Khodasevich's comment also strangely echoes Tsvetaeva's lyrical eroticization of her woman-lover in the tenth poem of "Girlfriend," where she calls her "Not a woman and not a boy, / but something stronger than me" (*Ne zhenshchina i ne mal'chik, / No chto-to sil'nei menia!*; Poliakova, *NOD*, p. 32).[47]

At the end of his review Khodasevich deals briefly and subjectively with Parnok's attitudes to love. He calls her poetic persona "fateful," both in her verse, a characterization for which he cites lyrical evidence, and in her life, an opinion for which he offers no support. He leaves his readers with a perception of Parnok that is again similar to the romanticized *femme damnée* image found in Tsvetaeva's "Girlfriend." Compare, for example, Khodasevich's comment, "She [Parnok] loves the fateful in life too. Her love . . . draws her to her ruin," and phrases from Tsvetaeva's declaration of love to Parnok in the first poem of "Girlfriend": "[I love you] For your inspired seductions / and dark fate" ([*Ia vas liubliu!*] . . . *Za vashi vdokhnovennye soblazny / I temnyi rok*; stanza 5) and "Because—despite all efforts meant to save you!— / you can't be saved" (*Za to, chto Vas—Khot' razorvis' nad grobom!— / Uzh ne spasti*; Poliakova, *NOD*, pp. 21, 22).

The last review of *Poems*, written by Maximilian Voloshin, a poet, leading light of the Silver Age, and good friend of Parnok's, appeared in 1917. Voloshin's comments are part of an article entitled "Voices of Poets," which he originally intended as an extensive general survey of contemporary Russian poets, a kind of new Annensky, only with voice (in the musical sense) replacing gender as the critic's organizing principle. Voloshin ended up narrowing his focus to two poetic voices, Parnok's in *Poems* and Osip Mandelstam's in *Stone* (*Kamen'*, 1913). It is hard not to see some sort of biographical subtext unconsciously at work in Voloshin's choice of these two poets. During the summer of 1915, when many of the lyrics in *Poems* were written, Parnok and Tsvetaeva were living at Voloshin's summer house *cum* poets' colony at Koktebel. Mandelstam was among the other guests, and because of his openly expressed infatuation with Tsvetaeva became involved in a poetic and personal rivalry with Parnok.

The inspiration for "Voices of Poets" comes from Voloshin's disagreement with Théophile Gautier's remark, "when a person passes away, his voice perishes more irretrievably than anything." Voloshin says Gautier disproved his own words in the poem "Contralto" (1849), which was inspired by the French poet's love for the diva Ernesta Grisi. He asserts, in contradiction to Gautier, "in verse a poet's voice continues living along with all its own intonations."[48]

Voloshin hears Parnok's unique sound in one of her love lyrics to Tsvetaeva, "Eyes unseeing stare anew" (no. 9). Parnok wrote this poem in August 1915, just after she and Tsvetaeva left Koktebel and the incipient triangular situations their love had aroused there involving Tsvetaeva's husband on one hand and her poetic "lover," Mandelstam, on the other. Voloshin dotes on "Eyes unseeing stare anew" as if he were personally involved with its addressee in the same sort of fatherly way as Gautier was involved with the daughter (his own) of the singer he celebrates in "Contralto." Voloshin quotes Parnok's poem to "Marina" in full and comments on it with impressionistic rapture: "[The poem] is uttered in a single breath, without pauses. . . . [I]t begins in a deep, female contralto and, gradually building in intensity, shifts from despair to a youthful summons, a girlish shout" ("Golosa poetov," pp. 545–46). There is a hint of the hermaphrodite in the opposition of "girlish shout" to "youthful summons," but for the most part Voloshin develops his impression of Parnok in a non-gender-marked musical metaphor of silence and full-voicedness.

Voloshin differs from Anonymous and Gertsyk in that he hears a "cry to life" in Parnok's book rather than "autumnal" sighs. Unlike them too, and less euphemistically than Khodasevich, he notes the poet's "passionateness" (*strastnost'*) in "Like a small girl." Though he quotes from the poem, he omits any lines where the feminine gender of the addressee is made explicit. Anonymous called this poem a "most cunning address to a female-lover" and used it to illustrate Parnok's "subtly sinful" eroticism, but he or she did not quote from it. Voloshin quotes from the poem to demonstrate Parnok's "profound passionateness" and the "penetrating quality" (*pronzitel'nost'*—an arguably "masculine" quality) of "all her words about love" ("Golosa poetov," p. 546). The implications of this statement, which reflects the Silver Age's view of Lesbians, are that the poet loves like a mannish woman and writes like a man. Voloshin actually enhances the gender ambiguity of Parnok's "penetrating" passionateness by quoting selectively so that the unambiguously Lesbian passion in the poem is not evident. His treatment of the poem replaces the wholly female eroticism depicted in it (maternal-daughterly, female-female, not male-female) with a decadently suggestive and stereotyped model of mannish Lesbian–young girl. Like Anonymous and Gertsyk, Voloshin exposes Parnok's sexuality only to reclothe and hide it in culturally approved decadent dress.

All four critics of Parnok's *Poems* try to put a straitjacket on the poet's Lesbian persona because she does not fit into her literary culture's typology of lyricisms. Their attempts to restrain the poet and "put her away" in some rational "literary" category reveal the deeper madness of their culture's attitudes toward Lesbian love. In describing Parnok's love lyrics, Anonymous becomes hysterical, Gertsyk obsessive. Khodasevich unsexes the woman poet to raise her to the status of human being and to separate her from bad poets, the "offspring of Sappho." And Voloshin ends on an ironical, not to say crazy, note, which, to continue his own musical metaphor, makes Parnok's "female contralto" sing from a male poet's opera:

Laid Out in Lavender

There cannot be any doubt: in these lyrics one hears that strange and disturbing voice of which Théophile Gautier said:

> Que tu me plais, o timbre étrange!
> Son double, homme et femme à la fois,
> Contralto, bizarre mélange,
> Hermaphrodite de la voix.
> ("Golosa poetov," pp. 546-47)

Thus Voloshin bows to the authority of his French mentor and concludes his discussion of Parnok by naming the Lesbian poet a hermaphrodite in the literary mold cast by Gautier, the poet who, DeJean notes, "contributed perhaps more than anyone to the lesbian's reduction to androgyny, simple source of sexual scandal, and prurient interest" (*Fictions*, p. 271). After exclaiming over the pleasure Parnok's bizarreness affords him, Voloshin moves on to his impression of Mandelstam's voice. Given his personal knowledge of Parnok's and Mandelstam's poetic and romantic rivalry over Tsvetaeva, one cannot help but hear a suggestively double-edged, if esoteric, irony in his description of Mandelstam as "a youthful bass, who might appear awkward and breaking like an adolescent" next to Parnok's "supple and developed female contralto" ("Golosa poetov," p. 547).

Conclusion

> Same as it ever was,
> Same as it ever was,
> —Talking Heads

If we look back over all the Silver Age perceptions of Lesbians and Lesbian love (excluding Parnok's) that we have examined here—and they are rather various on the surface—we are struck first of all by a sameness that overwhelms their diversity and puts the latter in question. The perceptions span a decade (1907–17) in Russia's cultural life, a decade of revolutionary ferment and change. Yet they begin and end on virtually the same note. Zinovieva-Annibal's fictional Lesbian lovers in *Thirty-Three Monsters* (1907) bear an uncanny resemblance to Voloshin's impression of the real, but fictionalized, Lesbian poet Parnok, in "Voices of Poets" (1917). The male critic's pleasure in and vicarious submission to Parnok's "strange and disturbing voice" comes from the same decadent model as Zinovieva-Annibal's narrator's perception of her Lesbian lover: "Vera is strange. But I would have submitted to her in everything."[49] The comparison demonstrates that neither time, nor the gender or sexual orientation of the perceiver, nor the genre he or she is writing in, nor his or her closeness to or distance from the Lesbian object of perception affects the way the Lesbian is perceived. At the end of the Silver Age, Lesbians remained the freakish, exotic, "foreign" hermaphrodites they were in Russian literature and criticism at the start of the period.

Second, and again excluding Parnok's perceptions, we note how consistently the model of the Lesbian as hermaphrodite is accepted and purveyed by Silver Age writers and critics who are personally not only not hostile to Lesbians but in most cases sympathetic to them. Zinovieva-Annibal, Annensky, Ivanov, Khodasevich, Gertsyk, and Voloshin all appear unaware of any negative or hostile aspects to the *fin de siècle* view of Lesbians they implicitly affirm. This unawareness strikes one especially in the case of Khodasevich, Gertsyk, and Voloshin: they were all close friends and admirers of the Lesbian whose work they reviewed, and clearly saw themselves as friendly rather than hostile critics. Their uncritical acceptance of the French decadent model of Lesbian love, their efforts to read it into Parnok's love lyrics, and their not seeing its irrelevance to her work suggest unconscious homophobia, and illustrate the triumph of literary style, medical authority, and cultural modeling over personal knowledge.

Against the Silver Age chorus of poets, her critics, and friends, Parnok's voice sounds truly revolutionary. Even in her first book, *Poems*, in which she was just beginning to liberate her voice from the collective sound of the age, we catch strains of a new, antidecadent perception of Lesbian love that her critics could not, or unconsciously did not want, to hear. This antidecadent perception is evident in such things as (1) the Lesbian poetic persona's search for a "fateful mistress" and "female companion-lover" (*podruga*) who is *not* an icon of the decadent femme fatale: "[I seek] not Isolde, not Cleopatra, not Manon and not Carmen!" (*ne Izol'du, ne Kleopatru, ne Manon i ne Karmen!*; Parnok, no. 43, p. 134); (2) her asking a woman lover to lead her *away* from death: "Oh, lead me away from my death" (*Akh, ot smerti moei uvedi menia*; no. 9, p. 114); (3) her joyful celebration of Spring: "Just like my first days" (*Slovno dni moi pervonachal'nye*; no. 2, p. 109) and "On the luxurious chestnut trees" (*Na kashtanakh pyshnykh ty*; no. 5, p. 111); (4) her anticipation of new growth despite the surrounding autumn: "A young stalk already shows green / in the gray hairs of last year's grass" (*Uzh iunyi zeleneet stebel' / v sedinakh proshloletnikh trav*; no. 10, p. 114); (5) her admiration of Sappho and celebration of Sapphic companionship and *creativity* (no. 38, no. 59); (6) and her repeated expression of Lesbian sexual power and fulfillment. Most striking of all, Parnok's poetic persona engages in no concealment. She does not hide her sex or her sexual orientation. She does not adopt a masculine persona to avoid being labeled a "female lyricist" or one of the "offspring of Sappho" by her misogynistic culture. Rather, she takes the offensive and asserts the liberation and creative empowerment she finds in her Lesbian femininity. With Lesbian feminist hindsight, one can see Parnok as having made an attempt to reclaim female, and female to female, lyricism from the male cultural establishment that defined, delimited, and degraded it.

In the last stanza of the first poem of "Girlfriend," Marina Tsvetaeva spoke of the "ironical charm" (*ironicheskaia prelest'*) of finding in Parnok a "you," a romantic addressee and a lover, who was "not a he." Starting in her first collection, *Poems*, Parnok's own love lyrics speak of an equally ironical charm, the charm of inscribing an "I," a romantic subject and a Lesbian, who is not a he. Her contemporaries and critics unfortunately did not share her sense of irony, or charm.

HELENA GOSCILO

Monsters Monomaniacal, Marital, and Medical

Tatiana Tolstaya's Regenerative
Use of Gender Stereotypes

■ Amidst the welter of grotesque relationships proliferating in Tatiana Tolstaya's fiction,[1] romantic-sexual liaisons particularly stand out as oxymoronic *mésalliances* cast in a Bakhtinian key.[2] More often than not, one or both partners involved seem highly implausible candidates for the type of coupling they contemplate, pursue, or enjoy, in large measure because social convention has habituated us to identify romantic scenarios automatically with beauty, glamour, success, and the like. Tolstaya, however, intentionally swims against the current of custom, for the temperamental idiosyncrasies and outlandish physical appearance that as a rule discourage association with romance invariably characterize her lovelorn and love-seeking personae. Thus Peters, the pastry-gobbling "glandular washout," doggedly and futilely woos modish young sophisticates with mumbled reminiscences of his plush rabbit and vague references to German culture ("Peters"); the maladroit, equine-faced Sonia, with pigeon toes and a sunken chest, perishes in a bombardment while saving her beloved Nikolai, without noticing that in actuality he is a vengeful female acquaintance ("Sonya"); Simeonov scorns the (s)motheringly amorous overtures of Tamara in favor of obsessive fantasies about a singer from the distant past who, in person, proves to be a mountain of gluttonous flesh now preoccupied solely with physical gratification ("Okkervil River"); 84-year-old Alexandra Ernestovna, a thrice-widowed monument to time's passage, with drooping stockings and an improbable hat of floral superabundance, still dwells elegiacally on her ancient decision not to run off with her devoted admirer many decades ago ("Sweet Shura"), and so forth. These "odd couples" are polemical antipodes to Pyramus and Thisbe, Romeo and Juliet, Dante and Beatrice, Héloïse and Abelard, and other canonic exemplars of exalted love. To dismantle the immemorial constructs generated by, and generating, such cultural icons, Tolstaya capitalizes on readers' standard (and prejudiced) expectations, only to subvert them, achieving strong tonal and emotional effects in the process.

That strategy of creative, irreverent sabotage likewise operates in a trio of narratives related to these works, yet distinct from them, which dethrone specifically gender stereotypes through ironic double-voicing, literalization of metaphor, and parodic interpolation of myth: "Hunting the Wooly Mammoth" (1985), "The Poet and the Muse" (1986), and "Fire and Dust" (1986).[3] The narrative impetus behind these stories derives from a reversal of all too familiar formulae that have long legislated heterosexual relations: for example, a woman's "female essence" can be realized only in marriage; everyone "has a right to personal happiness" (i.e., marriage); marriage necessarily means domestication, the preservation of "the sanctity of Home and Family"; beauty and the projection of inaccessible "virtue" constitute a woman's passport to the haven of marital bliss; and so on. In addition to satirizing such notions, Tolstaya's trio explicitly discredits the prescribed gender identities buttressing these hollow but hallowed *idées reçues*, namely: womanhood as Muse, as inspiration for artistic (i.e., male) creativity; as sacred vessel, decorative dreamer, self-abnegating nurturer, and pedestaled helpmate. In all these cases the female protagonists engage in the reflexive sociocultural mimetism common to insecure individuals whose mental agoraphobia or reticent intelligence motivates their uncritical capitulation to their culture's dominant values. These they internalize and disseminate in their turn, thereby upholding the constabulary of culture known as popular opinion or thought.

"Hunting the Wooly Mammoth" charts the narrow course of Zoya's relentless efforts to attain the universally sanctioned goal of "landing" a husband, optimally one with prestige ("Zoya didn't want to love without guarantees").[4] Within the presiding metaphor of the mammoth hunt, the hunter *cum* hospital receptionist Zoya initially sets her impersonal sights on a surgeon, but settles upon lesser game, the engineer Vladimir, as a compromise ("Zoya very much wanted to fall into a surgeon's embrace. But an engineer wasn't bad either," p. 53). Throughout, Zoya utterly dehumanizes Vladimir as an object defined exclusively in terms of her own teleology, and hence perceived as the adversary or prey earmarked for submission to her Purpose:[5] "She . . . hated the two-bearded Vladimir and wanted to marry him as soon as possible" (p. 55); "Oh, how disgusting he was! Marry him, hurry up and marry him!" (p. 56); "Zoya maintained a hostile silence . . . he, the viper, felt right at home" (p. 57); "What a louse Vladimir was. . . . After all there are rules of the hunt" (p. 60); "She had never particularly liked this man. No, why not say it—he had always repelled her. A little, powerful, heavy, quick, hairy, insensitive animal" (p. 62). This reduction of the male to a purely referential function (which Tolstaya intensifies by presenting him externally, through Zoya's eyes alone) exposes the dehumanizing aspects of objectification by self-positing subjects. Vladimir becomes co-opted and subsumed as alterity within an epistemologically imperialistic system that denies him all autonomy. (Paradoxically, that system originates in an internalized patriarchal structure that construes woman as Other.)

Zoya's solipsistic brutality communicates itself in the firmly grounded animal imagery that helps build the narrative's connective tissue. From the very outset, Tolstaya analogizes Zoya with a bee through the sound of her name ("Zoya's a beautiful name, isn't it? Like bees buzzing by," p. 51). A particularly apt, ambivalent association, given Zoya's delusive "sweetness" and her capacity to "sting," the image gains force through later repetition ("Zoya buzzed like a bee," p. 56). By contrast, Vladimir is equated with the hapless mammoth portrayed in his artist friend's symbolic painting, whose title the story appropriates: ". . . a wild craggy cliff, growths of cattails, and from the cattails emerges a wooly mammoth in slippers. Someone small is aiming at it with a bow and arrow. On one side you can see a cave: it has a light bulb hanging from a cord, a glowing TV screen, and a gas burner. Even the frying pan is drawn in detail, and on the little table there's a bouquet of cattails" (p. 59). The parallel requires little explication: just as in the larger scheme of things, so-called civilization and its progress effected the mammoth's extinction, so the time-honored ritual of conjugal domestication renders the free-roaming male a doomed species: "Zoya set traps: she'd dig a pit, cover it with branches, and nudge him, nudge him toward it" (p. 57). Even the slippers in the painting have precise relevance for Vladimir's circumstances: "In the fall Zoya bought slippers for Vladimir" (p. 56).

Finally, the dove and pigeon simultaneously evoked by the term *golub'* become Zoya's radically subjective and specious correlative from the world of nature invoked to validate her recipe for "happiness." Russian's failure to distinguish between the two (dove and pigeon) enables the image to connote spirituality and peace on the one hand and tamed subordination to human designs on the other. As an earthbound pragmatist, Zoya can conceive of only the "lower" connotations: "A pigeon/dove with a band around its leg landed on the window and looked severely into Zoya's eyes. There, there you are! Even a pigeon—a lousy, dirty bird—gets a band put on. Scientists *in white coats*, with honest, educated faces, Ph.D.s, take him, the little pigeon [*golubchik*, a diminutive of *golub'* that also means 'sweetie'], by the sides . . . the pigeon with the fiery *wedding band* arose out of the darkness" (pp. 60–61, emphasis added). The white coats recall Zoya's own garb in the hospital—a milieu that camouflages pain, dissolution, and death by a civilized veneer of sterility.[6] Through them, Tolstaya forges an eloquent parallel for Zoya's violent assault on Vladimir's selfhood under the paradigmatic guise of dispensing and seeking "happiness with the man she loves." The story's conclusion, however, tears aside the veil of convention through the grisly metaphor of a prehistoric cave in which Zoya lassoes her prey ("monster," "animal") and listens to it finally subside in defeat: "It puttered around for a while—whimpering, fussing, until it finally quieted down—in the blissful thick silence of the great ice age" (p. 62).

Although in a characteristically original twist Tolstaya reverses the gender roles in the classic metaphor of love as hunt,[7] and realizes the metaphor at several junctures, the effectiveness of these devices hinges on the reader's recognition of the image as a cultural stereotype. Moreover, that recognition empowers Tolstaya's concision and her audience's sensitivity to the double-voicedness of the narrative, which modulates constantly from Zoya's artless revelations of totalitarian impulses to the countervoice of ironic distancing. Both voices, in their contrasting ways, and the interplay between them expose not only Zoya's undebilitated vulgarity but also her egotistic pragmatism—her determination to "land her victim" at all costs. She does so by following the steps of a time-tested strategy which presupposes that a woman's beauty inherently entitles her simultaneously to the emblematic prerogatives of universal male adulation and a prestigious husband.

Zoya recruits her heaviest artillery from the arsenal of cultural history. It predictably consists of her looks and the simulation of elevated fragility and refinement. Thus during her first rendezvous with Vladimir at a restaurant she picks daintily at her dessert, "pretending for some intellectual reason that it wasn't very tasty" (p. 52). Later, she ostentatiously assumes a decorative pose of attitudinized contemplation, in a classic invitation to appropriation through the Male Gaze:[8]

[She would sit] languorously with a casual expression on her face, slightly mocking, slightly dreamy—her face was supposed to reflect the fleeting nuances of her complex spiritual life, such as exquisite sadness or some refined reminiscence; she would sit as if gazing off into space, her elbows gracefully resting on the table, and, her lower lip pouting, would keep sending lovely smoke rings up to the painted vaulted ceiling. She was playing fairy. . . . Zoya would get offended: wasn't she a princess, albeit unrecognized? (P. 53)

Tolstaya repeatedly emphasizes Zoya's lack of a subjective self. Conceiving of herself in purely visual, external terms through the series of scenes projected by her imagination, Zoya cannot separate herself from the perspective of the objectifying male viewer: as the physically disheveled, hence imperfect, decoration merely accompanying Vladimir on an outing, thus not in her "true role" (p. 53) of heart-stopping beauty; as the "original" of the photograph of herself she smuggles into Vladimir's wallet (p. 54); as the pièce de résistance at an artistic gathering and the "subject" of a portrait that causes a sensation (pp. 56–57); as the universally acclaimed idol once the portrait becomes famous and she as the "original" is sought after (p. 57); and, finally, as the incarnation of Unbounded Grief (*Bezgranichnaia Skorb'*) fit for depiction by a medieval artist (p. 59). Zoya's identity seeks definition through material representation. She walks through life, in fact, with an invisible mirror that obsessively checks her reflection at every potential encounter with a male subject.[9]

Although Zoya gives every evidence of tactical indefatigability on the battlefield of sexual politics, she actually joins the fray out of profound existential insecurity. Her very identity derives wholly from without, constituted by male attention as an acknowledgment of her desirability.[10] That contingent desirability constitutes her essence. Hence her loss of "self" both during the camping trip with Vladimir and his married coworkers ("All the engineers had their own women, no one gave Zoya special looks or said 'Oh!,' and she felt sexless, a camping buddy," pp. 54–55) and during their visit to Vladimir's painter friend: "The host's radiant but sort of unseeing gaze slid professionally over Zoya's surface. The gaze did not connect with Zoya's soul, as if she weren't even there . . . they both forgot about Zoya . . . Zoya wasn't here or anywhere else, she simply didn't exist at all" (p. 59). Her colossal self-preoccupation articulates itself in Zoya's crass, appurtenance-based ideal of conjugal life, wherein during Vladimir's absence she relaxes picturesquely on the couch in an elegant robe (imported), in front of a color TV ("let Vladimir buy her one"), by the rosy glow of a (Yugoslavian) floorlamp, and sips a light beverage as she smokes something extraordinary ("let the patients' relatives give her some as a gift"), anticipating a flirtatious call from the "ideal" surgeon with whom she will engage in badinage (p. 53).[11] Satisfaction within marriage is thus equated with conspicuous consumption, the luxury items to be deposited on the altar of female beauty. Unable to envision any desires, any world, in fact, beyond her affirmation as an enshrined gift to mankind, Zoya ineluctably degrades herself and Vladimir into commodities for barter on the market of dehumanized pseudosexual relations that Marxist feminists identify with paradigmatic patriarchal institutions. That Tolstaya conceives of Zoya's goal and *modus operandi* as a specific instance of a comprehensive cultural paradigm may be deduced from such comments as this: "But how to find out his intentions? Zoya didn't dare ask a direct question. *Many centuries of experience kept her from do-*

ing that. One bad shot—and it was over, write it off" (p. 57, emphasis added).

If "Hunting the Wooly Mammoth" spotlights the destructive consequences of manipulating life in accordance with internalized gender clichés, "The Poet and the Muse" goes still further by rendering those consequences literally fatal. Like the earlier story, "The Poet and the Muse" takes as its point of departure two cultural bromides, which the narrative proceeds to explode through double-voicing, literalized metaphor, "Homeric" catalogues, and ironic citation of biblical, folkloric, and mythic elements: (1) Woman as inspirational Muse and (2) everyone's "right to personal happiness" (*pravo na lichnoe schast'e* serves as a sardonic refrain). The story's female protagonist, Nina, and its plotline also echo "Hunting the Wooly Mammoth." As a doctor, Nina, like Zoya, belongs to the medical profession; she likewise chooses the victim of her implacable "love," launches a cold-blooded campaign to assume ascendancy over all aspects of his life, and ultimately succeeds in destroying it and eliminating him. Her presumption, which duplicates Zoya's, is that female beauty per se merits the automatic conferral of happiness: "Yet she'd certainly earned the right to happiness, she was entitled to a place in the line where it was being handed out.... It would only be fair for someone to sing her praises."[12] Whereas Zoya is given to checking her own image mentally, Nina observes herself quite literally in mirrors, to verify her superiority over her female "friends" with the "standard-issue" husbands for whom Nina harbors only contempt: "[She] would talk for a long time, eyeing herself all the while in the dark glass of the kitchen door, where her reflection was even more enigmatic, and more alluring in comparison with her friend's spreading silhouette" (pp. 36–37).

With clinical precision, Nina diagnoses her own needs, the vapid terms of which Tolstaya derides through (1) a listing device, which Flaubert used for comparable effect in *Madame Bovary*, and (2) a reaccented application of motifs from the fairy tale "The Feather of Finist the Bright Falcon": "She needed a wild, mad love, with sobs, bouquets, midnight phone vigils, nocturnal taxi chases, fateful obstacles, betrayals and forgiveness; she needed a—you know—an animal passion, a dark windy night, with street lamps aglow, so that the *classic womanly feat* would seem a mere trifle:

to wear out seven pairs of iron boots, break seven iron staffs in two, devour seven loaves of iron bread" (p. 36).[13] This condensation of externals, of threadbare props and symbolic gestures divorced from essence, along with the verb "seem" (*pokazat'sia*), provides an eloquent measure of Nina's entrapment in appearance and form. That misguided attachment acquires an additional edge in the dismissive comparison with the "classic womanly feat" from the fairy tale "The Feather of Finist the Bright Falcon," whose heroine undergoes genuine ordeals to regain the "bright falcon" of a man she loves with wholehearted, unselfish devotion.[14] The jarring contrast between Nina and the beauteous maiden (*krasnaia devitsa*) of the fairy tale reinforces the iron tension that the narrative sustains throughout between the superstructure of overblown ideals and extravagant "romantic" display on the one hand, and the base of savage repression activated by coarse, material self-interest on the other.[15] The contradictory nature of this hybridization is captured brilliantly by Tolstaya's satirical encapsulation of Nina's first encounter with the poet Grisha: "The near-corpse immediately abducted Nina's weary heart: the mournful shadows on his porcelain brow, the darkness around his sunken eyes, and the delicate beard, transparent like a springtime forest, all made for a magical scene. Invisible violins played a wedding waltz—and the trap sprang shut. Well, everybody knows how it usually happens" (p. 37).

Without a thought for reciprocity (crucial to love, but irrelevant to summary annexation), Nina instantly determines to give Grisha her heart. As Tolstaya reinvigorates the exhausted metaphor through literalization ("Nina . . . carefully took her heart from Grishunia's hands and nailed it to the bedstead," p. 37), she leaves pregnantly ambiguous at this stage the question of who better fits the role of savior, sufferer, and self-abnegator: "The thorny path lay ahead" (p. 115). That ambiguity feeds in part off Tolstaya's reversal of standard gender roles.

Feminist critics, starting with Laura Mulvey, have exhaustively documented a particular strain of both literature and the visual arts obsessed with the moment when a male subject "discovers" (or perhaps mentally "uncovers") the female object of his libidinal drives as she is sleeping or merely reclining in a vulnerable pose particularly attractive to the voyeuristic/sadistic mentality. Works as dissimilar as Matthew Lewis's *The Monk* (1796) and the gothic novels that sired it, John Keats's voluptuous *Eve of St. Agnes* (1819), and a host of *fin de siècle* paintings throughout Europe—not to mention countless examples of unabashed pornography—all depict anticipated possession through the male viewer's gaze directed at a prostrate woman, as a helplessly splayed object positioned for subjugation.[16] As the myth of Psyche and Cupid attests, the female variant of that scenario, in which the slumbering male form constitutes an object for female delectation, enacts less an assertion of sexual power than a need for reassurance, a settling of uncertainties.[17] By assigning Nina the active role and Grisha the passive function of reaction or resignation, Tolstaya embeds the male myth of possession within the larger narrative of romantic/marital entrapment. Like the heroes of the classic male formula, Nina unilaterally "chooses" Grisha on the basis of his looks (which stimulate conventional dreams fueled by bourgeois values) as the appropriate inhabitant of the doll's house in which she will psychologically incarcerate him. The unresisting Grisha, by contrast, seems indifferent to women's beauty (his affection for the talented but physically unprepossessing Lizaveta appears to surpass his feeling for the beautiful Agniya); fulfills the standard feminine role of nurturer when Lizaveta falls sick (p. 40); cries and gives freely of his emotions, which he readily expresses ("giving himself out by the handful," p. 40); responds passively and emotionally to psychological imperialism ("he was a frail thing; he cried a lot and didn't want to eat," p. 41); and succumbs to death for lack of toughness in withstanding the relentless attack on his selfhood. Like the frail, porcelain-browed virgin of fantasy abductions (Tolstaya briefly adverts to the experienced Nina's failed marriage and latest [?] affair, but divulges nothing about possible sexual/romantic involvements in his past), the gentle ("miagkii") Grisha struggles feebly, cries, and whimpers, but ultimately resigns himself to the seemingly inevitable. Diminutives in the story ("blazhennenkii," "slaben'kii," "rovnen'ko") are applied principally to him.

While saving Grisha's life in her capacity as doctor, Nina proceeds to devastate it as a woman, rearranging his entire existence, from the company he keeps to the poems he composes. Tolstaya uses military vocabulary to document Nina's merciless campaign of terrorism as she jealously edges his painter friend Lizaveta out of his life ("*destroying* Lizaveta turned out to be as hard as *cutting* a tough apple worm in half. When they came to fine her for violating the residence permit in her passport, she was already holed up in a different place, and Nina *sent the troops* over there . . . finally, Lizaveta evaporated to a mere shadow," p. 40, emphasis added); dismisses all Grisha's friends from the apartment she now shares with him ("Nina allowed Grishunia a final goodbye to his friends," p. 41); oversees Grisha's poetry ("once a week she checked his desk and threw out the poems that were indecent for a married man to compose," p. 42); and insists that he create with remunerative publication in mind ("You should be thinking about your poetry collection. We live in the real world," p. 41). In effect, Nina becomes his censor, his warden ("Men are men; you have to keep an eye on them," p. 42),[18] and, finally, his executioner.[19] His eventual death as an indirect consequence of her repressive machinations is prefigured by her early dream of possessing him wholly as an object—a goal that Tolstaya captures in several revealing passages, such as this, for example: "Oh, if she could only become the fully empowered mistress of the house once and for all, instead of just a casual, precarious girlfriend; if only she could put Grisha in a trunk, pack him in mothballs, cover him with a canvas cloth, bang the lid shut and sit on it, tugging at the locks to check: Are they secure?" (p. 40).[20]

Throughout, Tolstaya stresses the life-denying sterility of Nina's single-minded fixation on control, order, cleanliness, and "domestic" values: her apartment is "spotless"; the only detail we learn about her disappointing lover—Arkady Borisovich, a dermatologist (a profession inherently concerned with surface)—is his fanatical preoccupation with sanitary conditions, which manifests itself in compulsive hand scrubbing and a reliance on face masks and rubber gloves to ward off infection (unsuccessfully); she mistrusts the "great unwashed" of bohemian life; her "watchful gaze" ensures that guests wipe their feet carefully before entering the "crystal palace" (p. 41) of their domestic headquarters, maintained according to bourgeois precepts ("everything would be fine, . . . he'd be well fed and warm and clean," p. 41).

This straitjacketed order is systematically placed in diametric opposition to the carefree vitality of the artistic circle that Grisha,

Lizaveta, and Agniya typify—in Nina's hygienic eyes, a world of eccentrics and outcasts ("he [i.e., Grisha]—a carefree spirit ready to embrace any street mongrel, shelter any unsanitary vagrant," p. 40). The two worlds collide at every turn. Whereas Lizaveta abandons herself unconstrainedly to an inspiration resembling frenzy as she daubs her "Talonist" canvasses ("kogtizm"), Nina fastidiously protests, "Why can't she be more calm about it?" (p. 39). Whereas the ravishing actress manquée Agniya admires Grisha's openhandedness and deems him a genius, Nina shouts, "Did you understand me, sweetheart? Don't you dare write things like that!" (p. 41). Whereas Grisha prizes human contact to such a degree that in advance he sells his skeleton to the Academy of Sciences so that instead of lying alone in his grave "[he] would stand among lots of people . . . students—a fun crowd—would slap him on the shoulder, flick his forehead, and treat him to cigarettes" (p. 42), Nina despises his companions as "scum," "like trash from a vacuum cleaner." Like the totalitarian state of E. Zamyatin's *We*, Nina militantly repudiates whatever threatens strict regimentation, predictability, and ready-made, invariable patterns. To borrow the nomenclature of Zamyatin's famous binary opposition, Nina advocates entropy and does everything in her power to crush energy.

Characteristically, Tolstaya literalizes the metaphor "they speak different languages" to drive home the couple's utter incompatibility: Nina interprets all of Grisha's metaphorical *cris de coeur* literally. When he couches his desperate sense of suffocation in the cosmic imagery of a garden gone to seed, razed forests, and a door frozen fast against which he pushes to the pounding of red heels, Nina's instant jealousy reveals the philistine literalist whose cognitive faculties are confined to matter: whose red heels? Her nominal grief over Grisha's death, in fact, diminishes with her realization that his removal frees up space in the apartment, space such as that which another widow, for instance, happily converted into a showcase of bibelots, thereby profitably replacing one displayable object (a husband) with several.[21] Thus Tolstaya adumbrates the possible direction of Nina's future activity.

As in "Hunting the Wooly Mammoth," here too Tolstaya universalizes the heroine's case through such remarks as "she, a marvellous, ordinary woman . . . , who had fought for her personal happiness, *as we were all taught to do*" (p. 42). Or again, when Nina decided to "have" Grisha, "the trap snapped shut. Well, *everybody knows*, how it *usually* happens" (p. 37, emphasis added), Through such devices Tolstaya indicates that Grisha is a casualty of the annihilating force of cultural cliché and gender stereotype pushed inflexibly to their logical limit. If Grisha ultimately succeeds in eluding Nina's complete possession, he does so at the cost of his life, because the stifling environment of Nina's sexual colonization leaves room only for posthumous autonomy. In Grisha, Tolstaya portrays a transgendered Clarissa, an object possessed through violation.

"Hunting the Wooly Mammoth," then, dramatizes a ghastly mismating predicated upon blind adherence to ironclad convention. Tolstaya adds a new dimension in "The Poet and the Muse" by projecting a similar relationship against a background of bohemian camaraderie blithely indifferent to regulative blueprints of behavior. In "Fire and Dust," she posits that uninhibited, free way of life as a realizable alternative to yet another instance of "doomed domesticity" ruled by programmed thinking.[22] The two antithetical models of existence find embodiment in Rimma and Svetlana. As their names intimate, Rimma (*Rim* = Rome) has imbibed the "civic" values that assign primacy to marriage, family, and stability. Armed with her identity as wife and mother, Rimma defers all other experience as she leisurely dreams of a materially comfortable future that entails accumulation but neglects experiential growth ("In the meantime, life was not quite real, it was life in anticipation").[23] Conversely, her friend Svetlana (*Svet* = light or world) has a broader vision and ardently embraces whatever chance casts her way, without sparing a thought for possible consequences. Since the narrative proceeds chiefly from Rimma's point of view, the reader initially may align herself with Rimma's subjectivity, with her conformist values, and consequently may perceive the objectified Svetlana as a wild madwoman (*bezumnaia*) too indiscriminate with her sexual favors. Svetlana's indiscreet nickname of Pipka ("Little Cunt" or "Pussy"), her constant nakedness or near-nakedness ("half-dressed as always," p. 298),[24] her "black" mouth with its dreadful teeth,[25] and her association with fire all signal her potent sexuality ("yet lots of people liked her, and often at the end of a festive evening one of the men couldn't be accounted for: Pipka had whisked him away while no one was looking . . . to her place in Perlovka," p. 299). Pipka's enigmatic origins and disappearances ("No one knew where Pipka went, just as no one knew where she actually came from—she had simply shown up and that was that," p. 299), her bravura accounts of her fantastic adventures ("Boy, does she ever lay it on! A thousand and one nights!," p. 300), her mysterious, evocatively named dwelling ("that was the type Pipka usually carried off to her semifantastic Perlovka, if it actually existed," p. 300; "then Petyunya also vanished and the guess was that Svetlana had carried him off to Perlovka. Everyone who ended up there disappeared for ages, and when they returned, they were not themselves for quite some time," p. 304), and the dramatic legends she trails behind her[26] ultimately coalesce into a seductive image of life's infinitely rich possibilities, especially when one learns to subtract the distorting lens through which Rimma filters Svetlana's portrait. That plenitude Tolstaya (like James Joyce in *Ulysses* and T. S. Eliot in *The Love Song of J. Alfred Prufrock*) evokes through the ancient imagery of sea and sirens, in which context Rimma remains a shorebound spectator (associated with inert objects and the dust of the story's title),[27] leading a life of perpetual postponement ("Life had gone and the voice of the future was singing for others," p. 309; "And the *siren's* song, deceitfully whispering sweet words to the stupid swimmer about what wouldn't come to pass, fell silent forever," p. 310, emphasis added). Her antithesis, Pipka, whose elements are, tellingly, fire and water, immerses herself in the boundless sea of human experience, leaping into the maelstrom without hesitation. Rimma's smug condescension to Pipka ("is Pipka really human" expands into a motif) and her thoroughgoing conventionality erode as she gradually recognizes that her safe, orderly existence and philistine dreams have precluded her participation in such a life. For her, in fact, life in its full sense never eventuates.

To contrast two alternate worldviews and modes of conduct, Tolstaya resorts to gendered models. Rimma's oppressively code-affirming beliefs find expression in quintessentially "feminine" dreams of domestic acquisition: Ashkenazy's room with fresh curtains, a renovated kitchen, a handsome husband with a Ph.D. whose worth is gauged by the envy of her coworkers, clothes that will enhance her looks, and, for the children, activities rendered prestigious through their expensiveness, and so on. This upward mobility presupposes an essential stasis, with hearth and home as the impregnable nucleus of an expanding empire sanctioned by timeworn social habits. Svetlana's way of life, by contrast, entails constant peregrinations away from a *pied-à-terre* that sooner resembles a male harem than a domestic haven. Physical danger and vigorous sexual activity, the shedding of possessions (symbolized by her clothes), and receptivity to the unknown mark her multiple adventures in far-flung continents. Her periodic returns to Rimma's apartment, in fact, duplicate the structure of masculine movement in the majority of nineteenth-century Russian novels, where the arrival of the footloose male as the active principle triggers plot action.[28]

Once more, then, Tolstaya mocks convention by discrediting the paradigm of stable home, marriage, motherhood, and domestic cares that most cultures have touted as women's definitive route to self-realization. As a tenable alternative Tolstaya postulates what historically has been rejected as entirely inappropriate or "unnatural" for a woman: an unattached life exposed to risk and potentially spanning the entire gamut of human experience. Or, to recast the conflicting options in terms of literary genre, Tolstaya suggests that the tale of adventure, and not bourgeois drama, may offer a viable feminine narrative model. Such, at least, is the private epiphany at which Rimma arrives, spurred partly by Pipka's counterexample, which by story's end convinces Rimma that instead of seeking her own destiny she has marked time within the spurious safety of an untenable cliché.

Largely through Rimma, then, "Fire and Dust" topples the aureoled Soviet image of Woman as tirelessly beaming Wife and Mother immovably rooted in the Rock of Family Happiness.[29] Implicit in the ironic undercutting of institutionalized roles here, as in the other two stories of the trio, is a plea for individualism, openness, and multiplicity that is stylistically abetted by a prose of dazzling luxuriance.[30] All three narratives, in fact, polemicize with gender assumptions through a partly stylistic assault on "received wisdom" regarding the disposition of sexes ostensibly based on intrinsic, gender-marked traits. In dismantling the antediluvian mechanism of a gender assignment constructed by essentialization, Tolstaya extends her field of reference to encompass *all* forms of superimposition that constringe the life of the imagination and impede the discovery and expression of selfhood. Tolstaya's emphases, then, not only flout fundamental tenets of conservative Soviet ideology, but run counter to some of the regnant principles allying the majority of contemporary Russian women writers.

However susceptible some of Tolstaya's texts may be to a feminist reading, to label Tolstaya a feminist or an activist seeking feminist redress is to misrepresent her dominant concerns, as several interviewers have discovered.[31] It would be just as myopic or willful, however, to equate Tolstaya's fiction with her journalism or the opinions of her "interview persona." Anyone conflating these diverse categories or genres embarks on what Mary Jacobus has dubbed a "flight toward empiricism" that naively assumes "an unbroken continuity between 'life' and 'text.'"[32] Throughout exchanges between Tolstaya and Western journalists and scholars reticulate two leitmotivs that highlight an additional disjunction—the divergence between Russian women authors and their Western readers that also surfaced in the American reception of Natalia Baranskaya's *A Week Like Any Other* (*Nedelia kak nedelia*, 1969), over two decades ago:[33] (1) Tolstaya's vehement assertion that she does not align herself with feminism, adamantly opposes it as a reductionist phenomenon, locates its origins in the thwarted anger of overtly aggressive, sexually confused women, and detects no evidence of it in Russia;[34] and (2) the commentators' surprise or chagrin at what Westerners might well call conservative views on gender espoused by a writer with a deserved reputation for extreme liberalism, or, perhaps more accurately, subversive independence. That independence Tolstaya articulates forcefully and volubly, thereby incurring the censure of such ideologues as Vasily Belov and the right-wing contingent of the Writers' Union.[35] To those readers who had never heard Tolstaya dilate on women's issues, her apparently ultraconservative endorsement in the *New York Review of Books* of Francine du Plessix Gray's problematic volume entitled *Soviet Women: Walking the Tightrope* came as a shock.[36]

While readily conceding her "imperfect" knowledge of Western feminism even as she categorically dissociates herself from its perceived tenets, Tolstaya frequently voices ideas and analyzes culture in ways that converge with feminist interpretive strategies. For instance, the delay in Tolstaya's acceptance into the Writers' Union followed her spirited criticism of Belov's misogynistic novel *Everything Lies Ahead* (*Vse vperedi*, 1987) for being "against the idea of women as human beings. He thinks all women are devils who should be destroyed because they seduce poor men."[37] "Looking upon a woman as an evil vessel," objected Tolstaya, "betrays one's hypocrisy." Moreover, at a recent conference on contemporary Soviet literature, Tolstaya's lecture on "Beauty and the Hooligan: Elements of Russian Subculture" proposed that male cultural icons such as Stenka Razin, Sergei Esenin, and Vladimir Vysotsky achieved their heroic status through enacting conventional macho rites: ostentatious drinking and carousing, radical forms of violence against a female beauty, and the affirmation of a male brotherhood—all of which directly result in male bonding with the companions who explicitly or subliminally pressure the "hero" into complicity with this masculinist ethos.[38] A Westerner doubtless would characterize Tolstaya's comments on both occasions as a classic feminist critique of repressive patriarchal practices. Yet Tolstaya unequivocally denied that in pinpointing an archetypal misogynistic ritual she had (perhaps unknowingly) elaborated a feminist analysis of the phenomenon.[39] The stumbling block, then, is less feminist theory or praxis per se than the label "feminist." Discredited by class associations in earlier phases of Soviet history and still rendered suspect by disillusionment with any comprehensive political agenda, the term "feminism" as entertained by Russians is culturally overmarked and consequently stigmatized.[40]

Because Tolstaya's perceptions are profoundly steeped in her country's historicocultural traditions, she subscribes to various national myths (e.g., the age-old Russian cult of irrationality), while assessing their consequences in a spirit of ostensible impartiality. In short, she exercises her right to contradiction and paradox in defiance of a unitary self. Since the endless mediation intrinsic to fiction permits Tolstaya as prosaist to eliminate her own voice—recognizable from her interviews and journalism—the dogmatic imperatives of her nonauthorial persona dissolve in the amplitude of the fictional medium. With her fine-tuned sensitivity to the use, misuse, and abuse of discourse, Tolstaya in her prose pays homage above all to the formidable powers of language, ironizing the anesthetizing effects on the human psyche of catchwords, slogans, and myriad forms of ready-made phraseology symptomatic of the herd mentality, of an abrogation of individual responsibility. One cannot live outside language, into which, Tolstaya asserts, we are born.[41] Platitudes spawn and in their turn derive from automatic, unindividualized verbal usage inseparable from unexamined blueprints for human intercourse. Tolstaya's cognizance of that process explains why those texts in which her revulsion at cliché as philosophical and psychological imprisonment finds some form of articulation lend themselves admirably to a feminist reading.[42] For what could be more clichéd, after all, than our inherited monolithic conception of Womanhood?

PART III

The Maternal Body

JANE T. COSTLOW

The Pastoral Source

Representations of the Maternal Breast in Nineteenth-Century Russia

> *Quand la belle source coule égale et facile, quand l'enfant épargne sa mère et la dégage seulement de l'excès de la plenitude, elle tombe comme dans un narcotisme, un demi-rêve, où sa vie et la leur n'ont plus rien de distinct. Sa personnalité fluide lui échappe; elle est tous les trois à la fois, et surtout les deux qu'elle aime.* —Jules Michelet, "L'amour"
>
> *The usefulness of the breasts consists not only in the fact that they give great beauty and a pleasant appearance to the female sex, especially when both breasts are of average size, and are furthermore equal in size, rounded, supple, tender and white . . .*
> —Nestor Maksimovich-Ambodik, *Iskusstva povivaniia ili nauka o babich'em dielii*

■ At the beginning of his novel *No Where to Go* (*Nekuda*, 1864) Nikolai Leskov refers to an image from classical antiquity that registers much of the ideological and polemical weight of maternity for midcentury writers and readers. Leskov is describing the two young women, Lizaveta and Evgenia, who will be the heroines of his novel. The novel itself is one of a series of "antinihilist" texts that appeared in Russia in the 1860s.[1] The stories of Lizaveta and Evgenia are made to bear much of the ideational weight of *No Where to Go*: Lizaveta becomes a *nigilistka*, a participant in a Petersburg commune, a woman who spurns woman's traditional domestic role for the marginality and purported sexual freedom of the nihilists. Evgenia, on the other hand, becomes a paragon of virtue and domesticity, a mother and "angel in the house" who proves to be the embodiment of both maternal and civic virtue. In lampooning the radicals of the 1860s, Leskov is concerned with the family as central to social, political, and moral order; that the heroine of his novel becomes a mother—and that the *nigilistka* dies childless—is far from incidental.

The image from classical antiquity that Leskov appeals to at the novel's opening makes particularly succinct the larger operations and allegiances of this narrative, and focuses on the maternal body and its appropriation in ways that will be central to my discussion. Leskov writes: "Marina Abramovna [the girls' nanny] called Evgenia Petrovna a beauty not without reason. She was truly beautiful, and if an artist had needed to portray on canvas the famous daughter, nursing at the breast her father condemned to death, he would have found no better model [*naturshchitsa*] than Evgenia Petrovna Glovatskaya."[2] The exemplary heroine/mother is described at the novel's beginning as an exemplary daughter performing what only mothers can do: she suckles at her breast in a gesture/image that combines maternity and daughterly love, nourishment and symbolic salvation. In appealing to this figure of filial and civic virtue Leskov conjures an image of maternal love that is uniquely physical, but that also pronounces unabashedly who the maternal breast is *for*: woman's body, her capacities for maternal nutrition and nurturance, sustain the father. The physiology of maternity, the mother's body itself, belong to the father; Leskov's image extends to his heroine the beatitude of obedience to patriarchal order, an order threatened in his novel by *nigilistki* and their communes.[3]

Within the context of political and ideological disputes of the 1860s Leskov's text constitutes a particularly blunt admission of maternity as ideological ground, ground to be claimed by defenders of traditional roles for women within the traditional patriarchal family. If woman constituted a "question" (as in *zhenskii vopros*), it was one that originated in societal visions of her role as mother: even the liberal M. L. Mikhailov, in his groundbreaking discussion of women in the family and society, foregrounded not the possibility that women might not be mothers, but the question of how they might be better mothers if more liberally educated.[4]

The nursing woman is Leskov's image of womanly and filial duty: the essence of maternity concentrates for him in this image of the breast as sustainer of patriarchal order. Leskov's text is not alone in drawing on and creating powerful, complex associations with the maternal breast, and in proposing the breast as vehicle of feminine civic virtue. The attention of nineteenth-century gynecologists, and of Freudian psychology, focused on the uterus as origin and center of femininity; for the eighteenth century the breast captured most attention, symbolizing as it did women's role in the family (as suckler of children) and the capacity of women to attract men and forge the bonds of marriage.[5] The discussion of maternal nursing that opens Rousseau's *Émile* is in this sense characteristic; it served as authoritative text for advocates of women's traditional maternal role, and is clearly echoed in numerous Russian writers. Nineteenth-century Russia is in this perhaps indebted still to eighteenth-century France: for Leskov, for Tolstoy, for medical practitioners, and for social polemicists, it was woman's breast that represented her role in the family and society. The woman's breast emerges in their texts as locus of sentiment, desire, nostalgia, and nourishment—as that part of the body used to nourish and nurture various fantasies of power and privilege. What, in all this, the breast (as part of the body and as maternal experience) meant to women is at first glance harder to ascertain. But if I begin, by way of introduction, with an excursus into the ideological significance of the maternal breast, I will nonetheless return to texts by women, in whose words the mother's breast emerges as the site of economic and emotional contradictions left unremarked by mothers' sons.[6]

Both gynecologists and polemicists in nineteenth-century Russia assumed that it was a woman's duty to nurse her own children. Nestor Maksimovich-Ambodik, an eighteenth-century gynecologist and the author of a textbook for midwives, begins his discussion of the female breast with a statement of this maternal duty, a duty ordained both by Nature and by civil and moral law: "Finally, laws and ordinances themselves, civil as well as natural and moral, impel the fulfillment of this sacred duty of those who give birth [*sei sviashchennoi dolzhnosti rozhennits*]."[7] In nursing their children mothers follow both the law and the examples of suckling animals and the wives of "primitive peoples" (*Iskusstva povivaniia*, p. 165). The usefulness of maternal breast-feeding, Maksimovich suggests, extends both to the child and to the mother herself, who will thereby be spared those illnesses that befall "ladies [*gospozham*], who largely because of their capriciousness and laziness avoid this duty, and do not deserve the name of true mothers" (p. 164).

The anonymous author of a mid-nineteenth-century text on what we might call sexuality, *Man and Woman Apart and Together at Various Stages of Their Lives*, similarly assumes woman's natural and civil duty to nurse her children. The author urges women of "civilized" lands to imitate the wives of "primitive peoples" ("Negroes, Americans, Siberians"), who are held up as paragons of fertility and prodigious nursers: African women give birth to two hundred children, American women have been seen to have four breasts, native Americans and Negro women nurse their children until the age of three or four, "because they are good nurses [*potomu-chto oni khoroshie kormilitsi*]."[8] Maksimovich-Ambodik uses the language of science and analytical description; the author of *Man and Woman Apart* marshals bizarre pseudo-anthropological evidence—but for both authors the feminine/maternal ideal is embodied by the women of "primitive peoples."[9] Women are charged with sustaining humankind's original (but forsaken) closeness to nature; "primitive" women, the anonymous author suggests, suffer no pain in childbirth because they have not tasted of the fruit of good and evil.[10] Learned women are infertile or hysterical (the author, like most medical writers of the nineteenth century, identifies hysteria as a disease of the uterus):[11] by imitating "primitive women," by forsaking learning and suckling their children, the women of "civilized" Russia can remove Eve's sin, and return to fertile prelapsarian ignorance. Woman is not born to *eat* the fruit but to serve as fruit, herself to be consumed.

The possibility that women might *not* breast-feed their children introduces of course the figure of the wet nurse, and the interchangeability and instability of the maternal breast.[12] Women who refused to breast-feed—according to the author of *Man and Woman Apart*—act "against the laws of nature" in handing over their children to "hired hands [*naemnye ruki*]" (p. 49). While Maksimovich-Ambodik concedes that, for reasons of health or "other of life's circumstances," a woman might be unable to nurse her child, the anonymous nineteenth-century author views the possibility with horror, and raises the specter of ensuing social disorder and racial monstrosity. "It is evident that the use of wet nurses, which breaks the holiest of bonds, the bond of child and mother, is harmful for society's well-being, making children indifferent, disrespectful, and little devoted to their parents" (p. 54). His discussion of the ills of wet nursing ends with a cautionary tale of "white-skinned" English children, nursed in Jamaica by a Negro woman; the children, he assures the reader, will turn into creoles with dark skin. This author, like others, assumed that the child imbibed the soul of the woman with her milk:[13] despite his appeal to the ideal of "primitive" women, the author insists on maternal feeding to maintain racial and social purity. The severing of bonds and mixing of fluids implied by wet nursing "is harmful for society's well-being." The maternal breast becomes the cornerstone of social order, of racial and class distinction.

It is not coincidental that the author raises the prospect of filial revolt in connection with the maternal breast in 1859, at a moment when many voices, including women's, were calling for women's education and the liberation of women from traditional familial roles. Wet nursing, nihilism, and the destruction of the family are also conjoined in a potent and threatening nexus by Leo Tolstoy, in his 1863 play "The Infected Family" ("Zarazhennoe semeistvo"). What was at stake in these texts was the extent to which women were to be relegated to the realms of private, "natural" life—or be permitted to enter the public world, the world of culture and politics.[14] The focus on the maternal breast drew powerfully on associations with nature and woman's "physiological" destiny: Mikhailov too was obliged to acknowledge the maternal breast as sacred ground, though his intention was to stretch the metaphors of nursing and nourishment beyond the merely physical: "Of course no one can replace the breast or caresses or love of the mother for the child; but do you desire the development in the child of moral principles?" (*Zhenshchiny*, p. 9). The mother must be educated, Mikhailov argued, or one can ask of her no other part in a child's upbringing (*vospitanie*) than breast-feeding (*krome kormleniia grud'iu*, p. 30).

The idealization of the maternal breast, the injunctions against wet nurses, the unproblematic conflation of woman, nature, and nourishment are nowhere more forcefully played out than in Tolstoy's *Anna Karenina* (1873–77), a novel that in so many ways addresses the position of women in nineteenth-century Russian society. The duty of women to nurse their own children was for Tolstoy axiomatic: his wife, Sonya, records in her diaries their struggle at the birth of their first child, when Sonya, suffering from painful mastitis, weakened in her resolve to nurse the infant.[15] Tolstoy, on the other hand, was adamant, and the breast of his wife (as well as the infant-mother bond) became the occasion for a duel of pain and principle. Tolstoy won out: Sonya nursed through her pain, in a victory that is, again, hard not to see as symbolic of men's control of women's bodies. In this skirmish as in the novel he wrote ten years later, Tolstoy appropriated the breast—woman's "natural source"—to his own ideological ends.

The explicit semantics of maternal nursing in the novel revolve around Kitty, who nurses her child, and Anna, who doesn't. Kitty feels the flow of milk that binds her to her son; she *knows* her son with a knowledge grounded in physiology (the synchrony of hunger and fluid) that moves toward moral and spiritual intuition: "To Agatha Mikhailovna, to the nurse, to his grandfather, to his father even, Mitya was just a little human being requiring only material care; but for his mother he had long been a personage endowed with moral faculties with whom she already had a whole history of spiritual relations."[16] The bond of nursing mother and child here represents a privileged return to the unity of body and soul: the milk is a source of deep knowledge for both of them.

Anna, on the other hand, has no such privileged bond with her daughter by Vronsky: when Dolly visits them at their country estate, Anna explains her difficulties with an Italian wet nurse; the currently employed caregivers, a wet nurse and head nurse, are not "to be seen: they were in the next room, where they could be heard carrying on a conversation in the queer French which was their only means of communication" (p. 649). Against the physicality, intimacy, and preverbal communication of Kitty and son we have the foreign tongues and maternal remove of Anna, who shocks Dolly by not knowing where her daughter's toys are. Anna's refusal to nurse, her use of birth control, her preoccupation with "masculine" activities on the estate are but evidence of the depths of her estrangement from the self constructed of women's traditional role as mothers.

But if Kitty and Anna represent opposite poles of good and bad mothering, the nurturing and absent breast, it is Dolly and Levin who allude most fully to the significance of the maternal breast for Tolstoy. The third section of *Anna Karenina* orchestrates an extended meditation on the nature of work: the varieties of work—Koznyshev's intellectual labor, Karenin's bureaucratic travail, Vronsky's soldiering—are all held up against Levin's experience of unalienated labor in mowing with the peasants, an experience his economic treatises set out to articulate and build upon, an experience that stands as his only bulwark against the fear of death.[17]

This section of the novel also recognizes a parallel form of unalienated women's labor, in the person of Dolly. Tolstoy turns to his description of Dolly's life and work in the country immediately after his description of Levin's mowing. From the world and work of peasant men the reader is directed to the world and work of women. The description of Dolly's work as mother ends with her conversing with peasant women: their maternal experiences erase class boundaries; they share a common language; Dolly is "loath to part with the peasant women, so interesting to her was their conversation, so completely identical were all their interests" (p. 287).

Physical agricultural labor represents for Levin (and Tolstoy) the possibility of overcoming the alienation of urban bureaucratic life; the feminine equivalent of this is Dolly's work as mother, work that combines the physical, moral, and spiritual as did Levin's epiphanic mowing. In a letter of 1886 to Vladimir Chertkov, Tolstoy describes a woman's love for her infant as the love of a worker. Men and women, according to Tolstoy, perform different *kinds* of labor, but in both cases that labor must be informed with love and by immersion in the process itself: "This love for the child in infancy is not at all egoism, but is the love of the worker [*rabotnik*] for the work he performs as he performs it."[18] He goes on to compare the work of a woman mothering to his own work making boots: without love, the work would be spoiled. "Mothering" for Dolly is a process that is spiritual and moral as well as material; but it is the materiality of mothering, and the experience of breast-feeding, that creates for Dolly a bond with peasant women. Just as Levin's work erased boundaries of class, maternal "labor," properly construed, collapses differences among women, revealing a commonality that is, again, both physiological and spiritual.

Tolstoy's representation of this classless communality of mothers draws on some of the same assumptions found in Maksimovich and in the anonymous 1859 treatise. Like the "bizarre" *Man and Woman Apart*,[19] *Anna Karenina* assumes the identity of women, nature, and nourishment, an identity on which the possibility of Dolly's immediate rapport with the peasant women is based. Kitty shares this associative field: in the conversation that follows her chat with the peasant women, Dolly tries to get Levin to talk about Kitty, a topic he wants to avoid. What Levin talks about instead is the correct feeding regime to increase the productivity of milk cows (pp. 289–90). At some not-too-subliminal level we (and Levin) make the association of Kitty with abundant mammalian fluidity. For Tolstoy, as for Maksimovich and *Man and Woman Apart*, the models for maternal devotion are suckling animals and "primitive" women untainted by learning.

Unlike the earlier texts, however, this appeal to peasant women as ideals of maternity, nature, and unalienated femininity is made subversive of class distinctions, a polemical end that works against Tolstoy's apparent condemnation of wet nursing. Anna's use of a wet nurse and the *nigilistka*'s refusal to nurse in "The Infected Family" illustrate women's desire to control their own sexuality and enter the public world, and their refusal to submit to the constraints, both physiological and emotional, of maternity. Tolstoy's depiction of their refusal is unequivocally negative.

The section of *Anna Karenina* devoted to work begins, however, with a very different image of wet nursing, one that is fundamentally positive. In describing the meaning of the country and the peasantry for Levin, Tolstoy insists that the *narod* is not an object of idealization for his hero but "the chief partner in their common labor," and points to the origin of Levin's affection in the milk of his peasant nurse: "He regarded the peasant merely as the chief partner in their common labour, and in spite of all the respect and the affection that was in his blood for the peasant (imbibed probably, as he said himself, with the milk of his peasant nurse), he, as partner in their common labor, while sometimes enthusiastic over . . . these men, was often . . . exasperated with the peasant" (pp. 257–58). The effect of Tolstoy's syntax is to qualify unambiguous affection, but he nonetheless grounds the adult relationship in the irrational bond of infancy. His rhetoric mixes elemental fluids—blood and milk—and alludes to the notion that the soul of the one who nurses is sucked in by the child. What Tolstoy does here is to establish a physical basis for the erasure of class distinctions that Levin experiences in mowing. Woman's work in mothering and nursing is held up by Tolstoy as a form of unalienated labor: here it is the foundation for the unalienated bond that Levin himself will later come to know.

What these literary and polemical texts establish is a vision of the breast as pastoral object: the breast signifies an idyllic maternal-infant bond; the mother herself is a figure in and of nature; breast, mother, and child evoke the possibility of unalienated, alinguistic, harmonious existence. The mother's milk emerges, as does all of nature's bounty in pastoral, without human effort or intervention.[20] The breast also serves as pastoral object in these texts in a somewhat more specific sense, one I derive from Bakhtin: pastoral objects, Bakhtin writes in "Forms of Time and Chronotope in the Novel," are highlighted in pastoral "as objects not severed from the labor that produced them."[21] Women's work in mothering, the work of the body to reproduce and raise children, is not "productive" in the same sense as is men's work in the public sphere, a point Tolstoy inadvertently makes in his comparison of children and boots.[22] But in suckling their young, women produce a nutritive substance to be consumed, a substance that could be bought or sold (as wet nurses made painfully evident), but a substance that in issuing from the maternal breast remains, in Bakhtin's terms, "not severed from the labor that produced [it]." Wet nurses, to whom I will soon return, corrupt this idyllic situation by rendering economic and public what in the pastoral vision is private, untainted by commerce. The suckling mother nonetheless represents this pastoral moment when child, mother, body, labor, nutrition, are all one, and it is as part of a pastoral vision of society (and women's place in it) that the maternal breast enters the texts of Leskov, Tolstoy, and the author of *Man and Woman Apart*. The hostility or anxiety with which these men treat wet nursing derives at least in part from the power of the wet nurse to disturb this idyll by reintroducing economic relations and alienation. The wet nurse was a body and breast "rented" and put to use. In Maksimovich's gynecological text the wet nurse is a material object to be closely scrutinized before purchase; in the texts by women with which I want to close her body is the site of exploitation and painful moral choice.

The emphasis of Maksimovich's discourse is on the wet nurse's physical properties; his advice betrays the extent to which one purchased a *body* in "renting" (to recall the rhetoric of *Man and Woman Apart*) a woman's breasts. The child's health, Maksimovich points out, depends on the wet nurse's body: she should be carefully inspected naked (*Iskusstva povivaniia*, p. 172). She should be between 20 and 35 years old; she should have had a child herself not long ago (preferably not her first); and her periods should not have resumed since childbirth (pp. 173–74). She should have "average" sized breasts, with soft, uncalloused nipples. Maksimovich details four procedures for testing the woman's milk (pp. 174–75), and urges parents not to be stingy with payments. Finally, he insists that the nurse's skin be white; dark and yellow skins are signs of ill temper (p. 175).

Maksimovich laments that it is impossible to peek into "others' sacred inward parts [*chuzhie sokrovennye vnutrennosti*]," but his instructions for the inspection of potential wet nurses effectively rob them of privacy; they have become public bodies, items of economic exchange. As women's treatment of the nursing breast makes evident, they also become items of erotic exchange: even the maternal breast is not free from the appropriations of the male gaze.

There are three texts by women that I want to examine here: "On the Road" ("V doroge," 1896), a short story by Lidia Avilova; "Mother–Wet Nurse" ("Mat'–Kormilitsa," 1880?), a free translation by Anna Barykova of a poem in French by François Coppée; and the opening chapter of *The Talnykov Family* (*Semeistvo Tal'nykovykh*, 1847) by Avdotya Panaeva. The concerns that emerge most forcefully from these women's writings touch on the economic and erotic exploitation of women's bodies, and the material circumstances that lead women to work as wet nurses.

The Pastoral Source

Lidia Avilova, in "On the Road," tells the story of a woman going from her village to Moscow, hoping to find work as a wet nurse.[23] The conversations that make up the story take place in a railway station, as the woman waits with one young child for a morning train. She leaves two older children behind in the famished world of rural Russia, and most of the emotional and psychological power of this story derives from its portrait of a woman forced to desert her children in the hopes of money for "soft bread" (p. 221). Tormented by the haunting memory of a famished daughter denied bread, the woman copes with a terrible variation on the Solomonic dilemma, where love forces separation and renunciation.

The impact of Avilova's story derives from her concentration on painful maternal emotion (what has driven the woman to Moscow) and the woman's absolute vulnerability and naïveté. In the railroad waiting room she is made the emotional victim of two men, one young and one old, who seem to represent the forces who will prey on her henceforth: the older man is the voice of absolute morality, who does not enter into her terrible situation, has no access to her painful inner life and the realities of her choice, and yet passes judgment: "But how could you abandon your children?" (p. 221), a voice the woman can only counter with a fantasy of abundant earnings to send home. The other man in the waiting room is younger, and confronts her with the fate that seems to await her in Moscow. When the woman tells the older man she's going to Moscow as a wet nurse (*v mamki*), the younger responds by commenting that she's not bad looking, that he'd already noticed her; he later calls her a "beauty" (p. 222). The young man's words upset and frighten the woman.

The woman is going to Moscow to "rent" her breasts and sell her milk; the young man appraises her, however, not as a maternal vessel but as an erotic object. The exchange suggests both the equivocation of the male gaze directed at nursemaids' breasts and the possibility that, if she fails as a wet nurse ("You think there aren't many like you in the city?," p. 221), she might turn to prostitution.[24] Avilova's story refuses the pastoral representation of the maternal breast—her countryside is a place of hunger, cruelty, and death—and emphasizes instead the woman's economic and sexual vulnerability. In pointing to the double function of the breast, as object of male desire and infant succor, she highlights the contradiction Barykova explores in greater detail in the poem "Mother–Wet Nurse."

Barykova's poem is a translation of a poem by François Coppée, "Mère-nourrice," a circumstance that introduces the complexity of any translation's relationship to the original, and the nature of women's transmission of a male poet's words in particular. Barykova's translation is liberal, departing from the original in structure and imagery in ways I attempt to point out in notes to this essay. Barykova did an enormous amount of translation work; she insisted, however, that her choice of material was always motivated by philosophical and emotional kinship. She in fact refused to translate another of Coppée's poems on the same subject, "La Nourrice":[25] Barykova read the French poem at a moment when she herself was witness to a woman who had stopped nursing her own child in order to work as a wet nurse. Barykova was intensely critical of the woman, who did not need the money, and who was "condemning to certain death her own son." Barykova paints a pathetic picture of the mother feasting and flourishing while her child dies, a situation in which she felt some measure of guilt: "the mother is very happy with her fate—she chews away, swells up with tea and jam, gossips, is happy—as is fitting of any excellent wet nurse; and we all watch the slow murder of her child, we all take part in it, myself included."[26] The translation from Coppée that Barykova did complete presents a more sympathetic portrait of maternal labor, one in which economic realities are harsher, but where the mother refuses to abandon her child.

The focus of "Mother–Wet Nurse" is on the breast itself.[27] The poem is written in two parts: in the first part, the woman is an *artistka*, a performer in a tawdry café who displays her naked breast and shoulders to the paying public; in the second part of the poem, the same woman appears as a nursing mother, who turns from the narrator's gaze to offer her breast to her infant. Barykova plays on this duality—of performer/mother, public/private, seen/secret—in the structure of the poem and in the passage that serves as title. The "mother" offers freely what the "wet nurse" sells; the title brings the two together, while the poem itself recounts the narrator's surprise that this "public" woman whose body is for sale is *not* in fact a wet nurse (selling her maternal breast) but a mother.

In the first of the poem's two sections the woman's breast is object of male desire, offered "without shame"; in part two the nursing woman is represented as performing the "great sacred service of every woman" and as an image of the Madonna in whose sad eyes one sees God. Barykova clearly wants to hold on to the image of maternity as sacred: she calls her mother a madonna, and turns her from the narrator's gaze, creating a space of demure privacy that is absent in the original. But Barykova cannot deny— in fact the whole poem articulates—the economic conditions of women's labor, the ways in which women "work" with their bodies, the ways in which society converts women into "shameful goods" (*pozornyi tovar*). Barykova's mother is alienated from her child and from her own body by a society of men that exploits women's bodies for their own visual and oral pleasures. Barykova does not attempt to resolve the contradictions of this woman's life, but lets them stand as an indictment of society: the *artistka*, wet nurse, mother, Madonna, and God are all problematically one.

I have argued in these pages that for male writers in Russia the maternal breast signified a privileged pastoral moment, women's immersion in nature and physiology, her instinctual unity with the child. I would not want to imply that women were free of the longings implicit in such a vision (Barykova clearly embraces the rhetoric of sacred maternity), only that they might have *experienced* such pastoral visions differently.[28] Avdotya Panaeva, in her novel about her childhood, opens with an account of a child's funeral, juxtaposing an indifferent mother and a wet nurse who grieves for the child she nursed only because the death represents an economic loss. Panaeva's first chapter is heavy with maternal death, maternal absence, maternal indifference. But into this bleak narrative she inserts a long passage that fantasizes physical reunion with the mother. It is unclear whether the passage is memory or creation, whether it occurred in reality or in a dream. But coming fast on the heels of her description of a distant, unloving mother and of a wet nurse whose interests were purely fiscal, we read this imagined reunion as another of those "pastoral" dreams of the mother that mark men's texts:[29] "We were put to bed, but I couldn't get to sleep; I very much wanted to see Mama. . . . Suddenly I hear: Mama has come! I ran downstairs, and the first thing I did was to run to her. She seemed surprised by my happiness and kissed me. I started to cry. . . . Mama took me in her arms. I put my arms around her neck, held tightly to her and started sobbing worse than ever" (p. 105). What marks this moment as crucially different is the use to which Panaeva puts her pastoral vision, the role it plays in the longer narrative. For Panaeva, the pastoral mother does not refer to a social program; she is a nurturing presence who, in the larger narrative, simply never was. The pastoral maternal breast exists for only a brief moment, eclipsed by a long and horrendous narrative of abuse and indifference.[30]

The different use to which Panaeva puts her vision of reunion with the mother is, I think, an important one, crucial in understanding the way nineteenth-century ideology appropriated the maternal breast, and the way women may have experienced that appropriation. These women's texts suggest not that women were indifferent to such visions but that the economic and emotional realities of their lives meant that they could not indulge in fantasy for long. Jules Michelet, whose writings on women were greeted with such enthusiasm by Tolstoy, writes of the nursing mother as someone whose identity is lost in her child's. For Tolstoy and Leskov, for the author of *Man and Woman Apart*, the identity of the mother is submerged in the authors' own visions of social order. For Avilova, Barykova, and Panaeva, the mother's identity is not lost, nor does it dissolve in maternal milk: the mother herself is the site no longer of unalienated repose, but of contradictory longings and bitter reality.

BARBARA HELDT

Motherhood in a Cold Climate

The Poetry and Career of Maria Shkapskaya

■ The Mother Image remains timelessly static in Russian culture. From the Icon to the poem of remembrance by the grown child, it serves as a perfect construct of the male imagination, one sometimes also enthusiastically endorsed by women.[1] Its opposite—what French critics of our day call "feminine writing" (the transition or transferal of the feminine body into the text)—may appear to use similar imagery and lexicon, but such writing will always proceed differently: remythologizing, reflecting the displacements of the feminine, filling in the gaps of women's silence. If Marina Tsvetaeva's poetry has yet to be fully discussed as an innovative poetic embodiment of those disjunctures and silences, that of her contemporary Maria Shkapskaya has been virtually undiscussed. Shkapskaya began as a poet, but when she chose to continue to live and remain alive in the Soviet Union, she had to accept becoming a different kind of writer, a writer of prose sketches in a set journalistic mold rather than a writer of poetry in a new voice. For various reasons, other women writers of the 1920s made similar journalistic careers; however, none of the others left behind a corpus of poetry.[2]

As a writer of the feminine, Maria Shkapskaya chose as her poetic material the very voice and body of maternal authority that was becoming taboo in the chaos of competing "revolutionary" politics of the early 1920s and that was finally silenced and incorporated into the society of the Great Father. For all its protection and encouragement of certain kinds of writing by women that were useful to the myth of the common cause, Soviet Russia did not produce a poet whose writing is as powerfully feminine as Shkapskaya's until Elena Shvarts, a contemporary Petersburg poet whose work was only recently published, in a small booklet.[3] The peculiarly female-centered work of these poets includes a focus on the body from which their ways of thinking proceed. Both are religious, but not in the passive way acceptable for women in a patriarchal church. Both visualize and describe a female communality anathema to the communism of the patriarchal state.

Although Shkapskaya's journalistic prose was republished in the 1960s, the best of her writing, her postrevolutionary poetry, has been scarcely republished to this day, when so much else has come out.[4] Shkapskaya's poetry of the early 1920s includes all her best collections: *Mater Dolorosa* (*Mater Dolorosa*, 1921), *Drum of the Stern Lord* (*Baraban strogogo Gospodina*, 1922), *Blood-Gore* (*Krov'-ruda*, 1922), and *Earthly Crafts* (*Zemnye remesla*, 1925). There is clearly an ideological as well as a generic break between her poetry and her prose. Unpublished autobiographical writings found in her Moscow archive and letters to friends from their archives in Petersburg shed further light on this break. With this information, we can begin to understand why Maria Shkapskaya is perhaps Russia's most underrated poet. Our argument will focus on the mother as a female-generated image of flesh and blood, whose authority proceeds from the maternal body and subverts the power and authority of the male-generated abstract icon of the maternal. But it should be mentioned before we proceed that our study cannot be more than a preliminary attempt to broach topics that should be the subject of future books—for example, a comparative literary treatise on motherhood as conceived by the male and female poets of Russia, a Foucaultian study of Russian sexuality between 1890 and 1930, or a theory of Russian motherhood and female sexuality itself.

Shkapskaya's Moscow archive contains two pieces of autobiographical writing that are as deserving of publication as the rest of her work. One is handwritten and dated 1927/1930, with parallel uncollated variants.[5] The other is an authorized typescript dated December 1952. Had Shkapskaya lived a few more months, beyond the death of Stalin, would we have seen a third, different autobiography and a reborn poet? All that we have to help us answer this question are Shkapskaya's two attempts at self-writing, one of them written in the dark days shortly before her death. The following account is based on the first autobiographical sketch, supplemented by (and sometimes contrasted to) the later version.

The 1927 autobiography begins with her birth in St. Petersburg, on October 3, 1891, as a fourth-generation Petersburger, the oldest child in a large family of a low-ranking official (*chinovnik*) whose mother had been born a serf. Russian on her father's side and German on her mother's, Maria Mikhailovna Andreevskaya grew up

> in great poverty in those Petersburg slums that many people calling themselves Petersburgers often know nothing about . . . right near the city garbage dump, which for me and other children of the local poor was the source of existence: in it we gathered kindling to heat our corners, tin cans and rags to sell to ragmen. From the age of eleven I already looked out for myself—father was insane and mother paralyzed, and seven people had to be fed. (Pp. 7–8)

She had other jobs as well: "I worked in laundries, washed floors, wrote requests and letters at the post office, worked as an extra in a Ukrainian troupe at one rouble per show" (p. 18). While doing these kinds of work, she also finished school and, over her father's protests, attended the gymnasium with the help of her teacher, who initially paid for Shkapskaya's education out of her own pocket. Shkapskaya's generally "Dostoevskian" family and her mentally ill father made her a comparative streetchild among the more well-bred children of the gymnasium. She wrote in a rare autobiographical poem in *Blood-Gore*, "I stood up like Lot's wife" ("Vstala zhenoiu Lota"), about a visit to her father in the insane asylum, and his screams, which entered her own blood.

She married in 1910 upon finishing school, and took her husband's name. Although Shkapskaya's talents were already clearly literary, she spent two years in the Faculty of Medicine, out of a feeling of wanting to be useful to society. She had worked in socialist cultural circles even in her gymnasium years and was finally arrested and imprisoned in 1912 and again in 1913, then exiled, first internally in Russia and later abroad. A Moscow philanthropist intervened to finance an entire group of exiled young men and women, giving them money to finish their education abroad since they were not permitted to do so in Russia. Both Shkapskaya and her husband went to Toulouse.

With the outbreak of World War I the philanthropist's stipend ceased, and they were stranded in Paris without the right to return to Russia. But work was available in Paris, and there Shkapskaya developed both her journalistic and poetic talents, publishing in Russian newspapers and journals in Paris and also in Petrograd. She met Maximilian Voloshin, Nikolai Minsky, and Ilya Ehrenburg in Paris. Later, in 1920–21, she worked with Alexander Blok, and she names Elena Guro, Walt Whitman, and Francis Jammes as poets with whom she feels a sense of kinship. Shkapskaya notes that Arthur Schopenhauer, Sigmund Freud, and Charles Darwin were especially influential on her mode of thought. In the 1952 version she states that Ehrenburg, Vladimir Korolenko, and D. I. Zaslavsky helped her publish when she was abroad, and that Blok set her on the right path in the early 1920s. Others are not mentioned.

Shkapskaya returned to Russia in 1916, where she finished her term of exile in the provinces. She continued writing for *Day* (*Den'*) and during the civil war period traveled widely as their correspondent. In 1918 *Day* was closed down. By the summer of 1919 she had two children. She had qualified as a mental health nurse as a schoolgirl and worked during 1920–22 in the Pskov region for the central museum administration (*Glavmuzei*) trying to preserve churches and other buildings. Her first book of poetry, *Mater Dolorosa*, was published in 1921, and three other collections came out the following year. She traveled to Germany for part of 1923 and only in that year began to support herself fully by her writing. By 1927 she was an established writer and was acquainted with all others of that ilk, but still found the Writers' Union of that time a somewhat closed circle. Journalistic reportage enabled her to travel away from urban literary politics and, presumably, away from herself. She worked on Maxim Gorky's factory history project in 1932–36, and in 1937 moved to Moscow when her husband was transferred there. In the war years she took on an enormous amount of editorial work in spite of ill health. She died in 1952, overwork not being the only cause.

At the end of her first memoir of 1927 Shkapskaya observes that she feels she is "not a real poet [*poet ia nenastoiashchii*] and in literature an equally accidental wanderer as in all other spheres" (p. 15). She begins to criticize her own books as being all on one theme, reflecting "the eternal anxiety of the wanderer among things and events. Not too well anchored to firm ground and . . ." Here in self-doubt, which internalizes the criticism she had received from others, the line breaks off and the autobiography ends. In the later, uncollected, fragment (1930) she reiterates the phrase about not being a real poet, but also calls herself a lyric poet in a time that demands "sterner notes." So "now I no longer write poetry" (p. 12).

She might, like other more well-born poets, have written for the drawer; but it appears she did not. The revolution gave tangible benefits to people of the class she identified with, and she felt loyal to it. She lacked the sense of self-righteousness of poets like Anna Akhmatova, Osip Mandelstam, or Boris Pasternak. She mentions both her children and her books of verse as seeds planted for a better future. That future was not to come in her lifetime. There is much heroism in her survival and much more tragedy in the actual fate of her poetry. Evidence shows that she was willing to publish her poetry in any form whatsoever, in excerpts or as a single book. By 1928 all her old editions were sold out. She called them, in a private letter to A. G. Lebedenko, "ideologically unsound" ("ideologicheski ne vyderzhany").[6] The quotation marks externalize the certain criticism that would be applied to her lack of ideological firmness, criticism as inevitable in the future as it had been in the past.

A review of Shkapskaya's books in 1925 in *Red Virgin Soil* (*Krasnaia nov'*) gives a good idea of how she was willfully "misunderstood" as a decadent poet of female *toska* (anguish) with deliberately confusing verse forms, a poet who only occasionally came "out of her gynecological corner and reached an understanding of the fact that in the life of humanity there are more important questions than the lack of fulfillment of her maternal vocation by one or another woman."[7] Raising the specter of irrelevance to humanity in order to silence a woman writer is nothing new, but it had the force of official censure in the Soviet Union in 1925. Even earlier, in 1923, Gorky, who had formerly admired Shkapskaya's poetry, criticized her long poem *Reality* (*Iav'*) for its lack of pathos and its dryness—in other words, for exactly the innovative tone she had succeeded in striking.[8] Maria Shkapskaya survived after 1925 by ceasing to write poetry (four short poems, probably written previously, were published in *Red Virgin Soil* in 1929). Instead she wrote an approved form of prose, the *ocherk*, noted for its brevity and way of establishing solid links between writer/observer and subject/reality. This form gave her quite a different voice, one having little to do with her former voice. This transition from poetry to a certain, "real," kind of prose differs markedly from transitions made by other Russian writers (Ivan Turgenev, Vladimir Nabokov, Ivan Bunin) whose poetry *became* their prose.

Shkapskaya's sketches (over a hundred in the war years alone) are well-written, and occasionally we see flashes in them of her concern for women. Her description of the Women's Club (*Zhenklub*) in "A Week in an Old City" ("Nedelia v starom gorode," 1927) portrays the life of Uzbek women, married at eleven or twelve, bearing many children, intimidated against joining the new order. The author has sympathy for people in general that transcends the prescribed search for the progressive.

How did Shkapskaya herself view her life (1891–1952) and her writing career (1910–1952)? It is clear that she differentiated herself from her origins, describing them in a way that, even if fictional, provides an exercise in vocational teleology not unusual for a writer so far outside the norm. It may be that her painful identification with other women was a recreation of a painful childhood; but the reverse may be equally true. Shkapskaya always used her verbal intellect to earn a living: when she could no longer seek a new poetic language, she became a dedicated high-level journalist. While she remained visible as a writer, her poetic silence was more complete than that of Sophia Parnok, Akhmatova, or Tsvetaeva. The autobiographical writings give us little data on the thematic sources of her poetry. Their silence on the subject is an eloquent indication that the poetry must stand as its own "explanation."

Why were Shkapskaya's poetic embodiments of motherhood increasingly taboo in postrevolutionary Russian culture? Motherhood has overwhelmingly been used in modern Russian literature to generate images of patriarchal value, as icon to symbolize Russia, for example in Valentin Rasputin's *Farewell to Matera* (*Pro-*

shchanie s Materoi, 1985) or Alexander Solzhenitsyn's *Matrena's House* (*Matrenin dvor*, 1963). Here motherhood is disembodied and largely an abstraction, the mother becoming a potent symbol of a slaughtered nation and the narrator and the readers becoming, by implication, the surrogate children of that mother/nation. These images may well be related to mother-earth symbolism of pre-Christian Russia, but the suffering and forgiving mother seems more closely connected to Christianity. The women's lament is a form common to both.

Shkapskaya's use of the lamenting mother is related both to Russian folklore and paganism and to the Christian myth of the Virgin. She, however, reverses the terms of the metaphor. She does not compare Russia to a woman and then use this mother as a backdrop for the emotions of a son/narrator. Rather she situates the woman in Russia and keeps the focus on the woman, who, as a mother, includes both the child and the rest of society in herself. She envisions a sexually empowered motherhood centered in the female body and, even more importantly, in feminine conceptual space. She gives the mother an authoritative voice, one both lamenting and deeply critical of patriarchal society. This radical shift of perspective was undoubtedly what made Soviet critics of the time queasy and what has discouraged the publication of her poetry in a society that continues to symbolize, reify, and even valorize motherhood as long as it remains a nonfemale discourse. That is, fictional women and female narrators are expected "normally" to be good mothers. The only exceptions to the norm are outcast slatterns and madwomen—these are rare, though, and they constitute warnings. In women's writing virtually the same standards are maintained, although occasional sideswipes at useless, passive, or absent fathers are not only permitted but encouraged.

Motherhood in all its aspects and stages—fertility, pregnancy, birth, and nurturing—has been mythologized into a series of passive states that read as follows: women receive the seed, await the birth, submit to it in pain, watch as their children grow, and try to keep the family together. Women, the bearers of life, are rarely its interpreters: the meaning even of childbirth has been appropriated and named by men.[9] In Shkapskaya's poetry, however, men are bystanders and all readers onlookers to the closed configuration of mother and child. Motherhood is thus reclaimed as a function of woman's body, a condition voiced by the mother herself. The poems are female-centered monologues that at times enter into dialogue with various male interlocutors, including God and the absent fathers of the children.

Little feminist writing has yet emerged from Russia to deal with the peculiarities of the uses of the maternal in that society. Few major discussions of female sexuality, except in the context of pornography and eroticism, have appeared since the era of *glasnost*. It is to Western feminisms that we must look for supporting arguments and pluralistic debate that may shed light on the links between Shkapskaya's poetry and the maternal body. Anglo-American writers stress the practical and the cultural over the more philosophical and epistemological French feminisms.[10] Helena Michie's discussion of how motherhood was seen as a public duty and of how women rarely used the language of the body before the twentieth century applies well to Russia and states the non-French case: "the distance between the heroine's body and the words used to describe it are not simply *différance*, but an aggravated and deeply political instance of culture intervening between a subject and its representation."[11] Shkapskaya sought to overcome that distance in her poetry. Ann Ferguson's term "sex-affective energy" suggests a way of thinking about the peculiar intensity of Shkapskaya's love poems, which are directed at their own body-object, the child. These poems are far removed from the usual love poetry written for a putative sexual partner. The term sex-affective energy describes affectionate attachments that do not necessarily refer to particular objects or bodily functions, although they may do so. This theory enables feelings of parenthood and other forms of bonding to be related to the sexual as part of a more general category.[12]

On the French side, we have already mentioned Michel Foucault's work, which conceptualizes sexuality in relation to contemporary techniques of power used against it. Although Foucault cannot be considered a feminist thinker, his theorizing has proved valuable to feminists. If we substitute "motherhood" for "sexual relations" in his theory, Foucault's emphasis on the structures of power adds a useful dimension to the reading of Shkapskaya. We may turn to the work of Julia Kristeva for an even more specific analysis of the mother. The figure of the *mater dolorosa* inspired both the title of Shkapskaya's first unified book of poems (1921) and, coincidentally, Kristeva's brilliant essay "Stabat Mater" (1977), which juxtaposes, often in two typesets and columns on the same page, the author's own experience of giving birth to a son with her thoughts on the meaning of "stabat mater dolorosa" ("stands the mother, grieving"). Kristeva sees the figure of the grieving Virgin as expressing "the desire to experience within her own body the death of a human being, which the feminine fate of being the source of life spares her": since the Virgin must know about the resurrection, this alone explains her expression of pain at the foot of the cross.[13] Kristeva calls the mother's milk and tears "the metaphors of non-speech, of a 'semiotics' that linguistic communication does not account for."[14] Not milk and tears but blood, as we shall see, serves the function in Shkapskaya's poetry of communicating nonverbally the transmission of life through and from the body. Motherhood beyond metaphor is the great theme of Shkapskaya's poetry. She demythologizes previous concepts of mother—as Virgin, Motherhood, Earth—and then remythologizes them in several new ways.

Shkapskaya's poetry of 1913 to 1917, collected under the title *Evening Hour* (*Chas vechernii*, 1922) begins with a poem, "The Bible" ("Bibliia"), that can focus our discussion of her preoccupation with unifying human gestures through time and space as primarily feminized images. The poem feminizes patriarchal religion by considering the Bible both as a material object handled by women and as a text altered by its readers (some of whom are female).

Ее на набережной Сены
В ларце старуха продает,
И запах воска и вербены
Хранит старинный переплет.
Еще упорней и нетленней
Листы заглавные хранят
И даты нежные рождений
И даты трудные утрат.
Ее читали долго, часто,
И чья-то легкая рука
Две-три строки Экклезиаста
Ногтем отметила слегка.

Склоняюсь к книге. Вечер низок.
Чуть пахнет старое клише.
И странно делается близок
Моей раздвоенной душе
И тот, кто счел свой каждый терний,
Поверив, что Господь воздаст,
И тот, кто в тихий час вечерний
Читал Экклезиаст.
(P. 30)[15]

On the Seine embankment
An old woman sells it in a booth
Its ancient binding retains
The scent of wax and verbena.
Still more stubbornly and imperishably
Its title pages retain
The tender dates of births
The difficult dates of deaths.
It has been read long, frequently
And somebody's light hand
Has marked lightly with a fingernail
Two or three lines of Ecclesiastes.
I bend over the book. The evening hangs low.
You can barely smell the ink of the old printer's plate.
And to my bifurcated soul
Comes strangely near
Both the one who reckoned his every tribulation
Believing the lord would repay
And the one who in the quiet hour of evening
Was reading Ecclesiastes.

The old woman (as in an allegory of mortality) is located in the immutable selling place for old books, offering what has been a family Bible. The speaker can smell the binding, an experience linking her directly to the readers who came before her. Among these, one in particular has marked with a light (female?) hand two or three lines—no doubt the famous passage on the transitoriness of life. The permanence of names and markings contrasts with the reduction to ashes of human endeavor. Evening hanging low over the speaker seems almost to be reading over her shoulder, imparting a sense of urgency, of closure. As she reads, two interpretations suggest themselves: that of belief in God's vengeance and that of the recognition of nothingness. Thus the history of religion's use is recalled in the female speaker's "soul": when a double interpretation of the authoritative voice of the past is offered, that voice becomes both less authoritative and, paradoxically, more valuable.

The immediacy of the present moment is thus split into visions of other lives: the old woman who sells the book, the two who transmit their alternative readings of the text to the speaker, those whose births and deaths are recorded, and the marker of the text. The final reading of the Book (of life) contains all other readings. The speaker's own interpretation, however bifurcated, implies stoical acceptance, as does the epigraph to the collection *Evening Hour*, Zinaida Gippius's lines: "Words, like foam, / Are irrevocable and insignificant."

In the beginning of her poetic career, before the theme of motherhood had come to predominate, Shkapskaya was more abstractly interested in the continuity of generations, the markings of words in the flow of time, and the transmission of something valuable through women. The Bible was to remain an important source of imagery, and also seems to have greatly influenced Shkapskaya's poetic style. In her later poems, often written as prose but with lines marked by rhyme and in a loose *dolnik* meter, the poetic repetitions are evocative of the cadences of the Psalms. God is often invoked, as in the Psalms, even after the revolution. But God is also called to account. There is considerably less stoical acceptance in the poetry of the 1920s.

The collection of poetry published in 1921, *Mater Dolorosa*, consists of 22 poems delineating a progression from the fact of a dead child, through the mother's body, to a meditation on guilt both singular and collective, and finally to reflections on the nation and the Christ that presides over the bloodletting. The first line of the collection, "My child is dead" ("Nezhivoe moe ditia," p. 59), is followed by a string of negatives in nearly every line of the poem echoing the first one (literally: "Not living is my child"). The most positive line asserts, "Only in my heart is your quiet trace / Flesh out of flesh, vein out of veins" ("Tol'ko v serdtse tvoi tikhii sled, / Plot' ot ploti, ot zhilok zhilka"). The mother's body is no longer the bearer of life: it serves as the grave of her child. The poem employs a *kol'tso*, or ring verse form, as if to encircle the dead child firmly within the mother/speaker by a repeated final stanza. The second poem speaks more impersonally, though still with first-person pronouns, of the body not bearing its weight. The third poem, which describes the mourning mother as she follows the coffin, shifts to the female third-person pronoun "ona"; the speaker, whose persona is thereby detached from that of the mother, rejoins the mother only to ask rhetorically how she can walk without falling.

The fifth poem in the collection marks a major shift, reasserting the universality of motherhood—"We give birth to them ourselves in torment" ("My rozhdaem ikh v mukakh sami," p. 61)—and establishing the mother's authority over the child as stronger than God's. The mother literally orders God to wipe the "mortal sweat" from her child if He meets him and to tell him his mother gave permission for Him to do so. Thus her authority, even after death, if not her power over life and death, is the greater one. There is no father figure, even in death, not bound to obey the living mother.

In a later poem from *Drum of the Stern Lord*, "What are you doing there, old mother?" ("Chto ty tam delaesh', staraia mat'?" p. 78), the mother engages in dialogue with God, who has let her son die before her. At the beginning and end (after God reasons with her) she still wants to dig up her child. The dactyls underline the folk flavor of the dialogue, as does its *kol'tso* form. The use of the folk as of the biblical element applies the communality of their intonations to the common fate of women. The true common mother is a Mother of Sorrows, as she appears two poems earlier: "We are all Her children, we are all Her daughters, dancing in a ballet, standing in a line" ("Vse my Ei deti, vse my Ei docheri, tantsuiushchie v balete, stoiashchie v ocheredi," p. 77). The most exalted image of the Soviet female and the most everyday image are thus joined. At the end of this poem the children of the mother pray for *their* children, doubling the relation and adding a further dimension.

It is perhaps the anxious prayerfulness of her poetry, with God as its primary masculine addressee, that distinguishes Shkapskaya's poetry. A human masculine addressee rarely appears. The almost total exclusion of the lover is of course rare in the female lyric, which may use the masculine addressee the better to mirror the female self (as in Akhmatova's early lyrics) but rarely dispenses

Motherhood in a Cold Climate 249

with it altogether. Shkapskaya as a rule focuses on the self as mother or as mother and child, rather than as mistress. One exception, which begins with the words "How many women you've caressed" ("Kak mnogo zhenshchin ty laskal," p. 64), ends not with the lover as addressee but with God invoked to bear witness that the speaker is worthy of being called a mother ("ia zvat'sya mater'iu dostoina"). This is hardly a poem to flatter the male ego, although it was Maxim Gorky's favorite and was widely anthologized.

In a late *poema*, *Man Goes to the Pamirs* (*Chelovek idet na Pamir*, pp. 117–22), Man is also man, and he performs exploits at great cost to his wife and children. This long poem was placed at the end of Shkapskaya's last published collection, *Earthly Crafts*. It makes ambiguous obeisance to the heroic, muscular male worker of the socialist 1920s, who "eats on the go and sleeps on the go" ("Est' na khodu i spit na khodu") but has no time for children ("Ne do detei otsu").

Most of Shkapskaya's poetry, then, is situated entirely in a woman's world, a world of blood, toil, all-encompassing love for one's children, and solidarity with all other women, who are perceived as kindred. Shkapskaya uses the theme of motherhood to evoke sympathy, love, communality, nationhood, distress—in fact, a full range of human emotions involving the self, the other, and all others, but especially other women. The "dear sisters" of "O, sestry milye . . ." (*Mater Dolorosa*, p. 67) have no invisible threads binding them to another and look with envy "at the tired mother, with a child in her arms." Shkapskaya here addresses not a community of sisterhood based on mutual self-sufficiency, but rather a communality of understanding among women whose lives are diverse (mothers and nonmothers) but mutually sympathetic. This sympathy excludes men from the sister-mother-child configuration; nevertheless, the tiredness can be seen as a direct result of living in and working for a masculine world order that was proclaiming with upbeat rhetoric both the workplace and the home to be women's sphere and woman's duty. This existence produces not just physical exhaustion but profound alienation. The body itself can become alien, with a black enemy ("chernyi vrag," p. 63) bending over it. A "necessary" abortion—the latter word is not used in the poem "Yes, they say that it was necessary" ("Da, govoriat, chto eto nuzhno bylo," p. 67)—becomes a sacrifice out of the body and of the body, eventually invading the mother's dreams.

In the service of this communality, female figures like Eve and the Beautiful Lady are remythologized to incarnate the necessary feminine links in a chain of blood flowing through time and generations: "Everything flows—from our foremother Eve to days burdened with things, through each new womb, joining itself fully to new us's" ("Vse techet—ot pramateri Evy k otiagchennym veshchami dniam, cherez kazhdoe novoe chrevo, priobshchaias' vse k novym nam," p. 100). In this ultimate example of "feminine" writing, women alone are both the initiators and the vehicles for life itself, incarnating not just the womb but the new "us" in it. The process of joining overcomes the daily heaviness of things, another reference to *byt*, that constant feature of Soviet society that weighed especially heavily on women, and one more tedious still in times of scarcity. The length of the line moving from "everything" to "us" constitutes a single breath of life, like the process of giving birth without conception.

If Eve has always been a viable female figure in the poetry of both genders, the Beautiful Lady (the *Prekrasnaia dama* of the Symbolists) might seem a more difficult image for a woman writer to appropriate. Shkapskaya uses her not as inspiration to the spiritual male but as completion of a process of pro-genesis:

> Детей от Прекрасной Дамы иметь никому не дано, но только Она Адамово заканчивает звено.
> И только в Ней оправданье темных наших кровей, тысячелетней данью влагаемой в сыновей.
> И лишь по Ее зарокам, гонима во имя Ея—в пустыне времен и сроков летит, стеная, земля.
> (P. 99)

> To have children from the Beautiful Lady is given to no one, but only She completes the link of Adam's chain.
> And only in Her is the justification of our dark bloodlines, the thousand-year tribute inserted into sons.
> And only according to Her vows, driven in Her name, into the wasteland of times and terms the earth flies groaning.

M. L. Gasparov has termed this kind of Shkapskaya poetry "mock prose" (*mnimaia proza*), perhaps echoing Yuri Tynianov's definition of parody as *mnimaia poeziia*. The text is written like prose (or, as we said before, like biblical verse) but is actually a three-ictus *dolnik* with ABAB rhymes. Gasparov posits the author's wish to create a "casual, intimate, rapid speaking intonation," but suggests there may be other motivations for such a mode of writing.[16] To me, the breaking down of neat lines is in harmony with the essence of Shkapskaya's poetry, in which words mimic the continuum of life presided over by women. The "prose" format appears in her earliest verse and predominates in her later books.

Guilt and anxiety form an inevitable accompaniment to motherhood. At their most positive with Shkapskaya they can take the form of a prayer that one's children may ripen to full term:

> Господи, разви не встала я, егда Ты ко мне воззвах? Ведь я только петелька малая в тугих Твоих кружевах.
> Ведь мы только ягоды спелые в Твоем лесном туеске, цветы Твои белые в соблюденном Тобой песке.
> Твоими ржаными колосьями всходим из влажной земли в полях нашей скудной родины, в ее дорожной пыли.
> Но зреть под лучами теплыми дай нам время и срок, чтоб цветы встали в поле копнами, чтоб колос налиться мог.
> До срока к нам не протягивай тонких пальцев своих, не рви зеленые ягоды, не тронь колосьев пустых, ткани тугие, несканные, с кросен в ночь не снимай.
> —Детям, Тобою мне данным, вырасти дай.
> (P. 66)

> Lord, did I not stand up when You called to me? Truly I'm only a small loop in Your heavy lace.
> Truly we are but blind berries in Your woody little pot, white flowers of Yours in Your guarded woods.
> We rise up from the damp earth like Your ears of rye in the fields of our poor motherland, in the dust of her roads.
> But give us time and term to ripen under warm rays, so that flowers may rise in bunches in the field, so that the ear might ripen.
> Don't stretch out your thin fingers to us before it's time, don't tear off the green berries, don't touch the empty ears, don't remove the heavy weave unfinished from the frame in the night.
> Let the children given me by You grow up.

This poem is notable for its rhythm, syntax, imagery, and its clear division into two parts: description and prayer. The negative half of the prayer, with its implied anxiety for all that could go wrong, seems to speed the poem to a one-line conclusion that encapsulates its purpose. The subtle shifts in pronouns (I, you, we, *they*, i.e., the children), the buckling up of the first and last words ("Lord . . . give"), the continual variation of verblessness followed by verbs and their objects—all show complete mastery of style. The "folk" images from nature are totally appropriate, whether purely natural like the berries or crafted from nature like the lace, the birch pot, or the weaving frame. Woman's double ability to bear children and to create useful and beautiful artifacts (poetry being one by implication) forms the basis of her prayer for life.

The phrase "time and term" ("vremia i srok") is again crucial here. God and women seem to be in touch still with a time that the speeded-up, forward-marching tempo of the revolution is killing. Russia is still called Russia in the title of two poems; one of these is a small cycle of five lyrics, in the last of which she stands like a "stone woman" (*kamennaia baba*), one of those mysterious south Russian steppe female figures of worship, symbols of feminine permanence (p. 82). It is the figure of the mother who opposes state killings, whether those of revolutions in "To Louis XVII" ("Liudoviku XVII," pp. 84–85) or those of the tsarist autocracy (the son forcibly taken from the revolutionary Gesia Gelfman while she was in prison). "We are not implicated in that bloodshed" ("My k etoi krovi ne prichastny"), she writes. Shkapskaya's long poem of 1923 about an execution, *Reality* (pp. 88–93), incorporates both voices of the crowd straining to get a look and voices worrying about the effect on children, while the wife of the executed man tells her son quietly not to forget.

In this world of violence interrupting the flow of generations Shkapskaya treats the sexual act primarily as an act of conception, with children the "blind hostage to suffering and rage" ("slepuiu dan' stradaniiu i gnevu," p. 74). In the third poem of the "Russia" cycle sexual conjunction is allegorized: it occurs between Peter the Great and Russia, who conceives every night and gives birth the next day. Petrine history is continual rape of the body of the mother country, and, by implication, the revolution of 1917 continues the same process. Sex as the beginning of the birth process otherwise presided over by women alone forms an original use of the concept of sexuality. It is hardly akin to the free love of the 1920s, so much written about by men and women at the time in various ways. (Anna Akhmatova is the typical exponent of a sort of stylized male rapacity and female half-willed self-protection and half-knowing collusion.) In Shkapskaya the sexuality of motherhood has other dimensions, which emerge from the all-inclusive bond between mother and child that carries into the future lives of both for better or worse. Blood links have mysterious hidden potential that can be exploited artistically in a mythological as well as a historical context. They can be authoritarian, lamenting, or prayerful, as in the intonations of the poems already quoted. The opening of the body can entail either the blood of birth and continuity or the carnage and disruption of historical violence in Shkapskaya's poetry; increasingly it becomes the latter.

Shkapskaya was not antirevolutionary, but she was anticarnage. The word "blood" or one of its cognates appears in every poem of her collection *Krov'-ruda*, which means both "blood-ore" and "blood-gore," the latter as folk synonym. Blood is the key metaphor for all Shkapskaya's poetry—the vehicle for the flow of generations through historic and prehistoric time and the genealogical mystical archive within each individual. The poet's own body incarnates this slow and secret evolution in the poem beginning "Only the dress . . ." ("Tol'ko plat'e . . ."): "but how ancient is my body. / And what ancient secrets are preserved in my continuous bloodstream from the first days of the universe up until our days" ("no kak drevne telo moe. / I kakie drevnie tainy v krovi bessmennoi moei—ot pervykh dnei mirozdan'ia khraniatsia do nashikh dnei," p. 101). Spilling the blood of any human, especially a child's blood, is not merely an individual injustice but a break in the continuity of life. While not Orthodox, Shkapskaya's poetry is religious and even mystical. It is also revolutionary, although not in a way the October Revolution, when it consolidated its forces, was bound to admire. Her use of biblical imagery, her (defiantly) prayerful voice, her linking of injustice to postrevolutionary destruction of human life—all these could no longer be considered modes of expression compatible with an ideology that proclaimed progress, especially for women.

Her last published poem begins, "Don't leave inadequate traces or any work that is not completed" ("Ne ostavliai sledov nepolnotsennykh / I nikakikh nezavershennykh del"), and it ends with the image of a child as metaphor for her lost poetry: "the child born of meager caresses is unjoyful and even unlawful" ("Neradostno i nezakonno dazhe / Ot skudnykh lask rozhdennoe ditia").[17] Better, then, to cease having children/writing poetry and to consider the children/poems already in existence as seeds planted for a future time, the better future she refers to in her autobiographical notes. Shkapskaya may have linked poetry and motherhood in a single metaphor, but the motherhood she wrote about was real rather than symbolic. Like the real mother in the judgment of Solomon, she preferred to save her child (her poetry) by renouncing her claim altogether.

Shkapskaya's poetry demonstrates a new feminine potential for decentering societal norms. Motherhood is an "inside" phenomenon, for it is crucial to the life of society; but since it is primarily a female discourse it is also "outside." Images of male motherhood (as opposed to fatherhood, which usually means either procreation or legal status) are rarely connected to the male body in the same way. The mother-and-child configuration is a closed one, not penetrable except by physical force or force of law.

Motherhood in the social reorganization of the Soviet 1920s has barely begun to be chronicled.[18] Simultaneously empowering and devastating to women, the new state was not organized by or for them. The costs to women's bodies of sexual "liberation" and of abortion as the only alternative to child starvation have best been inscribed in the texts of Shkapskaya's poems. Shkapskaya's poems about guilty motherhood have as their basis the devastation and anxiety women felt about unborn children, those prematurely dead, and those surviving uncertainly, left in their care despite the rhetoric of caring by the state.

As for her actual children, Shkapskaya concludes her 1952 memoir with them, a daughter aged 24 and sons aged 34 and 32. First she catalogs their achievements, then suddenly she tells us that her younger son, who had been taken prisoner during the war, was sent to the labor camps in 1950. His mother writes: "His whereabouts at the present time are unknown to me. All this took place in Leningrad, where I have not lived for about 15 years now. It is, of course, the greatest sorrow of my life, and I feel very bitter not to have died a little sooner" (p. 25). Thus ends our tale of motherhood in a cold climate.

ERIC NAIMAN

Historectomies

On the Metaphysics of Reproduction in a Utopian Age

■ In the spring of 1925, the newspaper *Izvestiia* reported on a murder trial in the northern Ukraine that was arousing much interest. A peasant, Iosif Tsimbaliuk, was accused of braining his four children with a set of tongs. Apparently, Tsimbaliuk had acted from religious conviction. He had recently joined a sect inspired by the teachings of a local prophet, Kornei Kalamarchuk, who had been attracting followers throughout the Ukraine since well before the October Revolution. According to *Izvestiia*, Kalamarchuk's followers believed their leader to be Christ and were certain that when the "virgin" with whom he lived gave birth to a son, their lives would be prolonged by a thousand years, at which point Kalamarchuk would sit in judgment of all mankind. There was, however, one catch, a detail in Kalamarchuk's bible of which Tsimbaliuk claimed to have been ignorant when he had signed on: "Kalamarchuk's sect considers monogamy a sin and children 'evil spirits' [*nechist'*] who must be gotten rid of. Only those who are childless will receive 'grace.'"[1] On the stand, Kalamarchuk, also a defendant, justified this tenet by explaining that during the Last Judgment marriage and childbirth were prohibited. Both defendants were sentenced to eight years in jail.[2]

Kalamarchuk's religious teachings were portrayed by *Izvestiia* as "fanatical cruelty," which could not be tolerated, even on the margins of Soviet social life.[3] Events that evoke strong repugnance, however, are rarely as marginal as the outraged subject would suggest, and, indeed, within the broad contours of Russian millenarian culture Tsimbaliuk did not act alone. His mistake was in putting into action the technique that literary masters of the 1920s such as Andrei Platonov and Mikhail Zoshchenko were then employing as stylistic, philosophical, or even comic device. Tsimbaliuk erred in taking language literally, in "realizing" infanticidal metaphors that had rarely crossed the gulf separating philosophically totalitarian aspirations from what the Russians call *byt*: the category of nitty-gritty detail and everyday life.

By whom in the text of Russian religious thought was Tsimbaliuk aided and abetted? In turn-of-the-century Russia there had been a rich tradition of spiritual thinkers—noumenal revolutionaries—who devoured prospective children in their philosophies. For these men, the begetting of children embodied all that prevented humanity from attaining that utopian goal of absolute integral purity: immortality.[4] While early Soviet culture was the product of diverse influences, insight into the works of these philosophers can contribute to our understanding of the actions and images in which postrevolutionary society manifested its wishes and fears. Close attention to the sexual motives informing their writing can help us to orient ourselves better in the world of early Soviet desire.

The ostensible rationale for religious-utopian hostility to progeny is easy to understand. For Vladimir Solovyov (1853–1900) and Nikolai Berdyaev (1874–1948), birth represented the "bad infinity of physical reproduction";[5] it was a reminder of the change of generations and of the seeming inevitability of human decay. Berdyaev, who believed that "the opposition between love and childbirth is profound," declared: "birth is always the sign of the failure of the personality to attain perfection, of falling short of eternity. The one giving birth and the one who is born are subject to decay and imperfect."[6] As were many early-twentieth-century thinkers, Berdyaev had been strongly influenced by Nietzsche, and he eagerly seized upon Zarathustra's rallying cry: "I have never found a woman with whom I would want to have children, for I love you, eternity" (*Smysl tvorchestva*, p. 249). Nikolai Fyodorov (1828–1903), whose influence on Solovyov and Berdyaev was considerable but whom the latter criticized for his materialistic tendency to turn metaphysics into science, tended to depict the

Historectomies

fatal consequences of childbirth in a more medical vein. Agreeing with the proposition that "death ... is the transition of one creature (or of two uniting in a single flesh) into another by means of birth," he explained:

> In lower animals this is clear, obvious: within one cell embryos of new cells appear; as they grow, these latter cells rupture the mother cell and go out into the world. Here it is evident that the birth of children is also the mother's death. ... In this example the cell enters the world fully mature, but man is born immature; during feeding and upbringing he devours his parents' strength, feeding, so to speak, on their body and blood ... ; so that, by the time parents have finished bringing up their children, their strengths have been absolutely depleted and they die or enter a state of decrepitude approaching death. The fact that the murderous process does not occur within the organism, as with the single cell, but within the family, does not mitigate against the criminality of this affair.[7]

Part of the problem was that, in procreating, man was surrendering to nature. The philosophies of Solovyov, Berdyaev, and Fyodorov depended upon man's distinguishing himself from all other animals. Solovyov contended that man existed on several levels: natural, social, and divine. Procreation tended to occur on the first or second of these planes, and only by transcending procreation and infusing sexuality with the divine would man achieve immortality ("Smysl liubvi," p. 527). "As long as man reproduces like an animal," Solovyov asserted, "he will die like one" (p. 522). Fyodorov was obsessed with the conquest of nature, and he saw sexuality as part of the "blind force" that had placed man at the elements' mercy (*Filosofiia*, vol. 1, p. 314). Attacking Schopenhauer's celebratory assertion that this force was the key to immortality—Fyodorov renamed his predecessor's major work "The World as Lust" (p. 405)—he argued that man's task was to respond by an assertion of will assuming several forms: science would aid in overcoming droughts, for example, but the most impressive act of will would be the renunciation of sexual reproduction. Berdyaev quibbled with the first part of Fyodorov's solution. For him, the battle with nature and matter was akin to the exercise of "black magic." "White magic" was his answer. Rather than strive with "dead," hostile matter, man should transcend it. But

Berdyaev's goal *vis-à-vis* the elements was the same as his predecessor's: the power of man over nature (*Smysl tvorchestva*, pp. 51, 354).

The naive reader might here be tempted to interject that birth control would have been a mundane solution to these men's problems. In Western Europe contraception was heralded in the late nineteenth century as part of man's conquest of nature, proof of the rationalization of human passion.[8] Russian society in the early twentieth century, however, was on the whole extremely reluctant to let birth control infiltrate its language. The prevailing view at the turn of the century was expressed by Professor V. Bekhterev, of the Imperial Military Medicine Academy, when, in his introduction to August Forel's extremely popular *The Question of Sex* (*Polovoi vopros*),[9] he took issue with the Swiss psychologist's advocacy of birth control: "Neither the law nor society, in our opinion, should support sexual pleasure, if it has as its goal only pleasure and is not aimed at the production of offspring."[10]

While the early-twentieth-century Russian religious philosophers whom we have been considering did not subscribe to this popular justification of sexuality on the basis of reproduction, neither did they go against the prevailing tide and seek to liberate human pleasure. They endorsed the generally held view of love as an activity that should somehow bind the individual together with his fellow men, but they saw sexual intercourse as an unsatisfactory way of achieving this unity. Copulation divided as much as, if not more than, it unified. Present in most utopian thought is a striving for wholeness, and in sexual congress difference becomes most apparent at the very moment where the drive to obliterate it becomes most intense: "The flesh of two should merge together into a single flesh, they should completely [*do kontsa*] penetrate each other. Instead of this an act of transparent union occurs, too temporary and too superficial. The price that must be paid for fleeting union is still greater disunity.... In the differentiated sexual act itself there is already present a certain defectiveness and morbidity" (Berdiaev, *Smysl tvorchestva*, p. 228).[11]

Fyodorov, Solovyov, and Berdyaev all proposed ways of putting the pieces of sexuality and immortality back together. Fyodorov, as ever, had the most literal solution. Sexual intercourse should give way to chastity, and children should set about the complicated business of finding the bits of matter into which their parents had disintegrated. Then they would be able, literally, to bring prior generations back to life. Solovyov and Berdyaev settled on the solution of androgyny. For Berdyaev, who spells out his theory in much more detail, man's quest for the restoration of a lost androgynous ideal would culminate in an act of "creation" constituting the freely chosen union of man with God. This formulation, although elaborated more fully, was borrowed from Solovyov, who had asserted: "the path of the highest love, perfectly uniting male and female, spirit and flesh . . . is the union or mutual cooperation of the divine with the human, a process of godmanhood [*bogochelovecheskii*]."[12]

As Olga Matich has demonstrated in her surveys of the question, androgyny at the turn of the century was a growth industry. "While being acutely aware of the imminent collapse of the old order," she writes, "the Silver Age generation withdrew from traditional political activism and turned to the spiritual and private domains. As the esoteric ideal of inner personal harmony, androgyny was particularly appealing to those introspective Russian intellectuals seeking an ideal which was visionary and ahistorical."[13] "Visionary" and "ahistorical" claims, however, often reveal themselves as reactionary and context-determined. As we begin to look more closely at the language in which the utopian goal of androgyny is cloaked, we start to sense an underlying strategy and a repressive hidden agenda.

From the foregoing description, it would appear that the rejection of sexual intercourse in favor of androgyny or resurrection was a logical consequence of several desires whose fulfillment the act of copulation impeded: the desires for the elimination of childbirth, the distinction of man from animal, and the formation of what we might call "a more perfect union." Fyodorov and Berdyaev, however, display so much horror when discussing the forms and processes of the flesh that their reader may begin to wonder if this repugnance, rather than being an incidental detail, is not the base of their programs and all of the professed desires mere superstructure.[14] Fyodorov talks repeatedly of "the shame of birth" and ventures: "One might well guess how all the blood in a person must rush to his face when he learns of his origin, and how he must pale with horror, when he sees the end of a creature like himself. . . . If these two things do not kill a person on the spot, then it is only because he probably learns of them gradually and is not forced to appreciate the full horror and baseness of his situation all at once" (*Filosofiia*, pp. 312–13). In his philosophical autobiography Berdyaev confesses, "There is something hideous in the sexual act itself," and cites approvingly Leonardo's remark "the sexual organ is so hideous that the human race would die out if people did not fall into a state of possession [when reproducing]."[15] He recalls: "repugnance at the life of the species [Schopenhauer's term] belongs to the earliest and ineffable characteristics of my being. Pregnant women have always repelled me."[16]

Berdyaev's book *The Meaning of the Creative Act* (*Smysl tvorchestva*) pretends to glorify sexuality and to condemn asceticism, but while he may claim, "there is no getting away from sex" (p. 217), that impossible escape is precisely the project of much turn-of-the-century Russian religious utopian thought. Berdyaev glorifies sex only as he redefines it: "In the depths of sex, the creative act must conquer birth, the individual personality must defeat the species, and union in the spirit must triumph over natural union occurring in flesh and blood. This will be possible only with the appearance of a new, creative sex [androgyny], with the revelation of the creative mystery of man as a sexual being" (p. 237).

While Berdyaev was not original in his ascetic beliefs, he was *speaking* about asceticism in a new way. Throughout the Western world, language about sexuality had been overrunning bourgeois and intellectual culture for decades, but Russian society, late here as ever, was faced with a particularly intense assault of speculation about the inner man. Berdyaev's glorification of sexuality in effect permitted him to duck under the waves, to disguise a panicky, conservative cry for help as the latest fashion. Berdyaev's glorification of sex also located him in the center of a somewhat deceitful 40-year-old tradition in the "left" Russian intelligentsia. The advent of liberal, realist fiction had led to scandal with its advocacy of "free love" and its "awareness of the details of concrete, material existence, even the petty, ugly or revolting ones,"[17] but free love for Nikolai Chernyshevsky and his heirs had, ideally, involved very little physical mating, as Berdyaev was wont to point out.[18] Writing in 1908, a St. Petersburg doctor with Bolshevik

Historectomies

sympathies who believed that to the question "What Is to Be Done?" Chernyshevsky had given a "multifaceted, exhaustive answer in the spirit of the triumph of free sexual love" was able to assert confidently that the sexual ideal for the proletarian woman was the "Turgenev maiden," for whom not only premarital sex but also premarital kissing would be out of the question.[19] Moreover, Chernyshevsky's awareness of revolting details had not been incompatible with a wish to be rid of them. In his diary he wrote of his penis: "how disgusting that we've been given this thing."[20] In *What Is to Be Done?*, few of the earthy details that so fascinate the diarist Chernyshevsky are permitted to surface. The Crystal Palace is all glass and light, save for the chambers whither the lovers disappear to make love. These rooms, with their curtained doors and "luxurious carpets that devour sound"[21] are where the realist's penetrating gaze stops. Chernyshevsky's self-adopted grandchildren, the old Bolsheviks, while preaching the virtues of asceticism, would deny vehemently that they were ascetics, or indeed anything but materialists.[22] Berdyaev was part of a long tradition in the Russian intelligentsia that claimed to be redeeming "the flesh," "the real," or "matter," but that did so only by redefining these terms so as to exclude what had once been inherent in their definitions. A pair of boots may have been worth more than Pushkin, but only once the dirt had been carefully shaken loose.

Not surprisingly, progressives who seemed to be expanding their worlds to encompass the flesh also believed they were expanding the circle of socially significant beings to include women. Inclusion and exclusion often went hand in hand; what was permissible for Chernyshevsky's hero Lopukhov—relations with women as equals on various levels—was not permitted to contaminate the life of his superman Rakhmetov. Our philosophers did not escape the prevailing mentality of their age and intellectual tradition, which equated women with "flesh." Indeed, this equation was so "obvious" that it often had no need of affirmation and emerged in simple cadenced parallels. For Solovyov, the fifth, highest and androgynous path of love would unite "male with female, spirit with body."[23] The novelist Alexander Kuprin caricatured the widespread acceptance of this duality in Russian culture when in his scandalous novel *The Pit* (*Iama*, 1908–15) he had a weak male character say of his desire to reform a prostitute: "I am not talking about a woman but about a person, not about meat but about a Soul."[24] Moreover, the other negative term that these philosophers asserted man should seek to control by transforming sexuality—nature (*priroda*, etymologically related to *rody*, the process of birth)—was inevitably compared to a woman:

> Through maleness the human race communes with the Word; through woman—with the natural soul of the world. . . . The domination of the feminine over the masculine is that of the natural elements of the world over the Word. It has ever been revealed by mystical vision and religious consciousness that the fall of man was accompanied by his subjugation to woman, for the fallen angel acted through the female element. (Berdiaev, *Smysl tvorchestva*, p. 110)

Essentially, our three philosophers all accepted the prevailing tendency in Western Europe to view female sexuality as all-encompassing, to equate sexuality with femininity per se because sexuality supposedly had a far greater impact on a woman's life than it did on a man's. Berdyaev and Fyodorov, however, were more emphatic on this point. The former declared, "woman is the cosmic, global carrier of the sexual element, of all that is elemental [i.e., natural and bestial] in sex. The natural-procreative element of sex is the female element" (*Smysl tvorchestva*, p. 226). Belief about the nature of female orgasm served implicitly as evidence for this popular theory; Forel could not contain his amazement and disgust at lesbian sex, in which "orgasm follows orgasm, day and night, almost without a break."[25] For Berdyaev, the uninterrupted nature of female sexuality was not only a temporal but also a spatial phenomenon: "In man sex is more *differentiated* and *specialized*, but in woman it is spread over all the flesh in the organism, through the entire field of her soul" (*Smysl tvorchestva*, p. 226, emphasis added).

Berdyaev seems to have lifted this image from the Austrian suicide Otto Weininger, whose book *Sex and Character* created a sensation in Russia and Europe.[26] Weininger, whose fingerprints can be found all over twentieth-century Russian culture, had portrayed woman as a soulless creature who, because her sexuality was neither temporally nor topographically localized, was eternally in a state of arousal, receiving sexual pleasure from every object with which she came into contact (p. 279). For Weininger, every woman was part mother, part whore, and he heaped particular abuse upon those tending toward the former pole. Not only was maternal love "instinctive," "involuntary," "amoral," and "blind," it was also egotistical since directed only toward a woman's progeny, not toward all mankind (pp. 268–69). Weininger's popularity in Russia was no doubt due to a convergence of opinion on these matters. For Fyodorov, mothers were "base, sensual, and intolerant; their entire world is limited to the nursery" (*Filosofiia*, p. 323). Solovyov is willing to admit that maternal love is based on sacrifice, but he cannot forgive its role in condemning man to live among the beasts: "To a mother her child may be dearer than all else, but this is precisely because it is her child, just as with other animals; in other words, here the purported acknowledgment of an other's unconditional significance is in reality founded upon an external, physiological connection" ("Smysl liubvi," p. 510).

Significantly, Weininger, who, like Berdyaev and Solovyov, believed in the possibility of physical immortality, began his treatise with a lengthy exposition of the fundamentally bisexual nature of man. Bisexuality was a concept he had taken from Fliess and Freud,[27] but Weininger transformed it from a psychological to a metaphysical and biological notion; in his work, the term was the functional equivalent of the Russian religious utopians' androgyny, and he also paid lip service to the need to overcome sexual difference. For Weininger, however, the most valuable aspect of androgyny is that it entails the destruction of women (*Pol i kharakter*, pp. 421–23), and this is a view that Berdyaev shared. In the creative act that Berdyaev thought would presage his mystically whole, spiritually utopian "third age," women's creative act, maternity, would be "conquered" and matter would be "gotten rid of" (*Smysl tvorchestva*, p. 372). When he specified that in this new age, "femininity would be affirmed in its virginal aspect, and not in its maternal" (p. 240), he was trading two characteristics explicitly necessitating the concept "woman" (feminine, maternal) for an adjective that could also imply a man (virginal). He predicted confidently: "There will come . . . the end of the religion of the species, the religion of maternity and of matter, and there will be no power capable of preserving the maternal, material, organic life of the species or protecting it from doom" (p. 240). Just as Berdyaev did not attack "paternity," Fyodorov spoke nearly exclusively of the "resurrection of fathers." For both men the solution to man's mortality—whether androgyny or scientific resurrection—surreptitiously marginalized if it did not eliminate women, and their hostility toward the feminine leads one to suspect that this was their philosophies' cornerstone rather than a byproduct. Solovyov is certainly less open to this charge than his colleagues, but rhetorically he also suggests that it is more important that women become like men than the other way around. Once woman has been identified as matter and man as spirit, what else can the "spiritualization of matter" ("Smysl liubvi," p. 540) mean but the molding of the essence of femininity to remove all traces of the feminine?[28]

Here we come to the question to what extent and on what level our philosophers meant what they said. One can and usually does read philosophy as relating to a symbolic rather than physiological order. We can say that our philosophers marginalized women merely metaphorically, on a representational, linguistic level that relates only to symbols and a spiritual plane of meaning. But to limit our field of vision in this way, to accept the banishment of physical meaning from language that strongly implies physicality would be to read nearly as naively as that simple but penetrating reader who, several pages ago, asked about birth control. Moreover, these philosophers themselves failed to maintain a pristine distinction between the symbolic and the real. For the positivist Fyodorov this distinction never existed in the first place; his entire philosophy presents itself as a practical, scientific solution to the problems of reproduction and mortality. Even Solovyov, whose philosophy is the most ferociously antiphysiological of those considered above, offers zoological data as philosophical evidence and later argues that just because men have always died does not mean that immortality is physically impossible ("Smysl liubvi," pp. 493–94, 517). The diaries of Zinaida Gippius, whose views on sexuality were in many respects similar to Solovyov's, provide striking examples of the tendency of the mystically inclined in the intelligentsia to confuse philosophy with physiology even as they sought to keep these levels apart.[29]

The surfacing of a desire to be rid of women within the utopian project of being rid of history should remind us of the repressive nature of all utopian thought. Utopianism is never truly atemporal; its blueprints necessarily involve a rejection of the present and of all that is unpleasant in contemporary "culture," a word Berdyaev defined as that which makes man fail (*Smysl tvorchestva*, pp. 358, 434). The desire for a perfect future and the desire to be rid of the imperfect present are inseparable, just as dreams and their motivating wishes cannot be divested of the mechanics of repression. Turn-of-the-century Russian society, into which women were making substantial economic and political inroads, was no exception, and the reader of its culture should always look for what is being absented from the aspirations of its texts. In Berdyaev the repressive moment is not difficult to find:

The holy, mystical idea of androgyny has its dangerous caricature in hermaphroditism. *Turned inside out*, androgyny in "this world" [i.e., the world of matter, rather than of spirit] assumes hermaphroditic form. . . . Androgyny is man's likeness to God, his ascent above nature. Hermaphroditism is a bestial, nature-bound mixing of the sexes that has not been transformed into a higher form of being. The women's emancipation movement is in its essence a caricature, simian and imitative; in it there is hermaphroditic deformity and not androgynous beauty. . . . Woman, by mechanical imitation, out of envy and enmity, appropriates masculine characteristics to herself and becomes a spiritual and physical caricature. (*Smysl tvorchestva*, p. 238, emphasis added)

But if we read androgyny "inside out," we may find that it is a fearful reaction to and a repressive imitation of what Berdyaev calls hermaphroditism. Indeed, in all the cases we have so far considered, imitation and appropriation help to constitute immortality, as woman's reproductive function is replaced by its likeness. Fyodorov marginalizes "the cult of women" and of mothers (*materi*), deifying instead fathers and a paternalized concept of matter (*materiia*) as the dust of forefathers (*Filosofiia*, p. 445). He suggests "daughterliness" as a woman's proper function, and as an appropriate role model he suggests, among others, Antigone, whose name means "in place of a mother."[30] In Weininger, Berdyaev, and Solovyov, this appropriation of the maternal works in equally metaphorical ways, but here anatomy plays a much more obvious role. Weininger's answer to mortality is the male characteristic of genius, which he portrays as a state of universal receptivity. "The ego of the genius is universal apperception, a point in which all the infinity of space is already contained. The outstanding man contains within himself the entire world; genius is a living microcosm" (*Pol i kharakter*, p. 199). This sounds suspiciously like his descriptions of woman as an undifferentiated sex organ, copulating to varying degrees with every object around her, capable of being impregnated even from afar. And in fact Weininger is willing to admit that woman is a copy of genius: "A creature that carries out the sex act in every place and with all things can also be fertilized everywhere and by all things. In her, everything acquires life, for everything makes a physiological impression on her and enters into and is transformed into her child. In this sense ... one may compare her—on a baser, physical level—with genius" (p. 280). But here again we should seek to discover what is an imitation of what, to read the mechanics of copying, as our experience with Berdyaev suggests, "inside out." Weininger builds his notion of genius on characteristics stolen from women, one of the most important of which is depth: "Genius is identical with depth [or profundity], but let anyone try to connect 'deep' and 'woman' as definition and defined. Thus, female genius is a *contradictio in adjecto*, for genius has always been defined as the highest sort of virility, strikingly manifested, fully developed and achieving full consciousness" (p. 220). Weininger goes through mighty contortions here to recover depth—an aspect more usually associated with the female reproductive system—from woman. Engorged with genius, profundity becomes the phallic property that saves man from death.

The notion of genius as an all-encompassing phenomenon was an old, Romantic one, associated in German tradition with the protean figure of Goethe, in Russia with Pushkin. But in Weininger's system it was explicitly sexualized, and in this context an old feminine metaphor became part of a surgical strike against women. Berdyaev's theory of immortalizing creativity was also based on a rhetoric of all-encompassing filling and incorporation:

Man is a small universe, a microcosm that is the fundamental truth of human cognition and the fundamental truth made possible by the very possibility of cognition. The universe can enter into a man, be assimilated by him; it can be comprehended only because all the elements of the universe are present in a man, all its strengths and qualities, because a man is not a fractional part of the universe, but an integral small universe. (*Smysl tvorchestva*, p. 88)[31]

"Mystical experience," which was the genre from which his creative act emerged, was the speculum that "reveal[ed] the cosmos, the enormous universe, within man" (*Smysl tvorchestva*, p. 332). Here Weininger was only a minor source for Berdyaev, the most important being Solovyov's concept of "all-encompassing unity" (*vseedinstvo*). Solovyov's description of *"vseedinstvo"* is replete with the metaphoric language of love:

Already in the world of nature everything belongs to the idea [of *vseedinstvo*],[32] but her true essence demands that everything not only belong to her, that everything be included in her or embraced by her, but also *that she belong to everything herself*, that *everything*, that is, *all* private and individual creatures and, consequently, *each* of them, actually possess [*obladat'*] this ideal *vseedinstvo*, including it within themselves. ("Smysl liubvi," p. 542)

Yet in this spiritual orgy, incorporation and filling, not penetration, are the dominant images: the task of love consists in man's "being able, while remaining himself, to incorporate absolute content into his own form, to become absolute personality, but in order to be filled with absolute content (which in religious language is called eternal life or the Kingdom of God), human form must be restored (integrated) to its original nature [i.e., androgyny]" ("Smysl liubvi," p. 513). Indeed, man's task in achieving this state is to eliminate the spiritual hymen dividing him from all others: "Man, . . . being only one person and not another, can become everyone only by removing in his consciousness and life that internal border [*gran'*] that divides him from another" (p. 506). It is no coincidence that *vseedinstvo* is defined as "a certain manner of perceiving [or of "taking in," *vospriniat'*] and of appropriating to oneself everything else" (pp. 506–7). The entire utopian enterprise appears to be one of appropriation; in conquering the forces of history, man makes himself immortal not only by ridding himself of woman, but by retaining her womb and making it his own.

In capturing the womb, the utopian man does not stake any claims on female sexuality. As it has been defined by Berdyaev and Weininger above, female sexuality is fundamentally antiutopian; female arousal, unlimited by time or space, never escapes from history or geography, it is never ruptured, always present. Male sexuality, with its penchant for the "vulcanic" and its ability to become "absent" (the terms are Weininger's), purports, however, to be hostile to the cloying metonymics of female arousal. Rather, man, as these philosophers portray him, seeks his satisfaction on the wings of metaphor, which can equate sexuality or the human body with an image without necessitating temporary or spatial contamination. Male sexuality's purported separateness, its distinctness, is crucial to this metaphoric property, and it is also essential to traditional chiliastic and utopian imagery: the single event ending time, the island appearing on no map. Weininger and Berdyaev provide a further clue that this metaphoric dynamic may be related not only to traditional views of male orgasm but also to traditional male fears about male and female anatomy. All of Weininger's biological/metaphysical views are based, he admits, on the "crude" fact that "man has a penis, woman a vagina" (*Pol i kharakter*, p. 108). Weininger's work displays evident fears of anatomical loss, but he makes the possibility of castration into a virtue: "Since a man's sexuality is only an appendage and does not take up his whole life, it gives him the opportunity of psychologically distinguishing it from the general background and thus of comprehending it. A man may juxtapose himself to his sexuality and contemplate it isolated from the rest of him" (p. 107). With this, Weininger is off and running, and from this single fact he begins to "prove" that woman lacks the capacity to make detached, rational and moral judgments, lacks personality and lacks a soul.

Berdyaev also attempts to make a virtue out of the "differentiation" implicit in male sexuality, of man's ability to detach himself from sexual urges while incorporating "the entire plenitude of his personality's spiritual life independent of time" (*Smysl tvorchestva*, pp. 254–55). But this ability to achieve detachment also triggers fears of that detachment's becoming permanent, anxieties about metaphysical castration that surface in Berdyaev's work. Berdyaev, who confesses, "in the element of female love there is something awfully terrifying for a man, something threatening and devouring, like the ocean," further asserts, "[in] the field of male consciousness something emerges into the foreground, something else retreats, but nothing disappears, nothing loses its strength" (p. 255). Moreover, Berdyaev is extremely concerned with the problem of *otorvannost'* (isolation, or, more literally, detachment, from *otorvat'*, to tear off), particularly when he criticizes sectarianism, a concept that, in the context of Russian culture and the self-mutilating *skoptsy*, references castration: "Sectarianism is worse and more dangerous than individualism, for it creates the illusion of universalism; in it there is a seeming escape from separateness [*ot'edinennost'*], from individual isolation [*otorvannost'*]. The individualism of an isolated [*otorvannaia*] group is more difficult to overcome than the individualism of a single isolated [*otorvannogo*] person" (p. 190). The utopian's metaphoric reliance on the notion of a "velcro" organ is thus not without its already implicit dangers and fears. Here again, the poetics of "inside out" come into play. We have already discussed the repressive nature of the utopian enterprise, and the epitome of utopian metaphor is the device of metathesis. As Solovyov tells us, metathesis was in the service of utopians long before Butler's *Erewhon*: "[the Romans] believed in the legend that the true name of their eternal city should be read in the sacred . . . manner—from right to left—and then from strength it would be transformed into love. Roma . . . read in the original, semitic way is *Amor*."[33] Solovyov and Berdyaev were transposing anatomy into metaphysics and then reading the male body metathetically, or, as Berdyaev suggests, "inside out." The male sex drive, delighted and terrified by its physical "separateness," seeks metaphoric refuge in the image of a male-owned womb. Berdyaev explains emphatically: "Every mysticism teaches that the depths of a man are more than human, that in them is hidden a mysterious link with God and with the world. The true exit escape from self, from one's reserve and isolation [*otorvannost'*] is hidden within oneself and not outside, in that which is within, not without" (*Smysl tvorchestva*, p. 332). Solovyov's metathetics are even more anatomically correct. Human activity informed by the ideal of *vseedinstvo* releases "real spiritual-bodily currents," but he assures us, "the strength of this spiritual-bodily creativity in man is only the *turning inward* of that same creative strength which, in nature, being turned outward, has created the bad infinity of the physical reproduction of organisms" ("Smysl liubvi," p. 547).

Although the stream of postrevolutionary culture was formed

by many more philosophical currents than the one we are considering, the imagery and desires of early Soviet society cannot be fully understood without reference to the prerevolutionary philosophical assault on the female body. Sifting through the texts that early Soviet society generated, we repeatedly see the dynamic of male womb-appropriation at work, often in kaleidoscopic combination with other symbolic myths. It is not surprising, of course, that maternal imagery should have been mobilized by a nation obsessed with the birth of a new order and a new man. A decade before the revolution, the literary critic Akim Volynsky had declared: "the suffering and triumphant cry of mothers resounds in all revolutions of world importance, and it may be said that all genuinely fertile revolutions are a symbol of the world's maternity."[34] Symbols, however, like fertility, may be manipulated and controlled, and maternity's match to utopian aspirations in the Soviet period produced some curious offspring. There is no space here to provide a comprehensive family tree; for the time being we will merely acquaint ourselves with a few of the scions.

The revolution, Boris Pilnyak tells us, was a time when "women's muffs disappeared in Russia because women grew masculine."[35] It was a time when "children [were] not born to workers"[36] and when a man could "know the secret of a machine's birth."[37] Their breasts chopped off by White soldiers, Bolshevik women became martyrs to a utopian text's desire, while their Red Army brothers amused themselves trying on lingerie.[38] Literature of the 1920s is strewn with the corpses of children whose deaths, though mourned, fulfilled the culture's repressed and inherited authorial wish. And female pregnancy could still be depicted in terms intended to disgust, while those who failed to accept the changes of October cried: "I would tie all your women to their husbands' beds and tell 'em: give birth, you bitches!"[39] Trotsky noted a dangerous tendency in the 1920s to juxtapose the categories of *byt* (everyday life) and revolution,[40] and Kazimir Malevich, following in the footsteps of Berdyaev, considered the entire category of *byt* bourgeois,[41] but throughout the 1920s the unspoken equation beneath society's hostility toward this ontological category was "*byt* = woman."[42] The Komsomol press protested against this association and repeatedly excoriated the tendency of young Soviet men to treat women only as objects;

the organization's journalists saw in this tendency to marginalize women from the community of communist "subjects" the root of the much-criticized phenomenon of urban hooliganism.[43]

Our first exhibit (Fig. 1) is a particularly instructive example of how the surgical utopian myth was deployed. This poster by Mayakovsky and M. M. Cheremnykh dating from 1920 tells of a peasant woman who refuses to give a bread ring to a hungry Red soldier and who is devoured by the marauding Pole who defeats him. As Victoria Bonnell suggests, this poster uses the figure of the full-busted peasant to "exemplif[y] many of the negative attributes the Bolsheviks saw in this segment of the rural population: ignorance and political stupidity, blind self-interest, petty bourgeois greed."[44] Underlying this caricature, however, we find, virtually in parable form, the procreative dynamics we have been examining. The woman is surrounded by holes, and from this encompassing array of sexually charged items, attached to various parts of her body (here we should recall the myth of woman's undifferentiated sexuality), the soldier demands a hole for himself. The woman is subsequently eliminated (in an image projecting male castration fears?), and all that remains is a single bread ring: the survival of the female genitalia without woman. A tragic tale? Perhaps, but as the moral we see one man handing another a sack of flour that looks suspiciously like an egg. Woman's disappearance has led to a depiction of what we might call revolutionary ovulation.[45]

Our second exhibit is Andrei Platonov's story "Ivan Zhokh," first published in 1927. The line of utopian thinking that we have been following made its contribution to Platonov's work, and so, not surprisingly, dying children and womb imagery are central to his writing. In his novel, *Chevengur*, for example, a newcomer to the utopia notices that "from the sunny center of the sky nourishment was oozing to all men, like blood from a mother's umbilical cord."[46] Platonov was also, however, influenced strongly by Vasily Rozanov, a prerevolutionary, self-described antiutopian thinker who glorified human sexuality and woman's reproductive role, albeit from an extremely patriarchal position. In Platonov's use of womb imagery, indeed throughout much of his work, Berdyaev (or Solovyov), Fyodorov, and Rozanov seem to struggle with each other, so that, as in the passage cited above, it is unclear whether the umbilical cord is being appropriated for service to the utopian

Fig. 1. A colored lithograph created in 1920 by Vladimir Mayakovsky and M. M. Cheremnykh, titled *The Story of the Bread Rings* (*Istoriia pro bubliki i pro babu, ne priznaiushchuiu Respubliki*).

Historectomies

ideal (metonymy, indeed *the* metonymy, enslaved to metaphor) or whether the utopian ideal itself is not simply serving as a cover for a manifestation of sexual desire that an internal censor otherwise could not allow (metaphor pandering to metonymy). Rozanov's (and Gorky's, to cite a politically diametrically opposed figure with a similar respect for maternity) love of childbirth brings several children into Platonov's utopian world, but not surprisingly, they nearly always die, almost as a matter of course, for Berdyaev and Fyodorov are busy as subtextual midwives. But where Rozanov's vocabulary uses a rhetoric of purity to talk about the body, and even about the sex organs (he uses the word "pure" [*chistyi*] as frequently as does Chernyshevsky or Kollontai), Platonov is one of the first twentieth-century writers to ask himself whether he is valuing the flesh (that oppressed member of the body/soul dichotomy) as a good proletarian writer should. Platonov obsessively examines those boots to make sure that no dirt has been shaken loose.

"Ivan Zhokh" is essentially a story in two parts. The first tells how in the late eighteenth century a pretender named Ivan Zhokh leads a group of Old Believers in a rebellion against the empress and, having failed, takes them into Siberia to find refuge. In the second part, a group of communist partisans stumble upon the home of Zhokh's descendants—"Eternal-City-on-the-Far-Away-River"—and learn about its past.[47]

As the partisans near the city Zhokh built, they are in a desperate state, chased by Admiral Kolchak and "losing their last courage" (*muzhestvo*, literally "virility"). This loss apparently does not matter, for in the eternal city, resplendent with Greek architecture, there are no women and few noncastrated men. Castration, however, is not the founding act of sexual violence upon which the Old Believers have built their timeless walls. A native of Eternal-City-on-the-Far-Away-River gives the partisans a lesson in ahistory:

> Zhokh pretended to be Tsar Peter Fedorovich just like Emelian Pugachev. But Teshcha strangled Zhokh because Zhokh had gotten himself a wife from the Urals, where he had once lived and fought against Catherine the Great. This same Teshcha took pity on Zhokh's woman, for she was already with child. Later, she conceived a son from Teshcha as well. But no sooner had she given birth to his son, Georgy, than Teshcha cut out her uterus with a bread knife, and she died.[48]

Here, in its purest form, the hysterectomy is clearly visible as the operation that Man brings into play to put an end to reproduction and history. Platonov's utopian surgery may be more graphic than that of his predecessors. But even as he perpetuated a metaphor he was incarnating it, restoring flesh as he cut away at it, taking language seriously, like that misguided child-murderer, Iosif Tsimbaliuk.

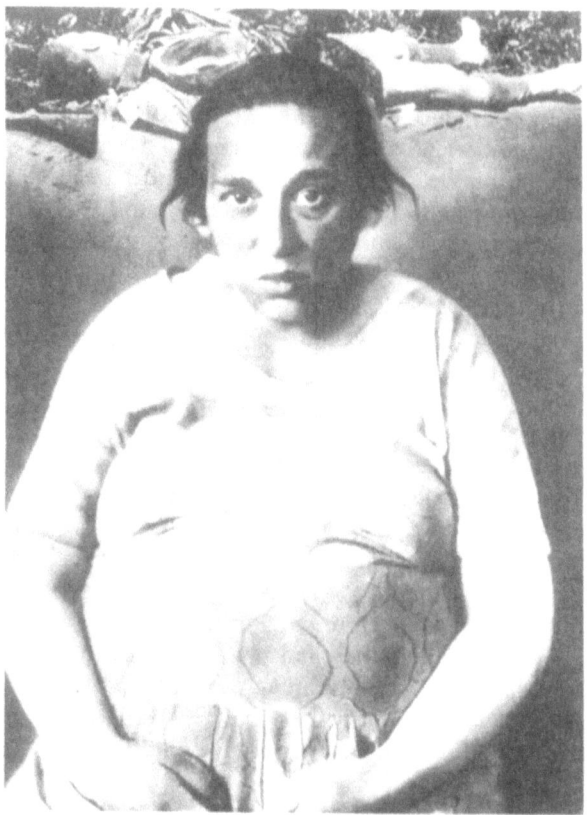

Fig. 2. A photomontage by John Heartfield, which was published in 1935 in the Soviet propaganda journal *USSR in Construction*. The image is captioned: "IN A CAPITALIST COUNTRY WHAT FATE AWAITS MY CHILD?" Reprinted from *USSR in Construction*, no. 6 (1935), p. 3.

Historectomies 275

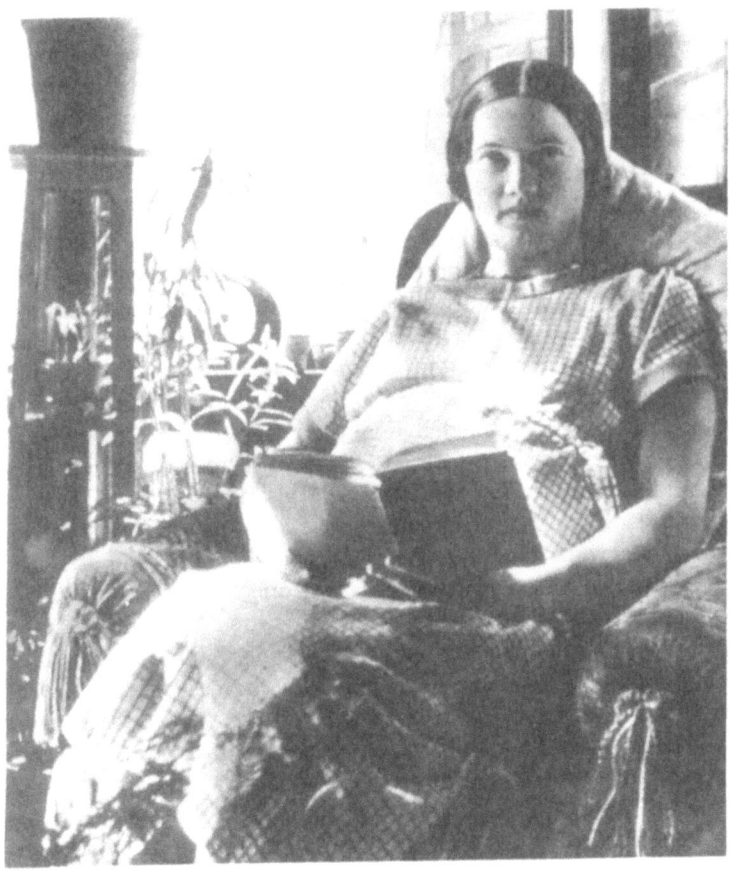

Fig 3. Photograph published in 1935 in the Soviet propaganda journal *USSR in Construction*. The photo is captioned: "IN THE USSR: MOTHERS! BEAR CHILDREN, FOR SOCIALISM NEEDS DIRECTING FORCES. BEAR CHILDREN, FOR A JOYOUS CHILDHOOD AND HAPPY LIFE AWAITS THEM." Reprinted from *USSR in Construction*, no. 6 (1935), p. 4.

By the mid-1930s, historectomies, one might expect, would no longer be present in the Soviet discursive arsenal. After all, this was the era when large families were rewarded, when abortion and divorce were made more difficult, and when the Soviet Union could take pride in the following "fact": "in not a single capitalist state has there been nor can there be anything even remotely resembling the enormous care for the woman-mother and for her children that is displayed by the government of our great socialist motherland and by the beloved leader of the nations of the world—Stalin."[49] Even here, however, the past has left its traces, as we can see by comparing Figure 2 and 3, which show pages from the Soviet propaganda journal *USSR in Construction*. Pregnancy in capitalism is not a pretty sight, ostensibly because war and poverty are a prospective mother's lot. In this photomontage selected to represent pregnancy under capitalism, however, we should not fail to notice that the pregnant body plays an important role in creating a sense of ugliness: the woman's belly is pushed to the fore, unmediated, into the viewer's face. In Figure 3, the pregnant belly is hidden; we have access to it only through a text, the book that the mother-to-be holds in her hands.[50] The title of the book is not clear, but we can easily surmise to whom the text—and what it covers—belongs. The page preceding the two photos made it clear that there is only one text that matters: the leader's words about the importance of the "New Generation" are presented in their authenticating original and are quoted in huge capital letters; beneath them is a hymn to the nation's love of children, which informs the reader, "THE SOVIET CHILDREN REPLY TO THIS TREMENDOUS LOVE AND CARE WHICH THE COUNTRY GIVES THEM BY THEIR LOVE AND LOYALTY TO THEIR FATHERLAND, TO OUR GREAT COMMUNIST PARTY, TO OUR LEADER COMRADE STALIN."[51] The cadence, leading from FATHERLAND to STALIN, explains why there is no father in the picture, and we can deduce from the place of the book just whose holy spirit has done the ideological inseminating. The womb, in short, is still being appropriated, even if it is no longer being excised. The premium now being placed on childhood necessitates that totalitarian language enter into potentially contaminating metonymic proximity to the female genitals and the womb, but it is still language, and language metaphorically used, that makes the purifying leap from genitalized text to Stalin and continues to raise physical relations to a higher, ideological plane where the uterus still belongs to MAN.

Notes

Notes

Costlow, Sandler, and Vowles: Introduction

1. Igor' Kon, "Seksual'naia revoliutsiia v kavychkakh i bez kavychek," a conversation and commentary prepared by Aleksei Samoilov, *Avrora*, no. 7 (1991), pp. 63–80; quotation from p. 75.
2. Eve Kosofsky Sedgwick, *The Epistemology of the Closet* (Berkeley, Calif., 1990), p. 29.
3. Michel Foucault, *The History of Sexuality, Volume I: An Introduction*, trans. Robert Hurley (New York, 1980), p. 4.
4. There are others of course, but the currency of these stereotypes is affirmed in the visual clichés that open a recent American film, *Moscow on the Hudson* (1984).
5. In advance of the symposium we encouraged participants to consider phenomena as diverse as the Russian baths and the visual representations of the body in painting, including icon painting. Foucault offers some remarkable insights into the ways that household architecture, for example, can participate in a regime of care for the body. See vol. 3 of *The History of Sexuality, The Care of the Self*, trans. Robert Hurley (New York, 1986), pp. 99–104.
6. See Sedgwick, *Epistemology of the Closet*, particularly "Introduction: Axiomatic," pp. 1–66.
7. Medieval historians and literary scholars have begun documenting more fully the sexual customs of pre-Petrine Russia. Eve Levin's paper in this volume is part of that tendency. See also her book, *Sex and Society in the World of the Orthodox Slavs, 900–1700* (Ithaca, N.Y., 1989); Christine D. Worobec, "Accommodation and Resistance," in Barbara Evans Clement, Barbara Alpern Engel, and Christine D. Worobec, eds., *Russia's Women: Accommodation, Resistance, Transformation* (Berkeley, Calif., 1991), pp. 17–28, esp. pp. 21–22; and, in the same volume, Eve Levin, "Childbirth in pre-Petrine Russia: Canon Law and Popular Traditions," pp. 49–59, where discussion of purification rituals is especially interesting in its effects on ideas about women's sexuality; and, in the same volume, N. L. Pushkareva, "Women in the Medieval Russian Family," pp. 29–43, esp. pp. 37–39.
8. Peter's reforms in this area have been little studied, despite the importance that he and his contemporaries granted them. This importance was in accord with Enlightenment views that saw the position of women in society and the treatment they received at the hands of men as indications of the barbarism or progress of that society. On Peter's reforms see

Dorothy Atkinson's "Society and the Sexes in the Russian Past," in Dorothy Atkinson, Alexander Dallin, and Gail Warshofsky Lapidus, eds., *Women in Russia* (Stanford, Calif., 1977), pp. 3–38; Nancy Shields Kollman, "The Seclusion of Elite Muscovite Women," *Russian History*, 10, pt. 2 (1983), pp. 170–87.

9. For Enlightenment thought on women in general see P. Hoffmann's *La Femme dans la pensée des Lumières* (Paris, 1977), and Sylvana Tomaselli's "The Enlightenment Debate on Women," *History Workshop Journal*, issue 20 (Autumn 1985), pp. 101–24; for an old but useful general introduction to Western attitudes to Russia see Albert Lortholary's *Le mirage russe en France au XVIIIe siècle* (Paris, 1951).

10. For foreign attitudes to mixed bathing see A. G. Cross, "The Russian *Banya* in the Descriptions of Foreign Travellers and in the Depictions of Foreign and Russian Artists," *Oxford Slavonic Papers*, n.s., 24 (1991), pp. 34–59; Levin, *Sex and Society in the World of the Orthodox Slavs*, pp. 195–97; and Judith Vowles's paper in this volume. Catherine II subsequently enacted a series of laws, often on the recommendation of foreign advisers, to keep the sexes apart in certain settings, including the baths, prisons, and hospitals, where they had formerly been housed together.

11. *Memoirs of Jacques Casanova de Seingalt*, trans. Arthur Machen, 6 vols. (London, 1894), vol. 5, p. 518.

12. For Michel Foucault's analysis of the role played by late eighteenth-century systems of knowing, see *The Order of Things: An Archaeology of the Human Sciences* (New York, 1970), pp. 217–302.

13. Thomas Laqueur, *Making Sex* (Cambridge, Mass., 1990), p. 5. Laqueur takes Foucault, among others, as a point of departure. As historian Lawrence Stone and literary scholar Jean Hagstrum have documented, the eighteenth century saw important changes in the ways in which love and sex were represented, bawdiness and an often playful eroticism giving way to a more puritanical and spiritualized love. See Stone's massive study *The Family, Sex and Marriage in England, 1500–1800* (New York, 1977), and Jean H. Hagstrum, *Sex and Sensibility. Ideal and Erotic Love from Milton to Mozart* (Chicago, 1980). One eighteenth-century writer who is often viewed as representing certain aspects of Enlightenment thought carried to their logical conclusion in the twentieth century is the Marquis de Sade; his work has recently attracted the attention of Viktor Erofeev. See his essay "Markiz de Sad, sadizm i XX vek," in Viktor Erofeev, *V labirinte prokliatykh voprosov* (Moscow, 1990), pp. 225–55. This essay, and a translation of Sade's *Justine* into Russian, drew the attention of a recent reviewer: see Aleksei Zverev, "Prestupleniia strasti," *Znamia*, no. 6 (1992), pp. 212–19, especially pp. 212–13.

14. I. R. Titunik, "Vasilii Trediakovskii and Eduard Limonov: Erotic Reverberations in the History of Russian Literature," in Kenneth N. Brostrom, ed., *Russian Literature and American Critics* (Ann Arbor, Mich., 1986), pp. 393–404.

15. V. Pokrovskii, *Shchegoli v satiricheskoi literature XVIII veka* (Moscow, 1903), and *Schchegolikhi v satiricheskoi literature XVIII veka* (Moscow, 1903). For a more recent account of eighteenth-century Russian literary attitudes, see Joe Andrew, *Women in Russian Literature, 1780–1863* (London, 1988), pp. 12–26.

16. M. M. Shcherbatov, *On the Corruption of Morals in Russia*, trans. and ed. A. Lentin (Cambridge, Eng., 1969).

17. Some of the newly available material about sex in contemporary Russia turns its attention to the "exotic" East rather than the "decadent" West. See, for example, *Tantra liubvi: Vostochnaia kul'tura seksa* (Leningrad, 1991); Chzhan' Zholon, *Dao liubvi* (Tallin, 1991). The popular literature about sex now widely available in Russia also features many volumes of translated essays or excerpts, some mixing East and West, contemporary and ancient. See, for example, R. G. Podol'nyi, ed., *Mir i eros: Antologiia filosofskikh tekstov o liubvi* (Moscow, 1991).

18. Compare the pointed observations of philosopher Marilyn Frye about the extant definitions of "lesbian" in her book *The Politics of Reality: Essays in Feminist Theory* (Trumansburg and New York, 1983), pp. 156–61.

19. See Titunik, "Vasilii Trediakovskii and Eduard Limonov," pp. 395–97. We give the date of the second edition of *Journey to the Island of Love* because, as Irina Reyfman points out, Trediakovsky tried to buy up and destroy copies of the first edition and it was the second that most readers knew. Reyfman gives a compelling argument for Trediakovsky's attractiveness to twentieth-century writers who sought models for their own acts of nonconformity; see Irina Reyfman, *Vasilii Trediakovsky: The Fool of the "New" Russian Literature* (Stanford, Calif., 1990), pp. 236–47; for her accounts of the editions of *Journey to the Island of Love*, see pp. 41, 151.

20. Georgii Gachev, "Russkii eros," in A. V. Gulyga, ed., *Opyty* (Moscow, 1990), pp. 210–46; the reference here is to pp. 211–12. Subsequent references are given in the text.

21. See, for example, Zbignev Lev-Starovich, *Seks v kul'turakh mira*, trans. I. I. Bogut, St. Lashin, and E. I. Filippova (Moscow, 1991), pp. 250–52; I. S. Kon, *Vvedenie v seksologiiu* (Moscow, 1990), pp. 317–32. A book that more explicitly ties the study of language to an investigation of sexual practices and attitudes is V. Kozlovskii, *Argo russkoi gomoseksual'noi subkul'tury: Materialy k izucheniiu* (Benson, Vt., 1986).

22. For the eighteenth century, see Titunik, "Vasilii Trediakovskii and Eduard Limonov," and J. L. Rice, "A Russian Bawdy Song of the Eighteenth Century," *Slavonic and East European Review*, no. 4 (1976), pp. 353–70.

23. For an intelligent analysis of how linguistic taboo has been working in recent cultural texts, particularly the differences between what is permissible in film versus what cannot be tolerated in elite literature, see Nancy Condee and Vladimir Padunov, "*Makulakul'tura*: Reprocessing Culture," *October*, no. 57 (1991), pp. 79–103, esp. pp. 89–91.

24. V. N. Voloshinov, *Freudianism: A Critical Sketch*, trans. I. R. Titunik (Bloomington, Ind., 1987), p. 90. These remarks are made in the context of a Marxist analysis of Freudianism and are directed against the emphasis placed on the explanatory powers of the sexual at the expense of economic, class, and cultural factors. As several of the papers here show—for example, Elizabeth Wood's paper on prostitution or Catriona Kelly's paper on misogyny in the *Petrushka* plays—these are not mutually exclusive, nor is the explanatory power of the latter adequate.

25. There is a parallel here to the frequent treatment of feminist thought in Russia as something Western and largely irrelevant. For intelligent accounts of this phenomenon, see Nina Belyaeva, "Feminism in the USSR," *Canadian Woman Studies*, 10, no. 4 (Winter 1989), pp. 17–19; Olga Lipovskaya, "Why Men Have Not Been Overcome: Or, 'the Costs of Emancipation,'" *Russia and the World*, no. 18 (1990), pp. 29–32; Helena Goscilo, "Domostroika or Perestroika? The Construction of Womanhood in Culture Under Glasnost," in Thomas Lahusen, ed., *Soviet Culture Today* (forthcoming); and Barbara Heldt, "Gynoglasnost: Writing the Feminine," in Mary Buckley, ed., *Perestroika and Soviet Women* (Cambridge, Eng., 1992), pp. 160–75. Better known are Francine du Plessix-Gray, *Soviet Women: Walking the Tightrope* (New York, 1989), and Tatyana Tolstaya's review of *Soviet Women*, "Notes from Underground," *New York Review of Books*, May 31, 1990, pp. 3–7. Many contributors to this volume (and many other Slavists) have also witnessed the resistance to feminism at recent conferences, for example the Fourth International Congress of Slavists held at Harrogate, England, in 1990, and the conference "Glasnost in Two Cultures," New York Institute for the Humanities, New York University, March 1991.

26. Other examples of such references to Catherine can be found in Brenda Meehan-Waters, "Catherine the Great and the Problem of Female Rule," *Russian Review*, 34, no. 3 (July 1975), pp. 293–307; and John T. Alexander, *Catherine the Great* (Oxford, 1989), especially the chapters "Nymphomania? Favorites and Favoritism" and "Epilogue: The Legend of Catherine the Great."

27. Mario Praz, *The Romantic Agony* (Oxford, 1933), pp. 207, 209–10.

28. Joseph Tenenbaum, *The Riddle of Woman* (New York, 1936), p. 74, as quoted by Diana Lewis Burgin in an earlier version of her essay. These visions of Russia as inordinately sexual participate in what has been identified as the discourse of Orientalism: Russia is rendered "East" in ways that Western-looking Russian intellectuals typically resent. For a good discussion that positions Russia between East and West, see Greta Slobin's treatment of sexual themes in Vasily Aksyonov's novel *Island of Crimea* (*Ostrov Krym*, 1981): "Revolution Must Come First: Reading V. Aksenov's *Island of Crimea*," in Andrew Parker, Mary Russo, Doris Sommer, and Patricia Yeager, eds., *Nationalisms and Sexualities* (New York, 1992), pp. 246–59.

29. An analysis of the ways in which definitions of woman as Other have been central to Western culture and thought forms the foundation of Simone de Beauvoir's classic *The Second Sex*, trans. H. M. Parshley (New York, 1952). Russian readers may be getting belated exposure to *The Second Sex*: it, along with Margaret Mead's book *Male and Female* (1949), is a point of departure for a survey of American feminist thought that appeared in Russia's leading journal of philosophy. See N. S. Iulina, "Problemy zhenshchin: Filosofskie aspekty (Feministskaia mysl' v SShA)," *Voprosy filosofii*, no. 5 (1988), pp. 137–47.

30. We refer to Berdyaev's *Russkaia ideia* (Paris, 1946), cited here in English translation from *The Russian Idea*, trans. R. M. French (Boston, 1962), and to an excerpt from his 1949 book *Self-Knowledge (Samopoznanie)* published in A. V. Gulyga, ed., *Opyty* (Moscow, 1990), pp. 422–74; and to Simon Karlinsky, "Russia's Gay Literature and Culture: The Impact of the October Revolution," in Martin Duberman, Martha Vicinus, and George Chauncey, Jr., eds., *Hidden from History: Reclaiming the Gay and Lesbian Past* (New York, 1989) pp. 347–64. Future references to these works will be made in the body of our essay.

31. See, for example, the selections from Rozanov included in the anthology *Russkii eros, ili filosofiia liubvi v Rossii*, ed. V. P. Shestakov (Moscow, 1991), pp. 106–50. In one passage, the volume even censors the word for masturbation (p. 143). A recent collection of Rozanov's writings, though broad in its reach (it includes literary essays, the important philosophical piece *Uedinennoe*, and some of Rozanov's letters), also omits his milestone treatment of homosexuality, *Liudi lunnago sveta* (1913). See Rozanov, *Sochineniia* (Moscow, 1990). *Liudi lunnago sveta* has now been reissued separately (Moscow, 1990). The full text of his "Mimoletnoe" was republished in *Kontekst 1989* (Moscow, 1989), pp. 182–230.

32. Other essays about sexuality in Russian culture by Karlinsky include "Gay Life in the Age of Two Josephs: McCarthy and Stalin," *The Advocate*, Apr. 28, 1983, pp. 37–39; "Russia's Gay Literature and History (11th–20th Centuries)," *Gay Sunshine* (San Francisco), nos. 29–30 (1976), pp. 1–7; "Gay Life Before the Soviets: Revisionism Revised," *The Advocate*, Apr. 1, 1982, pp. 31–34, as well as his book *The Sexual Labyrinth of Nikolai Gogol* (Cambridge, Mass., 1976; reissued in paperback, Chicago, 1992). For a bibliography of Karlinsky's work compiled by Molly Molloy, see *Russian Review*, 49, no. 1 (Jan. 1990), pp. 57–76.

33. Karlinsky employs the same forthrightness to describe Tsvetaeva's bisexuality in the revised edition of his biography *Marina Tsvetaeva: The Woman, Her World, and Her Poetry* (Cambridge, Eng., 1985).

34. See for example Olga Matich, "Androgyny and the Russian Silver Age," *Pacific Coast Philology*, 14 (Oct. 1979), pp. 42–50. For a discussion of the extent to which the ethos of midcentury radicalism was grounded in denying sexuality and private emotions, see Aileen Kelly, "Self-Censorship and the Russian Intelligentsia, 1905–1914," *Slavic Review*, 46, no. 2 (Summer 1987), pp. 193–213.

35. See also Barbara Alpern Engel, "St. Petersburg Prostitutes in the Late Nineteenth Century: A Personal and Social Profile," *Russian Review*, 48 (Jan. 1989), pp. 21–44; Laura Engelstein, "Gender and the Juridical Subject: Prostitution and Rape in Nineteenth-Century Russian Criminal Codes," *Journal of Modern History*, no. 60 (1988), pp. 458–95; Laura Engelstein, "Morality and the Wooden Spoon: Russian Doctors View Syphilis, Social Class, and Sexual Behavior, 1890–1905," *Representations*, no. 14 (Spring 1986), pp. 169–208; Richard Stites, "Prostitute and Society in Pre-Revolutionary Russia," *Jahrbücher für Geschichte Osteuropas*, no. 31 (1983), pp. 348–64. For work on images of the prostitute in contemporary Russian culture, see below.

36. The "woman question" in Russia is traditionally assumed to begin with the period of eased censorship inaugurated by the death of Nicholas I, in 1855. See G. A. Tishkin, *Zhenskii vopros v Rossii v 50–60 gg. XIX v.* (Leningrad, 1984); Richard Stites, *The Women's Liberation Movement in Russia: Feminism, Nihilism, and Bolshevism, 1860–1930* (Princeton, N.J., 1978); and Barbara Engel, *Mothers and Daughters: Women of the Intelligentsia in Nineteenth-Century Russia* (Cambridge, Eng., 1983).

37. Quoted in Stites, *Women's Liberation*, p. 46.

38. "Orthodoxy, especially Russian Orthodoxy, does not have its own justification of culture. There was in it a nihilistic element in relation to everything which man creates in this world" (Berdyaev, *Russian Idea*, p. 129). Berdyaev's association of this lack of a justification of culture and an asceticism of the flesh is made explicit in his discussion of Nikolai Chernyshevsky, whose moral (as opposed to sexual) concerns with human relationships Berdyaev deeply applauds. "The flesh," writes Berdyaev, "interested Chernyshevsky very little" (ibid., p. 109).

39. Vasily Rozanov, "People of the Moonlight," in *Four Faces of Rozanov: Christianity, Sex, Jews and the Russian Revolution*, trans. Spencer Roberts (New York, 1978), p. 121. Eric Naiman, in his essay in this volume, notes that Berdyaev and Chernyshevsky both express revulsion at the penis—Berdyaev by quoting Leonardo da Vinci and Chernyshevsky in confessing more privately to his journal.

40. Nikolai Chernyshevsky, *What Is to Be Done?*, trans. Michael Katz (Ithaca, N.Y., 1989). Page references to this edition will appear parenthetically.

41. As William Wagner points out in his notes to this edition, Chernyshevsky owes a considerable debt to Russian hagiography in his portrait of this "new saint" (*What Is to Be Done?*, p. 271).

42. On the power of Rakhmetov as a model for various Russian revolutionaries, see Irina Paperno, *Chernyshevsky and the Age of Realism: A Study in the Semiotics of Behavior* (Stanford, Calif., 1988), p. 30.

43. Gachev, "Russkii eros." The essay was written in 1966 but first published in the 1990 volume (see n. 20 above), along with essays by Berdyaev and Rozanov. The context of Gachev's publication indicates something of the Silver Age roots of nonofficial intellectual discourse in

Russia, and illustrates the extent to which questions of sexuality are being raised in a decidedly *philosophical* milieu.

44. It is in this distinction that Gachev makes explicit his (and Berdyaev's) differences with Freud: Freud's service, according to Gachev, lies in his having insisted, in a period of increasing technologization of life, on the inherent *chaos* that lies beneath the complexities and accretions of modern life. However, "Eros, in [Freud's] teaching about the *libido*, was narrowed to sex, and from this point of view all social and spiritual aspects of humanity's life and creativity became sublimated, transferred forms of sexual impulses" ("Russkii eros," p. 213).

45. Ibid. "Russkii eros" in fact ends with a meditation titled "Working the Land as Love" ("Zemledelie kak liubov'"), a passage that makes explicit the opposition between compassion and lust. This opposition, pity versus desire (*pozhalel* vs. *pozhelal*), brings with it other binary pairs: adolescent versus the "confidently male" (ibid., p. 241); penetration versus preservation; exploitation versus love.

46. If Gachev appears, on the face of it, to "eroticize" work, it is crucial to note that in his definition, eros is fundamentally disembodied. Some Western feminists have argued for a distinction between sex and eros as a way of *reclaiming* the body, but Gachev's impulse is the opposite: to relegate sex to a bodily realm that is denigrated, and to locate eros in a spiritual realm beyond matter. Among feminists for whom the distinction is important, see Ann Ferguson, *Blood at the Root: Motherhood, Sexuality, and Male Dominance* (London, 1989), pp. 78–82; Nancy Hartsock, *Money, Sex and Power: Toward a Feminist Historical Materialism* (Boston, 1985), pp. 166–69; Audre Lorde, "Uses of the Erotic: The Erotic as Power," in Laura Lederer, ed., *Take Back the Night: Women on Pornography* (New York, 1980), pp. 295–300, and widely reprinted.

47. Paperno, *Chernyshevsky and the Age of Realism*, pp. 127–31.

48. See Eve Kosofsky Sedgwick, *Between Men: English Literature and Male Homosocial Desire* (New York, 1985).

49. See for example A. Kelly, "Self-Censorship and the Russian Intelligentsia," and Engel, *Mothers and Daughters*. One can dispute Engel's interpretation of radical women as having had little interest in private, intimate life (this was a lively topic for discussion at the Amherst symposium), since many of these women were intensely important to each other and cultivated relationships that need further study. Some of the primary materials for such a study are easily available in *Five Sisters: Women Against the Tsar*, eds. Barbara Alpern Engel and Clifford N. Rosenthal (New York, 1977), and one might compare the close relations among imprisoned political women a century later as described in Irina Ratushinskaya, *Grey Is the Color of Hope*, trans. Alyona Kojevnikov (New York, 1988).

50. For a painfully immediate sense of how Kollontai experienced this treatment of her achievements, see her memoir *The Autobiography of a*

Sexually Emancipated Communist Woman, trans. Salvator Attanasio (New York, 1971), pp. 1–48. Originally published in German in 1927 as "Ziel und Wert meines Lebens," in Elga Kern, ed., *Führende Frauen Europas*, 1st ser. (Munich, 1927), pp. 258–86. We know of no Russian original.

51. Cited from excerpts from her notebooks from the years 1946–51, published in Aleksandra Kollontai, *Iz moei zhizni i raboty* (Moscow, 1974), p. 371. Compare a comment dated 1926: "the complete liberation of the working woman and the creation of the foundation of a new sexual morality will always remain the highest aim of my activity, and of my life" (*Autobiography*, pp. 47–48).

52. In her biography of Kollontai, Barbara Evans Clements notes: "In contemporary society, Kollontai asserted, women's inferiority was imbedded in the pattern of erotic love, the most private of human relationships. She accepted Engels's observation that bourgeois marriage was a fraud based on property and prostitution, but she added that it also destroyed individuality." Barbara Evans Clements, *Bolshevik Feminist: The Life of Aleksandra Kollontai* (Bloomington, Ind., 1979), p. 69.

53. There are surprising similarities between Kollontai's view of sexuality and oppression and those of Catharine MacKinnon, though perhaps not so surprising given the forthright dependence on Marxism in MacKinnon's theoretical writings. See Catharine A. MacKinnon, *Towards a Feminist Theory of the State* (Cambridge, Mass., 1989). A recent essay in Marxist theory cites Kollontai as an exception to the otherwise pervasive distancing from sexual matters found in Marxist texts. See Andrew Parker, "Unthinking Sex: Marx, Engels and the Scene of Writing," *Social Text*, no. 29 (1991), pp. 28–45.

54. See Clements, *Bolshevik Feminist*, pp. 228–231, which includes the dismissal of Kollontai's short stories as "bad fiction" (p. 231), and Beatrice Farnsworth, *Aleksandra Kollontai: Socialism, Feminism, and the Bolshevik Revolution* (Stanford, Calif., 1980), pp. 326–27, where she takes the fiction to be important principally for what it reveals about Kollontai's own life.

55. Two collections of Kollontai's essays appeared in the Soviet Union in the 1970s: *Izbrannye stat'i i rechi* (Moscow, 1972) and *Iz moei zhizni*. These collections distort her views about women, however, omitting any writing that urges sexual liberation.

56. An excerpt from Kollontai's 1923 book *The Position of Women in the Economy* (*Polozhenie zhenshchin v ekonomicheskom khozhiaistve*) is included in *Iskusstvo kino*, no. 6 (1991), pp. 105–9. This remarkable issue, which is devoted entirely to feminist writing, also includes translations from feminist film theorists who have been leaders in advancing new ideas about sexuality and culture (Judith Mayne, B. Ruby Rich, and Linda Williams), as well as original essays by Russian theorists and activists. We discuss some of those essays below.

57. This view is often imparted in Kollontai's essays, particularly

"Pervye shagi po okhrane materinstva" (in Kollontai, *Iz moei zhizni*, pp. 336–40), and in her notebook fragments, where she defines women as "citizen and mother" (ibid., p. 364). It can also be vividly felt in such fictional works as "Vasilisa Malygina" (1923), included in *The Love of Worker Bees*.

58. This is particularly evident in the introductory essay and in the concluding two selections on women and the peace movement in *Women and Russia: Feminist Writings from the Soviet Union*, ed. Tatyana Mamonova (Boston, 1984). Some of the essays in this volume appeared in Russian as *Zhenshchina i Rossiia* (Paris, 1980); some were first published in English in a British edition called *Woman and Russia* (London, 1980).

59. With regard to Russian lesbians, Mamonova broke a silence that had reigned among Russian intellectuals. Her *Women and Russia* volume included four contributions in a section entitled "Between Women." The 1990 issue of *Zhenskoe chtenie* devoted entirely to lesbian thinking is likely to raise more lively and more timely debate, however. See in particular its letter to Marina Tsvetaeva by lesbian activist and filmmaker Olga Zhuk, where Tsvetaeva's denunciation of lesbianism in her "Letter to an Amazon" ("Lettre à l'Amazone," 1934) is countered brilliantly: O. Zhuk, "Pis'mo k M. I. Tsvetaevoi," *Zhenskoe chtenie*, no. 6 (1990), pp. 79–85. This letter has remarkable affinities with two essays in this volume, Diana Lewis Burgin's, with its uncovering and affirmation of a lesbian poet's fate in the Silver Age, and Svetlana Boym's on Tsvetaeva—Zhuk addresses some of the same Tsvetaeva texts as Boym, including the *Tale of Sonechka*.

60. Ol'ga Lipovskaia, "Feminizm, ili 'izderzhki emantsipatsii'?," *Zhenskoe chtenie*, no. 3 (1988), pp. 57, 63–64.

61. Joanna Hubbs, *Mother Russia: The Feminine Myth in Russian Culture* (Bloomington, Ind., 1988).

62. George P. Fedotov, *The Russian Religious Mind, Volume I: Kievan Christianity* (Belmont, Mass., 1975; first published 1946), pp. 12, 13–15.

63. The debates were heated for several reasons: some participants felt strongly that discussions of the maternal were inherently acts of avoiding the sexual, and thus repetitions of the very anxieties about the erotic that had been asserted by some as typical of Russian culture; some participants simply disagreed with the terms with which motherhood was being described, finding them at once essentializing of the maternal and glorifying of it in a way that feminists, according to this view, ought to have found more suspect.

64. The most famous site of these views in Tolstoy's works is *The Kreutzer Sonata* (*Kreitserova sonata*, 1889), and it could be argued that this story has produced a disproportionate amount of generalization about sexuality in Russian culture. For a reading of *The Kreutzer Sonata*, see Barbara Heldt, *Terrible Perfection: Women and Russian Literature* (Bloomington, Ind., 1987), pp. 38–49. A discussion of *The Kreutzer Sonata* that addresses a wide range of cultural phenomena surrounding its

publication history and reception, and also compares it to other literary treatments of marriage and sex, is Peter Ulf Møller, *Postlude to "The Kreutzer Sonata": Tolstoy and the Debate on Sexual Morality in Russian Literature in the 1890s*, trans. John Kendal (Leiden, 1988). Cathy Popkin's paper in this volume suggests that the most erotically charged aspect of *The Kreutzer Sonata* may be its narrative format. For an approach to *Anna Karenina* that raises questions of sexuality and gender from a feminist perspective, see the recent work of Amy Mandelker, including "A Painted Lady: Ekphrasis in *Anna Karenina*," *Comparative Literature*, 43, no. 1 (Winter 1991), pp. 1–19, and "Feminist Criticism and *Anna Karenina*: A Review Article," *Tolstoy Studies Journal*, 3 (1990), pp. 82–103.

65. Leo Tolstoy, *What Is Art?*, trans. A. Maude (London, 1970), p. 190.

66. Gachev here quotes Maxim Gorky, who is in turn recalling a conversation with the elderly Tolstoy. For an English translation of Gorky's reminiscences of Tolstoy, see Maxim Gorky, *Reminiscences of Tolstoy, Chekhov and Andreyev* (New York, 1959). The passage quoted is found on pp. 12–13.

67. See Mary Poovey, *Uneven Developments: The Ideological Work of Gender in Mid-Victorian England* (Chicago, 1988); Peter Gay, *The Bourgeois Experience: Victoria to Freud*, vol. 1, *The Education of the Senses* (New York, 1984), vol. 2, *The Tender Passion* (New York, 1986). Both Poovey and Gay have extensive bibliographical annotations, and the literature of this subject is vast.

68. He also vividly rephrases Tolstoy's identification of the maternal with all that is to be valued in woman. For Gachev, "the question of how to plough (work) Russia's damp mother earth [*mat' syra*], how to be with her, live with her, is absolutely the same question as how the Russian man is to love the Russian woman, to be with her, to live with her" ("Russkii eros," p. 242).

69. Other examples might include Rozanov, Fyodor Sologub, Zinaida Gippius, and Alexei Remizov. For an analysis of the place of one of these writers, Remizov, in Russian traditions and taboos of writing about sexuality, see Greta N. Slobin, "Remizov's Erotic Tales: Stylisation and Subversion," in Nicholas Luker, ed., *The Short Story in Russia 1900–1917* (Nottingham, Eng., 1991), pp. 53–72.

70. Presumably Gachev has in mind Boris Kustodiev's impressive painting of a reclining nude, *The Beauty* (*Krasavitsa*, 1915), held in Moscow's Tretyakov Gallery. This nude, and Gachev's reference more generally, ought to be considered in the context of Kustodiev's paintings of full-bodied merchant wives in brilliantly colored dress. Their indulgence in gustatory pleasure (for example, in two paintings both called *The Merchant Wife at Tea* [*Kupchikha za chaem*, 1918 and 1920]) offers up a portrait for the viewer's visual delectation and oral fantasy.

71. Although Gachev places such writing at the beginning of the twen-

tieth century, this strain of thought exists earlier: his remarks echo those of Dostoevsky's Underground Man, as well as a scene in *Brothers Karamazov* in which the pure-hearted Alyosha is teased by his schoolmates with dirty stories and smutty pictures, against which he attempts to stop his eyes and ears. One might also note that Chekhov, a writer in the "decorous Russian tradition," was also capable of keyhole narrative. See for example his short story "At Sea" ("V more," 1883), in which two sailors (father and son, no less) spy on a honeymooning couple. See A. P. Chekhov, *Polnoe sobranie sochinenii i pisem*, 30 vols. (Moscow, 1974–82), vol. 2, pp. 268–71; for an English translation, see Anton Chekhov, *The Sinner from Toledo and Other Tales*, trans. Arnold Hinchliffe (Teaneck, N.J., 1972), pp. 21–24.

72. Gachev observes that the plight, weariness, age, and frailty of Russian women, whom he describes as wives or sisters rather than mothers, evoke in the husband and brother pity and the desire to comfort and care for them rather than the desire "to penetrate, tear, torment, rip open and plough up" ("Russkii eros," pp. 243–44). Ironically, his dismal view of sex resembles that of some feminists, for example Andrea Dworkin in her essays in *Intercourse* (New York, 1987); Slavists will find much of interest in the chapter on Tolstoy, "Repulsion" (pp. 3–20). What Gachev does not add (and what is noted in a number of papers) is that the exhaustion of the women he pities might be attributed to the heavy burdens of daily life (*byt*), including the bearing and care of children, small children as well as the adult man-child. In a lengthy footnote, however, he comments that it is in women's nature to create a home, to make life comfortable for men. This home, or blanket, "swaddles the man like an infant, and he lies warm and cozy in the original bliss of babyhood and childhood"; "childhood and babyhood he can experience only with a woman" (p. 229). These remarks are made in response to a disconsolate intellectual woman's questioning him whether this was what men really wanted.

73. For the Russian text of the tale (which we cite with page number references in our text), see Ivan Bunin, *Sobranie sochinenii*, 3 vols. (Moscow, 1984), vol. 2, pp. 379–382. An English translation is available in Ivan Bunin, *Wolves and Other Love Stories*, trans. Mark Scott (Santa Barbara, Calif., 1989), pp. 65–70.

74. It is worth noting how far traditional Slavophile notions of Russia as savior of the decadent, materialist West enter into these accounts of sexuality.

75. Sedgwick takes up the different definitions but intersecting workings of sex and gender in *Epistemology of the Closet*, pp. 27–35.

76. Considerable recent feminist scholarship has focused on the role of masquerade in the social construction of gender. See, for example, Judith Butler, *Gender Trouble: Feminism and the Subversion of Identity* (New York, 1990), pp. 46–54; Judith Butler, "Gender Trouble, Feminist Theory, and Psychoanalytic Discourse," in Linda J. Nicholson, ed., *Feminism/Postmodernism* (New York, 1990), pp. 324–40, esp. 336–39;

Marjorie Garber, "Fetish Envy," *October*, no. 54 (1990), pp. 45–56, an essay that also appears in her book *Vested Interests: Cross-Dressing and Cultural Anxiety* (New York, 1992); *Body Guards: The Cultural Politics of Gender Ambiguity*, ed. Julia Epstein and Kristina Straub (New York, 1991).

77. Nadezhda Durova, "Kavalerist-devitsa," in *Izbrannye sochineniia kavalerist-devitsy* (Moscow, 1988). The memoirs are available in English: Nadezhda Durova, *The Cavalry Maiden: Journals of a Russian Officer in the Napoleonic Wars*, trans. Mary Fleming Zirin (Bloomington, Ind., 1988). For an essay on Durova in English, see Tatyana Mamonova, "Nadezhda Turova: A Russian Amazon," in her *Russian Women's Studies: Essays on Sexism in Soviet Culture* (Oxford, 1989), pp. 19–25; there is a brief discussion here of Durova in the context of cross-dressing (p. 20).

78. For a good review of recent scholarship on women who dressed as men in order to serve in the military, see Margaret Hunt, "Girls Will Be Boys," *Women's Review of Books*, 6, no. 12 (Sept. 1989), pp. 11–13. She reviews Rudolf M. Dekker and Lotte C. van de Pol, *The Tradition of Female Transvestism in Early Modern Europe* (New York, 1989), and Julie Wheelwright, *Amazons and Military Maids: Women Who Cross-Dressed in the Pursuit of Life, Liberty, and Happiness* (London, 1989).

79. Shtakenshneider is quoted by Carolina de Maegd-Soep, *The Emancipation of Women in Russian Literature and Society* (Ghent, 1978), p. 75; "Emantsipatsii v teorii i na pratike," *Svetoch*, nos. 3–4 (1861), quoted in Maegd-Soep, *Emancipation*, p. 73. See also Carolyn G. Heilbrun, *Writing a Woman's Life* (New York, 1988), pp. 33–36.

80. Reprinted in Tishkin, *Zhenskii vopros*, 12th page of illustrations (unnumbered), following p. 176.

81. On George Sand's reception in Russia, see M. Elizarova, "Zh. Zand v russkoi kritike i literature," *Uchenye zapiski MGPI im. Lenina*, 31, no. 5 (1941), pp. 41–63; and Lesley Herrmann, "*Jacques* in Russia: A Program of Domestic Reform for Husbands," *Studies in the Literary Imagination*, 12 (Fall 1979), pp. 61–81. Turgenev's story "Correspondence" ("Perepiska," 1855) features a heroine identified as a "George Sandiste," who is reviled by provincial society. Ivan Turgenev, *Polnoe sobranie sochinenii*, 28 vols. (Moscow and Leningrad, 1960–67), vol. 5, pp. 159–91.

82. As with any of the examples we have offered in this introduction, many others could be given. The unresolvability of dress and gender, for instance, calls to mind Korobochka in Gogol's *Dead Souls* (*Mertvye dushi*, 1842) and Babichev in Olesha's *Envy* (*Zavist'*, 1927).

83. See Dmitri N. Shalin, "Glasnost and Sex," *New York Times*, Jan. 23, 1990, p. A23; Katerina Clark, "Not for Sale: The Russian/Soviet Intelligentsia, Prostitution and the Paradox of Internal Colonization," paper presented to the Second Annual Working Group on Contemporary Soviet Culture, University of California at Berkeley, 1991; Francis X. Clines, "Hotel for Young Lovers? Perestroika Turns Pale," *New York*

Times, July 8, 1991, p. A4; Sergei Chuprinin, "Peremena uchasti: Russkaia literatura na poroge sed'mogo goda perestroiki," *Znamia,* no. 3 (1991), p. 227; Elena Tikhomirova, "Eros iz podpol'ia," *Znamia,* no. 6 (1992), pp. 212–29.

84. Kon, "Seksual'naia revoliutsiia v kavychkakh i bez kavychek," p. 65.

85. In a PBS newscast of August 19, 1991, Madeleine Albright noted a survey of Soviet attitudes that showed that while more than 60 percent of respondents were in favor of democratization, far fewer believed that the country's problems could be solved democratically rather than through authoritarian imposition of solutions. The problems cited were economic conditions, law and order, and the "collapse" of public morality.

86. See Elizabeth Waters, "Restructuring the 'Woman Question': *Perestroika* and Prostitution," *Feminist Review,* no. 33 (Autumn 1989), pp. 3–19. Compare the comments of Ol'ga Lipovskaia, "Feminizm, ili 'izderzhki emantsipatsii,'?" p. 62, where she notes that antiprostitution campaigns did not even imagine that there was a question of demand in all of this, that they might have targeted male consumers if they actually wanted to curtail prostitution.

87. V. Kunin, "Interdevochka," *Avrora,* nos. 2 and 3 (1988), pp. 87–139 and 89–125, respectively. The story has been translated as *Intergirl: A Hard Currency Hooker,* trans. Antonina W. Bouis (New York, 1991). Petr Todorovsky directed the film version, also entitled *Interdevochka* (1988).

88. The nudity in the play was less a part of its shocking effect, and audiences became quickly blasé about nudity on stage, as Charles Isenberg reminded us. He recalled students rioting at a nude scene in the film *Shadows of Forgotten Ancestors* when it was shown in the mid 1960s at Moscow State University, "standing on their seats, whistling, and stamping" (letter, Nov. 5, 1991). There was still much public discussion about nudity in film when *Little Vera (Malen'kaia Vera,* 1987) premiered, although even then many letters to the editor noted that it was bizarre for filmgoers to be so distracted by a two-minute sex scene.

89. Our thanks to Peter and Susan Solomon, who made a copy of the film available to us. In a penetrating analysis of this film, Irina Bagrationi-Mukhraneli suggests that *To Die for Love* is more generally about the position of women in totalitarian society, about the relationship of freedom and love. Her essay is notable for its refusal to render prostitutes as alien, the sort of woman no respectable woman would see as a reflection of herself, and also for its synthesizing account of the history of images of women in Russian culture. See Irina Bagrationi-Mukhraneli, "Desakralizatsiia zhenshchiny," *Iskusstvo kino,* no. 6 (1991), pp. 36–41.

90. An excellent if painful chronicle of the Miss USSR contest was shown on the news program *Frontline,* Feb. 6, 1990; the typescript is available from ABC. Since then, Russians have sponsored a Miss Breast contest, replete with photographed contestants in national news publica-

tions. See Liudmila Sal'nikova, "Vpered k lichnoi zhizni," *Ogonek*, no. 44 (1991), pp. 14–16; Valerii Iakov, "Obnazhenie makhom," *Stolitsa*, no. 30 (36) (1991), pp. 31–34. For an excellent feminist analysis of beauty contests, see Ol'ga Lipovskaia, "Zhenshchina kak ob"ekt potrebleniia," *Iskusstvo kino*, no. 6 (1991), pp. 18–21. *Playboy* published "Women of Russia" in its Feb. 1990 issue, pp. 71–82, which also contributed to a new awareness of the potential for Russian women to pose in pornography.

91. Russian sources for several stories are cited below. For the plays, see L. Petrushevskaia, *Pesni XX veka* (Moscow, 1988) and *Tri devushki v golubom* (Moscow, 1989). For translations of Petrushevskaia's stories into English, see "Our Crowd," in Helena Goscilo and Byron Lindsey, eds., *Glasnost: An Anthology of Russian Literature Under Gorbachev* (Ann Arbor, 1990), pp. 3–24; "The Violin" and "Mania," in Helena Goscilo, ed., *Balancing Acts* (Bloomington, 1989), pp. 122–25 and 256–60; "The Overlook," in *Soviet Women Writing* (New York, 1990), pp. 275–300; "Through the Fields," in Sergei Zalygin, ed., *The New Soviet Fiction* (New York, 1989), pp. 235–38; "Nets and Traps," in Sigrid McLaughlin, ed., *The Image of Women in Contemporary Soviet Fiction* (New York, 1989), pp. 98–110; "A Modern Family Robinson," in Oleg Chukhontsev, ed., *Dissonant Voices: The New Russian Fiction* (London, 1991), pp. 414–24.

92. This is argued cogently in a recent paper on Petrushevskaya, Narbikova, and Erofeev: Helena Goscilo, "Body Talk in Current Fiction: Speaking Parts and (W)holes," a paper presented at the Second Annual Working Group on Contemporary Soviet Culture, University of California at Berkeley, 1991. Another very good recent piece on Petrushevskaya and Tolstaya is Natal'ia Ivanova, "Idei M. M. Bakhtina i grotesk v tvorchestve Liudmily Petrushevskoi i Tat'iany Tolstoi," paper presented at the "Glasnost in Two Cultures" conference, New York Institute for the Humanities, New York University, March 1991.

93. See Liudmila Petrushevskaia, "Po doroge Boga Erosa," *Literaturnaia gazeta*, July 3, 1991, p. 12. The story opens with a description of the undoctored woman as having receded into her body as into a shell.

94. Georgii Viren, "Takaia liubov'," *Oktiabr'*, no. 3 (1989), p. 203. This is a review of four stories Petrushevskaia published in 1988: "Svoi krug," *Novyi mir*, no. 1 (1988), pp. 116–30; "Ali-Baba" and "Gripp," *Avrora*, no. 9 (1988), pp. 138–45; and "Takaia devochka," *Ogonek*, no. 40 (1988), pp. 9–11. The plot possibilities mentioned above are from these stories and from "Skripka," *Druzhba narodov*, no. 10 (1973), pp. 151–53, and "Seti i lovushki," *Avrora*, no. 4 (1974), pp. 52–55.

95. Natal'ia Ivanova, "Vybor za kazhdym: Ob al'manakhe *Aprel'* i ne tol'ko o nem," *Zvezda*, no. 9 (1990), pp. 160–65.

96. Natal'ia Ivanova, "Zhizn' prekrasna?," *Iunost'*, no. 1 (1991), pp. 60–63.

97. Some of Erofeev's less shocking stories were included in the alma-

nac *Metropol'* (they were actually pretty daring for 1979): "A Fin de Siècle Orgasm," "Humping Hannah," and "A Creation in Three Chapters" are in the English version, *Metropol: Literary Almanac*, ed. Vasily Aksyonov, Viktor Yerofeyev, Fazil Iskander, Andrei Bitov, and Yevgeny Popov (New York, 1982), pp. 457–526. "The Parakeet" and "Anna's Body" are in Goscilo and Lindsey, *Glasnost*, pp. 367–82. For Russian originals, see Erofeev's collections *Telo Anny, ili konets russkogo avangarda* (Moscow, 1989) and *Russkaia krasavitsa* (Moscow, 1990).

98. Much of Limonov's work is available in English, including his controversial novel *It's Me—Eddie: A Fictional Memoir* (New York, 1983), published in Russian as *Eto ia—Edichka* (New York, 1979). An impressive essay that puts Limonov squarely in a Russian tradition of erotic writing is Titunik, "Vasilii Trediakovskii and Eduard Limonov." A. Zholkovskii has also written enthusiastically about Limonov in "Limonov na literaturnykh Olimpiks," *Sintaksis*, no. 29 (1990), pp. 150–60.

99. To cite but one such example, there are the humiliations inflicted on a naked and drunken woman by a group of men and women that disturb even Limonov's narrator in his "On the Wild Side," *Muleta*, vol. B (1985), pp. 212–39 (though the title is in English, this is a Russian-language text).

100. "Cherez kazhdye shest' dnei—voskresen'e" is included in Makarova's first book of stories, *Katushka: Povesti* (Moscow, 1978), pp. 5–72.

101. See Roman Timenchik, "Ty—chto? ili vvedenie v teatr Petrushevskoi," in Petrushevskaia, *Tri devushki v golubom*, p. 396.

102. See Julia Voznesenskaya, *The Women's Decameron*, trans. W. B. Linton (Boston, 1985), published in Russian as *Zhenskii dekameron* (Tel Aviv, 1987). This novel is in fact but one of many works by recent Soviet women writers set in a hospital: see Helena Goscilo, "Women's Wards and Wardens: The Hospital in Contemporary Russian Women's Fiction," *Canadian Woman Studies*, 10, no. 4 (Winter 1989), pp. 83–86. This essay explicates more fully than we do here the similarities between hospital and prison, and it includes some discussion of Makarova's "Preserving Life."

103. The heroine is more than once asked questions like "At what age did you become sexually active?" in rooms where she is far from the only patient, and just about the only satisfying scene in the entire tale is when one woman, having tersely responded that this is her thirteenth pregnancy and thirteenth abortion, simply loses it when she cannot answer the next question, about her blood pressure: "I am not a wind-up doll, I am a person." See Elena Makarova, "*Na sokhranenii,*" in her *Otkrytyi final* (Moscow, 1989), p. 119.

104. Liudmila Petrushevskaia, "Smysl zhizni," *Sintaksis*, no. 28 (1990), pp. 126–28, quotation from p. 126.

105. Nina Katerli, *Polina*, in her *Tsvetnye otkrytki* (Leningrad, 1986), pp. 96–181; the scene with Boria is most fully remembered on p. 145. For the scene where Polina is called to identify the dead body of her father, see pp. 110–13.

106. The turn to death as a figure for political and cultural commentary has roots in Russian culture: Eric Naiman's paper in this volume looks back to a period earlier in this century when a quest to give life to dead ancestors was replacing imagery of childbirth, particularly women's role in bearing children. Naiman's essay ends with a brief discussion of Andrei Platonov, author of many plots of death and decay. Platonov is being widely reprinted in Russia, particularly his bleaker tales and novels not available there previously, which may have been one influence on some of the recent writing discussed above. For a provocative essay on bodies, subjectivity, and seeing in Platonov, see Valery Podoroga, "The Eunuch of the Soul: Positions of Reading and the World of Platonov," *South Atlantic Quarterly*, 90, no. 2 (Spring 1991), pp. 357–408.

107. See Viktor Erofeev, "Pominki po sovetskoi literature," *Aprel'*, 2 (1990), pp. 274–82; and Ivanova, "Vybor za kazhdym," pp. 164–65, where she discusses the Russian language as dead in the hands of all too many contemporary writers.

108. Mikhail Rykhlin has argued that terror can generate cultural texts that function either by distancing themselves from this destruction of bodies or by creating scenes of compulsive exaltation. See his "Tela terrora (tezisy k logike nasiliia)," *Bakhtinskii sbornik*, vol. 1 (Moscow, 1990), pp. 60–76. Rykhlin's essay reads Mikhail Bakhtin's 1936 book on Rabelais and the murals of the Moscow metro system, and while in both cases he offers compelling insights into how bodies were represented during a time when bodies were being destroyed, a further value of his essay is its foregrounding of the hysterically celebratory tone that existed when logically we would expect profound mourning. Mary Russo, like Rykhlin, also uses Bakhtin's theory of carnival, but to remind us that the grotesque body that finds its most extreme imagining in death is gendered, often yet another disguise for the revulsion at all things embodied and thus female. See Mary Russo, "Female Grotesques: Carnival and Theory," in Teresa de Lauretis, ed., *Feminist Studies/Critical Studies* (Bloomington, Ind., 1986), pp. 213–29.

109. See Valeriia Narbikova, "Okolo ekolo . . . ," *Iunost'*, no. 3 (1990), pp. 10–25.

110. See Valeriia Narbikova's longest tale, *Ravnovesie sveta dnevnykh i nochnykh zvezd* (Moscow, 1990).

111. Valeriia Narbikova, "Ad kak Da, aD kak dA," in Larisa Vaneeva, ed., *Ne pomniashchaia zla* (Moscow, 1990), p. 328.

112. Elena Makarova, "Herbs from Odessa," is included in Goscilo, *Balancing Acts*, pp. 19–33. For the Russian original, see Elena Makarova, *Perepolnennye dni* (Moscow, 1982), pp. 38–55.

113. See Nina Sadur, "Pronikshie," in Vaneeva, *Ne pomniashchaia zla*, pp. 217–48.

114. Other Narbikova stories with characters who play against gender boundaries are "Probeg—pro beg," *Znamia*, no. 5 (1990), pp. 61–87; and "Ad kak Da, aD kak dA." For a different kind of writer's use of

androgynous characters (one lacking the critique of the maternal, for example), compare the poet Olesia Nikolaeva's story "Invalid detstva," *Iunost'*, no. 2 (1990), pp. 34–61. At quite the opposite extreme from Nikolaeva's demanding spirituality, Limonov plays creatively and impressively with the possibilities of gender in "Krasavitsa, vdokhnovliavshchaia poeta," *Sintaksis*, 29 (1990), pp. 139–49; the same story appeared in a Soviet youth magazine, albeit with all obscenities replaced by ellipses—see *Iunost'*, no. 2 (1991), pp. 32–36.

115. Xeroxed copies of *Zhenskoe chtenie* are being distributed in the U.S. by Helena Goscilo, Slavic Department, University of Pittsburgh. As of this writing, Lipovskaya is preparing a new women's journal to be more widely circulated.

116. These developments have been chronicled well by the American gay and alternative press. See, for example, Gary Indiana, "The Boys in the Baltic," *Village Voice*, June 26, 1990, pp. 31–32; Masha Gessen, "We Have No Sex: Soviet Gays and AIDS in the Era of Glasnost," *Out/Look*, no. 9 (Summer 1990), pp. 42–54; Julie Dorf, "Tema: On the Theme, Talking with the Editor of the Soviet Union's First Gay and Lesbian Newspaper," *Out/Look*, no. 9 (Summer 1990), pp. 55–59; Masha Gessen, "Comrade in Arms," *Out/Look*, no. 12 (Spring 1991), pp. 66–71. Our information about the 1991 gay and lesbian conference and film festival comes from a report on "All Things Considered," National Public Radio, Aug. 10, 1991; and from Julie Dorf and Masha Gessen, "Notes from the Revolution," *Tema International*, no. 2 (Autumn 1991), pp. 2–9.

117. As reported in Andrew Solomon, *The Irony Tower: Soviet Artists in a Time of Glasnost* (New York, 1991), p. 280.

118. See "Gay—Slaviane," *Ogonek*, no. 12 (1991), p. 23. Dorf and Gessen, in "Notes from the Revolution," observe that the 1990 gay and lesbian conference also attracted considerable media attention, some of it surprisingly neutral.

119. For examples from the visual arts, see Solomon, *Irony Tower*, pp. 280–82, where he describes one of Timur Novikov's creations, a version of the New York skyline made of invitations from New York gay clubs.

120. Harlow Robinson, review of *The Irony Tower*, in *The New York Times Book Review*, Sunday, July 28, 1991, p. 5.

121. Gessen, "We Have No Sex." See also Dmitri N. Shalin, "The Sexual Counterrevolution," *Boston Globe*, Aug. 18, 1991, p. A25. While Shalin looks at quite a wide range of sexual freedoms that are being hampered, he bases his discussion on what happened in 1990 when the Moscow City Council permitted the registration of a gay and lesbian organization, and he notes, "attacks on homosexuals are increasing throughout the country."

122. Rasputin, as quoted by Lionel Joyce in a letter to the editor, *New York Review of Books*, Apr. 11, 1991, p. 61. (Catriona Kelly confirmed

for us that the interview, included in a segment of *The Media Show* and presented by the journalist Emma Freud, was as Joyce described it.) One could note that the purity metaphor made its presence strongly felt in the essay about Rasputin by Peter Matthiessen to which Joyce was reacting (Matthiessen, "The Blue Pearl of Siberia," *New York Review of Books*, Feb. 14, 1991, pp. 37–47). Rasputin's other metaphor, of dead bodies (in his comparison of homosexuality to necrophilia), unfortunately resonates with the representations of gay men in the age of AIDS analyzed by British and American AIDS activists. See Simon Watney, *Policing Desire: Pornography, AIDS, and the Media* (Minneapolis, 1987); Simon Watney, "The Spectacle of AIDS," *October*, no. 43 (Winter 1987), pp. 71–86; and Cindy Patton, *Inventing AIDS* (New York, 1990), among many others.

123. See George Mosse, *Nationalism and Sexuality: Respectability and Abnormal Sexuality in Modern Europe* (New York, 1985). Not all ideological deployments of a rhetoric of purity have specific links to nationalism. In the Russian tradition, utopian thinking has been another important site. See Eric Naiman, "Of Crime, Utopia, and Repressive Complements: The Further Adventures of the Ridiculous Man," *Slavic Review*, 50, no. 3 (Fall 1991), pp. 512–20.

124. See also Rasputin's essay "Cherchez la femme," *Nash sovremennik*, no. 3 (1990), pp. 168–72, a paean to femininity as nurturing and maternal. He writes, "Caretaking is the essence of woman. Comfort, warmth, tenderness, humility, nourishing, faithfulness, softness, agility, mercy—this is what woman is made of" (p. 169). His essay is succeeded in the same issue by a more aggressive piece that calls directly for policing popular morals: Tat'iana Okulova, "'Nam dobrye zheny i dobrye materi nuzhny' . . . : Razmyshleniia o zhenshchine i 'zhenskoi teme' sovremennoi masskul'ture," pp. 173–87. Okulova's Russian nationalism also visibly shows its anti-Semitic leanings: "Isn't it time to call Russian what is Russian, Latvian what is Latvian, and Hebrew what is Hebrew? So as to tell the truth—and the truth is always interesting" (p. 186).

125. As quoted in *New York Times*, Aug. 20, 1991, p. A13.

126. As quoted in *New York Times*, Aug. 20, 1991, p. A13.

Levin: Sexual Vocabulary in Medieval Russia

1. Alison Macleod, *The Muscovite* (New York, 1971), p. 96.
2. Eve Levin, *Sex and Society in the World of the Orthodox Slavs, 900–1700* (Ithaca, N.Y., 1989), esp. pp. 36–78.
3. For a thorough treatment of the Western medieval tradition in sexuality, see James A. Brundage, *Law, Sex, and Christian Society in Medieval Europe* (Chicago, 1987).
4. See, for example, the autobiography of Archpriest Avvakum in N. K. Gudzii, *Khrestomatiia po drevnei russkoi literature XI–XVII vekov* (Moscow, 1962), pp. 492–93.
5. On Old Believer traditionalism, see Iurii M. Lotman and Boris A.

Uspenskii, "Binary Models in the Dynamics of Russian Culture (to the End of the Eighteenth Century)," in Alexander D. Nakhimovsky and Alice Stone Nakhimovsky, eds., *The Semiotics of Russian Cultural History* (Ithaca, N.Y., 1985), pp. 46–49.

6. Khozhdenie za tri moria Afanasiia Nikitina, *Pamiatniki literatury drevnei Rusi. Vtoraia polovina XV veka* (Moscow, 1982), pp. 450–51.

7. Joan Delaney Grossman attempted a comparison of high and low culture in her article "Feminine Images in Old Russian Literature and Art," *California Slavic Studies*, 11 (1980), pp. 33–70. She discusses attitudes toward sexuality at several points, but not in depth. For a discussion of semiotic models for the relationship between high and low culture and how they changed over time, see Lotman and Uspenskii, "Binary Models," pp. 30–66.

8. "A se grekhi," in S. I. Smirnov, *Materialy dlia istorii drevnerusskoi pokaiannoi distsipliny*, Chteniia obshchestva istorii i drevnostei rossiiskikh pri Moskovskom universitete, vol. 3 (Moscow, 1912), p. 46; A. Almazov, *Tainaia ispoved' v pravoslavnoi vostochnoi tserkvi*, vol. 3 (Odessa, 1894), p. 280.

9. Both meanings of *blud* may be found in the same text; cf. "Povest' o Savve Grudtsyne," in Gudzii, *Khrestomatiia*, pp. 406–9; Almazov, *Tainaia ispoved'*, pp. 153, 275.

10. Almazov, *Tainaia ispoved'*, pp. 145, 153.

11. A. Preobrazhenskii, *Etimologicheskii slovar' russkago iazyka* (Moscow, 1910–14), p. 31; Max Vasmer, *Etimologicheskii slovar' russkago iazyka*, 4 vols. (Moscow, 1964), vol. 1, p. 180.

12. *Pamiatniki literatury drevnei Rusi. Seredina XVI veka* (Moscow, 1985), p. 58.

13. "Ot pravil sviatykh apostol," in Smirnov, *Materialy*, p. 62; "Pravilo 'ashche dvozhenets,'" ibid., p. 65; Almazov, *Tainaia ispoved'*, p. 166.

14. "Pravilo s imenem Maksima," in Smirnov, *Materialy*, p. 54; Almazov, *Tainaia ispoved'*, pp. 143, 146, 148; N. S. Tikhonravov, *Pamiatniki otrechennoi russkoi literatury* (Moscow, 1863), vol. 2, p. 307.

15. A. V. Artsikhovskii and V. L. Ianin, *Novgorodskie gramoty na bereste* (Moscow, 1978), vol. 7, p. 131.

16. See, for example, TsGADA, F. 381, no. 173, ff. 209v–210: "God will judge fornication and adultery" (*liubodeem" bo i preliubodeiem" soudit' b"*).

17. *Ashche li mouzh' ot zheny sbloudit' ili zhena ot mouzha*, "Ot pravil sviatykh apostol," p. 62.

18. See, for example, the definition of sodomy in "Pravilo 'ashche dvozhenets,'" p. 66: intercourse with one's wife on top, with cattle, or with "anyone" anally. The penance is three years for a married man or eighteen weeks for a youth. See Levin, *Sex and Society*, pp. 197–99, for a discussion of the usage of the terms "sodomy" and "unnatural sex."

19. "A se grekhi," p. 47; "Pravilo 'ashche dvozhenets,'" p. 68.

20. "Voprosy i otvety pastyrskoi praktiki," in V. N. Beneshevich, *Pa-*

miatniki drevne-russkago kanonicheskago prava, Russkaia istoricheskaia biblioteka, vol. 6 (St. Petersburg, 1908), pp. 864–65; "Dva pravila monakham," in Smirnov, *Materialy*, p. 37; "Voprosy Kirika," article 30, in Smirnov, *Materialy*, p. 4; Almazov, *Tainaia ispoved'*, p. 143. Compare *upade sia na neiu*, "Iz sinaiskogo paterika," in *Pamiatniki literatury drevnei Rusi. XII vek* (Moscow, 1980), p. 132; *zhivut ne po zakonu s" zhenami*, "living with women not according to the law," "Poslanie mitropolita Fotiia v Novgorod (1410)," in Beneshevich, *Pamiatniki*, p. 272.

21. Tikhonravov, *Pamiatniki*, vol. 2, pp. 292–93, 297; "Voprosy i otvety pastyrskoi praktiki," p. 865; "Poslanie mitropolita Fotiia v Novgorod (1410)," p. 272; "Slovo o zhitii Dmitriia Donskogo," in Gudzii, *Khrestomatiia*, p. 180. See also Levin, *Sex and Society*, pp. 59–63.

22. "Zhitiia sviatago ottsa nashego Stefana byvshago v Permi," in Gudzii, *Khrestomatiia*, p. 188.

23. See, e.g., "Poslanie Iakova-Chernoriztsa k kniaziu Dmitriu Borisovichu," in *Pamiatniki literatury drevnei Rusi. XIII vek* (Moscow, 1981), p. 456.

24. Almazov, *Tainaia ispoved'*, pp. 146, 151.

25. *V kale bluda iako sviniia valiaiushesia i . . . iako skot*, "Povest' o Savve Grudtsyne," pp. 402, 406.

26. TsGADA, F. 381, no. 163, f. 63.

27. See, e.g., "Povest' o Savve Grudtsyne," p. 405.

28. "Skazanie o kniagine Ol'ge," in *Pamiatniki literatury drevnei Rusi. Seredina XVI veka*, p. 262.

29. "Povest' vremennykh let," in Gudzii, *Khrestomatiia*, p. 16.

30. A. V. Artsikhovskii, *Novgorodskie gramoty na bereste* (Moscow, 1978), vol. 6, pp. 76–77.

31. Ia. N. Shchapov, *Drevnerusskie kniazheskie ustavy, XI–XV vv.* (Moscow, 1976), pp. 96, 98.

32. "Poslanie Iakova-chernoriztsa," p. 458.

33. "Chin svadebnyi," in *Pamiatniki literatury drevnei Rusi. Seredina XVI veka*, pp. 186–88.

34. Ibid., p. 188; "Voprosy Ilii," article 21, in Smirnov, *Materialy*, p. 7; "Zhitie sviatago cheloveka bozhiia Aleksiia," in Gudzii, *Khrestomatiia*, p. 99.

35. "Izlozhenie pravilom apostol'skim i otecheskim," in Smirnov, *Materialy*, p. 59; "Sudy Solomona," in *Pamiatniki literatury drevnei Rusi. XIV–seredina XV veka* (Moscow, 1981), p. 78; Tikhonravov, *Pamiatniki*, vol. 2, p. 296.

36. "Ot pravil sviatykh apostol," p. 61.

37. TsGADA, F. 381, no. 173, f. 6v.

38. "Povest' o Petre i Fevronii," in Gudzii, *Khrestomatiia*, p. 234; "Voprosy Savy," article 4, in Smirnov, *Materialy*, p. 7; "Povest' o Karpe Sutulove," in Gudzii, *Khrestomatiia*, pp. 426–30; "Tri sviatitel'skiia poucheniia," in Beneshevich, *Pamiatniki*, p. 920; Almazov, *Tainaia ispoved'*, p. 145.

39. Tikhonravov, *Pamiatniki*, vol. 1, p. 299.
40. *Zhena vsedaiushchi na muzha*, "Nekotoraia zapoved'," in Smirnov, *Materialy*, p. 28.
41. "Pravilo o veruiushchikh v gady," in Smirnov, *Materialy*, p. 144; Horace A. Dewey and Ann M. Kleimola, *Zakon Sudnyj Ljudem (Court Law for the People)*, Michigan Slavic Materials, no. 9 (Ann Arbor, 1973), pp. 42–43.
42. Almazov, *Tainaia ispoved'*, pp. 152, 164, 175, 280; "A se grekhi," p. 48.
43. "Pravilo o veruiushchikh v gady," p. 142; Almazov, *Tainaia ispoved'*, p. 149.
44. Almazov, *Tainaia ispoved'*, pp. 151, 152, 164, 181.
45. "Pritcha o starom muzhe i molodoi devitse," in Gudzii, *Khrestomatiia*, p. 443.
46. Gudzii, *Khrestomatiia*, p. 239.
47. Almazov, *Tainaia ispoved'*, pp. 152, 155.
48. "Slovo o Ioanne arkhiepiskope velikago Novagrada," in Gudzii, *Khrestomatiia*, p. 209.
49. "Skazanie o Drakule," in Gudzii, *Khrestomatiia*, p. 230. The symbolism of rape involved in execution by impalement was not lost on the medieval author, who attributed to Dracula the comment "you are not a man, but a woman," on the occasion of the impalement of cowardly soldiers; see ibid., p. 228.
50. Manuscript division, Lenin Library, Fond 113, no. 412, ff. 4–4v.
51. See Levin, *Sex and Society*, pp. 195–97.
52. "The Ladder," in *Drevnerusskaia miniatiura* (Moscow, 1933), plate 50; "The Torment of the Prostitutes," in V. G. Briusova, *Russkaia zhivopis' 17 veka* (Moscow, 1984), p. 123; "The Damned," Uppsala University Library, Slav-71.
53. See, for example, "Bathhouse," in *Drevnerusskaia knizhnaia miniatiura iz sobraniia gosudarstvennoi publichnoi biblioteki imeni M. E. Saltykova-Shchedrina* (Leningrad, 1980); "St. George and the Dragon, with Scenes from His Life," *Novgorod Icons, 12th–17th Century* (Leningrad, 1980), plate 33; "The Baptism," *Novgorod Icons*, plate 157.
54. "Povest' o Savve Grudtsyne," p. 402. See also the tale of a monk incited to sin by the Devil: *diavol"* . . . *v"lozhiv" mnikha zlyi pomysl"*, TsGADA, F. 381, no. 173, f. 193v.
55. "The Fall," in Briusova, *Russkaia zhivopis'*, plate 115, showing both Eve and the Serpent with large breasts; "Scenes from the Life of St. Nicholas of Zaraisk," *Novgorod Icons*, plate 210, showing a demon with breasts and a face in the groin.
56. Levin, *Sex and Society*, pp. 45–55. Unlike those in Western Europe, witches in Russia were not frequently accused of carnal knowledge of demons. Indeed, 60 percent of accused witches in Russia were men. See Valerie Kivelson, "Through the Prism of Witchcraft: Townswomen in Seventeenth-Century Muscovy," in Barbara Evans Clements,

Barbara Alpern Engel, and Christine D. Worobec, eds., *Russia's Women: Accommodation, Resistance, Transformation* (Berkeley, Calif., 1991), pp. 74–94.

57. "Voprosy i otvety pastyrskoi praktiki," p. 867.

58. TsGADA, F. 381, no. 163, f. 180; see also "Poslanie Iakovachernorizta," p. 456; and "Pchela," in *Pamiatniki literatury drevnei Rusi. XIII vek*, p. 490, 510.

59. TsGADA, F. 381, no. 173, f. 1v; and TsGADA, F. 381, no. 163, f. 38v, from the *vita* of St. Eudokia, the repentant prostitute; "Pouchenie mitropolita Danila," in Gudzii, *Khrestomatiia*, p. 260.

60. See, for example, the "Letopisnaia kniga" of Prince I. M. Katyrev-Rostovskii, in Gudzii, *Khrestomatiia*, pp. 343–44.

61. TsGADA, F. 381, no. 162, f. 46.

62. TsGADA, F. 381, no. 163, f. 86; TsGADA, F. 181, no. 692, ff. 26v–30.

63. "Povest' o Karpe Sutulove," p. 426–30.

64. "Iz sinaiskogo paterika," p. 132.

65. TsGADA, F. 381, no. 163, f. 140v.

66. For example, see "Pouchenie filosofa, episkopa belgorodskago," in *Pamiatniki literatury drevnei Rusi. XII vek*, p. 404; "Pouchenie mitropolita Danila," p. 261.

67. *Domostroi* (Moscow, 1990), pp. 35, 57.

68. I have in mind here the work of Michel Foucault, *The History of Sexuality* (New York, 1980–86), and Helena Michie, *The Flesh Made Word: Female Figures and Women's Bodies* (New York, 1987).

69. L. N. Tolstoi, *Kreitserova sonata* (Moscow, 1900), p. 10.

70. Research in support of this article was conducted in the Soviet Union in 1981–82 and 1990 under the auspices of the International Research and Exchanges Board and the Fulbright-Hays program of the Department of Education. The granting agencies are not responsible for the views presented herein.

Vowles: Marriage à la Russe

I would like to thank Jane Costlow, Louis Goldring, Barbara Heldt, Joanna Hubbs, Cathy Popkin, and Stephanie Sandler for their comments and encouragement.

1. For a brief account of these changes see Dorothy Atkinson, "Society and the Sexes in the Russian Past," in Dorothy Atkinson, Alexander Dallin, and Gail Warshofsky Lapidus, eds., *Women in Russia* (Stanford, Calif., 1977), pp. 3–38, quotation from p. 26. See also Nancy Shields Kollman, "The Seclusion of Elite Muscovite Women," *Russian History*, 10, pt. 2 (1983), pp. 170–87; Richard Stites, *The Women's Liberation Movement in Russia: Feminism, Nihilism, and Bolshevism 1860–1930* (Princeton, N.J., 1978), pp. 11–15.

2. Charles-François-Philibert Masson, *The Secret Memoirs of the*

Court of Petersburg (London, 1805), pp. 266–67. Masson's *Mémoires secrets sur la Russie, et particulièrement sur la fin du règne de Catherine II et celui de Paul Ier* first appeared in Paris, 1800–1802. The English translation was made from a second edition that appeared in 1804 with additional material. To retain the flavor of the period, all quotations, unless otherwise stated, are taken from the English version. Where the English translator has censored Masson's text, the translations are my own, based on the 1804 edition reprinted in *Bibliothèque des mémoires relatifs à l'histoire de France pendant le 18e siècle*, vol. 22 (Paris, 1863).

3. Catherine Wilmot and Martha Wilmot, *The Russian Journals* (London, 1934), p. 217.

4. For details of Masson's life see *Biographie universelle ancienne et moderne* (Paris, 1820), vol. 27, pp. 428–31; and *Nouvelle biographie générale* (Paris, 1860), vol. 33, pp. 212–15.

5. There is a rich bibliography of literary and historical studies documenting changes in sexual manners and society in the eighteenth and early nineteenth centuries. Those I have found most useful here include: Nancy Armstrong, "The Rise of the Domestic Woman," in Nancy Armstrong and Leonard Tennenhouse, eds., *The Ideology of Conduct* (New York, 1987), pp. 96–141; Margaret Darrow, "French Noblewomen and the New Domesticity 1750–1850," *Feminist Studies*, 5, no. 1 (Spring 1979), pp. 41–65; Leonore Davidoff and Catherine Hall, *Family Fortunes. Men and Women of the English Middle Class, 1780–1850* (Chicago, 1987); Elizabeth Fox-Genovese, "The Ideological Bases of Domestic Economy: The Representation of Women and the Family in the Age of Expansion," in Elizabeth Fox-Genovese and Eugene Genovese, *Fruits of Merchant Capital* (Oxford, 1983), pp. 299–336; Jean H. Hagstrum, *Sex and Sensibility. Ideal and Erotic Love from Milton to Mozart* (Chicago, 1980); Joan B. Landes, *Women and the Public Sphere in the Age of the French Revolution* (Ithaca, N.Y., 1988); Judith Lowder Newton, *Women, Power, and Subversion. Social Strategies in British Fiction, 1778–1860* (Athens, Ga., 1981); Dorinda Outram, *The Body and the French Revolution* (New Haven, Conn., 1989), pp. 124–52; Mary Poovey, *The Proper Lady and the Woman Writer* (Chicago, 1984); Mary Poovey, *Uneven Developments: The Ideological Work of Gender in Mid-Victorian England* (Chicago, 1988); Maurice J. Quinlan, *Victorian Prelude: A History of English Manners 1700–1830* (Hamden, Conn., 1965 [1941]); Susan Staves, "British Seduced Maidens," *Eighteenth-Century Studies*, 14, no. 2 (Winter 1980–81), pp. 109–34; Susan Staves, "Where Is History but in Texts? Reading the History of Marriage," in John M. Wallace, ed., *The Golden and the Brazen World* (Berkeley, Calif., 1985), pp. 125–43; Lawrence Stone, *The Family, Sex and Marriage in England, 1500–1800* (New York, 1977).

6. Masson, *Mémoires secrets*, p. 204.

7. See Paul Hoffmann, *La Femme dans la pensée des Lumières* (Paris, 1977), and L. J. Jordanova, "Natural Facts: A Historical Perspective on

Science and Sexuality," in Carol P. MacCormack and Marilyn Strathern, eds., *Nature, Culture, and Gender* (Cambridge, Eng., 1980), pp. 42–69.

8. Quoted in Jordanova, "Natural Facts," p. 49.

9. On changing attitudes toward women, work, and property see Davidoff and Hall, *Family Fortunes*, and Elizabeth Fox-Genovese, "Women and Work," in Samia I. Spencer, ed., *French Women and the Age of Enlightenment* (Bloomington, Ind., 1984), pp. 111–27.

10. On conduct literature see Armstrong, "Rise of the Domestic Woman"; Michael Curtin, "A Question of Manners: Status and Gender in Etiquette and Courtesy," *Journal of Modern History*, 57 (Sept. 1985), pp. 395–423; Joyce Hemlow, "Fanny Burney and the Courtesy Books," *PMLA*, 65 (1950), pp. 732–61; Quinlan, *Victorian Prelude*, pp. 139–59.

11. John Gregory, *A Father's Legacy to His Daughters*, 4th ed. (London, 1774), pp. 50–51.

12. On women's economic powers and position see Davidoff and Hall, *Family Fortunes*; Susan Moller Okin, "Patriarchy and Married Women's Property in England: Questions About Some Current Views," *Eighteenth-Century Studies*, 17, no. 2 (Winter 1983–84), pp. 121–38; Poovey, *Uneven Developments*, pp. 51–88; Susan Staves, "Pin Money," *Studies in Eighteenth-Century Culture*, 14 (1985), pp. 47–77; and a later version of "Pin Money" that appears in Susan Staves, *Married Women's Separate Property in England, 1660–1833* (Cambridge, Mass., 1990).

13. Quoted by Staves, *Married Women's Separate Property*, p. 157. For other examples see Staves, "Pin Money."

14. Poovey, *Uneven Developments*, p. 52.

15. Gregory, *Father's Legacy*, p. 6.

16. The Wilmots' account echoes Gregory's fulminations against poor female conduct in his own society: "By the present mode of female manners, the ladies seem to expect that they shall regain their ascendancy over us, by the fullest display of their personal charms, by being always in our eye at public places, by conversing with us in the same unreserved freedom as we do with one another; in short, by resembling us as nearly as they possibly can.—But a little time and experience will show the folly of this expectation and conduct" (*Father's Legacy*, pp. 41–42).

17. Marc Raeff argues, from a different angle, for the influence of economic structures on the psyche of Russian *men* in "Home, School, and Service in the Life of the 18th-Century Russian Nobleman," *Slavonic and East European Review*, 40, no. 95 (June 1962), pp. 295–307.

18. For an account of the difficulties women faced in preserving innocence while gaining experience see Patricia Meyer Spacks, "Ev'ry Woman Is at Heart a Rake," *Eighteenth-Century Studies*, 8, no. 1 (Fall 1974), pp. 27–46.

19. For a description of the "wolfish age" see Newton, *Women, Power, and Subversion*, pp. 23–24; and Staves, "British Seduced Maidens."

20. These arguments are documented in Hoffmann, *La femme*; Jane Rendall, *The Origins of Modern Feminism: Women in Britain, France,*

and the United States, 1780–1860 (London, 1985), pp. 7–32; Sylvana Tomaselli, "The Enlightenment Debate on Women," *History Workshop Journal*, issue 20 (Autumn 1985), pp. 101–24; R. Meek, *Social Science and the Ignoble Savage* (Cambridge, Eng., 1976).

21. Masson, *Mémoires secrets*, p. 204.
22. See John Berger, *Ways of Seeing* (London, 1972), pp. 45–64, and Jane Sharp's essay in this volume for a critical reading of this tradition.
23. Masson, *Mémoires secrets*, p. 205.
24. Ovid, *Metamorphoses*, trans. Rolfe Humphries (Bloomington, Ind., 1955), pp. 90–93.
25. Masson, *Mémoires secrets*, p. 205.
26. Elizabeth Fox-Genovese traces the origin of arguments comparing women's relation to men with the relation of slaves to masters in "Property and Patriarchy in Classical Bourgeois Political Theory," *Radical History Review*, 4, nos. 2–3 (Spring–Summer 1977), pp. 36–59.
27. Masson, *Mémoires secrets*, p. 200.
28. Ibid.
29. Gregory, for example, encouraged modest dress in women by arguing: "A fine woman shews her charms to most advantage, when she seems most to conceal them. The finest bosom in nature is not so fine as what imagination forms" (pp. 55–56).

Kelly: A Stick with Two Ends

1. On "the circulation of social energy" see Stephen Greenblatt, *Shakespearian Negotiations* (Oxford, 1988), chap. 1.
2. James Clifford, *The Predicament of Culture* (Cambridge, Mass., 1988), p. 284.
3. Rosalind Coward, *Patriarchal Precedents* (London, 1983), p. 2.
4. Two English-language sources on women's involvement in rural rituals are Elizabeth Warner, *The Russian Folk Theatre* (The Hague, 1977), pt. 1, sec. 2, and Julia Vytkovskaia, "Women in Russian Mythology," in Carolyne Larrington, ed., *The Feminist Companion to Mythology* (London, 1992), pp. 102–17.
5. Several eighteenth-century texts dealing with sexual politics are given in I. P. Grebeniuk et al., eds., *Ranniaia russkaia dramaturgiia: P'esy liubitel'skikh teatrov* (Moscow, 1976), pp. 581–608.
6. The best-known use of the phrase "a stick with two ends" is perhaps in Dostoevsky's *The Brothers Karamazov*, bk. 12, chap. 10: "Rech' zashchitnika: palka o dvukh kontsakh," F. M. Dostoevskii, *Polnoe sobranie sochinenii*, 30 vols. (Leningrad, 1972–90), vol. 15, pp. 152–56.
7. See Catriona Kelly, *Petrushka: The Russian Carnival Puppet Theatre* (Cambridge, Eng., 1990), pp. 3–4.
8. One example of historians' tendency to underestimate the importance of entertainment in working-class Russians' lives is Diane Koenker, *Moscow Workers and the 1917 Revolution* (Princeton, N.J., 1981), p. 67,

where it is argued that almost the sole leisure activity of workers was drinking.

9. Jeffrey Brooks, *When Russia Learned to Read: Literacy and Popular Literature, 1861–1917* (Princeton, N.J., 1985), pp. 109, 160.

10. See, for example, Christine D. Worobec, "Victims or Actors? Russian Peasant Women and Patriarchy," in Esther Kingston-Mann and Timothy Mixter, eds., *Peasant Economy, Culture, and Politics of European Russia 1800–1921* (Princeton, N.J., 1991), pp. 177–206.

11. See Daniel K. Brower, "Labor Violence in Russia in the Late Nineteenth Century," *Slavic Review*, 41, no. 3 (Fall 1982), pp. 417–31.

12. A much fuller analysis is available in Kelly, *Petrushka*; see also Catriona Kelly, "From Pulcinella to Petrushka: The History of the Russian Glove Puppet Theatre," *Oxford Slavonic Papers*, 21 (1988), pp. 40–63.

13. On Guignol see J.-B. Onofrio, *Théâtre Lyonnais de Guignol: Nouvelle édition revue, corrigée et annotée par l'auteur* (Paris, 1890); on Judy see George Speaight, *A History of the English Puppet Theatre* (London, 1955; reprint: London, 1990).

14. A. Benua [Benois], *Moi vospominaniia*, 2 vols. (Moscow, 1980), vol. 2, p. 522.

15. O. Tsekhnovitser and I. Eremin, *Teatr Petrushki* (Moscow and Leningrad, 1927), p. 78.

16. P. N. Berkov, *Russkaia narodnaia drama XVII–XIX vekov: Teksty p'es i opisaniia predstavlenii* (Moscow, 1953), p. 116.

17. A. Putintsev, "Vanka: Sovremennaia narodnaia kukol'naia kamed'," *Voronezhskaia literaturnaia beseda*, 1 (1925), p. 7.

18. Tsekhnovitser and Eremin, *Teatr*, p. 61.

19. Ibid., p. 61.

20. D. A. Rovinskii, *Russkie narodnye kartinki*, 2nd ed., 2 vols. (St. Petersburg, 1900), vol. 1, p. 363.

21. Putintsev, "Vanka," p. 10.

22. Kelly, *Petrushka*, pp. 98–99.

23. A. F. Nekrylova and N. I. Savushkina, *Fol'klornyi teatr* (Moscow, 1988), p. 287.

24. Ibid., p. 280.

25. D. Grigorovich, "Peterburgskie sharmanshchiki," in D. Grigorovich, *Polnoe sobranie sochinenii*, 12 vols. (St. Petersburg, 1896), vol. 1, p. 13.

26. A. I. Alekseev-Iakovlev, *Russkie narodnye gulian'ia* (Leningrad and Moscow, 1948), p. 59.

27. Rovinskii, *Russkie*, vol. 1, p. 363.

28. Kelly, *Petrushka*, p. 60.

29. V. Doroshevich, *Sakhalin* (Moscow, 1903), p. 100.

30. N. Smirnova, *Sovetskii teatr kukol 1918–1932* (Moscow, 1963), p. 258.

31. S. Freud, *Der Witz und seine Beziehung zum Unbewussten* (1905; reprint: Frankfurt am Main, 1978), p. 78.

32. An example of an account of women's history where such uncomfortable questions are suppressed is David L. Ransel, *Mothers of Misery: Child Abandonment in Russia* (Princeton, N.J., 1988). On p. 11 Ransel celebrates the benefits of infanticide to subsistence economies in terms uncomfortably reminiscent of Jonathan Swift's famous pamphlet *A Modest Proposal*; on p. 102 Ransel argues that the Russian authorities were right to enforce "maternal responsibility" as a method of preventing infanticide in the late nineteenth century. In neither case does Ransel assess the human costs of such sweet utilitarian reasonableness, nor does he make any attempt to identify the contradictions inherent, given the terms of his own argument, in the enforcement of "maternal responsibility" on women precipitated into cities from "subsistence economies." "Why women laughed" is of course not the only counterintuitive question one could ask concerning popular texts. It would, for example, be very interesting to scrutinize the notion of masculinity in such texts. In some versions of *Petrushka* the title character beats and kills a male friend from his home village (*zemliak*) who has tried to renew friendly contact. Was this scene included because it was outrageous to established custom (working-class men in cities depended on *zemliak* networks for employment, housing, and social life), or because it was cautionary (intended to engender anxiety about certain kinds of male bonding)?

33. That the interpretation of carnival insults in some contexts may be extremely slippery is clear in, for example, Natalie Zemon Davis's instance of a sexual joke which provoked a murder; see her *Fiction in the Archives: Pardon Tales and Their Tellers in Sixteenth-Century France* (Stanford, Calif., 1987), p. 31.

34. The issues confronting feminist cultural criticism are extensively explored in Janet Wolff's new collection of essays, *Feminine Sentences: Essays on Women and Culture* (Oxford, 1990).

35. Germaine de Staël, "Les femmes qui cultivent les lettres," in her *De la littérature considérée en ses rapports avec les institutions sociales* (1800), ed. Paul von Tieghem (Geneva and Paris, 1959), pp. 331–42; E. Ann Kaplan, "Is the Gaze Male?," in Ann Snitow, Christine Stansell, and Sharon Thompson, eds., *Powers of Desire: The Politics of Sexuality* (New York, 1983), pp. 309–27.

36. On the incidence of domestic violence in Petersburg/Petrograd, see S. A. Smith, *Red Petrograd: Revolution in the Factories 1917–18* (Cambridge, Eng., 1983), p. 92. Those who have argued that such violence was acceptable to working-class women include Aleksandra Efimenko, who, writing in the 1880s, stated, "beating [the peasant woman] is not considered an abuse of power, but completely legal and natural to such an extent that the absence of beating is considered abnormal" (cited in Rose L. Glickman, *Russian Factory Women* [Berkeley, Calif., 1984], pp. 33–34). More recently, this line of argument has been restated by Anne Bobroff in her "Working Women, Bonding Patterns and the Politics of Daily Life: Russia at the End of the Old Regime" (Ph.D. diss., University of Michigan,

Ann Arbor, 1982). Bobroff argues that working-class Russian women were conditioned to bond to their husbands, however unsatisfactory the connection. (For a discussion of the problems raised by Bobroff's analysis and for a broad empirical treatment of representations of women in Russian popular texts, see Catriona Kelly, "'Better Halves?' Representations of Women in Russian Popular Culture, 1870–1910," in Linda Edmondson, ed., *Russian Women and Society* (Cambridge, Eng., 1992), pp. 5–31.

37. P. I. Lubaev, version of *Petrushka* recorded in 1925; quoted from a typescript in my possession.

38. Kaplan, "Is the Gaze Male?," p. 324.

39. The notion of shifting networks of control and repression is most extensively explored by Michel Foucault in *The History of Sexuality, Volume 1: An Introduction*, trans. Robert Hurley (New York, 1980).

40. An astringent analysis of the limitations inherent in Foucault's neo-Nietzschean pessimism was given by Terry Eagleton in his recent review of Stephen Greenblatt's *Learning to Curse*, *Times Literary Supplement*, Jan. 18, 1991, p. 7.

41. Cécile Dauphin et al., "Women's Culture and Women's Power: Issues in French Women's History," in Karen Offen, Ruth Roach Pierson, and Jane Rendall, eds., *Writing Women's History: International Perspectives* (London, 1991), pp. 107–33. This article is to my mind more incisive and stimulating than the better-known contributions of Joan Wallach Scott, collected in *Gender and the Politics of History* (Princeton, N.J., 1988).

42. On the post-Enlightenment tradition of education, see Valerie Walkerdine, "Reason and Gender," in her *Schoolgirl Fictions* (London, 1990), pp. 67–71.

43. Roger Chartier, *Cultural History: Between Practices and Representations*, trans. Lydia G. Cochrane (Cambridge, Eng., 1988), p. 125.

44. The paradigms applied here to the lives of working-class Russian women have some affinities with those explored by Simone de Beauvoir in *The Second Sex*, trans. H. M. Parshley (1949; reprint: London, 1988), though Beauvoir herself is concerned almost exclusively with bourgeois women, referring to working-class women only in terms of the stereotypical Marxist view that they enjoyed greater economic freedom, and hence greater freedom in every sense (pp. 141, 147).

45. Victoria Goddard, "Honour and Shame: The Control of Women's Sexuality and Group Identity in Naples," in Pat Caplan, ed., *The Cultural Construction of Sexuality* (London, 1987), pp. 166–93. For a similar argument on *bedu* women, see Jonathan Raban, *Arabia* (London, 1987), p. 141.

46. Genteelism among Russian working-class women is, like most aspects of their lives, a subject still requiring research. It is, however, a topos among nineteenth-century memoirists, in Russia as in the West, to suggest that dwellings in which women lived were better-regulated than those in

which men dwelt alone (see, for example, Grigorovich, "Peterburgskie sharmanshchiki," p. 13). For comparative material on the West, see Bonnie S. Anderson and Judith P. Zinsser, *A History of Their Own: Women in Europe from Prehistory to the Present Day*, 2 vols. (Harmondsworth, Eng., 1990), vol. 2, pp. 237–39.

47. Nigel Barley, *Not a Hazardous Sport* (Harmondsworth, Eng., 1989), p. 155.

48. Women workers as well as men practiced "carting out," a form of revenge on unpopular supervisors in which they were hooded, placed in a wheelbarrow, and suspended over a canal until demands were met; see Glickman, *Russian Factory Women*, p. 161; Smith, *Red Petrograd*, p. 193. "Staryi rabochii," author of the political pamphlet *Iz rabochego dvizheniia za Nevskoi zastavoi* (Geneva, 1900), p. 14, recounts how workers, apparently including women, inundated a manager with slops poured down from the fifth floor of their hostel. That women could also be active at home is suggested by the domestic murder statistics cited by I. Foinitskii, "Zhenshchina-prestupnitsa," *Severnyi vestnik*, 3 (1893), p. 115.

49. See Grebeniuk et al., *Ranniaia*, interlude no. 7; Claude Carey, *Les proverbes érotiques russes* (The Hague, 1972), nos. 14, 26, 108, 172, 183. A recent source on jokes includes several recorded from a schoolgirl: A. Lur'e, "Materialy po sovremennomu leningradskomu fol'kloru," in A. F. Belonsor, *Uchebnyi material po teorii literatury: Zhanry slovesnogo teksta: Anekdot* (Tallin, 1989), p. 118.

50. N. Simonovich-Efimova, *Zapiski petrushechnika* (Leningrad, 1981), p. 184.

51. T. Bulak, "Iz istorii komedii Petrushki," *Russkii fol'klor*, 16 (1976), p. 226.

52. Glickman, *Russian Factory Women*, p. 217. V. V. Krupianskaia and N. S. Polishchuk, *Kul'tura i byt rabochikh gornozavodskogo Urala kontsa XIX—nachala XX veka* (Moscow, 1972), pp. 64–65, argue that women workers often controlled the family finances. Two census enumerators, M. and O., estimated that practically all the working-class women whom they canvassed had children out of wedlock; see "Tsifry i fakty iz perepisi Sankt-Peterburga v 1900 godu," *Russkaia mysl'*, 23, pt. 12 (Nov. 1902), sec. 2, p. 92.

53. The tendency to see prerevolutionary Russian working-class women as victims was particularly marked in the 1930s: their miserable lot was then presented as a counterimage to the blissful condition of women under Stalin. See, for example, the speeches by working-class female delegates in *Pervyi vsesoiuznyi s"ezd Soiuza pisatelei SSSR: Stenograficheskii otchet* (Moscow, 1934).

54. Lissa Paul, "Dumb Bunnies: A Revisionist Re-Reading of *Watership Down*," *Signal*, 56 (May 1988), p. 119.

55. Robert Darnton, *The Great Cat Massacre* (Harmondsworth, Eng., 1985), p. 13.

56. There is no space here to consider whether women critics interpreting *Petrushka* might have been expected to have different views from their male colleagues. But it seems at first sight unlikely that the discourses of Russian academia and politics with which we are dealing here would have allowed the *expression* of divergent views, even had any been held.

57. A. Lunacharskii, *Teatr i revolutsiia* (Moscow, 1924), p. 61; M. Gor'kii, *Sobranie sochinenii*, 30 vols. (Moscow, 1953), vol. 23, p. 494.

58. On women workers as "backward," see Glickman, *Russian Factory Women*, pp. 172–73.

59. P. G. Bogatyrev, *Cheshskii kukol'nyi i russkii narodnyi teatr* (Berlin and Petersburg, 1923), and idem, *Voprosy teorii narodnogo iskusstva* (Moscow, 1971).

60. Mikhail Bakhtin, *François Rabelais and His World*, trans. H. Iswolsky (Bloomington, Ind., 1984). Bakhtin's approach has to date had an enormous influence on Western studies of popular culture, if not on Soviet studies of popular culture.

61. Ibid., p. 251.

62. Ibid., p. 240. This passage might, however, be assimilable for feminists in a utopian, rather than a historical, sense. It could be seen as advocating an anticlassical aesthetic of the body that would give full value to female bulges and orifices. This case has recently been argued by Ann Jefferson; see her "Bodymatters: Self and Other in Bakhtin, Sartre, Barthes," in Ken Hirschkop and David Shepherd, eds., *Bakhtin and Cultural Politics* (Manchester, Eng., 1989), pp. 152–77. Another convincing alternative reading, though in no sense a feminist one, is that this text is best regarded as a refraction of the actual circumstances of its production; see, for example, Mikhail Ryklin's article "Tela terrora: Tezisy k logike nasiliia," in *Bakhtinskii sbornik*, vol. 1 (Moscow, 1990), pp. 60–76.

63. It might be objected that the high numbers of migrant workers in Russian cities would have meant that the audiences of *Petrushka* were unlikely to be alienated from the traditional peasant society, with its emphasis on women's fertility. For reasons I have given elsewhere (Kelly, *Petrushka*, p. 39), I am disinclined to believe that recent migrants were a significant group in audiences for this text. And if they were, then the fertility ethic is likely to have impinged not only on their view of women but also on their view of men. In prewar rural Ireland, a comparable peasant society, spinsters and childless women had a low status, but so did bachelors and infertile husbands; see Eric Cross, *The Tailor and Ansty* (Dublin, 1979), p. 5, and Paul Henry, *An Irish Portrait* (London, 1988).

64. Michael Byrom, *Punch in the Italian Puppet Theatre* (London, 1983), p. 15. As Glickman, *Russian Factory Women*, p. 206, reveals, the "carnival" character of male workers' violence against their female colleagues made it no less threatening. Zemon Davis, *Fiction*, pp. 31–32, points out that male criminals might excuse their crimes by linking them

with carnival ritual; this strategy was not available to women, since involvement in carnival excess would have labeled them "bad women" in the first place.

65. Ol'ga Freidenberg, *Poetika siuzheta i zhanra* (Leningrad, 1936), p. 214.

66. Anna Nekrylova, "The Traditional Archetectonics of Folk Puppet Street Theatre," in *Proceedings of the UNIMA Symposium, Moscow 1983* (Moscow, 1983), p. 39.

67. Viacheslav Ivanov, "Ellinskaia religiia stradaiushchego boga," *Novyi put'*, 5 (1904), p. 34. Part of Ivanov's project was to restore to Russian society the lost *sobornost'* (consensus through ritual) of "primitive" societies. Elsewhere, in the essays "Drevnii uzhas" and "O dostoinstve zhenshchin" (in Viacheslav Ivanov, *Sobranie sochinenii*, 4 vols. and continuing [Brussels, 1979–], vol. 3, pp. 91–110, 136–47), he stresses that women are also to be involved in this joyous consensus. Ivanov's language, however, everywhere suggests that he envisages a passive, rather than an active, role for women. No doubt the beating of women as ritual (submission) is meant as the female, passive counterpart to the active self-sacrifice of the dismembered Dionysus, the male "suffering god."

68. Greenblatt, *Shakespearian Negotiations*, p. 1; Keith Thomas, *Religion and the Decline of Magic* (Harmondsworth, Eng., 1978), p. 800; Judith Hanna, *Dance, Sex and Gender* (Chicago, 1988), p. 34.

69. An instance of how emphasis on "ritual" can be used to conceal the nature of social marginalization is given in David Mayall's critique of Victorian ethnographers' views of "Gypsies": *Gypsy Travellers in Nineteenth-Century Society* (Cambridge, Eng., 1988), p. 77.

70. See Stephen Jay Gould, *Ontogeny and Phylogeny* (Cambridge, Mass., 1977), chap. 5.

71. On the importance of ritual readings of the popular theater to the symbolist theater, see Kelly, *Petrushka*, pp. 145–53.

72. Tsekhnovitser and Eremin, *Teatr*, p. 171.

73. Ibid., p. 159.

74. G. Tarasov, *Petrushka v shkole i pionerotriade* (Leningrad, 1930), p. 11.

75. Aleksandr K. Zholkovskii, "O genii i zlodeistve, o babe i vserossiiskom masshtabe (Progulki po Maiakovskomu)," in Aleksandr Zholkovskii and Iurii K. Shcheglov, *Mir avtora i struktura teksta* (Tenafly, N.J., 1986), pp. 225–79.

76. Eduard Limonov, *Eto ia—Edichka*, 2nd ed. (New York, 1982); Dmitrii Savitskii, *Niotkuda s liubov'iu* (Paris, 1986).

77. See Kelly, *Petrushka*, pp. 174–77.

78. Veronika Dolina, "Kukol'nik," in her *Stikhi* (Paris, 1987), p. 50.

79. On Percy Press, see Kelly, *Petrushka*, p. 210; Federico García Lorca, *El retablillo de Don Cristóbal*, in his *Obras III: Teatro I* (Madrid, 1980), pp. 153–81.

80. Blake Morrison, *The Ballad of the Yorkshire Ripper* (London, 1987).

81. A view of Soviet women's history that is a mirror image of official Soviet views in its crude reductionism has been much propagated recently by the well-known Russian writer Tatiana Tolstaya in her frequent public statements to the Western press.

82. On Belov et al. see for example Barbara Heldt, "Gynoglasnost: Writing the Feminine," in Mary Buckley, ed., *Perestroika and Soviet Women* (Cambridge, Eng., 1992), pp. 160–75. I have frequently been told by contacts in Russia and other parts of the former USSR that the availability of girlie calendars and suchlike reflects working-class tastes, which is to my mind a debatable proposition. What is certain is that the most vociferous advocates for the relaxation of censorship with regard to the representation of heterosexual relations are male intellectuals (notably Viktor Erofeev).

Sharp: Redrawing the Margins of Russian Vanguard Art

This paper is drawn from a chapter of my dissertation, "Primitivism, Neoprimitivism and the Art of Natal'ia Goncharova, 1907–1914" (Yale University, Department of the History of Art, 1992), and is based on research funded by the International Research and Exchanges Board and Fulbright-Hays grants. In addition to these foundations, I would like to thank Mary Chamot, Susan Compton, Elena Basner, my adviser Anne Hanson, Linda Nochlin, and Gleb Pospelov for their contributions and support.

1. Louis Octave Uzanne, *The Modern Parisienne* (New York, 1912), as quoted in Griselda Pollock, *Vision and Difference: Femininity, Feminism and the Histories of Art* (New York, 1988), p. 21. This quotation appears to summarize Cesare Lombroso's study of the "absence" of women of genius, which he ascribes to their innate psychobiological characteristics; see C. Lombroso and G. Ferrero, *La donna deliquente: La prostituta i la donna normale* (Turin, 1893), pp. 161 and 179–80. The citation of Lombroso is embedded within Octave Uzanne's text, pp. 127–28.

2. "Moskovskaia khronika: Delo obshchestva svobodnoi estetiki," *Rech'*, Dec. 23, 1910, p. 3, and "Bubnovaia dama pod sudom," *Protiv techeniia*, Jan. 4, 1911, p. 4. At the time of this publication, I have been unable to track actual trial documents.

3. "Brattsy-estety," *Golos Moskvy*, no. 69 (1910), p. 4 as quoted in V. Briusov, *Dnevniki 1891–1910: Zapisi proshlogo* (Moscow, 1927), pp. 191–92. A long passage from the *Golos Moskvy* article is also quoted by M. F. Larionov in "Gazetnye kritiki v roli politsii nravov," *Zolotoe runo*, no. 11/12 (1909–10), pp. 97–98.

4. Quoted except for the last sentence in Briusov, *Dnevniki 1891–1910*, p. 191. The rest is from Larionov, "Gazetnye kritiki," pp. 97–98.

5. "Boltuny literaturnye, / Poloumnye poetiki, / Netsenzurnye i burnye /

Provozvestniki estetiki, / Simvolisty-deklamatory, / Dekadentskie khudozhniki, / Khot' v iskusstve reformatory, / No v tvoreniiax sapozhniki . . . / Golosiat kak v truby mednye, / I ot breda netsenzurnogo / Lish' krasneiut steny bednye / U kruzhka literaturnogo . . . i.t.d.," published by an anonymous "Weg" (Briusov, *Dnevniki 1891–1910*, note to pp. 191–92).

6. "Delo obshchestva svobodnoi estetiki," p. 3, and "Bubnovaia dama pod sudom," p. 4.

7. Of the accused only Goncharova and Troianovsky actually appeared in court; see "Delo obshchestva svobodnoi estetiki." Konstantin Krakht was a sculptor and set designer with whom Goncharova had studied privately in Moscow in 1909. It was in his studio that she produced her first set designs for *Svad'ba Zobeida*, in that year. *Teatral'naia entsiklopediia*, ed. S. S. Mokul'skii (Moscow, 1961–62), vol. 2, pp. 66–67.

8. Larionov, "Gazetnye kritiki," pp. 97–98.

9. The Society of Free Aesthetics was founded in 1907 and functioned primarily as a sponsor for exhibitions, poetry readings, and lectures through 1917. A founding member of the society, Dr. I. I. Troianovsky (who was himself tried and who attended Goncharova's trial), became a serious collector of Larionov's work; by 1913 he owned at least nine paintings; see Il'ia Zdanevich (pseudonym Eli Eganbiuri), *Natal'ia Goncharova, Mikhail Larionov* (Moscow, 1913), pp. xvi–xvii. By 1913 Briusov had acquired at least one still life by Goncharova; see ibid., p. iv.

10. This account of changes in the censorship rulings is drawn from a 1913 survey of censorship and the press by V. Vodovosov, "Pokhod na pechat'," *Severnye zapiski*, no. 11 (Nov. 1913), pp. 183–95.

11. See *Rech': Ezhegodnik*, issues for 1912 and 1914, for lists of newspapers fined and editors arrested. Individual issues also listed arrests on a monthly basis; see, for example, "K polozheniiu pechati," *Rech'*, Aug. 5, 1912, pp. 1–2: "The past year has been a unique one in the life of even the long-suffering press. The surplus of fines and other repressions against those involved in the press has exceeded all previous years since the beginning of our constitutional epoch."

12. The artist I. Ia. Bilibin was placed under "administrative arrest" in January 1906 for publishing a caricature of Nicholas II, "Osel (Equus Asinus) v 1/20 nat[ural'noi] vel[ichiny]," in the third number of *Zhupel'*; see "Chronology," in Ivan Iakovlevich Bilibin, *Stat'i, pis'ma, vospominanie o khudozhnike* (Leningrad, 1970), p. 20. Vladimir Mayakovsky, a member of the RSDRP (Bolshevik party) from 1908, was arrested on three occasions, and served a prison term in 1909–10 for operating an illegal press. See *V. V. Maiakovskii*, ed. S. E. Strizhenova (Moscow, 1986), pp. 29–31.

13. "Delo obshchestva svobodnoi estetiki." The quotation is drawn from a press summary of Krakht's defense during the trial.

14. In October 1913, the League for Equal Rights for Women petitioned the Duma to cancel laws passed on December 25, 1909, regulating

prostitution. They argued: "even now all this has a corrupting effect and encourages the view that women are commodities, that it is permissible to buy and sell them and that prostitution is an acceptable trade for women." "Ob otmene reglamentatsii prostitutsii," *Rech'*, Oct. 17, 1913, p. 4.

15. The source for this summary is Vasilii Teplov's survey of legal actions taken by the Russian government during the years 1861–1910, "Piatidesiatiletie vysshego zhenskago obrazovaniia v Rossii," *Vestnik vospitaniia*, no. 9 (Dec. 1910), pp. 117–32.

16. The following is only one example. On May 21, 1873, a "government communication" was issued to call back all Russian women studying abroad, which explicitly connected political radicalism to immoral sexual behavior. The "communication" reads: "[Russian women] espouse communist theories of free love and under the guise of fictive marriage subvert the basic origins of morality and women's chastity to extreme ends." Teplov, "Piatidesiatiletie vyshego zhenskago obrazovaniia," pp. 125–26. According to Barbara Clements, by the 1870s, Russian women constituted 20 to 25 percent of the revolutionary underground. Barbara Clements, "Women in the Russian Empire," *The Modern Encyclopedia of Russian and Soviet History*, ed. Joseph L. Wieczynski (Gulf Breeze, Fla., 1987), vol. 44, pp. 20–21.

17. Richard Stites, *The Women's Liberation Movement in Russia: Feminism, Nihilism, and Bolshevism 1860–1930* (Princeton, N.J., 1978), pp. 423–26.

18. A complete account of the congress proceedings was published: *Trudy pervogo s"ezda pri zhenskom obshchestve v S-Peterburge, 10–16 dekabria, 1908 goda* (St. Petersburg, 1909).

19. "Beseda s N. S. Goncharovoi," *Stolichnaia molva*, Apr. 5, 1910, p. 3 (anonymous).

20. Ibid.

21. G. G. Pospelov, "Moskovskaia zhivopis' 1910-kh godov i gorodskoi fol'klor" (Ph.D. diss., Moscow State University, 1982), pp. 76–77. Pospelov draws his research material on the school from an unpublished manuscript of A. V. Lentulov's memoirs, held by the artist's family. See also Gleb Pospelov, *Karo-bube: Aus der Geschichte der Moskauer Malerei zu Beginn des 20 Jahrhunderts* (Dresden, 1985), pp. 57–58.

22. For a negative evaluation of Mashkov's nudes see A. Radakov in *Satirkon*, no. 19 (1910), and "Khudozhestvennye vesti," *Rech'*, Mar. 1, 1911, p. 5. Social sensitivity to the depiction of nudity in Russian high art was not, however, limited to figure painting by women. In early 1911, Serov's painting of the nude Ida Rubenstein was removed from view in the Russian Museum owing to public controversy over the image; see "Pis'mo V. Serova k M. Tseitlinu," in *Valentin Serov. Perepiska 1890–1911* (Leningrad and Moscow, 1937), p. 323. Two of Larionov's nudes were confiscated from his one-day exhibition at the Literary-Artistic Circle in December 1911 because their poses were considered by

the censors to be "too free"; see F. Mukhortov, "Progressivnyi paralich," *Golos Moskvy*, Dec. 9, 1911, p. 5.

23. Linda Nochlin, "Women Artists After the French Revolution," in *Women Artists 1550–1950*, exhibition catalogue, Los Angeles County Museum of Art (1976; reprint: New York, 1984), pp. 52–53. See also the more recent book by Charlotte Yeldham, *Women Artists in Nineteenth-Century France and England: Their Education, Exhibition Opportunities and Membership of Exhibiting Societies and Academies, with an Assessment of the Subject-Matter of Their Work and Summary Biographies* (New York, 1984), pp. 120–21.

24. The only statistics for the period on the presence of women in the Imperial Academy are given in newspaper accounts. According to these, during the academic year beginning September 1911 women constituted only 7.7 percent of those enrolled in the Imperial Academy (29 women out of 375 students). Jews were equally marginalized through the enforcement of a quota system; in the same year they numbered 34 or 9 percent. See *Rech'*, Nov. 8, 1911, p. 7.

25. This is discussed in chapter 4 of my dissertation, "Primitivism, Neoprimitivism and the Art of Goncharova."

26. Pollock, *Vision and Difference*, p. 45.

27. Like the excerpt quoted in the text above, the notice "Bubnovaia dama pod sudom" also indicates that the "God" was masculine: "By the way, the painting entitled *God* was an overly revealed male."

28. Zdanevich, *Goncharova, Larionov*, p. 16; Mary Chamot, *Gontcharova*, trans. Helen Gerebzow (Paris, 1972), p. 32; and idem, *Goncharova: Stage Designs and Drawings* (London, 1979), p. 9.

29. That Goncharova painted over the original (masculine) version of *God of Fertility* is not an unreasonable assumption; as her students in Paris noted, she frequently repainted earlier pictures (Tatiana Loguine, "Hommage à mes maîtres," in *Gontcharova et Larionov: Cinquante ans à Saint Germain des Près* [Paris, 1971], p. 230). Goncharova discusses repainting pictures in her 1912 diary as well. The January 8, 1912 entry states: "Yesterday what did I do? I finished painting, or in rough, repainted under Misha's [Larionov's] direction 'Bathing,' which I painted in the summer, in pink overcast sunset. . . . I don't like and don't know how to repaint my things, but I think that Cézanne painted [his works] for a long time, or rather repainted them several times." Cited from E. Ovsiannikova, "Iz istorii odnoi illiustratsii," *Panorama iskusstv*, no. 11 (1988), p. 248. Until the works are examined more thoroughly, however, no conclusion can be drawn to serve this argument.

30. For studies on the female spectator and the gaze and on the fetishization of the gaze, see Mary Ann Doane, "Film and Masquerade: Theorizing the Female Spectator," *Screen*, 23, nos. 3–4 (1982), pp. 77–88, and Laura Mulvey, "Visual Pleasure and Narrative Cinema" (1975), reprinted in *Art After Modernism: Rethinking Representation*, ed. Brian Wallis (New York, 1984), pp. 361–74.

31. Beatrice Farwell and Gerald Needham suggest that in composition and often in detail, the pornographic image and the whole history of the libertine print and photograph were grounded in the subjects and compositional motifs of high art. Beatrice Farwell, *Manet and the Nude: A Study in Iconography in the 2nd Empire* (New York, 1981), pp. 134, 147–55, 231–32; Gerald Needham, "Manet, 'Olympia,' and Pornographic Photography," *Art News Annual*, 38 (1972), pp. 80–89, esp. p. 81: "The mixture in 'Olympia' of an exotic odalisque setting with the very real, unexotic woman is typical of the photographs, which often sought a veneer of respectability by borrowing trappings from the nude paintings that proliferated in the Salon." The symbiosis between the two was further reinforced by the production, at least in France, of a genre of nude photo specifically for artists' use and sold only within the walls of the Ecole des Beaux Arts. Elizabeth McCauley points out that the line drawn between this "legally allowable photo" and the pornographic *carte* was not all that clear because it "depended on the definition of a 'natural pose' and was often violated, resulting in series of arrests and rejections by the depot legal censors" (Elizabeth A. McCauley, *A.A.E. Disderi and the Carte de Visite Portrait Photograph* [New Haven, Conn., 1985], pp. 106–9). Since, again, no research has been published on the transmission of these images from France and England to Russia, nor indeed on local production, I must assume that the Russian *sekretnye kartochki* were reasonably close reproductions or copies of their Western European counterparts. For other examples of European erotic and pornographic imagery see *Die erotische Daguerreotypie: Sammlung Uwe Scheid*, intro. Grant B. Romer (Weingarten, 1989), and writings by Abigail Solomon-Godeau: "Legs and the Countess," *October*, 39 (Winter 1986), pp. 65–108, and *Photography at the Dock: Essays on Photographic History, Institutions and Practices* (Minneapolis, 1991), pp. 220–37.

32. Ia. Tugendkhol'd, "Vystavka kartin Natalii Goncharovoi," *Apollon*, no. 8 (Oct. 1913), p. 72.

33. A. Gabhart and E. Broun explain as follows the title of an exhibition that they organized in 1972, Old Mistresses: Women Artists of the Past: "The title of this exhibition alludes to the unspoken assumption in our language that art is created by men. The reverential term 'Old Master' has no meaningful equivalent; when cast in its feminine form, 'Old Mistress,' the connotation is altogether different, to say the least." *Walters Art Gallery Bulletin*, vol. 24, no. 7, 1972, quoted in Roszika Parker and Griselda Pollock, *Old Mistresses: Women, Art and Ideology* (London, 1981), p. 6.

34. Pollock, *Vision and Difference*, p. 85.

35. Carol M. Armstrong, "Edgar Degas and the Representation of the Female Body," in Susan Suleiman, ed., *The Female Body in Western Culture* (Cambridge, Mass., 1986), p. 235.

36. The excerpt is from a review by "Dubl'-ve" titled "Futurizm i koshchunstvo," *Peterburgskii listok*, no. 73 (Mar. 16, 1914).

Wood: Prostitution Unbound

1. Leopold H. Haimson, "The Problem of Social Identities in Early Twentieth-Century Russia," *Slavic Review*, 47, no. 1 (Spring 1988), p. 1.

2. Sheila Fitzpatrick, "The Problem of Class Identity in NEP Society," in Sheila Fitzpatrick, Alexander Rabinowitch, and Richard Stites, eds., *Russia in the Era of NEP: Explorations in Soviet Society and Culture* (Bloomington, Ind., 1991), pp. 12–33.

3. On the female, and especially the "perverted" female, as symbol of danger in Western Europe, see Christine Buci-Glucksmann, "Catastrophic Utopia: The Feminine as Allegory of the Modern," in Catherine Gallagher and Thomas Laqueur, eds., *The Making of the Modern Body: Sexuality and Society in the Nineteenth Century* (Berkeley, 1987), pp. 220–29; and Bram Dijkstra, *Idols of Perversity: Fantasies of Feminine Evil in Fin-de-Siècle Culture* (Oxford, 1986).

4. In the symbolic logic of this period the prostitute stood in a relation of victimization and exploitation to her customers just as "Russia" (always a strongly female noun) stood in relation to Western and native capitalists seeking to fleece and denude her.

5. For further discussion of negative responses to the New Economic Policy in the women's party press, see E. Wood, "Gender and Politics in Soviet Russia: Working Women Under the New Economic Policy, 1918–1928" (Ph.D. diss., University of Michigan, 1991), pp. 276–358.

6. On prostitution in prerevolutionary Russia, see Laurie Annabelle Bernstein, "Sonia's Daughters: Prostitution and Society in Russia" (Ph.D. diss., University of California, Berkeley, 1987), and her essay "Yellow Tickets and State-Licensed Brothels: The Tsarist Government and the Regulation of Urban Prostitution," in Susan Gross Solomon and John F. Hutchinson, eds., *Health and Society in Revolutionary Russia* (Bloomington, Ind., 1990), pp. 45–65; Laura Engelstein, "Gender and the Juridical Subject: Prostitution and Rape in Nineteenth-Century Russian Criminal Codes," *Journal of Modern History*, no. 60 (1988), pp. 458–95; Laura Engelstein, "Morality and the Wooden Spoon: Russian Doctors View Syphilis, Social Class, and Sexual Behavior, 1890–1905," *Representations*, no. 14 (Spring 1986), pp. 169–208; Richard Stites, "Prostitute and Society in Pre-Revolutionary Russia," *Jahrbücher für Geschichte Osteuropas*, 31 (1983), pp. 348–64; Barbara Alpern Engel, "St. Petersburg Prostitutes in the Late Nineteenth Century: A Personal and Social Profile," *Russian Review*, 48 (Jan. 1989), pp. 21–44.

7. For the classic Marxist views on prostitution see Karl Marx, "The Economic and Philosophic Manuscripts," *The Holy Family*; Friedrich Engels, *The Condition of the Working Class in England*, and *The Origin of the Family, Private Property and the State*; and August Bebel, *Woman and Socialism*. Marx saw prostitution as a prime metaphor for exploitation and saw efforts to eradicate it as examples of bourgeois hypocrisy, views which, as we shall see, Lenin repeated in his works. For discussion

of these issues see Lise Vogel, *Marxism and the Oppression of Women: Toward a Unitary Theory* (New Brunswick, N.J., 1983), esp. pp. 44–45, 51–52, 74, 118; and Joan B. Landes, "Marxism and the 'Woman Question,'" in Sonia Kruks, Rayna Rapp, and Marilyn B. Young, eds., *Promissory Notes: Women in the Transition to Socialism* (New York, 1989), pp. 18–19.

8. V. I. Lenin, "Capitalism and Female Labour" (1913), in Robert C. Tucker, ed., *The Lenin Anthology* (New York, 1975), pp. 682–83.

9. V. I. Lenin, "The Fifth International Congress Against Prostitution," in Tucker, *Lenin Anthology*, pp. 683–84.

10. V. I. Lenin, "Tasks of the Youth Leagues (Bourgeois and Communist Morality)," *Pravda*, Oct. 5–7, 1920, in Tucker, *Lenin Anthology*, esp. pp. 667–68.

11. On the Bolshevik commitment to revolutionary transformation, see William G. Rosenberg, Editor's Introduction, *Bolshevik Visions: First Phase of the Cultural Revolution in Soviet Russia* (Ann Arbor, Mich., 1984), pp. 17–24 and passim; Abbott Gleason, Peter Kenez, and Richard Stites, eds., *Bolshevik Culture* (Bloomington, Ind., 1985); and Richard Stites, *Revolutionary Dreams: Utopian Vision and Experimental Life in the Russian Revolution* (New York, 1989).

12. A. Kollontai, *Sem'ia i kommunisticheskoe gosudarstvo* (Moscow and Petrograd, 1919), translated in Rosenberg, *Bolshevik Visions*, p. 87. Kollontai had first developed this approach in *Sotsial'nye osnovy zhenskogo voprosa* (St. Petersburg, 1909). She later repeated it in "Trudovaia Respublika i prostitutsiia," *Kommunistka*, 6 (1920), pp. 15–17, and in *Prostitutsiia i mery bor'by s nei* (Moscow, 1921).

13. V. A. Bystrianskii, *Kommunizm, brak i sem'ia* (Petrograd, 1921), p. 58.

14. F. Niurina, review of "Sud nad prostitutkoi," *Kommunistka*, 3/4 (1923), pp. 55–56.

15. T. Kuznetsova, "Ot mraka k svetu (Byl')," *Rabotnitsa i krest'ianka* (Moscow newspaper), 10 (Nov. 7, 1921), p. 4.

16. L. Trotskii, article in *Pravda*, July 13, 1923, translated by Z. Vergerova as "From the Old Family to the New," in Leon Trotsky, *Problems of Everyday Life* (New York, 1973), p. 36.

17. P. Lepeshinskii, article in *Molodaia gvardiia*, 3 (1923), cited in Mikhail Geller, *Mashiny i vintiki: Istoriia formirovaniia sovetskogo cheloveka* (London, 1985), p. 193.

18. S. Ravich, "Bor'ba s prostitutsiei v Petrograde," *Kommunistka*, 1/2 (June/July 1920), p. 23.

19. Bystrianskii, *Kommunizm, brak i sem'ia*, p. 59.

20. Vera Golubeva, "Rabota zhenotdelov v novykh usloviiakh," *Pravda*, Feb. 1, 1923, p. 3.

21. M. Reiser, letter to the editor, *Kommunistka*, 16/17 (Sept./Oct. 1921), p. 60.

22. A. Kollontai, "Novaia ugroza," *Kommunistka*, 8/9 (1922), pp. 5–9.

23. Note the play on the words for woman (*baba*) and wrecker (*vreditel'nitsa*).
24. Kollontai, "Novaia ugroza," p. 9.
25. See Christine Delphy, *Close to Home: A Materialist Analysis of Women's Oppression* (London, 1984), for one interpretation of the conceptual problem of left-wing activists' hostility toward the housewife and lady of leisure.
26. "Novaia ugroza," *Kommunistka*, 10/11 (1922), p. 57.
27. Bystrianskii, *Kommunizm, brak i sem'ia*, pp. 59–60.
28. "Mery bor'by s prostitutsiei," *Izvestiia VTsIK Sovetov*, Dec. 16, 1922, p. 3; Nikolai Aleksandrovich Semashko, *Health Protection in the USSR* (New York, 1935), pp. 109–12; Kollontai, *Prostitutsiia i mery bor'by s nei*.
29. Ravich, "Bor'ba s prostitutsiei," p. 22. Prostitutes were apparently sentenced not through the regular courts but by administrative order and accounted for as many as 60 percent of those incarcerated in the first year. See also Kollontai, "Trudovaia Respublika i prostitutsiia."
30. A party member (presumably male) could be purged from the party for frequenting prostitutes.
31. This situation of course is reminiscent of the developments discussed in Barbara Ehrenreich and Deirdre English's work, *For Her Own Good: 150 Years of Experts' Advice to Women* (London, 1979). The full extent of Russian women's ignorance of hygiene and health care is only now being plumbed, by David Ransel in his work on infant mortality in prerevolutionary Russia; see his *Mothers of Misery: Child Abandonment in Russia* (Princeton, N.J., 1988).
32. L. Fridland, *S raznykh storon: Prostitutsiia v SSSR* (Berlin, 1931), p. 43. This is reminiscent of Luise White's findings that the great sin of the prostitute under colonial rule in Nairobi was not so much her sexual seduction as her petty capital accumulation; Luise White, "A Colonial State and an African Petty Bourgeoisie: Prostitution, Property and Class Struggle in Nairobi, 1936–1940," in Frederick Cooper, ed., *Struggle for the City: Migrant Labor, the State, and Capital in Urban Africa* (Beverly Hills, Calif., 1983), pp. 167–94.
33. Michel Foucault has argued: "Sexuality must not be described as a stubborn drive, by nature alien and of necessity disobedient to a power which exhausts itself trying to subdue it. . . . [It] is not the most intractable element in power relations, but rather one of those endowed with the greatest instrumentality: useful for the greatest number of maneuvers and capable of serving as a point of support, as a linchpin for the most varied strategies" (*The History of Sexuality, Volume I: An Introduction*, trans. Robert Hurley [New York, 1980], p. 103). On the issue of interdepartmental rivalries in the sphere of social welfare see Bernice Madison, *Social Welfare in the Soviet Union* (Stanford, Calif., 1968).
34. Julia Kristeva, *Powers of Horror. An Essay on Abjection* (New York, 1982), p. 65.

35. Ibid., p. 4.
36. Ibid., pp. 157–73.
37. Ibid., p. 74.
38. Foucault, *History of Sexuality*, pp. 75–131.

Popkin: Kiss and Tell

1. Ross Chambers, "Histoire d'oeuf: Secrets and Secrecy in a La Fontaine Fable," *Sub-Stance*, no. 32 (1981), p. 67.
2. Barbara Herrnstein Smith, "Narrative Versions, Narrative Theories," in W. J. T. Mitchell, ed., *On Narrative* (Chicago, 1981), pp. 213–14.
3. Peter Brooks, *Reading for the Plot: Design and Intention in Narrative* (New York, 1984), p. 61. I deliberately omit the second member of the alliterative pair adduced by Brooks as the goal of the narrative drive (to seduce and to *subjugate*). His casual assumption that erotic engagement entails subjugation is problematic, to say the least, and he has been ably taken to task for his "male" model of desire by such critics as Susan Winnett (see her "Coming Unstrung: Women, Men, Narrative, and Principles of Pleasure," *PMLA* [Special Topic: The Politics of Critical Language], 105 [May 1990], pp. 508–18). Since I view seduction itself, however, as neither inherently male nor inherently objectionable, I provisionally adopt this aspect of Brooks's model for what it can tell us about the operation of narrative desire and discretion.
4. Ross Chambers, *Story and Situation: Narrative Seduction and the Power of Fiction* (Minneapolis, Minn., 1984), p. 11.
5. Iu. M. Lotman, *Struktura khudozhestvennogo teksta* (Providence, R.I., 1971), p. 278.
6. See his *120 Days of Sodom*, which in the final analysis is as much about storytelling as it is about the more lurid forms of pleasure it has made famous. In Marquis de Sade, *The 120 Days of Sodom and Other Writings*, trans. Austryn Wainhouse and Richard Seaver (New York, 1966), pp. 183–674.
7. Roland Barthes speaks of the reader's "passion for meaning" in his "Introduction à l'analyse structurale des récits," *Communications*, no. 8 (1966), p. 27.
8. E. M. Forster, *Aspects of the Novel* (London, 1927), pp. 17–18.
9. A. N. Afanas'ev, *Narodnye russkie skazki i legendy*, 3 vols. (Berlin, 1922), vol. 2, p. 380.
10. Ibid., p. 381.
11. A. P. Chekhov, *Polnoe sobranie sochinenii i pisem*, 30 vols. (Moscow, 1974–83), vol. 7, p. 342. All subsequent citations of Chekhov's work will refer to this edition, and will refer specifically to the *Sochineniia* unless otherwise indicated. Volume and page references appear in the text. The translations are my own.
12. Letter to Suvorin, June 16, 1891 (*Pis'ma*, vol. 4, p. 242).

13. Ryabovich's virtual invisibility in the billiard room strongly evokes the mortal insult sustained by Dostoevsky's underground man at the hands of a billiard-playing officer who, in order to continue his game, actually moves the underground man bodily from his spot without so much as noticing him. "Blows I could have forgiven," says Dostoevsky's character, "but not that he moved me from one spot to another without even noticing me." F. M. Dostoevskii, *Zapiski iz podpol'ia (Notes from Underground)*, in F. M. Dostoevskii, *Polnoe sobranie sochinenii*, 30 vols. (Leningrad, 1972–90), vol. 5, p. 128. Chekhov's Ryabovich, by contrast, is not particularly offended when he is similarly slighted; his treatment as a "nonentity" is perfectly consonant with his self-image.

14. War stories, as Lev Tolstoy demonstrates in *War and Peace*, are every bit as fundamental to military engagement as telling is fundamental to erotic activity. Soldiers, like lovers, are gripped by the desire to tell their stories, and the battles really only take on coherent (albeit distorted) form in their narrative treatments. See Gary Saul Morson, *Hidden in Plain View: Narrative and Creative Potentials in "War and Peace"* (Stanford, Calif., 1987), pp. 107–14.

15. As Rufus Mathewson points out in his treatment of Chekhov's "Beauties" ("Krasavitsy"), the sight of natural beauty in general and of beautiful women in particular is disquieting, saddening: "There is elevation in this feeling . . . but there is no desire, delight or enjoyment." Rufus Mathewson, Jr., "Intimations of Mortality in Four Čexov Stories," in William E. Harkins, ed., *American Contributions to the Sixth International Congress of Slavists*, Prague, 1968 (The Hague, 1968), p. 263.

16. A significant exception to this are the "passionate" kisses, even lovemaking, of Gurov and his lady friend in Yalta, reported dispassionately by the unobtrusive third-person narrator. "Dama s sobachkoi" ("Lady with the Little Dog"), Chekhov, vol. 10, pp. 131–34, 140–42.

17. Erica Jong, *Fear of Flying* (New York, 1973), p. 11.

18. "Fort-da" is Freud's name for the game of "disappearance and return" devised by a small child to master imaginatively his mother's absences. Sigmund Freud, *Beyond the Pleasure Principle*, trans. James Strachey (New York, 1961), pp. 8–10.

19. I. L. Leont'ev (Shcheglov), "On Chekhov," in *Chekhov v vospominaniiakh sovremennikov* (Moscow, 1954), p. 167.

20. L. N. Tolstoi, *Kreitserova sonata*, in L. N. Tolstoi, *Sobranie sochinenii*, 20 vols. (Moscow, 1960–65), vol. 12, p. 142.

21. The word *is* "prostyni," but in the context of the nearby bathhouse, beach towels are undoubtedly meant here rather than sheets. Still, by omitting the adjective in the usual expression (*kupal'naia prostynia*), Chekhov does leave us with the suggestion of sheets.

22. Tolstoi, *Kreitserova sonata*, in *Sobranie sochinenii*, vol. 12, pp. 142, 211.

23. William Labov found in his study of natural narrative that most

narrators have a dual project: not only do they represent a sequence of events, but they also actively attempt to persuade the listener that the tale is worthwhile; they work constantly to ward off the rejoinder "so what?," which would indicate that the narrative has failed. See his *Language in the Inner City* (Philadelphia, 1972), p. 366.

Boym: Loving in Bad Taste

1. Marina Tsvetaeva, "Geroi Truda," in Marina Tsvetaeva, *Proza* (New York, 1955). All translations from Russian are mine unless otherwise indicated.
2. Marina Tsvetaeva, "O liubvi," in Marina Tsvetaeva, *Sochineniia*, ed. Anna Saakiants, 2 vols. (Moscow, 1988), vol. 2, p. 276.
3. V. Voloshinov, *Freidizm* (New York, 1983), pp. 178–85.
4. Vladimir Nabokov, "Philistines and Philistinism," in Vladimir Nabokov, *Lectures on Russian Literature* (New York, 1981), pp. 309–15. I develop the history of *poshlost'* further in "Poetics of Banality," presented at the conference "Glasnost in Two Cultures," New York Institute for the Humanities, New York University, March 1991, to appear in Helena Goscilo, ed., *Fruits of Her Plume: Russian Women's Culture*, and in my forthcoming book *Common Places: Mythologies of Everyday Life in Russia*, to be published by Harvard University Press.
5. Michel Foucault, *The History of Sexuality*, 4 vols., trans. Robert Hurley (New York, 1988), vol. 2, p. 4.
6. Ibid.
7. Roland Barthes, *Le plaisir du texte* (Paris, 1973), pp. 88–89.
8. It came to my attention when this essay was virtually completed that in recent years Hélène Cixous has worked intensely on Tsvetaeva's poetry and prose and included her texts as part of the Études Féminins program in Paris in 1989–90. On "écriture féminine" see Hélène Cixous, "The Laugh of the Medusa," and Luce Irigaray, "The Sex Which Is Not One," both in Elaine Marks and Isabelle de Courtivron, eds., *New French Feminisms* (Brighton, 1980), pp. 190–217.
9. Quoted in Vsevolod Rozhdestvenskii, "Mariana Tsvetaeva," introduction to Tsvetaeva, *Sochineniia*, vol. 1, p. 36.
10. Osip Mandel'shtam, *Sobranie sochinenii*, 4 vols. (New York, 1971), vol. 2, p. 327. Paradoxically, the problem with the "poetess" is not only that she is not properly stylish and "classy," but also that she never goes beyond the mannerisms of style. Mandelstam insists that literary "femininity" is a matter of taste more than of biology or anatomy by ironically commenting in the same article that Mayakovsky, with his excessive futuristic lyricism, is in danger of becoming a "poetess." Mayakovsky wrote his own comments on literary femininity using Tsvetaeva again as a scapegoat: The "Komsomol girl came in with a strong intention to get, for instance, Tsvetaeva. One should tell her, the Komsomol girl, blowing away the dust from the grey book cover: 'Comrade, if you are interested

in gypsy lyricism, I would dare to offer you Selvinsky. The same topic, but look how well it is done! In one word, done by a man' ['Ta zhe tema, no kak obrabotana! Muzhchina']." Vladimir Maiakovskii, *Izbrannye sochineniia* (Moscow, 1985), p. 136. Maiakovskii's words suggest that it is often difficult to draw the line between cultural and biological issues, between the critique of poetic femininity and the insults directed at the woman poet. For further discussion see Svetlana Boym, *Death in Quotation Marks: Cultural Myths of the Modern Poet* (Cambridge, Mass., and London, Eng., 1991).

11. Iurii Tynianov, "O parodii," in Iurii Tynianov, *Poetika, istoriia literatury, kino* (Moscow, 1977), pp. 284–310.

12. Mikhail Bakhtin, *Problems of Dostoyevsky's Poetics*, trans. Caryl Emerson (Minneapolis, Minn., 1984), p. 195.

13. Sigmund Freud, "On Femininity," in Sigmund Freud, *New Introductory Lectures on Psychoanalysis*, lecture 33 (Harmondsworth, Eng., 1971).

14. Hans Georg Gadamer, *Truth and Method*, trans. Garret Barden and John Cummings (New York, 1975), pp. 33–39.

15. Immanuel Kant, *Critique of Judgement*, trans. Werner Pluhar (Indianapolis, 1987), pp. 68–73, 79–85, 126–41. In *Death in Quotation Marks* and in "Obscenity of Theory: Roland Barthes's 'Soirées de Paris' and Walter Benjamin's Moscow Diary" (*Yale Journal of Criticism* [Spring 1991]), I elaborate a concept of aesthetic obscenity that is applicable to Tsvetaeva's prose. The etymology of the word "obscene" is obscure: it can relate both to *obcaenum* (Latin *ob* [on account of] + *caenum* [pollution, dirt, filth, vulgarity]) and to *obscenum* (*ob* [in a relation of tension] + *scena* [scene, space of communal and ritual enactment, sacred space]). "Ob-scene" is defined as something "in a relation of tension" to the (aesthetic) scene. In the context of my work it points to something that has been perceived as culturally marginal and marginalized, as something played offstage with respect to the performance of a male genius. The *American Heritage Dictionary* defines "obscene" first as "offensive to accepted standards of decency or modesty" and second as "inciting lustful feelings, lewd." Perhaps it is the exposed genderedness of the "poetess's" writing, the laying bare of sexual difference, that offends the accepted universal standards of literary decency. Obscenity here is not a pornographic exposure but a manneristic sentimentality that disguises the fundamental lack. Barthes suggests in *A Lover's Discourse* that contemporary obscenity is not pornography or shocking transgression, but sentimentality, sentimentality that is less strange and therefore even more "abject" than Sade's classic example of transgression, the story of the pope's sodomizing of a turkey (*A Lover's Discourse*, trans. Richard Howard [New York, 1987], p. 175). It is this sentimental "lover's discourse," this excess of affect and lack of structure, that disrupts the aesthetic dignity of literary discourse and shapes the modern cultural myth of writing in the feminine.

16. Sasha Chernyi, "Poshlost'," in Sasha Chernyi, *Stikhotvoreniia* (Moscow, 1977), p. 6.

17. Anna Akhmatova, "We met the last time . . ." ("V poslednii raz my vstretilis' togda . . ."), in Anna Akhmatova, *Stikhi i proza* (Leningrad, 1976), p. 63.

18. Quoted in Simon Karlinsky, *Marina Cvetaeva, Her Life and Art* (Berkeley, 1966), p. 272. The American Association for the Advancement of Slavic Studies conference, the American Association of Teachers of Slavic and Eastern European Languages conference, and other Slavic conferences in the past few years have demonstrated an increasing interest in Tsvetaeva's poetry and prose in the work of many American Slavists: Olga Peters Hasty, Katherine O'Connor, Catherine Ciepiela, Greta Slobin, Stephanie Sandler, Michael Naydan, Jane Taubman, Laura Weeks, Pamela Chester, and others have greatly contributed to the recent reappraisal of Tsvetaeva's work.

19. Simon Karlinsky, *Marina Tsvetaeva: The Woman, Her World, and Her Poetry* (Cambridge, Eng., 1985), p. 97.

20. Laura Mulvey, "Visual Pleasures and Narrative Cinema," in Philip Rosen, ed., *Narrative, Apparatus, Ideology: A Film Theory Reader* (New York, 1986), pp. 198–210.

21. Marina Tsvetaeva, "Natal'ia Goncharova," in Marina Tsvetaeva, *Moi Pushkin* (Moscow, 1974), pp. 143–87.

22. Aleksander Griboedov, *Gore ot Uma*, in A. S. Griboedov, *Sochineniia* (Moscow, 1988), p. 66.

23. Marina Tsvetaeva, *Povest' o Sonechke*, in Marina Tsvetaeva, *Neizdannoe* (Paris, 1974). All references follow this edition.

24. Sofiia V. Poliakova, *Nezakatnye ony dni: Tsvetaeva i Parnok* (Ann Arbor, Mich., 1983). Diana Burgin's forthcoming book will give us a more in-depth view of Parnok's life and work.

25. Boris Tomashevsky, "Literature and Biography," in Ladislav Matejka and Krystyna Pomorska, eds., *Readings in Russian Poetics* (Ann Arbor, 1973), pp. 255–70.

26. Marina Tsvetaeva, "Zhivoe o zhivom. (Voloshin)," in Tsvetaeva, *Sochineniia*, vol. 2, pp. 166–224.

27. As the two Tsvetaeva scholars Kroth and Gove have observed, Tsvetaeva seeks to go beyond gender roles and gender limitations. See Antonina Filonov Gove, "The Feminine Stereotypes and Beyond: Role Conflict and Resolution in the Poetics of Marina Tsvetaeva," *Slavic Review*, 36 (June 1977), pp. 231–55, and Anya Kroth, "Dichotomy and *Razminovenie* in the Work of Marina Tsvetaeva" (Ph.D. diss., University of Michigan, 1977). Also see Kroth's article "Androgyny as an Exemplary Feature in Marina Tsvetaeva's "Dichotomous Poetic vision," *Slavic Review*, 38, no. 4 (1979), pp. 563–82. Kroth suggests that at the center of Tsvetaeva's "dichotomous vision" is the notion of androgyny, a desire for a "sexlessness of the soul," for ultimate reconciliation of the terrestrial sexes in one transcendental being. As Hélène Cixous pointed out in her

essay "Laugh of the Medusa," the concept of androgyny, dating back to Plato's *Symposium* and Ovid's *Metamorphosis*, is a very controversial one: in spite of its implied sexlessness and reconciliation, the root of the first syllable in the words "androgyne" and "hermaphrodite" always remains male. Moreover, "androgyny" suggests a final reconciliation of the sexes, the absence of conflict, of dialogue, an ultimate self-sufficiency.

Tsvetaeva's theoretical pronouncements, tinged with Romantic Platonism, might suggest the figure of the androgyne as an embodiment of the desire to transcend sexual stereotypes existing in culture. However, true to her defiant spirit, Tsvetaeva often deviated from her own critical pronouncements, and her writings remain controversially and unconventionally gendered. Tsvetaeva's gender theater is not necessarily "dichotomous" or "dualistic," but rather, truly dramatic, characterized by—to use Bakhtin's term—"heteroglossia," what we might call sexual multivoicedness or polysexuality. This polysexuality, like Dostoevsky's "heteroglossia" celebrated by Bakhtin, is not devoid of cultural prejudices and myths; in Tsvetaeva's case, it reveals many conflicting attitudes, especially with regard to relationships between women.

Burgin: Laid Out in Lavender

1. *Entsiklopedicheskii slovar'* (St. Petersburg, 1896), vol. 27A, p. 590. Unless otherwise noted all English translations of Russian originals (prose and poetry) used in this essay are mine.

2. See Laura Engelstein, "Lesbian Vignettes: A Russian Triptych from the 1890's," *Signs*, 15, no. 4 (Summer 1990), p. 814 n. 4. Engelstein includes three excerpts ("lesbian vignettes"), in English translation, from a study of female homosexuality entitled *The Perversion of Sexual Feeling in Women* (1895), by a Russian gynecologist, Dr. Ippolit Tarnovskii. Two of the excerpts concern Lesbians involved in criminal cases of the 1880s; one of the criminal Lesbians was also a prostitute. The third vignette is presented by Tarnovskii as the "autobiography" of an upper-class "mannish" Lesbian, who was somehow persuaded to tell Tarnovskii her life story and also submit to a gynecological examination. The latter is described, like several other medical probings of female genitals offered as evidence in Tarnovskii's texts, with pornographic detail. On the whole, Tarnovskii's "lesbian vignettes" merely add a Russian turn-of-the-century medical voice to what Alain Corbin suggests as a recognizable anti-Lesbian genre: "interminable pronouncements of doctors and magistrates on the proliferation of tribades in . . . bordellos and prisons"; these are of limited value to the historian of female homosexuality in Corbin's opinion because they principally provide evidence of "the fascination that the lesbian exerts on the . . . male imagination" (quoted by Joan DeJean, *Fictions of Sappho 1546–1937* [Chicago, 1989], p. 353 n. 73).

3. As Barbara Fassler has noted ("Theories of Homosexuality as Sources of Bloomsbury's Androgyny," *Signs*, 5, no. 2 [1979], pp. 237–

57), there is a tendency in all cultures to locate homosexuality far away from themselves in "foreign," exotic places. For Western European and Anglo-American cultures that often meant (and still means) viewing same-sex love as endemic to Asia, the Near East, and—ironically, from the Russian point of view that we are examining here—in Russia. For example, in a 1936 "clinical" study of female sexuality Dr. Joseph Tenenbaum makes the following comment: "In Czarist Russia, that country of sexual vices and excesses, homosexuality was deeply rooted and became a veritable epidemic at the beginning of the 20th century"; see Tenenbaum, *The Riddle of Woman* (New York, 1936), p. 74. Ancient Greece, of course, was widely identified as a pagan, homoerotic culture, particularly in Great Britain. The Sappho scholar Denys Page comments, "It is at least probable that Lesbos in [Sappho's] lifetime was notorious for the perverse practices of its women"; Denys Page, *Sappho and Alcaeus: An Introduction to the Study of Ancient Lesbian Poetry* (Oxford, 1987), p. 144.

4. DeJean, *Fictions*.

5. Elaine Marks, "Lesbian Intertextuality," in George Stambolian and Elaine Marks, eds., *Homosexualities and French Literature* (Ithaca, N.Y., 1979), p. 353.

6. I have heard the same attitudes expressed by older female members of the intelligentsia and scholars in the former Soviet Union who believe homosexuality is an intensely private, personal matter with no scholarly interest. Younger women of the region seem to take a more "Western" approach and have recently joined gay men in initiating (in St. Petersburg and Moscow) a more-or-less open struggle for the rights of "sexual minorities" (*seksual'nye menshinstva*).

7. Simon Karlinsky, "Russia's Gay Literature and History (11th–20th Centuries)," *Gay Sunshine* (San Francisco), no. 29/30 (1976), pp. 1–7.

8. Sof'ia V. Poliakova, *Nezakatnye ony dni: Tsvetaeva i Parnok* (Ann Arbor, Mich., 1983), p. 46. This book (cited below as *NOD*) also contains the texts of the poems in Tsvetaeva's cycle, "Podruga" ("Girlfriend"), from which I shall quote.

9. Parnok retains her unique position to this day. While Marina Tsvetaeva has written openly in poetry and prose about her experiences of loving women and has expressed her essentially anti-Lesbian views on Lesbian relationships in "Lettre à l'Amazone," she cannot in my opinion be considered a Lesbian poet in the fullest sense of the word: a poet who was a Lesbian in addition to treating the theme of Lesbianism.

10. I do not wish to enter into the contemporary debate in Western feminist and Lesbian feminist scholarship and writing on what a Lesbian is. My own position is middle-of-the-road. I reject a narrowly sexual definition of Lesbianism, but am also not comfortable with the different sort of limitation imposed by those who consider Lesbianism purely a political choice or philosophy of woman-identification. I like Mary Daly's definition of a Lesbian as "a Woman-Loving woman; a woman who has broken

the Terrible Taboo against Woman-touching *on all levels* [emphasis mine]; Woman-identified woman; one who has rejected false loyalties to men in every sphere," *Websters' First New Intergalactic Wickedary of the English Language* (Boston, 1987), p. 78. Following Daly's practice, throughout this paper I capitalize the word "Lesbian" "to indicate Woman-identification." I believe and, in fact, hope to demonstrate here that Russian Lesbians of the Silver Age were conscious of their difference from the majority of women and that this consciousness affected their writing, if only, in some cases, on the most basic level of forcing them to camouflage this fact of their biographies.

11. I would argue that the element of gender play in a *Lesbian* love lyric can only be developed to its fullest and most aesthetically pleasing if the sex of the poetic speaker *and* her beloved are both marked as feminine. Tsvetaeva provides an excellent example of Lesbian gender play in the last stanza of no. 6 of "Podruga":

Как я по Вашим узким пальчикам
Водила сонною щекой,
Как Вы меня дразнили мальчиком,
Как я Вам нравилась такой . . .

How I drew my sleepy cheek
Over your narrow fingers,
How you teased me for being a boy,
How I pleased you as a girl like that . . .
(Poliakova, *NOD*, p. 28)

The addressee ("you") has been previously identified as a woman, and the poetic speaker inscribes her feminine gender in this stanza in the feminine past-tense verbs "drew" (*vodila*) and "pleased" (*nravilas'*). The element of gender play and its erotic implications come across with particular subtlety and power in the grammatical gender contrast between *mal'chikom*, the instrumental case (demanded by the verb "teased") of the masculine noun for boy, and *takoi* (end of line 4), the instrumental case (demanded by the verb "pleased") of the feminine pronoun for "such a one," i.e., "a girl like that." These contrasting complementary masculine/feminine instrumentalities within the same female being, the poetic persona, reinforce a similar play contained in the last words of lines two and one: *shchekoi* (instrumental case of *shcheka*, "cheek," feminine), the means by which the female poetic persona puts her face in contact with her woman-lover in the aftermath of passion, and *pal'chikam* (dative plural of *pal'chik*, "finger," masculine), the implicit means by which the woman-lover addressee has touched her.

12. Hence the "double bind" of the Lesbian writer as described by Sharon O'Brien in her biography of Willa Cather: "either she could write as a woman, in which case she created a limited art, or she could write as a man, in which case she created an inauthentic art," as quoted by Carolyn G. Heilbrun, *Writing a Woman's Life* (New York, 1988), p. 96.

13. As of the writing of this essay, outside of my own and Sofia Poliakova's work on Parnok the only work by a Slavist on the subject of Lesbian writers and writing in Russia is, to my knowledge, Simon Karlinsky's general survey of homosexual writers in Russia. In addition to the article cited above, Karlinsky has recently published "Russia's Gay Literature and Culture: The Impact of the October Revolution," in Martin Duberman, Martha Vicinus, and George Chauncey, Jr., eds., *Hidden from History: Reclaiming the Gay and Lesbian Past* (New York, 1989), pp. 347–65.

14. Sof'ia V. Poliakova, "Vstupitel'naia stat'ia," in *Sobranie stikhotvorenii S. Ia. Parnok* (Ann Arbor, 1979), p. 91. Texts of Parnok's poems that are quoted in the present essay come from this, the only edition of her collected poems, and will be referenced in parentheses after the quotation with Parnok's name, the number of the poem, and the page on which it occurs.

15. DeJean has argued that Baudelaire "completely realigned literary lesbianism" and made "the lesbian . . . the heroine of modernism" (*Fictions*, p. 271). This model evolved from the hermaphroditic notion of female mannishness, of "woman devoting herself to intellectual creativity, woman perpetually virginal because she refuses men access to her body" (ibid., p. 274). DeJean therefore distinguishes Baudelaire's decadent *femmes damnées* from Verlaine's more "sensationalistic" portrayals. It seems to me that this distinction, while valid, should not be allowed to mask a more important *similarity* between these two male perceiver-poets: neither conceived of the Lesbian, whether heroine or nonheroine, as capable of full-fledged sexuality, because neither could, or wanted to, conceive of the possibility of sexual fulfillment for women without men.

16. Shari Benstock, *Women of the Left Bank: Paris 1900–1940* (Austin, Tex., 1986), p. 53.

17. Lidia Zinovieva-Annibal, *Thirty-Three Abominations*, trans. Sam Cioran, *Russian Literature Tri Quarterly*, no. 9 (1974), p. 113.

18. Zinaida Gippius [Anton Krainii], review of Zinovieva-Annibal's *33 Uroda, Vesy*, no. 7 (1907), p. 61. Evidence of the international notoriety achieved by Zinovieva-Annibal's novel can be found in the 1936 American study of female sexuality by Tenenbaum (cited above in n. 3). Tenenbaum notes: "In 1907 a novel appeared by the St. Petersburg actress, Sinowjewa-Annibal, called *Thirty-Three Monsters*. It dealt exclusively with Lesbian love" (*Riddle of Woman*, p. 74).

19. Innokenti Annensky, "O sovremennom lirizme: One," *Apollon*, Dec. 1909, p. 8.

20. Annensky, "Lirizme," p. 12. The pen name Solovyova chose for herself, Allegro, is curiously neuter. The editor's introduction to a selection of her poems in *Poety 1880–1890-kh godov* (Leningrad, 1972) notes, "the poetess herself explained the genesis of her pseudonym in her desire to make up for the lack of life energy which she felt in herself" (p. 357).

21. According to Russian anecdote and "formalized gossip" (Elaine

Marks's term, in "Intertextuality"), Gippius was rumored to be "physiologically a hermaphrodite," as Tatiana Mamonova notes in "Homosexuality in the Soviet Union," trans. Sarah Matilsky, in Mamonova's *Russian Women's Studies: Essays on Sexism in Soviet Culture* (Oxford, 1989), p. 130. In the context of Silver Age medical theories and decadent stereotypes, which identified the "mannish" Lesbian as a hermaphrodite-like Third Sex, this gossip about Gippius could be read as an allusion to the poet's Lesbian orientation.

22. Solovyova also writes about her attraction to "the impossible" (*nevozmozhnoe*) as a permanent feature of her journey through life, for example, in the 1900 poem, "On a Winter Road" ("Zimneiu dorogoi"): "Again the impossible, like blazing dawn, / Burns over the twilight of life; / My soul, as before, harkens avidly / To everything that it says" ("Opiat' nevozmozhnoe iarkoi zareiu / Nad sumrakom zhizni gorit; / Ia zhadno, kak prezhde, vnimaiu dushoiu / vsemy, chto ono govorit"), in *Poety 1880–1890-kh godov*, p. 362.

23. See Marina Tsvetaeva's later recollection of Solovyova and her lifelong lover, Natalia Manaseina, in *Mon frère féminin, Lettre à l'Amazone* (Paris, 1979), pp. 27–28.

24. Other critics of Solovyova's poetry drew indirect attention to the sterility and lifelessness created by her male persona. A critic of her first book, *Poems* (*Stikhotvoreniia*, 1899), points out the absence of "living human feeling" in her lyrics and seems to connect this shortcoming with the poet's implied intermediate status as neither male nor female. He admonishes her (and all contemporary poets) to let readers "see in you either a brother or a sister living not in some unearthly world of ethereal elves, but side by side with us, our joys, anxieties and sufferings" (L. Mel'shin, *Ocherki russkoi poezii* [St. Petersburg, 1904], p. 346).

25. Annensky was probably persuaded to review the unknown Vilkina's first book as a favor to her well-known and highly respected husband, Nikolai Minsky. Karlinsky describes Minsky as "a poet and playwright much interested in the Lesbian subculture" ("Literature and History," p. 3).

26. Rozanov, an influential writer and critic, argued in a 1909 journal article, "the essence of [male homosexual] relationships . . . lies in the humble, profound, exalted, spiritual love that arises between individuals of the same sex" ("Nechto iz tumana 'obrazov' i podobii, sudebnoe nedorazumenie v Berline," *Vesy*, no. 3 [1909], p. 57). Solomon's painting is reproduced in DeJean, *Fictions*, p. 226 and on the cover.

27. V. Rozanov, Predislovie, in Liudmila Vilkina-Minskaia, *Moi sad* (Moscow, 1906), p. 6.

28. Susan Gubar, "Sapphistries," *Signs*, 10, no. 11 (1984), p. 46.

29. Viacheslav Ivanov, *Alkei i Safo*, in his *Sobranie pesen' i liricheskikh otryvok v perevode Viacheslava Ivanova* (Moscow, 1914), p. 24. Elaine Marks has an interesting discussion in "Lesbian Intertextuality" of the role played by the Sappho model in fictions about women loving

women: "Although there is no evidence in Sappho's poems to corroborate the notion that she did indeed have a school, religious or secular, for young women, the gynaeceum, ruled by the seductive or seducing teacher has become . . . the preferred locus for most fictions about women loving women" (p. 357).

30. Greek texts of Sappho are cited from W. Barnstone, ed. and trans., *Sappho. Lyrics in the Original Greek with Translations by W. Barnstone* (New York, 1965), p. 16. The literal English translations of the original Greek are my own.

31. DeJean has an excellent reading of this poem in the appendix to her study *Fictions of Sappho*, pp. 322–25.

32. I am currently working on a study of Russian translations of Sappho from the eighteenth century through the Silver Age, which will focus in particular on the two complete translations of Sappho's fragments done by Ivanov (1914) and Veresaev (1915).

33. Parnok collected all her Sappho poems and imitations into *Roses of Pieria* (*Rozy Pierii*), which appeared in 1922. In one of these poems she comments on her Sapphic fiction-making:

> Так на других берегах, у другого певучего моря,
> тысячелетья спустя, юной такой же весной,
> древнее детство свое эолийское припоминая,
> дева в задумчивый день перебирала струны.
>
> Ветром из-за моря к ней доструилось дыханье Эллады,
> ветер, неявный другим, сердце ее шевелит:
> чудится деве—она домечтает мечты твои, Сафо,
> недозвучавшие к нам песни твои допоет.

> Thus on other shores, by another melodious sea,
> thousands of years later, in the same kind of young spring,
> remembering her ancient Aeolian childhood,
> on a pensive day a maiden ran her fingers over the strings.
>
> The breath of Hellada streamed up to her in the sea wind,
> a wind that others cannot feel stirs her heart:
> it seems to the maiden—she's dreaming out your dreams,
>   Sappho,
> singing through to the end your songs which have not sounded
>   down to us.
> (Parnok, no. 68, p. 147)

Unlike Ivanov, Parnok does note the controversy surrounding Sappho's sexuality, and implies, with obvious irony, that there is little to contend over—Sappho was a Lesbian in both the geographical and sexual senses of the word. In one poem she imagines Sappho asleep on her female companion's breast, dreaming of Aphrodite, whose divine voice speaks: "Here is what fame means, Sappho: / people argue to whom your eternal love songs—rapture of the gods!— / are addressed—to young men, or to maidens?" "Vot ona slava, Safo: / sporiat, komu tvoi vechnye—khmel' bogov!— / pesni liubovnye—iunosham, ili devam?" (no. 66, p. 146).

34. I use the term "external mediation" as defined and discussed by Rene Girard in *Deceit, Desire, and the Novel: Self and Other in Literary Structure* (Baltimore, 1976), p. 9 and passim.

35. Cited in Veronika Losskaia, *Marina Tsvetaeva v zhizni: Neizdannye vospominaniia sovremenikov* (Tenafly, N.J., 1989), p. 150.

36. The love affair behind Tsvetaeva's "Podruga" and the addressee of the poems in the cycle were established by Sophia Poliakova in her ground-breaking study *Nezakatnye ony dni* (see above, note 8). The title's phrase, "sunsetless days of yore," comes from Tsvetaeva's April 1916 good-bye poem to Parnok, "In days of yore you were like a mother to me" ("V ony dni ty mne byla, kak mat'," Poliakova, *NOD*, p. 99). I believe Tsvetaeva's "v ony dni" ("in days of yore") echoes intertextually with Parnok's "Like a small girl . . . ," in the last stanza of which she thanks Tsvetaeva for first coming to her "v te dni" ("in those days"). Parnok's poem also refers to the maternal tenderness that alternated with passion in her and Tsvetaeva's erotic relationship.

37. Quotes from Parnok, no. 82, p. 155. See my articles "After the Ball Is Over: Sophia Parnok's Creative Relationship with Marina Tsvetaeva," *Russian Review*, 47 (1988), pp. 425–44, and "Signs of Response: Two Possible Parnok Replies to Her *Podruga*," *Slavic and East European Journal*, no. 2 (1991), pp. 36–49.

38. The fifth review is a very brief one by a poet and friend of Parnok's, Konstantin Lipskerov, which exists in manuscript form in the Parnok Archive (TsGALI), and is quoted by K. Khudabashian, "Avtor libretto opery 'Almast' A. Spendiarova-Sofiia Parnok," in *Aleksandr Spendiarov: Stat'i i issledovaniia* (Yerevan, 1973), p. 195. Lipskerov, like Khodasevich (whom I discuss below), separates Parnok's verse from the "intimate chamber poetry of the majority of contemporary poetesses" as a way of praising her. Lipskerov finds that Parnok's Sapphic and Alcaean stanzas especially reveal the rarely met qualities of "mastery, firmness and masculine nobility" characteristic of "laconic speech." There are suggestions here of a view of Parnok as a "mascula Sappho" (see DeJean, *Fictions*, passim), an essentially hermaphroditic image.

39. This is the opinion of an anonymous critic in a review of Lokhvitskaya's first book in the journal *Russkoe bogatstvo*, no. 7 (1896), pp. 59–60. For more on Lokhvitsaya, and an attempt to save her reputation from the taint of sapphic eroticism, see Sam Cioran's "The Russian Sappho: Mirra Lokhvitskaia," *Russian Literature Tri Quarterly*, no. 9 (1974), pp. 317–35.

40. "Parnok, Sofia: Stat'ia o ee tvorchestve," archive of the publishing house Ogni, typescript, 5 unnumbered pages, Institute of Russian Literature, Leningrad.

41. Cited by Nancy Manahan, "Homophobia in the Classroom," in Margaret Cruikshank, ed., *Lesbian Studies, Present and Future* (Old Westbury, N.Y., 1982), p. 66.

42. The German Romantic writer von Arnim (1785–1859) was perceived by the poets in Gertsyk's circle, including Parnok and Tsvetaeva, as the eternal embodiment of female genius. Parnok, in her "Sonnet" (no. 28, p. 125), calls Tsvetaeva "Bettina," and I have shown that in the twelfth poem of "Podruga" Tsvetaeva quotes to Parnok von Arnim's oath of devotion to her romantic friend, the poet Karoline von Guenderode; see Burgin, "After the Ball Is Over."

43. Adelaida Gertsyk, "Sofiia Parnok: *Stikhotvoreniia*," *Severnye zapiski*, no. 2 (1916), p. 227.

44. Ibid., p. 228. With this comment Gertsyk unknowingly reveals that she, like Parnok, had not read Sappho in the original Greek.

45. Ibid., p. 229. Gertsyk's "flowers" seem like an allusion to Baudelaire's "flowers of evil"; her "willows" are a symbol of death and mourning. One should also note that she chooses to view as emblematic of Parnok's "autumnal poetry" a lyric that in fact ends with the promise of regrowth in the coming summer: "But won't heat flare in this same sky? / The foliage of these same oaks? / Already one young stalk shows green / Amidst last summer's greyhaired grass" ("No vspykhnet znoi ne v etom nebe l'? / V listve ne etikh li dubrav? / Uzh iunyi zeleneet stebel' / v sedinakh proshloletnikh trav"; no. 10, p. 114).

46. Vladislav Khodasevich, "Sofiia Parnok. *Stikhotvoreniia*," *Utro Rossii*, no. 274 (1916). I am grateful to Professor John Malmstad for drawing Khodasevich's review to my attention and providing me with a copy.

47. There is no evidence to support the possibility that Khodasevich read Tsvetaeva's "Podruga" in manuscript form. Their strikingly similar perceptions of Parnok appear to be a literary coincidence. This in turn seems to testify to the power of the Silver Age's hermaphrodite model of Lesbians.

48. Maximilian Voloshin, "Golosa poetov," republished in Maximilian Voloshin, *Liki tvorchestva* (Leningrad, 1988), p. 543.

49. Zinovieva-Annibal, *Abominations*, p. 95.

Goscilo: Monsters Monomaniacal, Marital, and Medical

1. On the grotesque in Tolstaya's fiction, see Helena Goscilo, "Tat'iana Tolstaia's 'Dome of Many-Coloured Glass': The World Refracted Through Multiple Perspectives," *Slavic Review*, 47, no. 2 (Summer 1988), pp. 280–90. On externally grotesque couplings, see Helena Goscilo, "Tolstajan Love as Surface Text," *Slavic and East European Journal*, 34, no. 1 (1990), pp. 40–52.

2. Such carnivalized pairings, of course, destabilize dogmatic distinctions and institutionalized hierarchies.

3. "Hunting the Wooly Mammoth" ("Okhota na mamonta," first published in *Oktiabr'*, no. 12 [1985], pp. 117–21) and "Fire and Dust" ("Ogon' i pyl'," first published in *Avrora*, no. 10 [1986], pp. 82–91)

appeared in Tolstaya's collection of stories, *Na zolotom kryl'tse sideli* (Moscow, 1987), translated into English by Antonina Bouis as Tatyana Tolstaya, *On the Golden Porch* (New York, 1989). The volume did not include "The Poet and the Muse" ("Poet i muza," *Novyi mir*, no. 12 [1986], pp. 113–19).

4. Tolstaya, *On the Golden Porch*, p. 57. All citations from "Hunting the Wooly Mammoth" refer to the Bouis translation, with changes where necessary to correct omissions and errors.

5. Zoya's motivation and her perception of the "love object" recall A. Tertz's *The Trial Begins* (*Sud idet*, 1956), wherein Karlinsky similarly equates Marina with his Purpose.

6. "Zoya worked in a hospital, in the information bureau, and she wore a white coat and thereby belonged a bit to that amazing, white, starched world. . . . And the king of this world is the surgeon" (pp. 52–53). In a recent interview with me in Moscow (May 31, 1988), Tolstaya acknowledged her animus against the medical profession, particularly its personal, intimate invasion of the body for "impersonal" reasons. That sense of violation by doctors communicates itself also in "The Poet and the Muse" and "A Clean Sheet" ("Chistyi list," first published in *Neva*, no. 12 [1984], pp. 116–26), in *On the Golden Porch*, pp. 77–99.

7. The topos of love as hunt can be traced to antiquity, when it enjoyed widespread use in the poetry of Ovid, Horace, and Virgil.

8. Feminist film theory first elaborated the notion that women frequently function as passive objects of male voyeuristic desire and possession within the subjective narrative of patriarchal (mis)representation in artistic form. The pioneering piece on the topic, which since has been superseded by somewhat subtler analyses in a more discriminating vein, is the article by the British feminist filmmaker and theorist Laura Mulvey, "Visual Pleasure and Narrative Cinema," *Screen*, 16, no. 3 (1975), pp. 6–18. For subsequent refinements of Mulvey's central thesis, see E. Ann Kaplan, *Women and Film: Both Sides of the Camera* (New York, 1983), especially the section entitled "Is the Gaze Male?," pp. 23–35; also Tania Modleski, *The Women Who Knew Too Much: Hitchcock and Feminist Theory* (New York, 1988), especially pp. 13–14. Mulvey herself has been revising her original insight: see Laura Mulvey, "Afterthoughts on 'Visual Pleasure and Narrative Cinema' Inspired by *Duel in the Sun*," *Framework*, nos. 15/16/17 (1981), p. 15, and idem, "Changes: Thoughts of Myth, Narrative and Historical Experience," *History Workshop Journal*, no. 23 (Spring 1987), pp. 1–19.

9. John Berger's ground-breaking study, *Ways of Seeing*, illustrates how consistently Western tradition has displayed women for the male spectator, who serves as a mirror for the woman's self-image. John Berger, *Ways of Seeing* (London, 1972), pp. 51–54.

10. Zoya represents a prime instance of the conventional female vicious cycle in which "women are accustomed to seeing themselves being seen, to valuing themselves according to others' evaluations of their

appearance, and then to being devalued for this 'narcissism.'" Judith Kegan Gardiner, "Mind Mother: Psychoanalysis and Feminism," in Gayle Greene and Coppelia Kahn, eds., *Making a Difference: Feminist Literary Criticism* (London, 1985), p. 128.

11. In this orgy of vulgar pleasure one recognizes the "mercantile psychology" of which Tolstaya spoke in an interview, deploring the addiction to brand names and fancy goods that she considers a hallmark of "feminine prose," which, she notes, "is mostly written by men." Tatyana Tolstaya, "A Little Man Is a Normal Man," *Moscow News*, no. 8 (1987), p. 10. Susanne Kappeler has commented cogently: "The remorseless diffusion of gender stereotypes, of readymade and imperative life-styles, of regulated uniform 'relationships'—the ideological diffusion of 'mind images' of humans—through the remorseless diffusion of their material basis—consumer goods—renders human subjects increasingly marginal." Susanne Kappeler, *The Pornography of Representation* (Minneapolis, Minn., 1986), p. 79.

12. Tatyana Tolstaya, "The Poet and the Muse," trans. Jamey Gambrell, *The New Yorker*, Jan. 15, 1990, p. 36. Further citations all refer to this translation, with occasional slight modifications.

13. Compare the passage with Flaubert's catalogue of the ingredients of the romances that exerted a fatal formative influence on Emma Bovary's impressionable and undisciplined imagination: "Ce n'étaient qu'amours, amants, amantes, dames persecutées s'évanouissant dans des pavillons solitaires, postillons qu'on tue à tous les relais, chevaux qu'on crève à toutes les pages, forêts sombres, troubles du coeur, serments, sanglots, larmes et baisers, nacelles au clair de lune, rossignols dans les bosquets, *messieurs* braves comme des lions, doux comme des agneaux, vertueux comme on ne l'est pas, toujours bien mis, et qui pleurent commes des urnes." Gustave Flaubert, *Madame Bovary* (Paris, 1957), p. 39. In translation, the passage reads: "They were all love, lovers, sweethearts, persecuted ladies fainting in lonely pavilions, postilions killed at every stage, horses ridden to death on every page, sombre forests, heart-aches, vows, sobs, tears and kisses, little skiffs by moonlight, nightingales in shady groves, 'gentlemen' brave as lions, gentle as lambs, virtuous as no one ever was, always well dressed, and weeping like fountains." Gustave Flaubert, *Madame Bovary*, trans. Eleanor Marx Aveling (New York, 1940), p. 42.

14. Tolstaya returns to the fairy tale for ironic comparison of motives when Nina starts hounding Lizaveta so as to eradicate her from Grisha's life. Tolstaya's text states: "Seven pairs of iron boots had Nina worn out tramping across passport desks and through police stations, seven iron staffs had she broken on Lizaveta's back, seven kilos of iron gingerbread had she devoured in the hated custodian's lodge: it was time for the wedding" (p. 40). The text of "The Feather of Finist the Bright Falcon" states: "three cast-iron staffs have I broken, three pairs of iron slippers have I worn out, three stone communion breads have I devoured, all in my con-

stant search for you, beloved!" ("tri chugunnykh posokha izlomala, tri pary zheleznykh bashmachkov istoptala, tri kamennykh prosviry izglodala—vse tebia, milogo, iskala!"), in A. N. Afanas'ev, ed., *Narodnye russkie skazki*, 3 vols. (Moscow, 1958), vol. 2, p. 239.

15. In this double-layered discourse, the style of the idealistic 1840s seems grafted onto the utilitarian values of the 1860s, creating an inner tension that evokes the clashing worlds of the fathers and sons captured in Turgenev's and Dostoevsky's generational novels: *Fathers and Sons* and *The Possessed*.

16. Dijkstra's compellingly argued thesis that *fin de siècle* culture harbored erotic fantasies of feminine evil is richly supported by the plethora of reproductions in his book, which diagnoses, *inter alia*, the period's inordinate fascination with prostrate women who are sleeping or merely sprawling languidly in poses calculated to stimulate libidinous thoughts in the viewer. In some cases, sickness, which enjoyed an unprecedented cult at the time, accounted for the women's lying in bed. Frailty and consumptiveness were deemed desirable in women as evidence of their purity, whereas health and vigor, as masculine traits, compromised the "feminine essence." Bram Dijkstra, *Idols of Perversity* (New York, 1986), esp. pp. 25–63. For additional insight into the cult of invalidism, see the chapter entitled "The Sexual Politics of Sickness" in Barbara Ehrenreich and Deirdre English, *For Her Own Good* (New York, 1978), pp. 101–40.

17. Lev Tolstoy's *Anna Karenina*, which examines sexuality and possession of diverse sorts, synthesizes the two in a powerful scene in which Anna gazes avidly at the sleeping Vronskii, whom she views as lover, enemy, and victimizer even as she herself victimizes him.

18. The Russian text in *Novyi mir* omits this sentence, which is translated by Jamey Gambrell in the English version from Tolstaya's manuscript.

19. The motif of fatality that accompanies their misunion is introduced at the very outset and repeats itself throughout the narrative: "Grisha beat his porcelain brow against the wall and cried out that fine, all right, he was prepared to die, but after his death—you'll see—he'd come back to his friends and never be parted from them again" (p. 41); "Only he was a frail thing: he cried a lot and didn't want to eat, . . . whimpered and made up poems that offended Nina, about how motherwort had sprouted in his heart, his garden had gone to seed, the forests had burned to the ground, and some sort of crow was plucking, so to speak, the last star from the now silent horizon, and how he, Grishunia, seemed to be inside some hut, pushing and pushing at the frozen door, but there was no way out" (pp. 41–42); "He roamed the apartment and muttered— muttered that he would soon die, and the earth would be heaped over him" (p. 42).

20. This passage is also pertinent: "Oh, to wrest Grisha from that noxious milieu! To scrape away the extraneous women who'd stuck to him

like barnacles to the bottom of a boat; to pull him from the stormy sea, turn him upside down, tar and caulk him and set him in dry dock in some calm, quiet place!" (p. 40).

21. The startling capacity to add a human being to one's collection of objects, which Marxist feminists view as inherent in bourgeois patriarchy, likewise defines the Duke in Robert Browning's *My Last Duchess* and Gilbert Osmond in Henry James's *Portrait of a Lady*.

22. Nina Katerli offers a comparable contrast in her novella (*povest'*) *Polina* (first published in *Neva*, no. 1 [1984]), which otherwise bears scant resemblance to Tolstaya's story.

23. Tatyana Tolstaya, "Fire and Dust," trans. Jamey Gambrell, in Sergei Zalygin, ed., *The New Soviet Prose* (New York, 1989), p. 299. With minimal modifications, I rely on this fine translation by Gambrell in preference to Antonina Bouis's version in *On the Golden Porch* (pp. 100–115), which is riddled with inaccuracies.

24. See also: "There they supposedly ravished her, knocked out half her teeth, and abandoned her, naked, on the seashore in a pool of oil" (p. 299); "Still completely naked, she and the ethnographer, who called her Svetka-Pipetka . . . , holed up in an abandoned watchtower, dating back to Shamil's time" (p. 299).

25. It is possible that Tolstaya is familiar with the tradition, dating at least from Chaucer's time, of associating gaps in teeth with sexuality. See, for instance, the following lines from Chaucer's "Wife of Bath," which find a clear resonance in the specifics of Pipka's fate: "She knew all about wandering—and straying: / For she was gap-toothed, if you take my meaning." This passage, as Walter Skeat observes, equates "gap-toothed" with lascivious. Walter Skeat, ed., *The Complete Works of Geoffrey Chaucer* (1894; reprint: Oxford, 1961), p. 44. That opinion is echoed by John H. Fisher, who agrees that physiognomists interpreted gaps between teeth in a woman as indicating "a bold, lascivious nature." John H. Fisher, ed., *Complete Poetry and Prose of Geoffrey Chaucer* (New York, 1977), p. 18.

26. Pipka's final disappearance is surrounded by dramatic ambiguity: "Some people knew for a fact that she'd married a blind storyteller [Homer's shade!] and had taken off for Australia—to shine with her new white teeth amid the eucalyptus trees and duck-billed platypuses above the coral reefs, but others crossed their hearts and swore that she'd been in a crash and burned up in a taxi on the Yaroslavl highway one rainy, slippery night, and that the flames could be seen from afar rising in a column to the sky" (p. 310).

27. The dust here, as in Byron's poetry and countless other texts, carries the rich connotation of mutability, reminding one of human mortality ("from dust to dust") and thereby lending a certain urgency to the issue of how one should spend the limited time at one's disposal. Rimma and Svetlana embody the quintessential Tolstayan contrast of matter/impermanence and spirit/transcendence, also elaborated in Tolstaya's "Sonya,"

"Okkervil River," and other narratives. On this, see Goscilo, "Tolstajan Love as Surface Text."

28. True to age-old prejudices and actual conditions in Russia of the nineteenth century, a staple of countless novels of the period with a gentry estate as the chief locus is the arrival on the scene of the male protagonist as a catalyst to action and narrative momentum. In the majority of cases he departs (through travel or death), while the heroine in whose life he has caused tremendous upheaval remains as part and parcel of the stable environment. See, for instance, *Eugene Onegin*, *A Hero of Our Time*, *Dead Souls*, *Rudin*, and *A Common Story*, to name but a few.

29. Tolstaya's namesake, Lev Tolstoy, authored "Family Happiness" ("Semeinoe schast'e," 1859), the classic nineteenth-century Russian fictional manual for woman's "natural self-fulfillment." Total immersion in her uxorial and particularly maternal duties, Tolstoy contended, is what brings a woman "family happiness." As in other spheres, Soviet ideology has trodden in Tolstoy's footsteps, championing family structures and rewarding prodigious feats of reproduction by monetary aid and decorations.

30. The most lush sequences in the narrative tend to occur in summaries of Pipka's fabled adventures and in descriptions of Rimma's daydreams, both of which affirm the vividness of a varied, intensely felt life.

31. See, for instance, David Remnick, "The Literary Limits of Glasnost," *Washington Post*, Apr. 18, 1988, esp. p. B6, col. 6; Tolstaya, "A Little Man Is a Normal Man," p. 10; and Tatyana Tolstaya, "In a Land of Conquered Men," *Moscow News* (Sept. 24–Oct. 1, 1989), p. 13: "I take a special interest in one type of Russian woman whom I constantly come across: a miserable, unenlightened tyrant craving power and happiness. 'Happiness' is one of the key words in Russian cultural mythology." During interviews Tolstaya emerges as a vociferous opponent of feminism, yet she readily conceded that she has no familiarity with feminist scholarship when I maintained, in a talk entitled "Tolstaya's Women" at a conference on contemporary women's fiction that she, like most Russians, has a poor grasp of what constitutes feminism in the West (Conference on Soviet Women Writers, coordinated by Anthony Vanchu, University of Texas at Austin, Nov. 1989).

32. Mary Jacobus, "Is There a Woman in This Text?," *New Literary History*, 14, no. 1 (Autumn 1982), p. 138.

33. Whereas Westerners enthusiastically hailed *A Week Like Any Other* as an early feminist statement, Baranskaya herself has protested such an interpretation, claiming that her work, on the contrary, portrays "the power of love." Personal interview in Moscow during spring 1988. Nelly Furman has argued, "from a feminist viewpoint the question [for the textual reader] is not whether a literary work has been written by a woman and reflects her experience of life, or how it compares to other works by women, but rather how it lends itself to be read from a feminist position." Nelly Furman, "The Politics of Language: Beyond the Gender

Principle?," in Greene and Kahn, *Making a Difference*, p. 69. The majority of Russian readers (and writers), however, subscribe to the primacy of authorial intentionality.

34. Tolstaya is unaware, apparently, that 1990 witnessed the establishment of the Center for Gender Studies at the Academy of Sciences in Moscow and knows little about Tatiana Mamonova, Julia Voznesenskaya, and the other feminists who in 1980 fell afoul of the authorities and were expelled from the Soviet Union. She has not heard of such current activists as Anastasia Posadskaya, *de facto* organizer of the Gender Center; Olga Lipovskaya, editor of the unofficial women's publication *Zhenskoe chtenie (Women's Reader)*; Olga Voronina; Tatiana Klimenkova; and other Soviet intellectuals committed to the feminist cause.

35. Tolstaya's outspokenness regarding Belov doubtless swayed the vote against her when she was nominated for acceptance into the Writers' Union, which was then dominated by the notoriously conservative faction of Russian literati. The organization finally admitted her in October 1988.

36. Tatyana Tolstaya, "Notes from Underground," trans. Jamey Gambrell, *New York Review of Books*, May 31, 1990, pp. 3–7.

37. Cited in Anne Williamson, "Tatyana Tolstaya: A Soviet Author Speaks Out, Loud," *Wall Street Journal*, May 11, 1989, p. A12.

38. Conference on Contemporary Soviet-Russian Literature, held at Texas Tech University, Lubbock, Texas (Oct. 4, 1990).

39. Tolstaya made this denial during a private exchange after the conference in Lubbock.

40. On this, see David Ransel, *Women's Studies Newsletter*, published at Indiana University, 1989. For a sobering summary of Soviet misconceptions about Western feminism, see Nina Belyaeva, "Feminism in the USSR," *Canadian Woman Studies*, 10, no. 4 (Winter 1989), pp. 17–19.

41. Peter I. Barta, "The Author, the Cultural Tradition and Glasnost: An Interview with Tatyana Tolstaya," *Russian Language Journal*, 44, nos. 147–49 (1990), p. 268.

42. Authoring those texts, of course, does not vouchsafe Tolstaya membership in any feminist group. My reading does not intend to promote or demote Tolstaya to the rank of feminist, but suggests that perspectivism, irony, and subversive verbal play in her fiction dethrone cultural paradigms (including gender stereotypes) and implicitly posit the liberating potential of multiplicity—possibly the broadest and most beguiling goal shared by thoughtful feminists.

Costlow: The Pastoral Source

1. On the antinihilist novel, see Charles Moser, *Antinihilism in the Russian Novel of the 1860's* (The Hague, 1964).

2. Nikolai Leskov, *Sobranie sochinenii*, 11 vols. (Moscow, 1956) vol. 2, p. 10.

3. Leskov refers to the story of Mycon and Pero, drawn from Valerius Maximus (*de Factis*, 1st century A.D.). The elderly Mycon, wasting away in prison, was breast-fed by his daughter Pero. Perry Preston, *A Dictionary of Pictorial Subjects from Classical Literature* (New York, 1983), p. 183.

4. M. L. Mikhailov, *Zhenshchiny, ikh vospitanie i znachenie v sem'e i obshchestve* (St. Petersburg, 1903). G. A. Tishkin discusses the range of polemics on women's role in society and as mother in *Zhenskii vopros v Rossii v 50–60 gg. XIX v.* (Leningrad, 1984).

5. I draw here on L. J. Jordanova's discussion in "Natural Facts: A Historical Perspective on Science and Sexuality," in Carol P. MacCormack and Marilyn Strathern, eds., *Nature, Culture, and Gender* (Cambridge, Eng., 1980), pp. 49–50. It is worth noting a "return to the breast" among post-Freudian feminists (Julia Kristeva, Hélène Cixous), as well as Nancy Chodorow's caution against over-focusing on the breast. Chodorow's work suggests that the child's bond with a nurturing parent is not based on relationship to the breast. See her *The Reproduction of Mothering: Psychoanalysis and the Sociology of Gender* (Berkeley, Calif., 1978), pp. 57–76.

6. Virtually no work has been done by social historians on the practice of breast-feeding and the use of wet nurses in prerevolutionary Russia. Jessica Tovrov, in her work on the Russian family, makes only passing reference to wet nurses, as if they were of inconsequential significance for the child when compared with the *niania*. Jessica Tovrov, *Action and Affect in the Noble Russian Family from the Late 18th Century Through the Reform Period* (Ph.D. diss., University of Chicago, 1980), p. 152. David Ransel also makes some reference to wet nurses, but only incidentally, in discussing the development of systems of foundling homes in eighteenth- and nineteenth-century Russia. David L. Ransel, *Mothers of Misery: Child Abandonment in Russia* (Princeton, N.J., 1988). The topic has been more attentively studied by historians of Europe and the U.S. See, for example, George D. Sussman, *Selling Mothers' Milk: The Wet-Nursing Business in France, 1715–1914* (Champaign, Ill., 1982), and Sally G. McMillen, *Motherhood in the Old South* (Baton Rouge, La., 1990).

7. Nestor Maksimovich-Ambodik, *Iskusstva povivaniia ili nauki o babich'em dielii* (St. Petersburg, 1784–86), p. 165.

8. *Muzhchina i zhenshchina vroz' i vmeste v razlichnii epokhi ikh zhizni* (St. Petersburg, 1859), pp. 51–52. While it would be difficult to ascertain for whom the anonymous author wrote the book, it is worth noting that at least one Russian writer read it: the censor who gave permission for the volume's publication was Ivan Goncharov.

9. These authors do not consider the possibility that actual practice among "primitive women" might be less ideal than their imagination of it. David Ransel, in his study of child-care practices among peasants in the Russian empire, sketches a far less idyllic picture: Russian peasants

routinely introduced solid food when the baby was a few days old and unable to digest it; the fact that women returned to fieldwork immediately after giving birth meant that infants might be nursed only early in the morning and late at night. See David L. Ransel, "Child Care Cultures in the Russian Empire," in Barbara Evans Clements, Barbara Alpern Engel, and Christine D. Worobec, eds., *Russia's Women: Accommodation, Resistance, Transformation* (Berkeley, Calif., 1991), pp. 113–32.

10. The author is surely guilty of racism in denying to "primitive" women—whether Africans or Russian peasants—the experience of pain.

11. "Vot pochemu zaniatie naukami i chteniem stol' pagubny dlia zhenshchin, potomu-chto ono otvlekaet ikh zhiznennye sily k mozgu, i takim obrazom lishaet polovye organy estestvennoi ikh sily." ("That is why scholarship and reading are so harmful to women, since they deflect their vital strength to the brain, thus depriving their sexual organs of their natural strength.") *Muzhchina i zhenshchina*, p. 43. The notion that women possessed a limited amount of bodily energy, and that the development of the brain occurred at the expense of reproductive organs, was widely held in the nineteenth century. See Barbara Ehrenreich and Deirdre English, *For Her Own Good: 150 Years of the Experts' Advice to Women* (New York, 1978), pp. 113–18.

12. Maksimovich-Ambodik (*Iskusstva povivaniia*) allows for the possible use of cow's or goat's milk in feeding the infant, an option that was fraught with danger because of problems of hygiene. See Ransel, "Child Care Culture," and Sussman, *Selling Mother's Milk*, p. 11. A safe substitute for human milk was available by the end of the nineteenth century, as is evidenced by the article in Brockhaus and Efron that discusses the relative merits (and economies) of a wet nurse and Nestle's. See "Vskarmlenie," in *Entsiklopedicheskii slovar'. Izd. Brokgausa i Efrona* (St. Petersburg, 1890–1904), vol. 3, pp. 404–5.

13. Sally McMillen, in her study of nursing practices in the American South, refers to similar assumptions: "A few doctors believed that breast milk communicated the characteristics of the lactating woman and that wet nurses thus posed another risk." McMillen, *Motherhood*, p. 113.

14. One of the concerns of M. L. Mikhailov in his series of essays on women was to refute the notion that women's physical "disabilities" (connected to menstruation, pregnancy, and childbirth) precluded the possibility of cultural and intellectual attainments. Mikhailov, *Zhenshchiny*, pp. 12–23.

15. *The Diaries of Sophia Tolstoy*, trans. Cathy Porter (New York, 1985), pp. 22–24.

16. Leo Tolstoy, *Anna Karenin*, trans. Rosemary Edmonds (New York, 1978), pp. 816, 817.

17. This section of the novel begins and ends with references to work: "Sergei Ivanich Koznyshev wanted a rest from intellectual work" (p. 257); "the one thread to guide [Levin] through the darkness was his work, and he clutched at it and clung to it with all his might" (p. 377).

18. Lev Tolstoi, *Polnoe sobranie sochinenii*, 90 vols. (Moscow, 1928–58), vol. 25, p. 413.

19. The term "bizarre" is Richard Stites's, who discusses the volume's indebtedness to Proudhon and Michelet; see Richard Stites, *The Women's Liberation Movement in Russia: Feminism, Nihilism, and Bolshevism, 1860–1930* (Princeton, N.J., 1978), p. 40.

20. One might in fact see lactation and the production of milk as a model for the beneficence of (Mother) nature in pastoral. On the absence of work in pastoral see Renato Poggioli, *The Oaten Flute* (Cambridge, Mass., 1975), pp. 1–41.

21. Mikhail Bakhtin, *The Dialogic Imagination: Four Essays*, ed. and trans. Michael Holquist and Caryl Emerson (Austin, Tex., 1981), pp. 233–34.

22. The issue is one that concerns Mikhailov, as well: "k kakoi kategorii truda, proizvoditel'noi ili neproizvoditel'noi, sleduet otnesti trud nosheniia v svoei utrobe i potom kormlenie rebenka? Ili eto dazhe i ne trud, a prazdnost', za kotoruiu, kak vozmezdie, sleduet ne tol'ko lishenie prava na golos v obshchestve, no i polneishee lishenie svobody." ("How should one categorize bearing a child in the womb and then nursing it—as productive or unproductive labor? Or is it leisure rather than work, in reprisal for which comes not only the loss of one's right to a voice in society but the full loss of freedom.") Mikhailov, *Zhenshchiny*, p. 18.

23. The story was first published in 1892 in *Peterburgskaia gazeta*; it has recently been reprinted in *Pisateli chekhovskoi pory* (Moscow, 1982), pp. 218–22. Lidia Avilova (1864–1943) was the author of numerous short stories, corresponded with Chekhov, and helped in the transcription of his works for publication. She was the sister of the publicist and Tolstoyan F. A. Strakhov.

24. According to a recent discussion, 40 percent of the prostitutes in St. Petersburg at the end of the nineteenth century had formerly worked as domestic servants—a category that includes nurses (*nianki*). Barbara Alpern Engel, "St. Petersburg Prostitutes in the Late Nineteenth Century: A Personal and Social Profile," *Russian Review*, 48 (Jan. 1989), p. 28. Engel's research suggests that Avilova's story of a mother is not unlike the experience of many rural women who came to the city for reasons of economic hardship: their destitution, isolation, and economic/sexual vulnerability easily led to prostitution.

25. Coppée's poem tells the story of a woman whose husband, a drunkard, forces her to abandon her child and go to work as a wet nurse in order to make money to buy him drink. When the woman returns, their child has died from neglect. *Oeuvres de François Coppée*, 5 vols. (Paris, 1907), vol. 2, pp. 3–14.

26. Barykova's letters were excerpted by the editors of the 1910 edition of her poetry, the Tolstoyans Vladimir and Anna Chertkov. Anna Barykova, *Stikhotvoreniia* (Moscow, 1910), p. 22.

27. This focus on the breast is Barykova's alone; where Coppée uses generalized language Barykova repeatedly focuses on the breast and plays on metaphors of eating and consumption. In Coppée, the actress's appearance is described thus: "Une assez belle fille, oui, mais tres effrontée, / Montrant toute sa gorge et l'offrant au public." ("A fairly pretty girl, true, but very brazen, / Showing all her breast and offering it to the public.") Barykova's rendering manipulates poetic form and metaphor to create an implicit contrast with the "unseen" moment of the infant's nursing: "S ulybkoi klaniaias', ona nakhal'no grudi / I plechi golye pokazyvala vsem,— / Kak budto podnosila publike na bliude / I ugoshchala imi . . ." ("Bowing with a smile, she brazenly showed everyone her naked breasts and shoulders, / As though she brought them to the public on a tray, for a treat.") The *grudi–na bliude* apposition makes the visual erotic encounter into an oral one as well. Barykova, *Stikhotvoreniia*, pp. 187–89 and Coppée, *Oeuvres*, vol. 5, pp. 143–46.

28. Mary Poovey discusses the "uneven" way in which ideology was "experienced differently by individuals who were positioned differently within the social formation (by sex, class, or race, for example)." See Mary Poovey, *Uneven Developments: The Ideological Work of Gender in Mid-Victorian England* (Chicago, 1988), pp. 3–4.

29. Avdot'ia Panaeva, *Semeistvo Tal'nikovykh* (Leningrad, 1928), pp. 104–5.

30. For recent discussions of Panaeva's novel see Barbara Heldt, "Codes for Russian Women in Autobiographical Fiction: Prophecy and Lament," paper read at Conference on Women in Russian History, Akron, Ohio, Aug. 1988; and Mary Zirin, "Forgotten Beginnings. Early Depictions of Russian Girlhood: Nadezhda Durova, Avdot'ia Panaeva and Nadezhda Sokhanskaia," unpublished manuscript.

Heldt: Motherhood in a Cold Climate

My profound thanks to M. L. Gasparov for all his help.

1. See Barbara Heldt, *Terrible Perfection: Women and Russian Literature* (Bloomington, Ind., 1987); see also Joanna Hubbs, *Mother Russia: The Feminine Myth in Russian Culture* (Bloomington, Ind., 1988), for what one scholarly critic called the "stance of a feminist neo-Slavophile" (Lindsey Hughes, in *Times Higher Education Supplement*, Jan. 27, 1989, p. 18). A representative anthology of sanctioned and sacrosanct works on motherhood is *Mat': Stikhotvoreniia russkikh i sovetskikh poetov o materi* (Moscow, 1979). It contains poems by 113 authors, some female.

2. Charlotte Rosenthal has called my attention to an article by Vera Inber that relates disingenuously how four different women writers (Larisa Reisner, Marietta Shaginian, Shkapskaya, and Zinaida Richter) "saw themselves working . . . in the sphere of Soviet journalism": *Zhurnalist*, no. 11 (1927), p. 23.

3. See my article "The Poetry of Elena Shvarts," *World Literature*

Today, 63, no. 3 (Summer 1989), pp. 381–83. For Shvarts's verse, see Elena Shvarts, *Stikhi* (Leningrad, 1990); idem, "Istoricheskaia shkatulka," *Vestnik novoi russkoi literatury*, no. 2 (Leningrad, 1990), pp. 65–81. Two collections were published in the West: Elena Shvarts, *Tantsuiushchii David* (New York, 1985); idem, *Trudi i dni Lavinii, monakhini iz ordena obrezaniia serdtsa* (Ann Arbor, Mich., 1987). Perhaps this judgment will be modified when more women's poetry is published, e.g., the poems by O. Cheremshanova quoted in T. L. Nikol'skaya's excellent article "Tema misticheskogo sektantstva v russkoi poezii 20-kh godov XX veka," in *Puti razvitiia russkoi literatury* (Tartu, 1990), pp. 157–69. An anthology of one hundred women poets of the Silver Age, edited by Nikol'skaya and Ol'ga Kushlina, is in the final stages of preparation: *Sto russkikh poetess. Serebrianyi vek* (St. Petersburg).

4. A recent anthology includes six earlier poems but describes them as "saturated with decadent feelings" (V. V. Uchenova, ed., *Tsaritsy muz: Russkie poetessy XIX-nachala XX vv.* (Moscow, 1989), pp. 369–72 and 434. Eighteen poems, with a one-page introduction by V. Iu. Bobretsov, appeared in *Russkaia literatura*, no. 3 (1991), pp. 219–22, and sixteen poems from Shkapskaya's archive, with a four-page introduction by M. L. Gasparov, appeared in *Oktiabr'*, no. 2 (1992), pp. 168–71.

5. TsGALI, fond 2128, opis' I, ed. khr. 157. All numbers in parenthesis refer to pages (*listy*) from this archive. Insofar as verification has been possible, it would seem that much in the autobiographies was intended to establish credentials to protect Shkapskaya's family. I am grateful to Marina Ledkovsky, whose own research, including interviews with people who knew Shkapskaya's brother Ivan (b. 1894), provides entirely different sources on and views about the Andreevskii family. According to these sources, they lived comfortably. All translations are my own.

6. GPB, fond 1077, ed. khr. 652. I am grateful to Catriona Kelly for this letter.

7. G. Lelevich, review in *Krasnaia nov'*, no. 1 (1925), pp. 311–12.

8. Mariia Shkapskaia, *Puti i poiski* (Moscow, 1968), p. 12.

9. See Barbara Heldt, "Men Who Give Birth: A Feminist Perspective on Russian Literature," in Catriona Kelly, Michael Makin, and David Shepherd, eds., *Discontinuous Discourses in Modern Russian Literature* (London, 1989), pp. 157–68.

10. For criticism of the French theorists by an American scholar see Domna Stanton, "Difference on Trial: A Critique of the Maternal Metaphor in Cixous, Irigaray, and Kristeva," in Nancy K. Miller, ed., *The Poetics of Gender* (New York, 1986), pp. 157–82.

11. Helena Michie, *The Flesh Made Word: Female Figures and Women's Bodies* (New York, 1987), p. 84.

12. See Ann Ferguson, *Blood at the Root: Motherhood, Sexuality and Male Dominance* (London, 1989).

13. Julia Kristeva, "Stabat Mater," in Toril Moi, ed., *The Kristeva Reader* (Oxford, 1986), p. 175.

14. Kristeva, "Stabat Mater," p. 174. Kristeva has written two other works on motherhood. "Motherhood According to Giovanni Bellini," in Julia Kristeva, *Desire in Language* (New York, 1980), pp. 237–70, gives a definition of motherhood that is too intellectualized as dichotomy (presence/absence) to be of use here, but chapter 3 of her book *Powers of Horror: An Essay on Abjection* (New York, 1982) contains a brilliant account of the suppression of maternal authority.

15. All page numbers refer to the only published, nearly complete collection of her poetry: Mariia Shkapskaia, *Stikhi*, ed. Boris Filippov and Evgenia Zhiglevich (London, 1979).

16. M. L. Gasparov, *Uchebnyi material po literaturovedeniiu. Russkii stikh* (Tallin, 1987), pp. 14–15.

17. *Krasnaia nov'*, no. 10 (1929), p. 133.

18. For basic reading see Gail Warshofsky Lapidus, *Women in Soviet Society* (Berkeley, Calif., 1978), chap. 2, and Mary Buckley, *Women and Ideology in the Soviet Union* (Ann Arbor, Mich., 1989).

Naiman: Historectomies

The author would like to express his appreciation to Victoria Bonnell, Boris Gasparov, Christina Kiaer, Anne Nesbet, Irina Paperno, and the editors of this volume for their comments and assistance. Financial support was provided by the Social Science Research Council.

1. "Delo sektanta Tsimbaliuka," *Izvestiia*, no. 47 (Feb. 26, 1925), p. 4.

2. V. Tkachuk, "Delo religioznykh izuverov," *Izvestiia*, no. 53 (Mar. 5, 1926), p. 4.

3. Ibid.

4. These thinkers are not utopians in the classical sense; they did not provide elaborate outlines for the structure of an ideal society. Rather, their work falls squarely into the "absolutist" (*totalitarnaia*) and eschatological tradition that Nikolai Berdyaev was later to claim played a crucial role in the development of Russian thought. See Nikolai Berdiaev, *Russkaia ideia* (Paris, 1970) (first published in 1946), pp. 33, 195; English translation, *The Russian Idea* (London, 1947), trans. R. M. French. By the word "utopian" I refer to thinkers who believed or strongly implied belief in the possibility of human spiritual perfection and in the consequent literal ability of man to achieve immortality.

5. Vladimir Solov'ev, "Smysl liubvi," in his *Sochineniia*, 2 vols. (Moscow, 1988), vol. 2, p. 547; English translation, *The Meaning of Love*, trans. Jane Marshall (New York, 1947). The essay was first published in 1892–94.

6. Nikolai Berdiaev, *Smysl tvorchestva* (Paris, 1983) (first published in 1916), p. 229; English translation, *The Meaning of the Creative Act*, trans. Donald A. Lowrie (New York, 1962). Berdyaev's use of gender here is interesting: "rozhdaiushch*ii* i rozhdaemyi tlennyi i nesovershennyi," a masculinization of the birth act, to which we shall return.

7. Nikolai Fedorov, *Filosofiia obshchego dela*, 2 vols. (Vernyi, 1906), vol. 1, p. 313.
8. Peter Gay, *Education of the Senses*, vol. 1 of *The Bourgeois Experience: Victoria to Freud*, 2 vols. (New York, 1984), p. 256.
9. Between 1907 and 1912, Forel's book appeared in at least four Russian translations in editions totalling at least 38,000 copies. As late as 1928, the book was published in Kharkov in yet another translation. *Knizhnaia letopis'* (St. Petersburg and Moscow, 1908–13, 1929).
10. V. Bekhterev, "Predislovie," in Avgust Forel, *Polovoi vopros* (St. Petersburg, 1908), vol. 1, p. vii. Commentators from both the left and the right, while accusing each other of immorality, all joined in the assault on pleasure.
11. For a very similar statement, see Solov'ev, "Smysl liubvi," p. 522.
12. Vladimir Solov'ev, "Zhiznennaia drama Platona," in his *Sochineniia*, vol. 2, p. 619. The essay was originally published in 1898.
13. Olga Matich, "Androgyny and the Russian Religious Renaissance," in Anthony M. Mlikotin, ed., *Western Philosophical Systems in Russian Literature* (Berkeley, 1979), pp. 165–66. See also her article "Androgyny and the Russian Silver Age," *Pacific Coast Philology*, 14 (Oct. 1979), pp. 42–50.
14. Boris Paramonov wittily makes this same point in his pursuit of "homosexual" models in turn-of-the-century culture: "The resurrection of ancestors is a dubious affair, which in any case will require a great deal of time, but Fyodorov tells us that it is already high time we abandoned our wives." See his "*Chevengur* i okrestnosti," *Kontinent*, no. 54 (1987), p. 345.
15. Nikolai Berdiaev, *Samopoznanie* (Paris, 1983), pp. 83–84; English translation, *Dream and Reality: An Essay in Autobiography*, trans. Katharine Lampert (New York, 1951).
16. Berdiaev, *Samopoznanie*, pp. 89–90.
17. Irina Paperno, *Chernyshevsky and the Age of Realism: A Study in the Semiotics of Behavior* (Stanford, Calif., 1988), p. 44.
18. Berdiaev, *Russkaia ideia*, p. 112.
19. A. P. Omel'chenko, *Svobodnaia liubov' i sem'ia ("Sanin" kak vopros nashego vremeni)* (St. Petersburg, 1908), pp. 24–25, 46–47. Turgenev's heroines, it should be noted, were usually members of the gentry and never proletarians.
20. N. G. Chernyshevskii, *Polnoe sobranie sochinenii*, 16 vols. (Moscow, 1939), vol. 1, p. 82.
21. N. G. Chernyshevskii, *Chto delat'?* (Leningrad, 1975), p. 290.
22. See, *inter alia*, "VI Vsesoiuznii s"ezd RLKSM," *Pravda*, no. 157 (July 13, 1924), p. 4 (Krupskaia); "Plenum TsKK. O partetike," *Pravda*, no. 230 (Oct. 9, 1924), p. 3 (Iaroslavskii); "Uchitel'stvo i Komsomol," *Izvestiia*, no. 28 (Feb. 4, 1925), p. 4 (Bukharin).
23. Solov'ev, "Zhiznennaia drama," p. 619.
24. A. I. Kuprin, *Sobranie sochinenii*, 6 vols. (Moscow, 1958), vol. 5, p. 166.

25. Forel, *Polovoi vopros*, vol. 1, p. 261.
26. Between 1908 and 1912 Weininger's book appeared in at least 39,000 copies and four translations. The Russian literary critic Akim Volynsky recalled: "The book's appearance in 1903, soon after its author's suicide, evoked an uproar in society, it was like the explosion of a grenade. All the papers, journals, people of different scholarly professions, students, everyone was in turmoil." A. K. Volynskii, "Madonna," in Otto Veininger (Weininger), *Pol i kharakter* (St. Petersburg, 1909), p. xiv. Volynsky's failure to distinguish Russian from European reaction indicates that the fascination with Weininger was part of a transcontinental mode. The anxiety of influence is apparent in Berdyaev's treatment of Weininger. He says in a footnote: "Weininger has remarks of intuitive genius concerning female psychology, but they are spoiled by his bad, weak enmity towards femininity" (*Smysl tvorchestva*, p. 432).
27. See David Abrahamsen, *The Mind and Death of a Genius* (New York, 1946), pp. 43–45.
28. In Solovyov's cosmogony, "the eternal feminine" is defined as what God both separates and does not separate from himself: "in relationship to God, it is a passive unity, female, since here eternal emptiness receives the fullness of divine love" ("Smysl liubvi," p. 533). Solovyov claimed that in perfect love the male lover would see—and not in a transitory manner—the eternal feminine in his earthly female beloved. However, the disastrous attempts of the Symbolists to infuse Solovyov's teachings into their lives and writings reveal how easy it was for the eternal feminine to coexist with hatred for real women. See, *inter alia*, V. F. Khodasevich, *Nekropol'* (Brussels, 1939), pp. 16–17, 68–69, and Zinaida Gippius, *Zhivye litsa*, 2 vols. (Prague, 1925), vol. 1, pp. 16–19. Berdyaev, perhaps with the experience of the Symbolist generation in mind, claimed that the concept of the eternal feminine was itself inherently flawed because the eternal feminine provided no escape from the female sexual element. Unless philosophers abandoned the eternal feminine for an androgynous ideal of virginity, he urged, man would never "be fully emancipated from immersion in the feminine sexual element, in magnetic and engulfing (*zasasyvaiushchaia*) sexual polarity" (*Smysl tvorchestva*, p. 224).
29. On Gippius and Solovyov, see Olga Matich, *The Religious Poetry of Zinaida Gippius* (Munich, 1972), pp. 66–69. For Gippius's diary, see Temira Pakhmuss, "Dnevnik Zinaidy Nikolaevny Gippius 'O byvshem,'" *Vozrozhdenie*, no. 217 (Jan. 1970), pp. 56–78, and Zinaida Gippius, "O byvshem," *Vozrozhdenie*, nos. 218–20 (Feb., Mar., and Apr. 1970), pp. 52–70, 57–75, and 53–75 respectively. English translation, Zinaida Gippius, "About the Cause," in *Between Paris and St. Petersburg: Selected Diaries of Zinaida Hippius*, ed. and trans. Temira Pachmuss (Urbana, Ill., 1975), pp. 101–78.
30. Robert Graves, *The Greek Myths*, 2 vols. (Harmondsworth, Eng., 1960), vol. 2, p. 380.
31. The word Berdyaev uses for man in this passage, *chelovek*, is gen-

der neutral, but throughout *Smysl tvorchestva* woman (*zhenshchina*) is the marked member in the male/female dichotomy, and gender-neutral terms should be read as those purified of femininity.

32. Solovyov's substitution of "idea [*ideia*] of *vseedinstvo*" for "*vseedinstvo*" itself allows him to accord the concept feminine gender in this passage.

33. Solov'ev, "Zhiznennaia drama," p. 612.
34. Volynskii, "Madonna," p. xx.
35. Boris Pil'niak, *Mashiny i volki* (Leningrad, 1925), p. 19.
36. Ibid., p. 93.
37. Ibid., p. 74.
38. A. S. Serafimovich, *Zheleznyi potok* (Moscow, 1960), pp. 115–16, 134. This work was first published in 1924.
39. Fedor Gladkov, "Tsement," *Krasnaia nov'*, no. 6 (1925), p. 61.
40. L. Trotskii, *Voprosy byta* (Moscow, 1923), p. 3.
41. See Aleksandar Flaker, "Byt," *Russian Literature*, 19, no. 1 (1986), pp. 4–5.
42. This equation was often implicit in the manner in which Soviet society divided the world. In 1924 and 1925 *Knizhnaia letopis'*, the official list of all books published in the USSR, listed the following under the same heading: "*Byt*. The Situation of Woman. Folklore." Occasionally, children's diseases were also included in this listing. *Knizhnaia letopis'* (Moscow, 1924–25).
43. See, for example, L. Sosnovskii, "Razvenchaite khuliganov," *Komsomol'skaia pravda*, no. 216 (Sept. 19, 1926), p. 2. On the role of sexuality in the campaign against hooliganism, see E. Naiman, "The Case of Chubarov Alley: Collective Rape, Utopian Desire and the Mentality of NEP," *Russian History*, 17, no. 1 (1990), pp. 1–30.
44. Victoria E. Bonnell, "The Representation of Women in Early Soviet Political Art," *Russian Review*, 50, no. 3 (1990), pp. 285–86.
45. For more on women in Maiakovskii's work, see Aleksandr K. Zholkovskii, "O genii i zlodeistve, o babe i vserossiiskom masshtabe (Progulki po Maiakovskomu)," in Aleksandr K. Zholkovskii and Iurii K. Shcheglov, *Mir avtora i struktura teksta* (Tenafly, N.J., 1986), pp. 228–54.
46. Andrei Platonov, *Chevengur* (Moscow, 1988), p. 208.
47. Part 1 ends with Zhokh giving the order to his men to head east beyond the Urals. First, however, his follower and eventual rival, Teshcha, dismounts in order to relieve himself. As he is rustling about in the bushes, he speaks to Zhokh the first part's final words: "we have to look for an uninhabited land . . . there we'll find our earthly haven" (Andrei Platonov, *Epifanskie shliuzy* [Moscow, 1927], p. 88). It is from this utopian wish, spoken at a moment where the text could not be closer to the body and the earth, that the eternal city is born. One might take this excretory moment as a hint that Platonov will accept all the consequences of the flesh in his utopia. We soon learn, however, that the closer Plato-

nov's text gets to the body, the more sharply it mutilates the human form.

48. Platonov, *Epifanskie shliuzy*, p. 105. The reader should note that Teshcha's name means "mother-in-law," a concept in which maternal status exists only through the agency of a patriarchal institution.

49. V. K. Nikol'skii, *Sem'ia i brak v proshlom i nastoiashchem* (Moscow, 1936), p. 68.

50. Note the symbolic correspondence between the dead boy in the background of the "capitalist" photo (Fig. 2) and the phallic highrise building in the background of the "U.S.S.R." photo (Fig. 3).

51. *USSR in Construction*, no. 6 (1935), p. 2.

Index

In this index an "f" after a number indicates a separate reference on the next page, and an "ff" indicates separate references on the next two pages. A continuous discussion over two or more pages is indicated by a span of page numbers, e.g., "pp. 57–58." *Passim* is used for a cluster of references in close but not consecutive sequence.

Abstinence, medieval terminology for, 45
Academy, the, *see* Moscow School of Painting, Sculpture, and Architecture
Aesthetics, and female writing, 163, 321n15
Afanasiev, Alexander, 142
"Agitation trials," 132
Agitprop theater, 93–94
Agnos, Art, 35
AIDS, 35–36
Akhmatova, Anna, 161, 164
Albright, Madeleine, 291n85
"All-encompassing unity" ("*vseedinstvo*"), 267, 269
Andreevskaya, Maria Mikhailovna, *see* Shkapskaya, Maria
Androgyny: lesbian writing and, 186, 197, 199–201, 202; Silver Age views of sexuality and, 259–65 *passim*; concept of, 322n27. *See also* Hermaphroditism
Annensky, Innokenti, "Contemporary Lyricism," 184–88
Anti-Lesbian genre, 323n2
Armstrong, Carol, 121
Arnim, Ludwig Joachim von, 330n42
Art, *see* Nude painting; Vanguard art; Visual arts
Art-historical terms, assumed masculine subject of, 121, 160–63, 314n33
Artsybashev, Mikhail, 19
Asceticism, 260

Augustine, Saint, 42
Avilova, Lidia, 339n23; "On the Road" ("V doroge"), 232–34, 236
Bagrationi-Mukhraneli, Irina, 291n89
Bakhtin, Mikhail, 157, 161f, 231, 294n108
Bakmeteff, Marie, 63f
Baranskaya, Natalia, 218, 335n33
Barley, Nigel, 86
Barney, Nathalie Clifford, 192
Barthes, Roland, 159
Barykova, Anna, "Mother–Wet Nurse" ("Mat'–Kormilitsa"), 232, 234–35, 236
Baudelaire, Pierre Charles, 326n15
Beautiful Lady, as poetic figure, 250–51
Beauty: as literary sexual motif, 50–51; *Petrushka* puppet plays and, 78–79; in Chekhov, 146, 319n15; Tsvetaeva's treatment of, 165f; "unnaturalness" of lesbian love and, 181–82; male artist's perception of, 182; subversion of gender stereotypes and, 208–9, 210; masculinist ethos and, 219
Beauty contests, 29, 291n90
Beauvoir, Simone de, *The Second Sex*, 283n29, 306n44
Belov, Vasily, 95, 218f
Benstock, Shari, 188
Berdyaev, Nikolai, 8–18 *passim*, 256–72 *passim*, 344n28; *Russian Idea* (*Russkaia ideia*), 13, 342n4;

The Meaning of the Creative Act (Smysl tvorchestva), 260
Biblical imagery, 245–47, 253
Binary oppositions, 285n45
Bisexuality, 167, 169, 182–83, 263
Blok, Alexander, 164; "The Twelve" (*Dvenadtsat'*), 124–25
Blood metaphor, 253
Blud, usage of word, 44–45
Bobroff, Anne, 305n36
Body, the: as term, 1–2; Russian imagery for, 2; indifference to, in contemporary writing, 31–33; boundary definitions of, 134. *See also* Maternal body; Maternal breast; Women's bodies
Boehme, Jacob, 10
Bogatyrev, P. G., 90
Bogomil heresy, 47
Bonnell, Victoria, 271
Boym, Svetlana, 11, 22, 156–76
Breastfeeding: injunctions against wet nursing and, 224–32; ideological significance of, 225–26; historical work on, 337n6; substitutes for, 338n12
Breasts, in medieval sexual iconography, 49, 299n55
Briusov, Valery, 156f, 165
Brooks, Peter, 140
Broun, E., 314n33
Bulak, T., 87
Bunin, Ivan, 19; "Mordvinian Sarafan" ("Mofdovskii sarafan"), 20–22
Burgin, Diana Lewis, 11, 17, 22, 171, 177–203
Bystriansky, Vadim, 127, 131
Byt (everyday life), 250, 256, 270

Cabanis, Pierre-Jean-Georges, 56, 62
Capitalism, and prostitution, 125–31 *passim*, 317n32
"Carting out," 307n48
Casanova de Seingalt, Count Giacoma Girolama, 4–5, 8
Castration, 268–69, 273
Cather, Willa, 325n12
Catherine II, 4, 8, 280n10
Censorship, 95, 97–98, 100–101, 283n31
Chambers, Ross, 140
Chamot, Mary, 108f
Chartier, Roger, 85

Chekhov, Anton P., 11f; "Peasant Women," 142–43, 147; "The Kiss," 143–55
Cheremnykh, M. M., 271, 272
Cherny, Sasha, "Poshlost'," 164
Chernyshevsky, Nikolai, 12–16; Berdyaev's reading of, 13–14; What Is to Be Done? (*Chto delat'?*), 13–16, 26, 37, 260–61
Children, love poems of mother to, 244; early Soviet views of, 256–57. *See also* Motherhood; Reproduction
Chodorow, Nancy, 337n5
Christianity, *see* Roman Catholic Church; Russian Orthodoxy
Cixous, Hélène, 159, 173, 320n8, 322n27
Clements, Barbara Evans, 286n52, 312n16
Clifford, James, 74
Communist Party, 125–26, 129–31
Companionate marriage, 15
"Compensatory" strategies, 85–86
Contemporary, The [*Sovremennik*] (journal), 23, 24–26
Conventionality, *see* Gender stereotypes
Coppée, François, 234, 339n25
Corbin, Alain, 323n2
Costlow, Jane T., 1–38, 223–36
Coward, Rosalind, 74

Daly, Mary, 324n10
Dancing, medieval view of, 51
"Dark literature" (*chernukha*), 30
Darnton, Robert, *The Great Cat Massacre*, 88
Dashkova, Princess Ekaterina, 53
Death: maternal imagery and, 21–22, 32, 257, 294n106; sexuality and, 21–22, 32–33; the body and, 32–33
Decadence, and Silver Age lesbian writing, 181–87 *passim*, 193, 195, 200
DeJean, Joan, 178, 180, 192, 201
Democratization, 291n85
Demonic imagery, 49–50
Desire: vs. pity (*pozhalel* vs. *pozhelal*), 20, 285n45, 289n72; folk magic in narratives of, 33–34; medieval terminology for, 46–47; and discretion, in narrative, 139–55

Index

Dijkstra, Bram, 333n16
Discretion, and narrative desire, 139–55
Dolina, Veronika, 95
"Doll parasites" (*babochki vreditel'-nitsy*), 130
Doroshevich, V., 81
Dostoevsky, F., 30, 37, 169, 289n71
Douglas, Mary, 134
Dress, *see* Masquerade
Drunkenness, 51
Durova, Nadezhda, *The Cavalry Maiden* (*Kavalerist-devitsa*), 22–24, 26
Dworkin, Andrea, 289n72

Ecclesiastical literature, and medieval sexual vocabulary, 43–44
Economic independence, of early-nineteenth-century Russian women, 57–66 *passim*
"Écriture feminine," 159, 173
Efimenko, Aleksandra, 305n36
Ehrenreich, Barbara, 317n31
Eighteenth century, images of sexuality in the, 4–5, 6–8
Elagin, Ivan, 94
Emergency Committee, 36–37
Engel, Barbara Alpern, 285n49, 339n24
Engelstein, Laura, 323n2
English, Deirdre, 317n31
Erofeev, Viktor, 30, 33
Eros, for Gachev, 19–20, 285n46
Eroticism: female, 156, 159, 171–76, 188, 262; literary, 156, 159
Eroticization: and contemporary Russian culture, 27–28, 37–38. *See also* Sexualization
"Eternal feminine," concept of, 344n28
Euphemisms, medieval, 44–48
Eve, as poetic figure, 250

Fairground genre, 92–93
Farwell, Beatrice, 314n31
Fedotov, Georgy, 18
"Female poetry," male-defined notions of, 184–88
Female sexuality: masquerade and, 23; prostitution and, 133–35; female writers and, 156, 159; lesbian writing and, 179, 181–82, 188, 194; conventionality and, 215–16; contemporary discussion of, 244; motherhood and, 252–53, 262–63; postrevolutionary utopian philosophy and, 261–64, 267–69
Female writers: female eroticism and, 156, 159; "poetess" as term and, 160–63. *See also* "Feminine writing"; Lesbian writing; *and specific writers by name*
Feminine ideal, and eighteenth-century Russian society, 54–72
"Feminine writing," 237–38, 242–44, 250
Femininity: exaggerated, as masquerade, 22; art and, 121; female poets and, 162–63, 198, 320n10; Tsvetaeva and, 164–65
Feminism: of Kollontai, 16–17; contemporary, view of sexuality in, 17–18; in mid-nineteenth century, 24–26; Goncharova and, 102–3; sexual behavior and, 102–3; in prerevolutionary period, 103; Silver Age lesbians and, 178; Western, 219, 282n25, 335n31; contemporary resistance to, 219, 282n25. *See also* Women's liberation
Feminist critique: of popular culture, 74, 82–84, 88; approaches to art history and, 107, 121; Tolstaya's work and, 211–12, 218, 219–20. *See also* Parnok, Sophia
Femme damnée, 182f, 198, 326n15
Ferguson, Ann, 244
Fertility ritual, 91–92
Fin de siècle period, *see* Silver Age
First All-Russian Women's Congress (1908), 103
Fitzpatrick, Sheila, 125
Folk magic, 33–34
Folk traditions, and seduction model for narration, 141–42
Forel, Avgust, 262
Forster, E. M., 141
Foucault, Michel, 1–3, 7; *History of Sexuality*, 6, 134–35, 317n33; liberation and repression and, 15; conceptualization of sexuality and, 158–60, 244
Free trade, and prostitution, 131
Freidenberg, Olga, 91f
Freud, Sigmund, 263; Voloshinov's cri-

tique of, 157–58; "On Femininity," 162–63; Gachev and, 285n44
Freudianism, 7, 282n24
Furman, Nelly, 335
Fyodorov, Nikolai, 256–64 passim, 271f

Gabhart, A., 314n33
Gachev, Georgy, 7, 14–21 passim, 285n46
Gadamer, Hans Georg, 163
Galin, Alexander, Stars in the Morning Sky (Zvezdy utrennego sveta), 29
Gap-toothed women, 334n25
Gasparov, M. L., 250–51
Gautier, Théophile, "Contralto," 199, 201
Gay political activity, 34–35
Gender difference: sexual experience and, 3f; masquerade and, 22–26; nude art genre and, 26, 98f, 104–7, 116–23; in eighteenth-century Europe, and Russian society, 54–72; representation of, in popular culture, 73–84 passim; vanguard art and, 98–99, 102–6, 113, 116, 121–23; reaction to NEP and, 131; Parnok's poems and, 196–97; androgynous characters and, 294n114
Gender relations, in Petrushka puppet plays, 77–80
Gender stereotypes: Tolstaya's subversion of, 204–20; conventionality vs. independence in women and, 215–17, 223–24
Gender vs. sexuality, 22–26
Genius, sexualization of, 265–68
Gertsyk, Adelaida, 196–97
Gessen, Masha, Out/Look, 35
Ginzburg, Evgenia, Journey into the Whirlwind (Krutoi marshrut), 32
Gippius, Zinaida, 185, 195, 247, 264, 327n21
Glasnost, 27f, 33, 37
Glickman, Rose L., 308n64
God, as poetic male addressee, 247, 248–49
Goddard, Victoria, 86
Gogol, Nikolai, 10
Golden Fleece, The [Zolotoe runo] (art journal), 100
Golub', as term, 207
Golubeva, Vera, 129

Goncharov, Ivan, 337n8
Goncharova, Natalia, 26; trial for pornography, 97–102, 123; God (Bog), 99, 107–9, 111; Same, 99; specific nude paintings by, 99, 107–17 passim; press interview of, 103–4; life-study genre and, 104–22; Water Nymph (Rusalka), 107, 110; Tsvetaeva's essay on, 166–67; repainting and, 313n29
Gorbachev, Mikhail, 36
Gorky, Maxim, 89, 240f, 249, 288n66
Goscilo, Helena, 22, 204–20
Greenblatt, Stephen, 92
Gregory, John, Father's Legacy to His Daughters, A, 58–66 passim, 302n16, 303n29
Griboedov, Aleksander, Woe from Wit (Gore ot uma), 166–67
Grigorovich, D. V., 81
Grossman, Joan Delaney, 297n7
Guilt, and motherhood, 247–48, 251–52

Hagstrum, Jean, 280n13
Haimson, Leo, 125
Health Commissariat, 132, 133
Heartfield, John, 275, 276
Heldt, Barbara, 11, 18, 20, 237–54
Hermaphroditism, 197, 199–201, 202, 265, 326n15, 327n21, 330n47. See also Androgyny
High culture, 43–44, 52, 117, 314n31. See also Nude painting
Homophobia, 195, 197, 202
Homosexuality: history of, in Russia, 10–11; Russian legal system and, 24; contemporary views of, 35, 324n6; as "foreign," 324n3. See also Gay political activity; Homophobia; Lesbianism
Hospitals, 31–32, 35–36, 293n102
Hubbs, Joanna, Mother Russia, 18

Iconography, 49f
Immortality, and transcendence of sexuality, 257, 258–59, 263, 265–67, 342n4
Impalement, execution by, 49, 299n49
Inber, Vera, 340n2
Individualism: sexuality and, 157–58, 269; vs. conventionality, 215–17

Infanticide metaphors, 256–57
Invalidism, cult of, 333n16
Ippolitych, Ippolit, 149
Isenberg, Charles, 291n88
Iskra [*The Spark*] (journal), 24–26
Iskusstvo kino (journal), 286n56
Iurodivye, 49
Ivanov, Viacheslav, 92, 188–91, 309n67
Ivanova, Natalia, 30
Izvestiia (newspaper), 255

Jack of Diamonds group, 98, 100, 105
Jacobus, Mary, 218
Jong, Erica, 147
Justification of culture, and Russian Orthodoxy, 13, 284n38

Kalamarchuk, Kornei, 255–56
Kalinin, Roman, 35
Kaplan, E. Ann, 83–84
Kappeler, Susanne, 332n11
Karlinsky, Simon, 8, 9, 10–11, 15, 37; affirmation of sexuality and, 16; liberation vs. repression and, 23–24; Tsvetaeva and, 164f, 169; homosexuality and, 178, 326n13
Katerli, Nina, *Polina*, 32
Kelly, Catriona, 12, 31, 73–96
Keyhole narrative, 19–20, 288n71
Khodasevich, Vladislav, 197–98, 330n47
Khudozhnitsa ("artist"), 121
Kissiloff, General, 63
Kissing: narrative as, 139–40; Chekhov's "The Kiss" and, 143–55; lesbian sex and, 183–84
Kollontai, Alexandra, 9, 16–18, 127, 130–31; *Social Bases of the Woman Question*, 103
Kon, Igor, 1, 28
Kraft, Konstantin F., 100, 101–2
Kristeva, Julia, 134, 244–45; "Stabat Mater," 245
Kroth, Anya, 322n27
Kuprin, Alexander, *The Pit* (*Iama*), 261–62
Kustodiev, Boris, 288n70

Labov, William, 319n23
Language: assumed masculine subjects of art terms and, 121, 160–63, 314n33; cliché and, 220. *See also* Russian language
Laqueur, Thomas, 6
Larionov, Mikhail, 101–5 *passim*, 312n22
League for Equal Rights for Women, 311n14
Ledkovsky, Marina, 341n5
Lenin, V. I., 11, 126–27, 129
Lepeshinsky, P., 128
Lesbianism, 177–78; silence regarding, 24, 287n59; *fin de siècle* stereotypes of, 177–83 *passim*, 193, 195, 197, 201–2; Silver Age literary perceptions of, 180, 181–94; antidecadent perception of, 202–3; defined, 324n10
Lesbian writing: in contemporary Russia, 34–35; *fin de siècle* views of lesbianism and, 178–80, 194; identification of, 179–80; decadence and, 181–86 *passim*, 193, 195, 200; male-defined notions of "female poetry" and, 184–88, 197–98; gender play in, 325n11. *See also* Parnok, Sophia
Leskov, Nikolai, *No Where to Go* (*Nekuda*), 223–25, 231, 236
Levin, Eve, 7, 27, 41–52
Liberation, 22–26, 36. *See also* Repression-liberation patterns; Women's liberation
Limonov, Eduard, 31, 94
Linguistic taboo, 281n23
Lipovskaya, Olga, 18, 34f, 295n115
Lipskerov, Konstantin, 329n38
Lira Safo [*Sappho's Lyre*] (journal), 34
Little Vera [*Malen'kaia Vera*] (film), 291n88
Lokhvitskaya, Mirra, 195
Lotman, Yuri, 141
Love: association of sex with, 46, 157; vocabulary for, 157; Tsvetaeva's novella structure and, 170–71; concept of "all-encompassing unity" and, 267
Love poems, of mother, 244
Love song genre, 6, 161f
Lunacharsky, A., 89

McCauley, Elizabeth, 314n31
MacKinnon, Catherine, 286n53
McMillen, Sally, 338n13
Makarova, Elena, 31; "Preserving Life" ("Na sokhranenii"), 31–32, 33–34; "Herbs from Odessa" ("Travy iz Odessy"), 33
Maksimovich-Ambodik, Nestor, 225–27, 230, 232, 338n12
Male brotherhood, 13–14
Male gaze: gender stereotypes and, 208–9; maternal breast and, 232f, 234–35
Male sexuality, 268–69
Malevich, Kazimir, 270
Mamonova, Tatiana, 17–18, 327n21
Man and Woman Apart and Together at Various Stages of Their Lives (anonymous), 226, 230f, 236
Mandelstam, Osip, 161ff, 199, 201, 320n10
Marks, Elain, 327n29
Marriage: abstinence and, 45; gender relations in early 1800s and, 53–72; rural ritual and, 75; Tolstaya's satirization of conventionality and, 205–15
Marxism: Kollontai and, 16, 286n53; prostitution and, 126, 315n7
"Masculineness of the women," in early-nineteenth-century Russia, 55–57, 66
Masculinity: in Chernyshevsky, 13–14; in Gachev, 14; nineteenth-century feminism and, 26; in Goncharova's art, 118–21, 166; of key art-historical terms, 121, 160–61; Tsvetaeva and, 166; perceptions of lesbian writing and, 185–86, 200
Mashkov, Ilya, 105, 111, 113, 116
Masquerade, 22–26
Masson, Charles-François-Philibert, *Mémoires secrets sur la Russie*, 53–60 *passim*, 65–72 *passim*
Maternal body: transcendence and, 4; Gachev's view of, 14; revulsion toward, 18, 20–22, 260; Tolstoy's view of, 18–19; sexuality and, 18–22; indifference to, in contemporary writing, 31–32; ideological significance of, 224–32, 236; Shkapskaya's poetry and, 244–54; Soviet appropriation of, 274–76.

See also Breastfeeding; Reproduction; Women's bodies.
Maternal breast, 20; nineteenth-century representation of, 223–36; as pastoral object, 231–36 *passim*; male gaze and, 232; post-Freudian feminists and, 337n5
Mathewson, Rufus, 319n15
Matthiessen, Peter, 296n122
Mayakovsky, Vladimir, 271f, 320n10
Medieval period, Russian sexual vocabulary in, 41–52
Metathesis, 269
Michie, Helena, 244
Mikhailov, M. L., 224, 227, 338n14, 339n22
Mikhailovsky, A. N., 30, 105
Minsky, Nikolai, 327n25
Mirianin, Lev, *Whack on the Nut*, 93–94
Mirsky, D. S., 164
Misogyny: in *Petrushka* puppet plays, 12, 73–96; urban vs. rural manifestations of, 75–76; methodological problems in research on, 76–77; as sanctioned by tradition, 92; association of women with reactionary politics and, 93–94; Kollontai and, 130–31; aesthetic, and Tsvetaeva, 172; Silver Age perceptions of lesbianism and, 184; in contemporary literature, 219
Moral purity of women, 59–62, 72
Morrison, Blake, 95
Moscow School of Painting, Sculpture, and Architecture, 98, 101, 105–6
Motherhood: contemporary Russian feminists and, 17; patriarchal ideology and, 224–32; feminine writing on, 242–44; guilt and, 247–48, 251–52; female sexuality and, 252–53, 262–63. *See also* Breastfeeding; Maternal body; Maternal breast; Myth of the maternal; Reproduction
Mulvey, Laura, 165, 211
Muratova, Kira, 30
Myth of the maternal: Kollontai and, 17; sexuality and, 18–22; contemporary representation of the body and, 33; Barykova and, 235; feminine writing and, 237; postrevolutionary Russia and, 242–43

Index

Nabakov, Vladimir, 158
Naiman, Eric, 9, 11f, 18, 255–76, 294n106
Narbikova, Valeria, 34; "Around Environ..." ("Okolo ekolo..."), 33
Narrative, seduction model for, 139–55
Naturalness, concept of, 74; lesbian love and, 181–82
Necrophilia, 36, 183
Needham, Gerald, 314n31
Nekrylova, Anna, 91
New Economic Policy (NEP), sexualization of, 125–31 *passim*, 135
Nietzsche, F. W., 256
Nigilistka, 223f, 230
Nihilism, 223–24, 227
Nikitin, Afanasii, 43
Nikolaeva, Olesia, 295
Nineteenth century: Silver Age and, 10–12; post-1861 reforms and, 12, 13–15; gender relations in early 1800s and, 53–72; representation of maternal breast in, 223–36. See also Silver Age
Nochlin, Linda, 107
Novel genre, 6
Nude painting: by woman artists, 26, 98f, 104–7, 116–23; public display of, 106, 312n22; in academic genre, 115–16, 117; vanguard compositions and, 116; Kustodiev's *The Beauty* and, 288n70
Nudity: Russian baths and, 5, 49, 66–72 *passim*; medieval views of, 49; on stage, 291n88

O'Brien, Sharon, 325n12
Obscenity, literary, 167–68, 171, 321n15
Ogonek (journal), 29, 35
Okulova, Tat'iana, 296n124
Orientalism, 281n17, 282n28
Orloff, Count Alexis, 63
Ovid, 67, 68–69

Paganism, 51
Page, Denys, 324n3
Panaeva, Avdotya, *The Talnykov Family* (*Semeistvo Tal'nykovykh*), 232, 235–36
Paramonov, Boris, 343n14

Parnok, Sophia, 22, 161, 171, 178–79, 324n9; affair with Tsvetaeva, 171, 193–94; Silver Age critical response to, 180–81, 194–201; Sappho poems of, 191–93, 328n33; *Poems*, 191–202 *passim*
Parody, 161–63
Paul, Lissa, 88
Perestroika, 36–37
Peter I, 5, 53, 252
Petrushevskaya, Lyudmila, 31; "Down the Road of the God Eros" ("Po doroge Boga Erosa"), 29–30; "The Meaning of Life" ("Smysl zhizni"), 32
Petrushka puppet plays: misogyny in, 12, 73–96; representation of women in, 71–80, 82; women as spectators and, 73, 80–88 *passim*; description of, 77; violence against women in, 77–80; why women laughed at, 82–86; "class war" reading of, 89–90; critique of early interpretations of, 89–93; formalist reading of, 90; Bakhtin-inspired reading of, 90–92; Soviet period and, 93–95
Pilnyak, Boris, 270
Pity vs. desire (*pozhalel* vs. *pozhelal*), 20, 285n45, 289n72
Platonov, Andrei, 294n106; "Ivan Zhokh," 271, 273–74
Playboy (magazine), 292n90
Poe, Edgar Allen, 162
Poet, as term, 160–63
"Poetess": as term, 121, 160–63; Tsvetaeva and, 165, 167–68, 169
Poetry: role of women in, 162; of Shkapskaya, 237–54
Poliakova, Sophia, 171, 180–81, 326n13, 329n36
Political radicalism: denial of sexuality and, 13–14, 15, 283n34, 285n49; gender ambiguity and, 24–26; artists and, 98–99, 311n12; sexual freedom and, 102–3, 312n16; women and, 312n16. *See also* Gay political activity; Reactionary politics
Pollock, Griselda, 107
Poovey, Mary, 60
Popkin, Cathy, 11f, 139–55
Popova, Lyubov, 107

Popular culture: relation to high culture, 43–44, 73–74, 297n7; women's involvement in, 73, 75, 86–87; rural rituals and, 75–76; urban, 75–77; representation of Bolshevik revolution in, 127–28. *See also Petrushka* puppet plays
Pornography: Goncharova's trial for, 97–102, 104, 117–18; high art and, 117, 314n31; erotic "postcards," 117–18, 119f, 314n31
Poshlost, concept of, 158, 163–64, 174, 320n4
Pospelov, Gleb, 105
Possession: and nonpossession, paradox of, 174–75; male myth of, 211–12
Postrevolutionary Russia: anxieties about sexuality in, 124–35; feminine writing and, 242–43. *See also* Soviet culture; Utopian thought
Power: gender difference and, 26, 82–84; fantasy of, in *Petrushka* puppet plays, 81–82; ideological, in police and courts, 101
Praz, Mario, *The Romantic Agony*, 8
Press, Percy, 95
Profilaktorii (medical asylums), 132
Prostitution: Tolstoy and, 19; contemporary treatment of, 28–29, 291n89; medieval representation of, 44, 50; prostitute as victim and, 125, 126–27, 133, 315n4; women's section of Communist Party and, 125–26, 129–31; campaigns against, 126, 133f, 317n29; regulation of, 126, 311n14; official postrevolutionary policy on, 131–32; sexuality of the prostitute and, 133–35; economic hardship and, 339n24
Purity metaphor: in Soviet culture, 27, 36–38; Rasputin and, 36, 296n122; utopian thinking and, 296n123. *See also* Moral purity of women; Utopian thought

Raeff, Marc, 302n17
Ransel, David L., 305n32, 317n31, 337n6, 337n9
Rasputin, Valentin, 6, 36, 95, 242–43
Reactionary politics, association of women with, 93–94

Red Virgin Soil [*Krasnaia nov'*] (journal), 241f
Religion, *see* Russian Orthodoxy
Remizov, Alexei, 288n69
Repression: of women, and heterosexual sex, 17; utopian thought and, 263–65, 269
Repression-liberation patterns: history of homosexuality and, 10–11; gender difference and, 11–12; post-1861 reforms and, 12; nineteenth century and, 12–16; masquerade and, 23–24; *glasnost* and, 37
"Repressions" [*Repressii*] (pre-revolutionary censorship), 101
"Repressive hypothesis," 2
Reproduction: feminist vs. male writers and, 17; early Soviet hostility toward, 255–58. *See also* Maternal body; Maternal breast; Motherhood; Myth of the maternal
Reyfman, Irina, 281n19
Riabushinsky, Nikolai, 100
Richardson, Samuel, 60
Ritual, in rural theater, 75
Rogneda, Princess, 46–47
Roman Catholic Church, 42
Rousseau, Jean Jacques, *Émile*, 225
Rovinsky, D. A., 79
Rozanov, Vasili, 9, 16, 186f, 271, 327n26
Russia, contemporary, sexual discourse in, 27–36
Russian baths, 5, 49; Masson's description of, 66–72 *passim*
Russian Journals, The (Catherine Wilmot and Martha Wilmot), 54–66 *passim*
Russian language: inadequacy of sexual vocabulary in, 6–7, 172f; linguistic play and, 33; medieval sexual vocabulary and, 41–52; literary use of connotation in, 207. *See also* Art-historical terms; Language
Russian Orthodoxy, 13, 18, 27, 42, 284n38
Russo, Mary, 294n108
Rykhlin, Mikhail, 294n108

Sade, Marquis de, 30, 141, 280n13
Sadur, Nina, 34
Sand, George, 24, 26

Index

Sandler, Stephanie, 1–38
Sappho, 177f, 180, 198, 324n3, 327n29, 328n33; Ivanov's translation of, 188–91
Sappho's Lyre [Lira Safo] (journal), 34
Savitski, Dmitri, 94
Sectarianism, 269
Sedgwick, Eve Kosofsky, *The Epistemology of the Closet*, 3
Seifullina, Lydia, 94
Sekretnye kartochki (erotic "postcards"), 117–18, 119f, 314n31
Semiradsky, Konstantin, *Choosing Between the Slave Girl and the Precious Vase*, 115–16
Serebriakova, Zinaida, 107
Serov, Valentin, 106, 312n22
Seventeenth Echo (Semndtsatoe ekho) (Tatarinova, ed.), 35
Sexual explicitness: in contemporary Russia, 27–31; medieval penitential terms and, 48–49
Sexual identity, ambiguity in, 167, 169, *See also* Androgyny; Hermaphroditism
Sexual intercourse: marital, in medieval period, 45, 47–48; Soviet utopian philosophy and, 258–60
Sexuality: as term, 1–2; as Western phenomenon, 6–8, 28–29, 36f, 157; accounts of, in Russian culture, 8–18; nineteenth century sublimations and, 13–16; nineteenth century affirmation of, 16–18; myth of the maternal and, 18–22; vs. gender, 22–26; medieval euphemisms for, 41–52; association of love with, 46, 157; postrevolutionary anxieties about, 124–35; postrevolutionary utopian views and, 255–61; male, 268–69. *See also* Female sexuality
Sexualization: of New Economic Policy, 125–31 *passim*, 135; of genius, 265–68. *See also* Eroticization
Sexual motifs in literature, 49–51
Shadows of Forgotten Ancestors (film), 291n88
Shakhverdiev, Tofik, *To Die for Love (Umeret' ot liubvi)*, 29, 291n89
Shalin, Dmitri N., 295n121
Sharp, Jane A., 11f, 17, 26, 97–123

Shcherbatov, M. M., *On the Corruption of Morals in Russia (O povrezhdenii nravov v Rossii)*, 6
Shkapskaya, Maria, 20, 237–54; prose vs. poetry of, 237–38, 242; autobiographical writings of, 238–41, 254; *Blood-Gore*, 239; poetry of, 240–42, 244, 245–54; *Evening Hour (Chas vechernii)*, 245–47; *Mater Dolorosa*, 247–48, 249; *Drum of the Stern Lord*, 248; *Earthly Crafts*, 249; *Man goes to the Pamirs (Chelovek idet na Pamir)*, 249
Shtakenshneider, Elena, 24
Shvarts, Elena, 238, 341n3
Silence: cultural injunction to, 2, 9–10; regarding lesbianism, 24, 287n59
Silver Age, 10–12; perceptions of lesbianism in, 180, 181–94
Slavery, 66, 70–71
Smith, Barbara Herrnstein, 140
Society of Free Aesthetics (*Obshchestvo Svobodnoi Estetiki*), 99–100, 104, 311n9
Sodomy, 45, 297n18
Solomon, Peter, 291n89
Solomon, Simeon, 186
Solomon, Susan, 291n89
Solovyov, Vladimir, 168, 256f, 261–71 *passim*, 344n28
Solovyova, Poliksena, 185f, 326n20, 327n22, 327n24
Solzhenitsyn, Alexander, 243
Soviet culture: "dark literature" in, 27; rhetoric of purity and, 27, 36–38; sexuality of women and, 27; misogyny in, 93–95; postrevolutionary anxieties about sexuality in, 124–35; policy on prostitution in, 131–32; Shkapskaya's poetry and, 240–42, 253; marginalization of women and, 254, 255–76; utopian thought and, 255–76; appropriation of maternal body in, 274–76. *See also* Postrevolutionary Russia; Utopian thought
Sovremennik [The Contemporary] (journal), 23, 24–26
Spark, The [Iskra] (journal), 24–26
Spiritualization, 13–16, 21

Staël, Germaine de, 83
Stone, Lawrence, 280n13
Story of the Bread Rings, The [*Istoriia pro bubliki i pro babu, ne priznaiushchuiu*] (poster by Mayakovsky and Cheremnykh), 271f
Storytelling, *see* Narrative
Sublimation, and reforms of post-1861 period, 13–15
"Subversive" strategies, 85f
Sumarokov, Alexander, 6
Symbolic vs. real, 264
Symbolist movement, 181, 344n28

Taboo, *see* Homophobia; Linguistic taboo; Silence
Tarasov, G., 94
Tarnovskii, Ippolit, 323n2
Taste, and female writing, 161, 163f, 170–71
Tellability, 149–52, 154
Tenenbaum, Joseph, 324n3, 326n18
Theme, The [*Tema*] (newspaper), 34f
To Die for Love [*Umeret' ot liubvi*] (Shakhverdiev film), 29, 291n89
Tolstaya, Tatiana, 22, 30, 34; "Date with a Bird" (Svidanie s ptitsei"), 34; grotesque liaisons in fiction of, 204–5; subversion of gender stereotypes and, 204–20; "The Poet and the Muse," 205, 210–15; "Fire and Dust," 205, 215–17; "Hunting the Wooly Mammoth," 205–10, 215; feminism and, 219, 335n31, 336n34, 336n42
Tolstoy, Leo, 15, 37, 153, 335n29; *Anna Karenina*, 8, 228–31, 288n64, 333n17; mother Russia and, 18–19; *What Is Art?* (*Chto takoe iskusstvo?*), 19; *The Kreutzer Sonata* (*Kreitserova sonata*), 52, 287n64; "The Infected Family," 227, 230; war stories and, 319n14
Tomashevsky, Boris, 172
Trediakovsky, Vasily, 6–7; *Journey to the Island of Love* (*Ezda v ostrov Liubvi*), 7, 281n19
Triangular relationships, 15
Troianovsky, I. I., 311n9
Trotsky, Leon, 128, 270
Tsimbaliuk, Iosif, 255
Tsvetaeva, Marina, 22, 237, 287n59, 324n9; *The Tale of Sonechka* (*Povest' o Sonechke*), 156, 160, 164–65, 167–76; "The Hero of Labor," 165; ambiguous viewpoint of, 165, 167, 169; "Natalia Goncharova," 166–67; novella structure and, 169–70; affair with Parnok, 171, 193–94, 203, 329n36; "Girlfriend" ("Podruga"), 193, 198, 203, 329n36
Tugendkhold, Yakov, 119–21
Tynianov, Yuri, 161, 250–51

USSR in Construction (propaganda journal), 274–76
Utopian thought: postrevolutionary views of sexuality and, 255–76; marginalization of women in, 263–65, 270–71; repressive nature of, 263–65, 269; womb imagery in, 271–74; purity metaphor and, 296n123; "utopian" as term and, 342n5

Vanguard art, and gender difference, 98–99, 102–6, 113, 116, 121–23
Venereal disease, 132
Venetsianov, Alexei, 111f
Verlaine, Paul, 326n15
Victorian culture, 19
Vilkina-Minskaya, Liudmila, *My Garden* (*Moi sad*), 186–88
Violence: contemporary representations of sexuality and, 29–31; in Soviet society, 36–37; against women in puppet plays, 77–80, 83, 91–92; working-class women and, 83, 305n36; revolutionary, and Shkapskaya, 252–53. *See also* Castration
Visual arts: gay political activity and, 35; censorship in, 97–98; involvement of women in, 121–23, 313n24
Vita of St. Barbara, 50–51
Vita of St. Ripsimia, 50
Vivien, Renée, 192
Voice of Moscow [*Golos Moskvy*] (newspaper), 99–100
Voloshin, Maximilian, 176; "Voices of Poets," 199–200, 201–2
Voloshinov, V., 7f, 157–58
Volpin, *An Amateur Performance* (play), 93
Volynsky, Akim, 270, 344n26

Index

Vowles, Judith, 1–38, 5, 53–72
Voznesenskaya, Julia, *Women's Decameron (Zhenskii dekameron)*, 31
"Vseedinstvo" (concept of "all-encompassing unity"), 267, 269

Wanting (*khocheti*), sexual sense of, 46–47
War stories, 319n14
Waters, Elizabeth, 28
Weininger, Otto, *Sex and Character*, 262–63, 265–66, 267f
Western culture: Russia's relation to, 3, 4–8; early-nineteenth-century views of Russian society and, 53–72; prostitution and, 125–31 *passim*; lesbianism and, 178; Russian women writers and, 218–19; feminism and, 219, 282n25, 335n31; views of female sexuality in, 262
Wet nursing, 20; nineteenth-century injunctions against, 224–32; women's work and, 229–31, 233; physical properties of wet nurses, 232; historical work on, 337n6
White, Luise, 317n32
Wilamowitz-Moellendorf, Ulrich von, 188–89
Wilmot, Catherine, 53f, 58–65 *passim*, 69
Wilmot, Martha, 53, 54–55, 59ff, 63–65, 69
Witches, in Russia, 299n56
"Woman question," 165; sexual representation in the 1860s and, 12–13; masquerade and, 24–26; sexual freedom and, 103; origin of, 224, 284n36
Womb imagery, in utopian thought, 271–74
Women: repression of, and heterosexual sex, 17; eroticism between, and masquerade, 23; views of European women on early-nineteenth-century Russian women, 57–65; working-class, 83, 86, 305n36, 306n46, 307n53; poetic role of, 162; conventionality vs. independence in, 215–17, 223–24; education of, 224, 227, 338n11; sisterhood among, 249–50; elimination of, in utopian thought, 263–65, 270–71; ignorance of hygiene, 317n31. *See also* Female sexuality; Female writers; Femininity; Lesbian writing; Lesbianism; Maternal body; Motherhood
Women's bodies, contemporary images of, 28–29
Women's liberation, 227; Kollontai's social programs and, 16–17; masquerade and, 24–26
Women's Reader [Zhenskoe chtenie] (journal), 34f, 287n59, 295n115
Wood, Elizabeth A., 12, 17, 27, 124–35
Work: physical labor as sublimation and, 13–14, 15; nature of, 229–30; of women, as maternal, 229–31
Working-class women, 83, 86, 305n36, 306n46, 307n53

Zaitsev (puppeteer), 87
Zamyatin, E., *We*, 214
Zdanevich, Ilya, 107ff
Zenovia, Prince, 64
Zhenskoe chtenie [Women's Reader] (journal), 34f, 287n59, 295n115
Zholkovsky, Alexander, 94
Zhuk, Olga, 287n59
Zinovieva-Annibal, Lidia, 188; *Thirty-Three Monsters (Tridtsat' tri uroda)*, 182–84, 201–2

Library of Congress Cataloging-in-Publication Data

Sexuality and the body in Russian culture / edited by Jane T. Costlow, Stephanie Sandler, Judith Vowles.
  p. cm.
Includes bibliographical references and index.
ISBN 0-8047-2113-0 (cl.) : ISBN 0-8047-3155-1 (pbk.)
1. Sex customs—Russia—History—Congresses.
2. Sexuality in popular culture—Russia—Congresses.
3. Sex in literature—Congresses. 4. Russian literature—History and criticism—Congresses.
5. Russia—Social life and customs—Congresses.
I. Costlow, Jane T. (Jane Tussey), 1955—
II. Sandler, Stephanie, 1953—   . III. Vowles, Judith, 1956—
HQ18.R9S49   1993
306.7'0947—dc20   92-47410
                                    CIP

∞ This book is printed on acid-free, recycled paper.

Original printing 1993

The authorized representative in the EU for product safety and compliance is:
Mare Nostrum Group
B.V Doelen 72
4831 GR Breda
The Netherlands

www.ingramcontent.com/pod-product-compliance
Lightning Source LLC
Chambersburg PA
CBHW021816300426
44114CB00009BA/199